PSYCHOANALYSIS

AND

THE SOCIAL SCIENCES

PSYCHOANALYSIS AND THE SOCIAL SCIENCES

VOLUME 2

Managing Editor
Geza Roheim, Ph.D.

Editorial Board

Marie Bonaparte, Paris
Henry A. Bunker, M.D., New York
John Dollard, Ph.D., New Haven
Erik H. Erikson, Ph.D., San Francisco
Paul Federn, M.D., New York
J. C. Flugel, B.A., D.Sc., London
Angel Garma, M.D., Buenos Aires
Heinz Hartmann, M.D., New York
Imre Hermann, M.D., Budapest
Edward Hitschmann, M.D., Cambridge

Ernest Jones, M.D., London
Clyde Kluckhohn, Ph.D., Cambridge
Ernst Kris, Ph.D., New York
R. Money-Kyrle, M.A., Ph.D., London
Sandor Lorand, M.D., New York
Karl A. Menninger, M.D., Topeka
Herman Nunberg, M.D., New York
Clarence P. Oberndorf, M.D., New York
Oskar Pfister, Ph.D., Zurich
Fritz Wittels, M.D., New York

Gregory Zilboorg, M.D., New York

Assistant Editor
Gertrud M. Kurth, Ph.D.

INTERNATIONAL UNIVERSITIES PRESS, INC.
NEW YORK   NEW YORK

Copyright 1950, by Geza Roheim, Ph.D.

Manufactured in the United States of America

CONTENTS

INTRODUCTION

Raymond de Saussure   Psychoanalysis and History 7

Part One: ANTHROPOLOGY

Marie Bonaparte	Notes on Excision	67
George Devereux	Heterosexual Behavior of the Mohave Indians	85
Warner Muensterberger	Oral Trauma and Taboo. A Psychoanalytic Study of an Indonesian Tribe	129
Geza Roheim	The Oedipus Complex, Magic and Culture	173

Part Two: ESTHETICS

Harry B. Lee   The Values of Order and Vitality in Art 231

Part Three: HISTORY

Henry Lowenfeld   Freud's *Moses* and Bismarck 277

Part Four: SOCIOLOGY

Gertrud M. Kurth	Hitler's Two Germanies. A Sidelight on Nationalism	293
Roger Money-Kyrle	Varieties of Group Formation	313

Introduction

PSYCHOANALYSIS AND HISTORY
By Raymond de Saussure, M.D. (New York)

Freud's Contributions

(1) *Psychoanalysis in Itself*

It is amazing that psychoanalysis has not been systematically applied by historians, because in itself the method is historical. Of course, the healing process is an emotional one, relying on the repetition principle and the transference but in the case of Dora, like in many others, Freud has insisted on establishing complete anamnestic data of the patients and on the difficulties the analyst will encounter in his task due to the repressed emotions and memories. For the doctor, and partially for the patient, analysis is a reconstruction of the past, with all its emotional richness. At the same time the psychological determinism which is the underlying hypothesis of the method gives an explanation of the past and the present. This social aspect of psychoanalysis has been well stressed by Glover: "In a sense, therefore, a psychoanalysis is a sociological investigation, revealing in detail every one of an individual's characteristics as a social being. It is even in a sense a sociological experiment, since during the process fresh social adaptations make their appearance; moreover, since the analyst is unconsciously identified with a number of other persons, the scope of this sociological inquiry is not limited, as might appear, by the fact that only two persons take part in it."[1]

From the time of Aristotle, three functions have been ascribed to history: (1) The accurate establishment of events; (2) the creation of historical laws resulting from the comparison of those events; (3)

---

[1] Edward Glover: Man, the Individual. In Ernest Jones, *Social Aspects of Psychoanalysis*. Williams and Noyate, London, 1924, p. 43.

the artistic or emotional reanimation of the past. In a way we could say that psychoanalysis assumes those three functions for it is a historical study of the living being. If this is so, psychoanalysis has something to contribute to history.

Psychoanalysis is a causal experience which helps toward a better knowledge of our ego and its development just as history facilitates the understanding of the present days. By catharsis and by the reintegration into the ego of emotions formerly repressed, psychoanalysis creates for the individual another past, one which allows him a better future. On the social level, a philosopher has defended a similar idea concerning history.

"We really question whether the historical like the natural sciences do develop according to a cumulative and progressive rhythm or whether, on the contrary, each society rewrites its history, for it chooses and recreates its past."[2]

By daily practice Freud and his pupils have acquired a special skill for interpreting the deep significance of unconscious manifestations. This talent has served Freud to shed new light on the infantile conflicts of Leonardo da Vinci and to explain by them many riddles of the artist's life. It was not only in biographies that this method was applied, for Freud used it in a convincing way to build up some historical hypotheses.

Historians admit that Moses' name is Egyptian and not Jewish. Freud has backed this hypothesis with a purely psychological demonstration. Starting from Rank's book, *Der Mythus von der Geburt des Helden*[3] (The Myth of the Birth of the Hero), he first remarks that Moses in contradiction to other heroes was born in a humble family and then adopted by the Pharaoh's daughter. Rank's thesis can be summarized as follows: A hero is a man who stands up valiantly against his father and in the end victoriously overcomes him. He was born against his father's will and saved in spite of his father's evil intentions. The family romance is expressed in the following way: The child's first years are governed by a grandiose overestimation of the father. Kings and queens represent the parents. Later on, under the influence of rivalry and disappointments, a critical attitude toward the father sets in. The two families of the myth,

---

[2] Raymond Aron, *Introduction à la philosophie de l'histoire*. Paris, Gallimard, 1938, p. 10.
[3] Vienna, Deuticke, 1908.

the noble as well as the humble one, therefore both represent his own family as it appears to the child in successive periods of his life. From this we may conclude that the first family, the one by whom the babe is exposed to danger is the fictitious one; the second who adopted the hero is the real one. "If," says Freud, "we have the courage to accept this statement as a general truth, then Moses is an Egyptian—probably of noble origin, whom the myth undertakes to transform into a Jew." The above argument is a striking example of a psychoanalytic observation supporting a historical hypothesis.

This is not the only instance where Freud has tried to supplement the lack of documentation by a psychological hypothesis.

(2) *The Exclusion of the Moral Judgment*

Before Freud, historians tried to be objective and to narrate the succession of events refraining from giving a moral appreciation to men or events. However, the historian has a tendency to write with his political prejudices and easily indulges in some kind of moral judgment. The therapist living before Freud's era also thought it his duty to give some moral standards to his patients.

It was not only for technical reasons and to allow the patient to become conscious of his repressed wishes that Freud refrained from any moral judgment, but also because he was convinced of the psychological determinism which made a man act in a neurotic or perverse way.

Instead of criticizing some aspects of a civilization, the psychoanalyst tries to discover the reasons for these trends. In order to clear up conflicts between nations or social groups, it becomes more and more necessary to be better informed on the psychological causes of political attitudes, on the functions that a group may have for sublimation, on discharge or projection of personal conflicts, and on the interplay of groups in national life.

(3) *Individual and Social Psychology*

At the beginning of this century, Freud was one of the psychologists who contributed the most to a real revolution of psychology. Instead of describing the different psychic faculties of our mind as isolated functions, as special compartments, he showed that they were all interrelated and that the interesting fact was not, for instance, the succession of early memories which we were able to reproduce, but the underlying unconscious emotions which explain why certain scenes of the past are retained and others repressed. He transformed the static atomic into an active psychodynamic psychology.

He did not only insist on this interplay of the functions of our mind, but he also described the individual in function with his environment. He shifted the interest from the individual to the unconscious connections which bind people together. The object of study was no longer the individual *per se* but the underlying system that ties together the members of a group. If we take an individual at a given moment, the forces within him form a system which has a certain equilibrium, at least as long as the individual is normal. Any pressure, coming from within like hunger or from without like danger or a social stimulus will change the equilibrium. Similarly, but in a much more complicated and varied way, every society has a psychodynamic equilibrium and this unstable system of forces changes as a reaction to pressure from within or without. Within a given family structure, we have a system of adjustment which bears consequences on the individual as well as on the social life. This adjustment is an emotional psychodynamic equilibrium. The object of the psycho-historical studies is to observe the variations of those family structures and their concomitant variations in the individual character and the social institutions.

The main object of psychoanalysis is to study how the individual emotions are interlinked with social structures and vice versa.

The borderline that divides the psychology of the individual and of the group is non-existent. Maybe this has not been stressed enough, so far. Freud, in introducing that new standpoint has given a greater unity to the different disciplines studying man and, in so doing, has accomplished a great revolution, some consequences of which we shall study a little later.

Freud described human behavior as a sort of compromise between the ego (reality function), superego (introjected social function) and id (instinctual function). Once more he showed the close connection between the individual and society and the impossibility of studying one without the other. For instance, we know that the first object-relation of the child is the mother. From her attitude will depend for years, perhaps for life, the child's attitude toward reality. Does this phenomenon belong to the realm of the individual or of society? And what should we say about such mechanisms as identification, projection, introjection and their consequences on the group and the individual psychology? In the past, psychology and sociology were sharply delineated; today they are constantly interlinked.[4]

Psychology and sociology study the same object: human behavior. Psychology has to study the action of the environment on the individual as well as the action of the individual on the group formation. In the future it will be impossible to differentiate between these two disciplines.[5]

Freud made from the study of man the study of a biological unit reacting to its environment. From this point of view also, he en-

---

[4] Zilboorg has shown for other reasons the close relations of both disciplines:
"The consideration of psychiatric factors in social life grew out of the consideration of social factors in psychiatric conditions. As a result, we find that the social scientist is forced more and more to engage in psychiatric speculations; he therefore becomes an amateur psychiatrist. The psychiatrist on the other hand enters more and more into sociological speculations; he tends to become an amateur sociologist." (Gregory Zilboorg, Psychiatry as a Social Science. *Amer. Journ. of Psychiatry*, Vol. 99, Jan. 1943, p. 585.)
But Zilboorg does not blame sociologists or psychiatrists for this. He understands that these two fields are more and more interlinked and have to be studied in close connection.
"The terms social adjustment and social adaptation became legitimate terms in psychiatry; the criteria of social adjustment, from the subjective point of view of objective behavior, became the major criteria of our clinical evaluations. The psychological history of the individual as a social being and the psychological history of society itself became the chief objects of investigation." (Gregory Zilboorg, *loc. cit.*, p. 587.)

[5] How much both problems are interlinked is clearly expressed in the following quotations:
"The process of civilization is a constant restricting of primordial nature and its replacement by a man-made reality which contains and reflects his instincts and conflicts. Just as man reacts biologically to changes in his environment, so must he respond to changes of psychic climate with varying attempts of adjustment. At the same time the manner in which the satisfaction of the instincts, their sublimation and the defenses against them are achieved, depends in part upon the given reality or social condition. While culture demands adjustment from the individual, it is also the process which furnishes the different means of adjustment."
"The struggle with man-made civilization leads to the same formation of theories and ideologies. These have the same function as religious concepts, but can fulfill it only insufficiently and are constantly endangered through reality. The function and the background of such ideologies are often difficult to penetrate in the individual patient, because they represent a normal attempt at a solution at the present stage of civilization, because they seem to be relatively rational, and, above all, because analysts themselves participate in such ideologies. However, in many cases they contain the essential emotional conflicts of the unconscious, in its most disguised form and then appear as the cardinal resistances in analysis." (Henry Lowenfeld, Some Aspects of a Compulsion Neurosis in a Changing Civilization. *Psa. Quart.*, Vol. XIII, 1944, pp. 11 and 15.)

larged and unified the human sciences. His was a bio-psychological point of view which has given a new impulse to psycho-somatic medicine.

Even politics and economics which may have their own methods will have to yield to the Freudian point of view. In individual psychology we attribute economic failure to psychological factors. In the same way, in the last analysis the good and bad labor organization or the fair distribution of raw material are psychological problems.

(4) *Totem and Taboo* [6]

In the previous sections we have studied how Freud's thought has influenced in a general way the *humaniora*, and how the new foundations of psychoanalysis had *ipso facto* an influence on sociology or history. Let us now examine the more direct contributions that Freud made to history.

In *Totem and Taboo* we find two fundamental contributions:

(a) The discovery that the totemic organization at least at its beginning was a defense against the oedipus wishes, and that in later organizations the taboos surrounding the king were defenses against the unconscious desire to kill the father.

By this brilliant demonstration Freud opened a new way to study the links between family structure, personal conflicts and social structures. He observed several phenomena that we shall find even in much more complicated social structures. They are: (a) that the infantile repressed conflict is projected into the social environment; (b) that the neurotic is not only compelled to repeat the repressed emotions but also to recreate a social environment which gives him symbolically the same social frame he had in his childhood; (c) that this new social structure is utilized as defense mechanism against the repressed wishes, as a frame that promotes the sublimation of these early emotions. The history of humanity could be written from this point of view and its meaning would be: how man finally acquired mastery of his own emotions and could place himself objectively in the world.

We cannot hope to outline all the implications of these few observations. They would mean an entirely new approach to history. However, the aim of this paper is to show some of the new perspectives which derive from these premises.

---

[6] Translated by A. A. Brill, New York, Dodd, Mead & Co., 1919.

(b) The second contribution in *Totem and Taboo* concerns the hypothesis of the primal horde.

I personally think that Freud's hypothesis of the primal tribe, of its mutation in a clan of equal brothers and of the guilt they experienced is correct, but Freud's description has something unnecessarily dramatic, in the sense that he describes it as an event which happened once and sealed the human fate. We are more inclined to think that it happens very often, and that finally in several instances the brother organization became predominant. Economic reasons have perhaps facilitated such transformations because several tribes in periods of drought had to live together and the number of oppressed sons increased. Anyhow those speculations are useless as we have no means to prove them.

I am less inclined to follow Freud in the use he made later of this hypothesis in *Group Psychology and the Analysis of the Ego* as well as in *Moses and the Monotheism*. Freud's idea is that the unconscious of the human mind always kept a sort of vague memory of this early event and that therefore the feelings of the primal horde and the guilt its members experienced can be reanimated under certain circumstances.

Instead of imagining some racial, emotional archetype, it seems simpler to find the origin of these feelings in the childhood of every man as Roheim said a long time ago.[7] We know that the child during the oedipal phase feels deprived of his mother because of the presence of his father and this is practically the same emotional situation as in the primal horde where a male is deprived of a woman because of another male.

(5) *Group Psychology and the Analysis of the Ego*[8]

From the historical point of view, the two main theoretical ideas of this work are (1) that the mob formation or some social organizations may require regressive mechanisms of the individual, (2) that the psychodynamics of a group can be described. When I discuss the problem of magic I shall come back to this problem of mass psychology and therefore I do not want to elaborate further on the subject here.

---

[7] Geza Roheim: *The Riddle of the Sphinx*, London, Int. Psa. Library, 1934, p. 234.

[8] Translated by James Strachey, London, Hogarth Press, 1922.

(6) *The Future of an Illusion*[9]

Freud has taught us to consider religion as the expression of a neurosis. It is a collective rationalization which helps the repression and sublimation of our impulses and which, in some cases, brings about the liquidation of guilt feelings. The symbols of the same religion are used in varied ways, in accordance to the neurotic needs of the individuals; for some, religion will be used for sublimation; in others it will aggravate character distortions.

In the discussion of historical developments many analysts have attributed great influence to an ideology (religious or political) in the shaping of a civilization. After a few generations, the problem of course arises of knowing whether the individual conflicts maintain alive an ideology or whether the ideology creates the same conflicts in every generation. Both assumptions are true. I personally am inclined to think that the conflicts of the individual are the formative element within an ideology; it is not so much the dynamics of the ideology as such that is responsible for keeping alive its emotional or suggestive power but the way, for instance, parents make use of an ideology to coerce their children.

As mentioned above, we also see that two successive generations may feel differently about the same symbols. The repressing function of a symbol becomes with time more a suggestion of sublimation. The coercive action of an ideology comes from an ambivalent attitude towards the parents; the fear of letting the aggression overwhelm the tender feelings brings the individual to stick dogmatically to the parental ideology and to impose it on the next generation as a defense mechanism. As we shall see later the socialization of a conflict is a defense mechanism. The evolution of a civilization is not shaped by an ideology, but by the way the latter is utilized by the successive generations in order to express their conflicts or attempts at adjustment.

(7) *Civilization and Its Discontents*[10]

In this book Freud has given a great many ideas which are not always systematically related to one another. We shall discuss some of them.

---

[9] Translated by W. D. Robson Scott, London, Hogarth Press, 1934.
[10] Translated by Joan Rivière, London, Hogarth Press, 1930.

He shows that one of the processes of civilization is due to the sublimation of love, man giving up part of his attachment to the love object in favor of generous feelings given to all neighbors. From a methodological point of view, it is astounding that Freud did not describe the genesis of those processes in childhood. In reading *Civilization and Its Discontents* one gets the impression in many instances that culture is a phenomenon concerning the adult, while we know, and this is the essence of Freud's contentions, that nothing happens which does not have its roots in childhood. All actions are manifold. When a child succeeds in a new activity, he may repeat it to get more attention and love from the parents, but he also finds a personal narcissistic satisfaction and when the parents for one reason or another withdraw part of their affection, it is normal for the child to go back to this satisfactory activity as a means of comfort. Similarly, the brother or the sister or the neighbor child are good substitutes for the parents, when the latter are too busy to stay with their child. Individual needs drive people to agglomeration and not as Freud puts it: Civilization requires agglomeration.

The methodologic reproach which should be made to this essay is that Freud constantly uses the concept of civilization as an abstraction which has a causal influence on the cultural processes, as an entity which has a will in itself.

". . . From all this we might well imagine that a civilized community could consist of pairs of individuals such as this, libidinally satisfied with each other, and linked to all the others by work and common interests. If this were so, culture would not need to levy energy from sexuality. But such a desirable state of things does not exist and has never existed; in reality, *culture is not content* with such limited ties as these; we see that *it endeavors* to bind the members of the community to one another by libidinal ties as well, that *it makes use of every means* and favors every avenue by which powerful identifications can be created among them, and that it extracts a heavy toll of aim-inhibited libido in order to strengthen community by bonds of friendship between members. Restrictions upon sexual life are unavoidable if this object is to be attained."[11]

I underline such expression as: *"Culture is not content with such limited ties, etc."* Personal needs of a part of the society, the parents, for

---

[11] *Civilization and Its Discontents.* London, Hogarth Press, 1930. pp. 80, 81.

instance, and not the culture as such are the dynamic causes of the cultural restrictions.

Of course, it could be objected that nobody knew it better than Freud and that he himself described our aggressive impulses as the cause of the inhibiting factors of our civilization. Nevertheless I think it is wrong to express oneself in such general terms which omit the most interesting part of the dynamic description.

Let us now stress the positive results of this important work. One concerns the role of aggression, its sublimations and the defenses with which the ego opposes it; the other concerns the internalization of the environment and its dynamic survival in the superego. Both are key problems to understanding the structure of a civilization. The core of Freud's doctrine is that the price of progress in civilization is paid in forfeiting happiness through the increase of the sense of guilt. Instituting restrictions is the basis for culture and is therefore opposed to a certain degree to the happiness of individuals.

Civilization is the social environment in so far as it is organized (at least Freud constantly uses the term in that sense). The main element of this environment, in primitive cultures, is the family. There the individual wishes of the child are entirely curbed by the egotism of the adult who tends to keep for himself the females and the best part of the food. Civilization as a process of gradual improvement tends on the contrary to give more and more an equal share to all individuals in the group. Culture used in that sense is far from being frustrating; it tends to seek more gratifications from the environment.

Freud does not make clear where he uses the term "civilization" in the sense of social environment and where he uses it as a process of social development. This essay attempts to describe the two forces at stake: aggression and aim-inhibited love; but it does it in a general way which, except for the problems of introjection and guilt, fails to show the real place where they meet. At the start, the social environment has considerably limited the individual gratifications and because of the repetition compulsion the young generation could free itself only very gradually. The process of civilization is parallel to the process of maturation of the individual. This process did not follow a constantly ascending road. For economic and psychological reasons, the social coercions have frequently to be re-enforced. We shall outline later our ideas about civilization. We just wanted to point out here a difficulty of Freud's position, which is well expressed in the following quotation:

"So in every individual the two trends, one towards personal happiness, and the other towards unity with the rest of humanity, must contend with each other; so must the two processes of individual and cultural development oppose each other and dispute the ground against each other."[12]

History From The Psychoanalytic Point Of View

For the past years the trend has been toward studying more and more the history of civilizations and less and less the dull succession of events. If history is the recreation of the past, psychoanalysis applied to it will tend to study every one of its conscious and unconscious aspects. Even non-psychoanalyst authors have stressed lately the greater unity of human sciences.

"When what we now roughly designate as science has been fully assimilated into our cultural stream, we shall perhaps no longer use the word as we do today. When that time arrives, as I have no doubt it will, the subject of this book will be fused into the age-old problem of understanding man and his works: in short, *'secular education'*."[13]

We cannot sharply differentiate and study politics, economics, sociology, mythology, the history of sciences as independent aspects of the past; for instance, historians accept the fact that the object of their studies is to trace the causes of a single event, while sociological studies have as their object to find the causes of events susceptible to repetition.

In the analysis of an individual, we find also events which happened only once and others which repeated themselves. The latter generally are the result of some fixation or some repetition compulsion and psychoanalysis is particularly interested in detecting their causes. Nevertheless psychoanalysis remains interested in the event which is unique and does not repeat itself.

Jekels[14] has shown that Napoleon was an enemy of France and that he changed his feelings toward this country the day when Louis XVI (father symbol) was killed. From that day on the union of his little island Corsica with France (the mother symbol) became his goal. It is

---

[12] *Op. cit.*, pp. 135-136.
[13] James B. Conant, *On Understanding Science*. New Haven, Yale University Press, 1947, p. 2.
[14] *Imago*, 1914, I-IV.

easy to understand the influence on world history of this turning point in Napoleon's life. There we have a typical example of a unique event which is enlightened by psychoanalysis.[15]

Mythology gives us many data on the unconscious of a civilization. Its study has been used to this effect by Rank, Wittels, de Saussure, and Marie Bonaparte in her recent book on the *Myths of War*.[16]

Marie Bonaparte, studying various myths which seem to have existed in every country at war, has brought an exceedingly interesting contribution to psychoanalysis and history. Analyzing those myths, she has described the unconscious affects at stake which are revealing of the affective atmosphere during the war. Those myths give a pretty good idea of the functions of antagonistic groups and their utilization for the socialization of conflicts. It would be interesting to study all sorts of myths during peace time, for instance, the false ideas, illustrated by examples of what the children think of their parents, myths which exist between two families or two social groups which are in rivalry, false stories about the royal or any outstanding family.

The very fact that, in order to give a good picture of the past, so many aspects of a civilization must be studied has prevented analysts from giving us a complete study of a culture. It is more in the field of anthropology, that we have seen these attempts to characterize a civilization and describe its different aspects. Several years ago I tried to show for what psycho-sociological reasons science was born in ancient Greece and not in one of the other civilizations flourishing at that time. Many essays have been written on the Nazis and on Fascism. We shall come back to some of them later. What can be said is that they are all very incomplete and that if history were to be written from a psychoanalytic point of view, many more facts would have to be accumulated on the prejudices, the religious beliefs, the legal aspects, the way some philosophical or scientific questions are raised, and so on. In other words, history from the psychoanalytic point of view means: what are the fundamental emotional attitudes of a time and how did they reflect on the social structure and the cultural patterns?

---

[15] Another example is the relationship of Napoleon and Talleyrand which is well described by Edmund Bergler. (See Ed. Bergler: *Talleyrand-Napoleon-Stendhal-Grabbe,* Vienna, Internat. Psa. Verlag, 1933, p. 36.)

[16] Marie Bonaparte, *Myths of War*. London, Imago Publ. Co., 1947.

Psychoanalysis and Historiography

As Raymond Aron pointed out, every generation rewrites history from its point of view. Carlyle emphasized the role of big men; Auguste Comte wanted to incorporate history in the natural sciences; Marx declared that the succession of events was entirely dependent on economic factors. Similarly it would be a mistake to explain history entirely from a psychoanalytic point of view.

When we describe an individual from a psychological point of view we know that some hereditary and constitutional factors play a role; we also know that an accident or a disease may handicap a man. Nevertheless more important than the accident is the way the person reacts to it. To President Roosevelt infantile paralysis was a challenge; to others it might have meant a breakdown. In a factory two men have lost a finger; the one will rejoice that he lost only one, the other will be shy and withdraw from society. The same is true in the growth of civilizations. During certain periods, defeat, economic difficulties, hard physical conditions will be taken as challenges and will re-enforce the strength of the nation, while at other times these very same conditions will precipitate decay. Only the psychological background may be responsible for those different reactions.

Some psychoanalysts have taken the humble attitude that they should not write about history because they do not know enough about economics or sociology. I do not agree with this. Psychoanalysis sheds light on many historical problems and the psychoanalyst is not a professional historian. He is an expert in his own branch and emphasizes the psychological causes of an event, just as the economist stresses economic and demographic arguments. Very often economists wanted to explain every phenomenon by economic causes and a closer study then showed they were wrong. Many of them, for instance, interpreted the large emigration from the Greek mainland in the seventh century B.C. as an economic necessity due to the growth of population. But, as Guiraux has shown,[17] this was not the case and we know that it was more a psychological cause, namely, the overpowering authority of the father in the family which led the children to escape from the mainland. The professional historian has the double task of establishing the facts that the specialists will interpret and of weighing the arguments of the different specialists to appreciate how far in a given

---

[17] *La Propriété foncière en Grèce.* Paris, 1893, p. 86.

problem the physical conditions of a country, the economic, demographic and psychological conditions have shaped this event.

The psychoanalyst has to uncover a psychological causality which does not mean that he has a blind spot about the other causes. If in describing President Roosevelt's life the psychoanalyst analyzes the chain of psychological causes, it does not mean that he denies the organic impairment brought by his illness; it only means that his goal is to make a psychological study of his character and to emphasize this side of his personality. From this point of view the analysts should pay much greater attention to history, politics, sociology and collective mental hygiene problems.

Such a point of view has been adopted by Ernest Jones, for instance. In his essay on Ireland[18] he writes: "It is the object of this paper to suggest along psycho-analytic lines that one important factor effecting this difference, the geographical factor of the countries, operates in a more subtle and complex manner than might be suspected. In so doing it is clear that we are deliberately isolating one factor only and have no intention of underestimating the numerous other well-recognized ones, historical, dynastic, economic and so on."

Now that we have emphasized the limitations in the study of psychoanalysis applied to history, we may also stress in what direction our science will influence historiography at the end of this century.

For a long time biographies have consisted in the narration of the great achievements of a man and the description of the qualities which helped his success. Freud has shifted the interest of the biographer to the underlying unconscious conflicts. The causes behind the scene became more important than the facts.

So with the life of a nation. The interest is shifted from the political events to the underlying unconscious causes which may explain a great number of facts, from the civilization to the keys which help to understand it.

Macroscopic Interpretation of History

Freud has given a clue and a starting point for a great field of research when in *Totem and Taboo* he demonstrated that there is a connection between the early infantile conflicts and the social institu-

---

[18] Ernest Jones, *Essays in Applied Psychoanalysis,* London, Hogarth Press, 1923, p. 398.

tions of a people, namely, that in the totem organization (at least in its origin) the taboo not to kill the totem and not to marry a woman of the same clan were defenses against the early oedipal wishes.

I have shown elsewhere[19] that the complete passivity of the early Greek civilization was also a defense against the desire to kill the father. In order to protect himself, the father had to have more and more despotic power and the greater his power the greater the defense against the criminal desire of the child. This comes to a certain limit and then the vicious circle is broken. In the Greek civilization it did because of the transformation of an agricultural into a city civilization and because of the great emigration to the colonies. The Greek, the Latin and all civilizations arising from our Middle Ages give good opportunities to study the connections between the father's authority and certain patterns. It is obvious that while in the Middle Ages this authority was very great, the whole structure of the society and of the church was organized so that everybody was always dependent upon a higher lord and nobody was really free. The cultural result of such a civilization is that in research work people rely on the tradition and on moral authorities like the Bible, Aristotle, Hippocrates, Galenus, and so on, and not on experience. The emotions of submission, fear and revolt are expressed in the collective art of the cathedrals. In the literature if some knight revolts at the beginning of his career, the greatest emotion lies in his later submission to God. Compliance to the father remains the goal of life. A strong homosexual trend arises from this organization. The life in monasteries, the crusades are examples of this trend.

In the cultural field, we can observe that for centuries the great majority of people were trained according to obedience and not according to experience. Of course, some outstanding minds, like Bacon, Locke, Descartes, and many others, freed themselves but they remain exceptions. Even in the eighteenth century, when the nobility was so free in many ways, we observe strong tendencies to obedience. Let us give as an example the *"Mémoires de l'Académie de Médecine"* of the 1770's. The great majority of the authors, when they had a new theory, did not try to prove it by facts but by a great number of quotations of recognized authorities. Let us, for instance, consider French psychiatry, before and right after the French Revolution. It illustrates two kinds of civilizations. Of course, it would be easy to find exceptions

---

[19] *Le Miracle Grec.* Paris, Denoël, 1939.

to my statements as we can imagine that before the Revolution some forerunners existed and that afterwards some conservative minds remained untouched by the great social change.

Those restrictions being clear, we can characterize French psychiatry of the eighteenth century under five headings:

(1) Every statement was backed by a great many quotations of antiquity and of earlier authors.

(2) A great many attempts were made to guess what Nature was instead of observing and experimenting. At that time the adult behavior was supposed to be very rational and in order to comply with the adult mind it became compulsive for many scientists to have a rational explanation for every phenomenon. To accept a doubt and to acknowledge that there is something we do not know presupposes a great emotional security which was exceptional in the middle of the eighteenth century. At the time when the microscope was discovered, the majority of physicians still accepted the idea of the animal spirits carrying the nerve energy through the whole of the nerve channels. Any section of the nerve would have shown that such channels do not exist, but nevertheless, since this idea had the backing of Descartes and many other authorities, we find it stated as a fact even by the best neurologists of the time, like Tissot of Lausanne, Boissier Sauvages, etc.

(3) Interest in general ideas.

The eighteenth century was more philosophical than scientific. The father's authority had been undermined to a large extent among the nobility and the high bourgeoisie. A certain liberalism started and two successive generations could find a common ground in rational behavior, the son behaving so that the father could not reproach him. (I have observed such defense mechanisms in the young Brazilian generation trying to free themselves from still very autocratic fathers.) Very soon the abstract rational law replaces the father's authority. This law serves several functions: (1) To free the son from his father, (2) to fulfill the remaining complying tendencies and free the individual from guilt, (3) to represent a part of reality and bring about a better adjustment.

But these people still stick to the general law in a compulsive way. Therefore they have a tendency to discard all exceptions to the law and to be interested only in general ideas and very little in facts.

A consequence of this attitude is that they write books with ideas but without facts. For instance, at the time that I describe the Abbé Richard wrote a book[20] on dreams without exemplifying any of his contentions with a dream, or Jean Dumas wrote a book on suicide without any case history.[21]

(4) The exclusion of the irrational or isolated fact.

The consequence of this rational attitude was that the child, the insane, the psychopathic character, the poor, the criminal—the exception in science—were of no interest. Only the common denominator with the father, the rational idea had value. For this reason, the insane persons were not really studied in the eighteenth century.[22] The society was only interested in discarding them and most of the time they were jailed with criminals. They were irrational people and for this reason of no interest.

(5) All psychological studies were hampered by confusion between soul and mind. A certain fear to disobey God or the demands of religion compelled the physician of that time to hold the insane responsible for his irrational acts and to punish him. Psychiatrists indulged in long philosophical dissertations about mind and soul in an unsuccessful attempt to free pathological observations from theological prejudices.

In contradistinction to what we just stated, French psychiatry during the Revolution was characterized by the following trends:

(1) Freedom from tradition.

The old authors are no longer or very rarely quoted (I am especially referring to psychiatrists like Pinel, Cabanis, and, in a certain measure, Esquirol).

(2) Experimentation and observation become important.

(3) Interest is directed to specific facts.

The possibility of stressing the importance of a fact which contradicted the general law certainly had to do with the social revolu-

---

[20] L'Abbé Richard, *La Théorie des songes*, Paris, 1766.
[21] Jean Dumas, *Traité du suicide*, Amsterdam, 1773.
[22] In the sixteenth and seventeenth centuries in France repression was greater, but the city life was less developed and sophisticated; the possibilities of escaping from the family were more numerous; therefore life was less rational and more emotional. The interest in human passions was much larger than in the eighteenth century.

tion, giving to the adult child as much recognition as to the father. We even see a shift in the scientific interest. While the books of the eighteenth century were full of general ideas, the post-revolutionary books contained wonderful observations and Pinel, for instance, succeeded in discarding entirely the philosophical discussions about insanity which poisoned the works of his forerunners.

Many sciences came to light with this reversal of emotional attitudes and the sudden interest in facts.

(4) This interest in the outcast (child, poor, criminal, insane) manifested itself in a practical way in many instances: Reform of the educational program, homes for poor people and beggars, new hospitals, and so on. We can say that the motto of the French Revolution *Liberté, Egalité et Fraternité* is the result of a revolution within the family. Freedom from the father which brought liberty and equality between the two successive generations forced replacement of the father's authority by the authority of experience.

This sense of equality increased the sense of equity,[23] therefore gave a greater sense of brotherhood to the idealistic generation of the French Revolution.

(5) At least in the field of science, nature observation and experimentation dominated the theological thoughts.

This comparison between the French psychiatry of the middle and the end of the eighteenth century is but one example among many which could be cited to show connections between certain family attitudes and certain cultural patterns. This difference between pre- and post-revolutionary science is especially clear in psychiatry which is a more conservative field. In other sciences, like physics or chemistry, the interest in the facts developed before the Revolution. This does not contradict my thesis, as it is obvious that in a large measure the family structure changed before the Revolution, this latter being only a consequence of the former change. But with the explosion of the Revolution and the wars which started soon afterwards, the family structure received a new blow, the consequence of which was to free the coming generation more completely from medieval culture.

It seems that all civilizations where the father's authority was strong developed special characteristic features. For instance, the traditions will prey on the social life, the institutions and people in

---

[23] See Piaget, *The Moral Judgment of the Child,* London, Kegan Paul, 1932.

authority (governmental officers, doctors, teachers, etc.) will be highly respected, the will of a dead person is observed, and everybody considers it a duty to leave a will; the law is harsh and allows for no exceptions; collective ideas like religious beliefs, national prejudices, family traditions are much stronger than personal will. The strong-willed man, free of the prejudices of his class has to emigrate or become the scapegoat of society. No divorce, no tolerance for neurotic fancies, the collective traditions with the general ideas they imply are always stronger. Instead of science there is a kind of "rational abstractionism". We mean by this term the psychological school known as the ideologists. Instead of describing facts they explain everything by abstractions. The most representative author of this group is Collineau. For instance, take his definition of "memory":

"The intellectual and affective movements may press more or less strongly, more or less often on the same object, on the same subject, on the same things, and as soon as these things make a sufficient impression on our sensitive organs, or our moral agents, they present themselves to our mind, willingly, or as a result of instinctual habit. That phenomenon is the memory."[24]

In other words, we can always describe a civilization according to the ratio: individual versus society, society being here the same as the father. In the lectures I gave a few years ago in the New York Institute of Psychoanalysis, I suggested to call this ratio *Libidinal Index of a Civilization.*

Practically, this index would measure the superego of a cultural unit with all the libidinal implications it has. For instance: the stronger the father's authority, the stronger the homosexual trends (sublimated or not).

When the father has despotic power, he generally considers the woman, like the children, as unreasonable and forces the child to repress strongly his oedipus wishes.

We have described some aspects of a civilization from the angle of the father's authority. Other trends could be emphasized. Recently in his book on the *Origin and Function of Culture*[25] Roheim criticizes the materialistic view that culture is a rational adjustment to environment. This element, of course, exists, but is secondary in development.

---

[24] See Collineau: *Analyse physiologique de l'entendement humain,* Paris, Baillère, 1843, p. 30.
[25] Geza Roheim: *The Origin and Function of Culture,* New York, Nervous & Mental Disease Publ. Co., 1943.

Roheim abandons the idea that a civilization is a neurosis, he admits that today it is rather a reaction formation which is largely used as a sublimation.

Many psychoanalysts have given descriptions of cultural patterns, referring to family structures but without trying to build up a method which could be used systematically and improved with time. Others, however, in keeping with the lines of this macroscopic interpretation of history have made interesting contributions or remarks, drawing parallels between personal character conflicts, familial and social structures.[26]

Speaking of the many societies with exclusively male membership in national German life, Wittels says that they operate as a defense against homosexuality by sublimation of this tendency. He then adds:

"As long as the covenant remains strong in its aims and practices, it succeeds in its sublimation. If it is weakened as a result of a clash with unusual social forces the homosexual drive breaks through—all the more strongly since the specific energy of the drive was continuously fed to grow in the group."[27]

Now let us come to a very different aspect of psychoanalysis applied to history.

In his charming essay on the Island of Ireland Jones has tried to show that for her inhabitants she has always been described as a symbol of motherhood. "We found there the fountain of life, the golden apples, children come from it and return to it. Heroes set out to secure the wonderful Cauldron of Re-Birth, a typical womb symbol, just as elsewhere they did for the Holy Grail."[28] De Valera, in a speech on February 22nd 1920 said: "There were people who held Ireland was a mother country, and would never consent to making her a kind of illegitimate daughter." Jones thinks that England failed to recognize how important it is to Ireland to remain a mother country and therefore failed in her policy toward her neighbor island. Curiously enough Jones did not elaborate on this theme to show that England too was an island and a mother symbol. There lies the reason why she could not treat her sister Ireland on an equal footing. Even from

---

[26] See for instance: Eider: Psychoanalysis and Politics, in: Jones: *Social Aspects of Psychoanalysis*, pp. 158-159; or Erikson: Hitler's Imagery, *Psychiatry*, 1942, p. 480, or Flugel, *Psychoanalytic Study of the Family*, p. 127.

[27] Fritz Wittels, Collective Defense Mechanisms against Homosexuality. *Psa. Rev.*, XXXI, 19, 1944.

[28] Ernest Jones, *Essays in Applied Psychoanalysis*, London, Int. Psa Press. 1923.

a strictly psychoanalytic point of view many other reasons should be mentioned as contributing factors of this historical discord.

Microscopic Interpretation of History

(1) *Introduction.*

We have just given a few samples of psychoanalytic interpretations applied to history. Every analyst interested in that field has followed his intuitions and has shed light on one aspect or another of the problem. But the time comes where we should develop a method and acquire a more systematic approach to the social and cultural problems.

Very few physicians at the end of the eighteenth century, after the discoveries by Lavoisier of combustion or after Bichat's studies on the tissues, understood the revolution which started in medicine. For a long time the macroscopic diagnoses continued to be the essential part of medical art. Today the greatest field of medical research is dependent upon the microscope.

Today's attempts to apply psychoanalysis to history or sociology are similar to the macroscopic clinic and as time goes on a method will be found which will give with much greater accuracy the connection between personal conflicts, the structure of the family, the organization of the state, the layers of the society and the cultural patterns of a civilization.

A few years ago, Heinz Hartmann wrote: "In theory one should be able to utilize the results of personal analysis of which a large number are now available in order to study many of the current sociological problems. Each of these analyses gives us an unparalleled insight into the intimate relations between the personality structure and the social structure. But the experiences of psychoanalysis in this respect up to this time have not been used in a systematic manner."[29] A similar idea has been expressed by Erikson:[30] "Men who share an ethnic area, an historical area or an economic pursuit are guided by common images of good and evil. Infinitely varied, these images reflect the elusive nature of historical change; yet in the form of contemporary social models, of compelling prototypes of good and evil,

---

[29] Lorand, Ed., In: *Psychoanalysis Today,* p. 337.
[30] Erikson, Ego Development and Historical Change, *Psa. Study of the Child, II,* p. 339.

they assume decisive concreteness in every individual ego's development. Psychoanalytic ego psychology has not matched this concreteness with sufficient theoretical specificity."[31]

These assertions, especially those of Hartmann, are very true. They originate from two facts:

1. That those observations are very scattered,

2. That we lack a system of grouping them. We know how to make wide generalizations and how to observe one patient, but we do not yet know how to connect those two sets of observations and how to coordinate the great amount of isolated sociological data that we collect from individual analyses. To find a better connection between individual reactions and social patterns will be the object of a microscopic interpretation of history.

(2) *Psychodynamics of a Culture.*

Every science which has tried to express itself in a dynamic system has a unit. These units combine to create compounds which will organize themselves in systems.

It could be discussed what in human energy is the simplest unit? Is it a need? An emotion like fear, pleasure, or anger? In our opinion the most practical unit is the affect. An affect is any connection between an emotion and the outside (physical or social) world. We call emotions any appetitive, rejecting, pleasurable or inhibitive reaction. Let us give different forms of affects. Peaches are invested by an appetitive affect if people like to eat them; a skunk is invested by a repelling affect because of its odor. A lovable child is invested with a positive affect by normal parents, and so on.

Any affect has three components: (1) An emotion; (2) a representation of the outside world; (3) a potential action. As is well known in psychology, any emotion tends to be released by action. For many reasons, the energetic charge of an affect is not immediately and generally not entirely discharged. The introjected representation of the outside world is also periodically reinvested. The result of this is that our memories are not a collection of indifferent representations, they are an energetic system with different affective charges.

---

[31] See also the last chapter (VII) of Alexander, *Our Age of Unreason*, or Fromm, Appendix to *Escape from Freedom.*

As a cell of our body is the center of a chemical system absorbing oxygen, iron and other useful products and rejecting carbon dioxide and other wastes, so our instinctual needs fix in our mind new potentialities of gratification and repel unpleasant objects. The psychic representatives of stimuli are invested by our desires, or, expressed in another way, our needs are channeled in new gratifying representations of the outside world which helps at the same time to gratify (by displacements) and stimulate the function.

Any energetic charge of an affect can be set in motion either from within (activated by a physiological, emotional or intellectual need); or, from without, by the reality of the object acting as "agent provocateur" or suggesting and re-enforcing the dynamic charge of the affect. The affect can also be set in motion by association of ideas or emotions which reanimate old experiences and vitalize or "dynamize" the affect.

The experiences of life and especially the early experiences of childhood create a system of emotions which has a certain fixity. According to their degree of rigidity they are called emotional patterns or complexes.

Reactions to a flexible emotional pattern (which can change according to reality) are called behavior; reactions to a rigid complex are called neurotic behavior. The best known of these are the oedipus and the castration complexes. They shape a great number of other emotional reactions, their fixity is an obstacle to a normal adjustment to reality and they cause all sorts of defense mechanisms.

The totality of emotional patterns of any individual forms his character. This synthetic system of reactions is always more or less dominated by emotions but in normal people the systematization takes place in a great measure according to logical principles and reality demands. We are now speaking of normal characters, while the systems which are predominantly under the tyranny of some complexes and their defense mechanisms are called neuroses or psychoses. In such cases the external stimuli instead of arousing normal, adjusted reactions to a given situation, reanimate older situations with the set of emotional patterns which originated at the time when they were first and unsuccessfully experienced. The result is that in so far as the man is well adjusted, his mind has introjected the physical world as it is, with its natural order; but at the same time its different parts are invested with different affects according to the feelings of pleasure, of safety or of danger that those realities can engender.

In so far as the individual is neurotic, he introjects the social patterns of his environment and approaches reality with his own conflicts.

To exemplify this, the man who was educated with a normal approach to sex will consider different women as possible objects for his sex needs and will make a choice that corresponds to a maximum of happiness and pleasure. On the other hand, a man raised by a castrating mother who has a jealous fixation on her son will rationalize the situation and look at girls with fear and suspicion; he will remain fixed on his mother, or make a choice of a frustrating woman under whose dependence he will live.

These phenomena are well known to the analysts and it is unnecessary to multiply the examples.

Let us summarize what we said as follows:

Individual Structures		*Social Reactions*
Affect	(Emotion + outside representation)	Reaction
Emotional patterns	(Adjusted system of affects)	Normal behavior
Complexes	(Fixed system of affects)	Neurotic behavior
Character	(Organization of emotional patterns)	History of a life
Neuroses	(Complexes + Defense Mechanisms)	

All the reality a man has experienced is invested with affects. This system of investment will change according to his age. The infant especially has oral investments, later the child has a phallic investment, and so on. Once the man is an adult, the world is invested according to the different needs of his body and of our culture. People who have similar ways of sublimation or defense mechanisms have a similar investment system and form cultural groups.

The more primitive a civilization, the more intense and symbolic is its investment system. For instance, in societies with a strong castration complex, the magic power (the mana which has a symbolic phallic value) plays a great role and many objects are invested with it. In very differentiated societies where the facilities for the gratification of biological needs are great, the world is more and more invested with intellectual or scientific curiosity. But even behind this objective research we often find neurotic investments.

The psychological predisposition that neurotic parents inflict on their children may last several generations if nothing happens to straighten out the young generation. This leads to similar rationalizations in parents and children and creates real family ideologies.

These family neuroses may take different forms and they have not yet been sufficiently studied.[32]

As we observe neurotic family patterns, we observe neurotic cultural patterns which give similar emotional reactions to a group or a nation. This means that the group shares the same affects or has the same affective investment of reality.

Not all those affects are pathological in nature, as Hartmann has shown. Many are normal and are shared by every member of the human race. As we have shown elsewhere, those affects will give predominant value to certain items of a civilization. Where, for instance, the libidinal index is low, the respect of a dead man will be great; in more differentiated culture, the respect will be shifted to the living man. A closer study of the civilizations will show how much all our concepts are animated by emotional values.

A modern civilization has always different layers, each of them having a different system of values. This very often helps the development of an individual and the interplay of those layers also determines the history of a country. When a man enters a society governed

---

[32] See, for instance: Laforgue, La névrose familiale; Leuba, La famille névrotique et les névroses familiales. *Rapport présenté au IXe congrès des psychanalystes de langue française.* Paris, Editions Denoël, 1936.

by a rigid structure (feudalism, autocratic regime, etc.), he has to adjust himself to it in order to survive. When the civilization is more differentiated, different layers with different systems of investments are at his disposal. If he was educated under a strong paternal authority and wants to free himself from the imagery and the affects of his childhood, it is easy for him to find political, social or scientific groups which are already adjusted to more liberal standards and have already created a system of affects in accordance with more democratic views. The man makes a conversion and identifies himself with the new group whose imagery gives him at once the means and the strength to give up the old ideology. Contact with the new group has a catalytic effect on the catharsis of old emotions and may help many people to go through the liquidation of neurotic trends provided that those are not too strongly rooted. A man goes through different ideologies before he reaches maturity and steady adjustment to life.

As Erikson has expressed it:[33] "A child has quite a number of opportunities to identify himself more or less experimentally with real or fictitious people of either sex, with habits, traits, occupations and ideas. Certain crises force him to make radical selections. However, the historical era in which he lives offers only a limited number of socially meaningful models for workable combinations of identification fragments. Their usefulness depends on the way in which they, simultaneously, meet the requirements of the organism's maturational stage and the ego's habits of synthesis."

(3) *The Socialization of Affects.*

In the last paragraph we have seen that every individual is a sort of energetic system answering to the stimuli of the outside world and that some neurotic patterns become familial. It is obvious also that some ideologies (political or religious) or social organizations (factories, stores, offices, societies, and so on) by their requirements of the individual will have the same claims as the family had on the children and therefore will be chosen by the adult individual who was conditioned to them in his childhood. These social organizations will be new units maintaining normal or abnormal emotional patterns. They have been created by individuals according to the emotional patterns they had acquired in their childhood. But this unconscious reproduction is not the only way of socialization of our affects.

---

[33] Erikson, Hitler's Imagery, *loc. cit.*

Let us try to describe some of these processes of socialization.

(a) Displacement of the affect on other people

Freud has described the part of Eros in the social ties as being essentially an aim-inhibited sex drive. No doubt that this displacement plays a great role. However, we know, from Freud himself,[34] that an object fulfils a great many functions. The mother after having been the provider of the food and the oral gratifications, becomes a source of security. These functions may be extended to other people. The need of security becomes a need in itself; its gratification helps the child to establish confidence in himself and to express his emotions, instead of repressing them. But, if the mother is an object of fear to the child, this fear will be extended to other people and the child will have more difficulty in becoming secure.

All those facts are well known to analysts, but their social implications have not been completely formulated. The man who has been conditioned to fear in his childhood, will react as an adult by isolating himself or by trying to dominate other people. In so doing he becomes a source of insecurity for others. If many people react the same way in a nation, for instance, we find that a great number of social organizations (education at school, colleges, universities, army, management of offices, hospitals, factories, and so on) will reflect this emotional pattern which will also shape part of the political organization. The discovery of these emotional patterns in a great number of social activities of a country, the way they develop in new patterns is the object of the microscopic interpretation of history.

(b) Introjection and projection

In my opinion introjection and projection are primary processes of the unconscious, like symbolization, displacement, etc., which may be utilized sometimes as defense mechanisms.

Freud has taught us that prior to normal thinking, the child has hallucinations, which means, for instance, that when it is hungry, it anticipates by hallucination part of the feeding process. At first, these hallucinations certainly are very partial, are more kinesthetic sensations than representations of the outside world. However, the latter must appear, first in a confused way, then more accurately. These hallucinations are introjections of the outside world, which are pro-

---

[34] See his latest theories on anxiety.

jected later in reality and compared with it. Through thousands of these reality tests our inner world becomes more and more like the outside world.

This fact may partially explain the repetition compulsion in so far as the child is led to seek what he hallucinated and later what he experienced.

These processes of introjection and projection are as valid in the emotional life as they are in our intellectual adjustment. The emotional experiences, good or bad, have to be repeated once they have been introjected.

Freud has given two very different descriptions of the instinct, one of which he unfortunately applied to the death instinct but it keeps its full value for the emotional patterns. It reads in this connection: "An instinct would be a tendency innate in living organic matter impelling it towards the reinstatement of an earlier condition."[35]

In order to reproduce the same emotional patterns, the individual has to find (in so far as his later adjustment has not freed him from the early emotions) the same type of individuals as those who conditioned his childhood and to recreate social organizations where he can find the same dependency and submission but also the same protection that he experienced in his first years.

This process of introjection and repetition compulsion is increased in any conflicting situations where hatred, repressions, guilt feelings bring greater complications. This is the case in the superego formation. There is the real clue to understanding how society shapes the individual and how the latter shapes his social environment.

If man is enclosed in such a vicious circle, how is it that the structure of society still changes?

The core of emotions which is projected into social environment belongs to the early repressed experiences of the first years. But the child has another source of social experiences whose importance has been stressed especially by Piaget.[36] When he has to deal with younger siblings, he very often acts towards them as the parents or the older siblings acted towards him. But, in societies where the child is trained for years with children of his own age, he is acting (in cases where he can free himself of his earlier experiences) on an equal footing

---

[35] Freud, *Beyond the Pleasure Principle*. Translation by C. J. Hubbach, Int. Psa. Press, 1922, p. 42.

[36] Piaget, *The Moral Judgment of the Child*. London, Kegan Paul, 1932.

with his comrades. The completely different relationships that he forms on these occasions will clash with the old emotional patterns of submission and eventually bring him to act according to the real characters he meets and not according to a stereotyped pattern. In many societies the paternal authority is too great to allow the relationships of equal footing to overstep the relations of subservience.

The idealized father, internalized in the superego, is then projected on a political or religious authority.

Eder quotes Blackstone's formula: "The sovereign is not only incapable of doing wrong; he can never mean to do an improper thing; in him is no folly or weakness." Commenting on Blackstone, Eder adds[37]: "Put briefly, it is the maxim that the king can do no wrong and its genesis is: I am like my father—I can do no wrong. This ego-ideal splits off and is projected onto the father of his people —the king. The reverence that doth hedge a king is thus the reverence unconsciously paid to our ideal self. It must be borne in mind that this feeling may be displaced onto a number of persons or ideas; there may be, so to say, many kings—many projections of the original identification . . . "

In such societies, of course, the priest, the schoolmaster, the doctor, the boss of a business, all have the character of the idealized father,

(c) Identification

Freud has shown that identification occurs with the loss of the beloved object or as a process of neutralization of aggression. I am interested here in pointing out the social implications of identifications.

In the process of identification the individual incorporates not only a great part of the feelings of his model but also attitudes and ideas which are interwoven with these feelings. Therefore when several persons identify themselves with a family, national or religious figure, they accept the same ideology and they tend to reinforce the common feelings with all their practical and intellectual implications.

"Ideologies are not the creation of a single individual," says Schilder,[38] "but are created by social intercourse. The pattern starts with the relations between child and parents and is continued through-

---

[37] Eder: "Psychoanalysis in Relation to Politics" in Ernest Jones: *Sociological Aspects of Psychoanalysis,* p. 187.
[38] Paul Schilder: *Goals and Desires of Man.* New York, Columbia University Press, 1942, p. 53.

out all the life. The processes going on are extremely complex. By identification, individuals take into themselves other persons with their ideologies and may change their own ideologies in accordance with their attitudes towards these other persons. An individual who has become the carrier of an ideology tries consciously to impart this ideology to others, but he may not even be conscious of such a wish. Such a wish may originate from his deeper tendencies but it will not be weaker because of it. The mere fact that an ideology exists has social significance. Human beings have to influence each other whether they want to or not. A large part of the ideology is transmitted from person to person and even from one generation to another, as tradition. There may or may not be a definite formulation, but the ideology will finally express itself in customs and ceremonies."

When several persons have been conditioned by similar experiences of childhood they will idealize their father in the same way and find a national hero of whom they will make a common paternal figure.

Freud has well described the formation of such a collective super-ego.[39]

These collective identifications bring a great number of common affects to people who share the same ideology. After a few generations, the young people feel too different to be able to project their conflicts onto the old ideology. The older people, being threatened in their beliefs, increase their dogmatism and the younger depart. The schisms occur frequently and are important to the historian. They express in a symbolic way the emotional evolution of a few generations. Under the impact of some catastrophe subsequent generations will reinvest the older ideology.

We psychoanalysts are better acquainted with the projection of personal conflicts on political events than on other frames of projection, but no doubt that these other frames are as important as the political scene in judging the emotional significance of an epoch.

In the history of sciences we all know that there exist periods when a science passes from one system of references to another. At those periods you see characteristic facts.

(1) A leader breaks with a tradition. For instance, Lavoisier breaks with the flogiston theory and describes the chemical processes

---

[39] Freud, *Civilization and Its Discontents* (Rivière transl., p. 136).

of combustion. Bernheim breaks with the idea of hypnotic sleep and stresses the importance of suggestion and persuasion. Freud breaks with the idea of the hypnoid and explains the neuroses in terms of conflicts within the personality.

(2) The new conception is a revival of an earlier concept which is re-introduced in a more elaborate way and demonstrated by new facts.

For instance, the idea of conflict has been stressed by the church to explain the unhappiness of the people. It was introduced in psychopathology by many German doctors at the end of the eighteenth century, it was well described as a genetic factor of neuroses by Descuret in France in 1841, it is often mentioned by Breuer, but it gained its real significance only through Freud.

(3) For a period of time, scientists, attached to the old conception, rationalize their defense of it and deny the new facts. The most striking example of this kind happened at the Academy of Medicine in Paris when Pasteur fought for his idea of asepsis and the surgeons answered: "Either the microbes exist and we kill them with our knives, or they do not exist—why bother with the microbe myth?" Psychoanalysts also know the rationalizations that so many psychologists and psychiatrists have opposed to the unconscious or to the sex-life of the child.

(4) The followers of the new leader have a tendency to reject as no good all the last defenders of the old theory. In its growing phase, psychoanalysis has rejected hypnosis and few people have given Breuer the credit he deserves.

Even in the field of science our emotions find a way of expressing themselves: the last vestiges of an oedipus rivalry are imprinted in the choice of a scientific lore. Those who could not detach themselves from the guilt and remained dependent on their father have to stick to the old conception, while those who revolted or freed themselves, enjoy demonstrating the truth of the new ideas.

Maybe we should even go further and say that the new leader should have some aggressiveness to impose a new vocabulary and a new frame of references on his contemporaries.

Very often the new facts of a new lore were known, but as long as they were not systematized and socialized in a movement of research, they remained without influence on the thoughts of the contemporaries.

Only when they acquire an emotional significance for the unconscious of a group do they assume a certain strength of conviction in their use as weapons in the fight and sublimation of unconscious conflicts.

(d)   The adjustment to reality

The socialization of affects takes place also because the social environment is part of reality. A growing child is surrounded by people who try to seduce him, to boss him, frighten him and, of course, he wants to play on others the tricks that others play on him. As in other fields, a method of trial and error teaches him the best way to handle his neighbor. But only if he is free from unconscious conditionings will he be able to vary his emotional reactions and adjust himself.

(e)   The socialization of the conflict

In the process of socialization we should distinguish between two steps. A man may identify himself with another man or with a group. This second step of socialization is normal and increases self-confidence. A child may tell a story to his mother, but is unable to tell it in front of his class. A woman is able to sing alone in her living room, she is unable, however, to do it before an audience. Acting in common helps the control of emotions in front of a group and re-inforces identification with one's fellowmen. Therefore among primitive people many activities are collective. Identification with a group gives security, reminds one of the family and belongs to a normal process, but it may also help the assertion of neurotic trends.

For instance, a masculine woman after having challenged her boy friends individually will join an aggressive group of feminists, identifying herself with a group of women who have the same difficulty. Or, a paranoiac, after having fought his father or one of his substitutes will create a group fighting a father's symbol.

This socialization of the conflict may re-inforce any perversion (religious masochism, political sadism, etc.) or any defense mechanism.

In this process there are many transitions between normal sublimation and neurotic trends. Even in the history of sciences we see that often new ideas triumph because they were discovered or rediscovered by a man with paranoiac tendencies who had an urge to impose them on others. Mesmer, for instance, was such a personality and helped scientists to accept the reality of hypnotic phenomena.

(f) Attempt to describe a method

If we try to follow the same path that Freud took in *Totem and Taboo*, we must try to find (1) the characteristics of a family; (2) the main and general conflicts resulting from this structure; (3) the defense mechanisms attempting to overcome those conflicts; (4) the projection of these conflicts and defense mechanisms both in the structure of the state and in the pattern of civilization; (5) the action of traumas (war, revolution, industrial discoveries, and so on) on the normal frame of projection of the conflicts. Without formulating clearly the method, many authors have alluded to such connections and some have attempted a more or less systematic work in that direction.

We could quote many passages of Flugel's writings showing this connection between a strong father's authority and a strong state, a liberal father and a liberal state.

If we want to progress in this field of psychoanalysis applied to history we must leave those generalities and start studying facts, for instance, take several civilizations with strong paternalistic family structures, compare the family structures, the conflicts expressed in different cultural patterns and the state structures. From such comparisons, we shall be able to improve our method. We also should try to show the parallel evolution of the family structure, the state organization and the cultural patterns.[40]

(g) Family structure and personal conflicts

Every analyst has met in his career men who stem from families dominated by a tyrannic father, and has seen developed in the son compulsions to revolt overcompensated by compliance compulsions which lead to great passiveness.

Many civilizations started with a family structure in which the father was omnipotent. The fear of disobeying made men build a social and cultural (religious) frame in which they had constantly to obey an authority. Due to poverty and primitiveness of such societies the houses are usually small, the sexual contact between children and adults great, therefore the oedipus feelings are strongly aroused and have to be equally strongly repressed or sublimated.

In such societies a strict code of ethics prohibits hatred of the father, the consequence of which is to force the child to see only

---

[40] I tried to do this in *Le Miracle Grec*, but it should be done in much greater detail and for a great number of cultures.

the good side of his father and to identify with him. This constant moral endeavor to turn hatred against one's defects and to deflect i' from the father leads to a progressive sublimation where the hatred economy is better dealt with. But the child has also alloplastic defenses, like leaving the house and escaping to another country where he can develop more initiative, and new forms of displacement or sublimation. In civilizations where money exists, the child becomes more successful than his father and finds in this revenge an appeasement for his earlier conflicts.

When we study the evolution of such civilizations, we see that grosso-modo they undergo three phases: (1) the father is stronger than the son, the culture is marked by a dogmatic faith in religious beliefs, the king has a religious and political power; (2) the father is still highly respected but the adult son feels his equal and the father has a tendency to trust him. The cultural patterns tend to a certain ethic and artistic perfectionism—general and rational ideas tend to overthrow the religious superstitions; (3) the son becomes more important than the father, the civilization goes through rapid changes, the scientific and individualistic point of view becomes predominant.

All these social changes are slow. They are the work of a constant sublimation process. But at a time, when a new ideology is formed and when a liberal government is desired by a group, this new ideology will help the socialization of the conflict with the father. Different political shades will express the different "nuances" of this conflict.

In the frame of this paper, we cannot describe the gradual transformation of the family, the gradual change of individual conflicts and their repercussions on the government structure and the cultural patterns, but this is really what should be done to improve the method. However, great caution is necessary in the interpretation of facts. For instance, Flugel identifies the conservative political ideas with introjections of father figures and superego activities while he describes the leftists' activities as ego-syntonic, which is an erroneous oversimplification. It is true that the decrease of the father's authority facilitates a more liberal civilization, but it is not true that the leftists can be entirely identified with ego-syntonic people. A great number of them have a compulsive behavior of revolt with destructive tendencies, just as rightists may have a compliance compulsion. Furthermore, Flugel describes the leftist primarily loyal to the group and the conservative to the leader. This depends greatly on the position of the left or the right. Where a political party represents a minority (right or left), it has a tendency to express revolt and to be directed by a leader, which shows how much those groups are utilized for personal conflicts. A son in a leftist family may express his revolt in joining a rightist political party. It is the task of the microscopic interpretation of history to describe the interplay of different social layers, their political belief, their family structures and conflicts.

The problem becomes interesting when the generalities stop being true and we have to face a more complex reality. It is doubtful that we already have the necessary material to describe the details of a political structure or of a cultural medium of a modern civilization; however, such attempts should be made in order to improve the method and to see more concretely the gaps in the present investigations and how to supplement them.

From this angle, it would be particularly interesting to study a period like the Restoration period in France in 1830. For forty years the country had been shaken by the Revolution and by the Napoleonic wars.

Different family structures gave rise to different political attitudes and different layers in the revolutionary movement. Many rich families of the eighteenth century had lost their patriarchal structure. The more liberal ideas about education published by Locke, Fontenelle, Rousseau, had lessened the father's despotic attitude. Men educated in these new ideas became the idealistic contributors to the French Revolution, others did not help directly to political freedom but to new scientific ideas, giving to their contemporaries a new pattern of culture. Another type of revolutionists like Marat or Robespierre had a personal conflict with the father and projected it onto the political stage. A great number of others did not during their childhood receive much affection from parents who were members of a spoiled nobility whose chief goal was to have a good time. Those children suffered from rejection and swelled the ranks of dissatisfied people. Many of them were happy to become heroes of the Napoleonic wars.

The Revolution itself brought uncertainty for a few years. Lack of security, tight food conditions and the long imperial wars started new difficulties. For fifteen years husbands were dragged away from their homes, many died, many were crippled, syphilis became a terrible social disease. As a result, many men and women were longing for order and peace. The old feudal ideal with a strong monarchy was brought back. However, many could not adjust themselves to such an order after the chaotic years of the Revolution and the Empire.

Several traditions were alive in the society of the thirties: (1) a revival of the old monarchy; (2) a group still longing for the glorious days of the Napoleonic era; (3) a revolutionary tradition whose aim was less a revolt than the democratic ideal.

During that period we find very different cultural patterns. A strong return to abstract philosophy. A current of mystical ideas. A scientific attitude in which observation and experimentation became more and more rigorous.

The study of a large number of biographies of that time would be of great interest and help to show the interplay of family conflicts, social ideologies, political group formations, cultural patterns. Those different currents were fighting each other during the whole nineteenth century.

(h)   The break in the projection

As long as the early conflict is projected on an identical sociological screen (let us say, for instance, that the parental couple is projected onto the royal couple) a similar process of sublimation and a certain unit of civilization develops.

Two things may happen:

(1) A break in the projection pattern from within, which means a new political ideology forming a scission in the primitive national ideal and making it possible for the younger generation to oppose the older one by joining an opposition group. From that point on the apparent historical fact will be the interplay of these groups and the supremacy of one or the other. But behind that the most dynamic forces which move these groups are the individual conflicts and the way they utilize the collective ideologies. The different ideologies fighting each other and after a time certain leftist groups going back to the right bring compromises and a certain stability despite the political differences.

(2) Another break in the projection pattern can occur from without. A long war breaks the family structure, increases the freedom of youth, mixes all classes of the society, the consequence of which is that the younger generation is left with aggressive tendencies without having a socially constructive outlet to express them. This explosion of hostility brings also self-punishment tendencies and the result is a

strong sado-masochistic culture with many regressive trends. Where such a break occurs, all the ordinary channels of sublimation which were used during adolescence and all the social structures on which the individuals had projected their conflicts disappeared with the war, the man is left alone with his passions. He can no longer, as did the preceding generation, project his repressed infantile conflicts on a corresponding social organization; the aggressions are actualized and set free by the fact that they are detached from their old social structure, the individual is overwhelmed by them (traumatic situation); being put in an emergency situation, he has to regress, acting out a great part of his aggression or going back to more primitive social organizations in which he rationalizes his regressive behavior. Here again we can only indicate the macroscopic aspect of such breaks, but through analytic and biographic material it should be established what were the main cultural patterns and how the social trauma acted to modify them. We also feel that a better knowledge of those social phenomena will help in understanding some of the neurotic processes. Every time that such breaks take place in a cultural pattern, the aggression has to be displaced on scapegoat groups. Those have been especially studied with the new wave of anti-Semitism, that Nazism has created. The kind of attack directed against those groups is essentially irrational as Simmel and others have shown.

The necessity of finding a scapegoat is not only due to displaced revenge feelings but also to a psycho-dynamic problem of fear. Every dictatorship has a police force which spies on all the actions of the party members. The more responsibility a man has, the more watched he is. For this reason he has to fear the government, but, on the other hand, he does not dare to express this fear; very often he does not even dare to become conscious of it. The result is that he projects this fear and this hostility against the enemies within or outside his country. This, for instance, is greatly responsible for the misunderstandings between Russia and the United States. This also makes it possible in such times to spread social and racial prejudices very quickly.

A similar phenomenon takes place in small communities where the father's authority is still very strong and where the sons displace their fear of the father on neighbors and replace family hostility by gossip.

Prejudices against political parties often have this same origin. This has been demonstrated in a more experimental way on children by Lewin.[41]

As an obsession or a taboo may extend from one object to another, a conflict extends from personalities to groups of personalities. For instance, a Jewish patient one day mentioned in his free associations his seeing a Jew with a dark sun-tan, when coming to town on the train. He said he had felt ashamed and thought that surely all non-Jews on the train would object to these Jews going to Florida, spending money, and often being so noisy. He admitted later that he would have thought in the same way had the passenger been a woman.

With this special emotion of surprise, described by Theodor Reik, he understood that the dark man was his father and the woman his father's secretary and mistress; both used to go together to Florida. He had to conceal this fact from his mother, thus had to share the guilt of his father. Then he extended his feelings to all Jews.

The socialization of the conflict is a defense mechanism, a description of a great many of them will make us more acquainted with some cultural patterns and will help to fill the gap between personal analyses and social behavior.

Simmel has described another aspect of the connection between individual and society.

"There is an inner relationship between individual character development and collective character development. Before the individual can reach the level of his own civilization, he must first repeat within himself in an accelerated and abbreviated manner all the historical phases through which his culture has passed."[42]

This idea which was already expressed by Stanley Hall and Freud is partially true, but does not by any means represent the only relationship between the individual and society.

(i) Analysis of some methodological errors

I have no derogatory intentions in quoting critically some authors who otherwise have often been pioneers in this difficult field. I feel that pointing out some errors may clarify the method which still is at its beginning. The subject has been tackled in many ways; some seem more successful than others.

---

[41] Quoted by Dollard, *Frustration and Aggression,* pp. 87-88.
[42] Simmel, Ed.: *op. cit.,* p. 34.

After an interesting study on the psychodynamics of frustration and repressed aggression, John Dollard has tried with his colleagues to describe Democracy, Fascism and Communism in terms of frustrations, aggressions and gratifications. It did not work quite satisfactorily because the problem was expressed in too general a form, it became too difficult to determine which frustrations lead to which aggressions. In many cases, the frustrations rising from a social system are not those which have built up the aggressiveness of individuals. To make fruitful such research one has first to study the structure of the family in the years preceding such a regime and then study the family conflicts and their projection on the social environment. René Laforgue, in a book on Talleyrand[43] writes: "The consequence of the suppression of the monarchy's authority was to reintroduce within the ego of every Frenchman this authority which disappeared on the outside. We could say that this seemingly suppressed coercion was replaced by an unconscious coercion acting as a superego. This would explain why the Frenchman obeys a sort of unwritten law which is dictated to him by a national ideal of perfection."

This quotation shows two fundamental methodological and factual mistakes: (1) It is not the suppression of the king's authority, but the destruction of the father's authority which has helped to build up a mature self-reliance and only because many men possessed this internalized authority were they able to suppress the king's authority. (2) The second mistake consists in starting from the general ideologies of a country to explain the individual, instead of describing the national ideology as a final expression of individual trends or conflicts. Of course, a national ideology helps to shape the adult mind and after having been the projection of personal conflicts of a group, finally helps to form the personality of subsequent generations. But here also the active process takes place within the family; because the father accepted it, the son by identification or revolt will accept or reject it.

This way of starting from a supposed national characteristic brings Laforgue to a third mistake which is to describe as specifically French a trend which is more a sign of psychological maturity than of French nationality.

---

[43] René Laforgue, *Talleyrand*. Geneva, Ed. du Mont Blanc, 1947.

Another mistake that we find in the writings of many analysts consists in describing in conscious terms unconscious processes.

Example: "But under the leadership of Hitler, she (Germany) decided to cling to a few German absolutes, with monomanic pride, determined ignorance and blind brutality. She felt she had to free herself from all the relativity of values which comes from too wide a cultural experience."[44]

Even if the Nazis were compelled to rationalize such a regression in an ideology, they did not decide such evolution deliberately. They were driven to revolt against their fathers and this part of their culture which inhibited their revolt. If a regicide is elaborating an ideology to rationalize his crime, we know that in a great majority of cases his ideal was not the real motivation of his murderous action, but his ideal like his crime were symptoms of a displaced oedipus complex. It is a common mistake to overemphasize the causal influence of an ideology. The rationalization and the action have a common psychodynamic origin and the rationalization has only a secondary effect in the sense that it helps a new ego-synthesis and allows a warded-off drive to be reintroduced into the ego. On a social or political level, such a new rationalization has to be stressed with all the tools of modern propaganda in order to counteract the old cultural inhibitions.

Erich Fromm, whose book contains excellent theoretical remarks failed to apply them when he discussed the time of the Reformation. He writes:

"On the whole, it seems safe to say that Calvin's adherents were recruited mainly from the conservative middle class, and that also in France, Holland and England his main adherents were not advanced capitalistic groups but artisans and small business men, some of whom were already more prosperous than others but who, *as a group, were threatened by the rise of capitalism.*

"To this social class, Calvinism had the same psychological appeal that we have already discussed in connection with Lutheranism. It expressed the feeling of freedom but also of insignificance and powerlessness of the individual. It offered a solution by teaching the individual that by complete submission and self-humiliation he could hope to find new security."[45]

---

[44] Erikson, Hitler's Imagery, *loc. cit.*
[45] Erich Fromm, *Escape from Freedom,* New York, Farrar and Rinehart, 1941, pp. 86-87.

Fromm's error is to think that capitalism as such threatened the individual and helped the formation of what he calls the social character.

Increased opportunity to free oneself from poverty increased the desire to free oneself from the father's authority. The ideology of the Reformation brought the individual nearer to his God (father) by the suppression of the ecclesiastic hierarchy. But this gain in freedom had to be paid for by other submissions as a guilt compensation. The reason why many Protestants became rich people was not because of the moral effort required by the new religion, but because money became the way to free oneself from the father's authority by being more successful than he. This successful rivalry with the father had to be paid for by a greater religious submission. Even the idea of predestination could be looked at as a denial that the man was responsible for his success and his victory over his father. The dogmatism and moral rigidity of the first generations of reformers was a defense against the idea of a complete revolt.

Alexander justly emphasized that sociology should be founded on individual emotions. He wrote many pages which are in line with what we consider the right method, showing for instance the connections between the child's dependence and social cohesion; but like many others, he has a great difficulty in sticking to the method and he expresses himself as though general causes would act directly on the social medium. They react on the family structure and then on the individual and only later on the social medium; this explains what has been called the social lag. Let us exemplify this methodological error. Alexander writes "There is ample evidence that social cohesion decreases in the opposite situation when security and plenty prevail. Therefore rich and powerful nations often tend to decline. When secure, people become more selfish and pursue their own interests, without consideration for others, which shows that individualism is stronger and more deeply rooted than coöperation and is relinquished only under external threat."[46]

In itself the observation is right, but described in those general terms, it misses the most important phenomenon. In a rich society the father does not need to control the children so much and very often he has many interests outside the family which lead him to neglect them. The latter, feeling rejected, reject society, and increase

---

[46] Alexander, F.: *Our Age of Unreason*, New York, Lippincott, 1942, pp. 248-9.

the process of individual interest prevailing on group safety. (For lack of space I am over-simplifying a complicated process. I limit myself to indicate the direction in which it should be studied.)

We are aware that the description we have given of a microscopic interpretation of history is very imperfect.

The Psycho-Anthropological Approach

In the first volume of *Psychoanalysis and the Social Sciences*, Géza Róheim has given a brief survey of the work of many anthropologists such as Margaret Mead, Bateson, and many others who have attempted to characterize the cultural structure of a country, under the assumption that common standards in the way of raising children create unconscious emotional patterns for countries. Those studies became especially numerous during the war as they could promote the understanding of allies or enemies.

They intend, of course, to give a synchronic picture, the general characteristics of one time, and they have succeeded in so far as the studied countries presented unity enough to neglect the description of the different social layers which compose them.

We cannot summarize here the numerous valuable books of the psycho-anthropological school. Their method has been described in the books by A. Kardiner and Margaret Mead as well as in papers by Douglas Haring and Geoffrey Gorer.[47]

Does a Neurotic Culture Exist?

In raising this question I take it for granted that the original and true sense of the words civilization and culture is lost and that nowadays they are synonymous. Civilization in the past meant the slowly accumulated experience of a society and culture, the intellectual experience of man. The Germans who have mixed so many things, have mixed the true meaning of those two words in calling "Kultur" what the others called "civilization."

"It seems pointless and indicative of a lack of understanding of the process of cultural development to speak of a neurotic culture, as is sometimes done. Different epochs offer man various methods of overcoming the problems arising from his biological instincts. He seems to need certain general concepts to make it possible for him to keep his equilibrium in the difficult situation between instinct and

[47] See bibliography.

danger. These concepts contain his childhood problems on an enlarged scale and at the same time offer solutions for them. In epochs of cultural stability the tensions reach a balance and the individual born in such a period lives out his childhood conflicts in later life in a more objective way. As long as the adult struggled above all with the unknown and the dangerous in nature and the cosmos, the religious world concept proved a satisfying solution—a world concept, with a monotheistic world image and the development of a universal stable moral order, which sought its center outside reality and independent of it."[48]

I would like to start with this challenging quotation of Henry Lowenfeld. Before we give a direct reply to this contention let us say a few words about normalcy in individuals. We accept the fact that a normal adult tends to be directly adjusted to reality, which means that as much as possible he does not adjust himself to authorities and images of reality, which are only current scientific or philosophic prejudices, but he tries to have a direct understanding of people and situations. He is able to gratify satisfactorily his organic, emotional and intellectual needs, either in taking what he needs from the environment or in modifying the latter in such a way that he need not remain frustrated. Like everybody, he has some repetition compulsions from childhood, but he gives up many of them in a spontaneous way; and despite them he has the capacity of getting adjusted to new circumstances. This man may have projected the family structure on the social environment but he freed himself of this early imagery to face reality and give his strength to rebuild the social world more as it should be than as it was.

If every man were endowed with such freedom toward his past, it would be possible to build up a better world but this is not the case. A great majority of people have to obey repetition compulsions reinforced by obedience forced upon them in their childhood and therefrom rebuild the emotion molds which have formed their own emotional patterns. In periods of prosperity, the potential aggression between two successive generations may be decreased by sublimation. But for different reasons, a civilization may follow another pattern of growth and instead of going from a despotic to a liberal family structure, may reinforce a neurotic family trend which will be projected on the environment and make more difficult for the

---

[48] Lowenfeld: *op. cit.*, pp. 14, 15.

members of this family to rid themselves from the pattern of their early emotions. Complete normalcy in an individual is an ideal concept, but people offer enough variations in their adjustment to make it possible to consider some of them normal and others neurotic.

Just the same, all civilizations do not give the same chances of adjustment to reality and, therefore, we may consider them as more or less developed or more or less neurotic. This same question was raised by Freud himself.[49]

The criterion of being adjusted to the environment is only partial. No progress could be possible if nobody would fight the prejudices and show new ways to get adjusted more directly to reality. All civilizations do not grant the same opportunities of adjustment. For instance, in a well-diversified and liberal society it is easier for a man to adjust himself to reality than in a coercive society which forces the individual to adjust himself first to the pattern of this civilization. To give an example, in the sixteenth century it was impossible for Galileo to assert freely that the world was round. Nevertheless people of the sixteenth century could gratify their instinctual drives in a large measure, but the kind of civilization prevailing did not permit free thinking; it inhibited the progress and imposed the acceptance of the cultural belief of that time rather than the experimental truth. Such facts speak more for a delay in the development of a civilization than for a neurotic culture.

Quite different is the case of a civilization whose family structure should create a certain type of culture and which is hampered from creating it by some external factor breaking the normal course of its development. All of a sudden the solutions of the past generation with their neurotic trends but also with their sublimation potentialities are not available and the new generation loaded with strong emotions has to find new ways of abreaction. Unprepared for such a task, many men of such a country fail to adjust themselves and regress into a more neurotic behavior. If such failures are numerous and a leader appears who offers a regressive type of culture (which means that his followers have to adjust themselves more to his coercion than to reality) a neurotic culture will arise.

We agree with Lowenfeld when he writes: "In epochs of cultural stability tensions reach a balance and the individual born in such a period lives out his childhood conflicts in later life in a more

---

[49] Freud: *Civilization and Its Discontents,* (Trans. Rivière) p. 141.

objective way." But when outside circumstances break the frame of the old society, the projection of early childhood conflicts with the environment becomes impossible and a great many individuals fail to find the right adjustment.

In a society whose development is not broken by a trauma, the ways of instinctual distortions and sublimations imposed by the family find their natural projection in the social institutions. Therefore, the man who follows this line appears to be adjusted, even if those social institutions and cultural patterns are not fully adjusted to reality. When society is well diversified, a man belonging to the conservative class who deserts his fellowmen to join a more progressive political party will often be considered as maladjusted by the people of his class, just because he broke the regular frame of projection of his family. As long as we do not accept the fact that the different society structures are not equally adjusted to reality, we form a conventional idea of normalcy in admitting as normal the man who is adjusted to his social background.

To explain our point of view, nothing is better than to have a glance at what happened in Germany in these last decades, a subject which intrigued more than one analyst. I apologize because I am forced to sketch the subject instead of giving a full description of the psychological process. (I have given some aspects of this problem in other articles.) In 1914, in Western Europe and even in Austria despite the imperial regime, a growing liberalism in the children's education and in the social structure could give hope for a better social adjustment. However, Germany was divided into two cultural streams: the one deeply attached to the feudal system with Junkers, army people and a certain conservative middle class which established a parallel to the feudal hierarchy in university dignitaries, in hospital doctors (*Oberarzt, Unterarzt, Assistent,* and so on), in the bureaucracy, etc.; the other one coming from town's people tended to more democratic ideas. The feudal group felt threatened by the growing liberalism and this, among many other causes, started the first World War. A great number of boys adjusted to their family and social structure were displaced. They had to live in changed circumstances during war time and for economic reasons could not later go back to their homes.

Before the first World War, the normal outlet for the aggression roused by the father's domination was to turn a great part of it masochistically into homosexual compliance, the man enslaved himself to a boss, an officer or any authority, and in order to make the obedience less painful he developed an increasing perfectionism (another sublimated outlet for his aggression) which satisfied him and the authority on which he was depending. From childhood on the older brothers had a certain authority over the younger siblings, and could take revenge on them for the beating they received from their father. This continued in the social structure of the adult, where the man tried to get the attention of the superior (to identify himself with the big brother or the father) and to be harsh towards the underdog (revenge on the younger siblings). The army, the bureaucracy, and many other institutions were ideal to act out such affects. This submission on one side and the aggression on the other side allows an equilibrium between revolt and guilt and satisfies also other instinctual demands.[50]

It would be easy to elaborate on the subject, and show how this fact shaped the social structure and many cultural patterns of old Germany. The war destroyed this stratification of the society and left the soldier coming back with the task of coping with an extraordinarily intense feeling of revolt (in the childhood against the father, now projected against the present political and social environment), an intense guilt feeling for this aggression, a need of submission to neutralize this guilt, an old rivalry with the father expressed in the desire to accomplish grandiose things, very little professional training. The inability to channelize these overwhelming impulses in new, constructive, cultural patterns increased the number of neuroses and depressions and the desire to escape in some sado-masochistic adventure which could purge them from the inner tension of non-acted-out emotions. The revolutionary feelings destroyed all the sublimation patterns of old Germany and the perversions or primitive drives broke through. This has been confirmed by the analysis of pre-Nazi Germans:

---

[50] Freud, *Civilization and Its Discontents*. Translation of J. Rivière, p. 90. Conflicts of groups:

"There is an advantage, not to be undervalued, in the existence of smaller communities, through which the aggressive instinct can find an outlet in enmity towards those outside the group. It is always possible to unite considerable numbers of men in love towards one another, so long as there are still some remaining as objects for aggressive manifestations... The Jewish people, scattered in all directions as they are, have in this way rendered services which deserve recognition to the development of culture in the countries where they settled; but unfortunately not all the massacres of Jews in the Middle Ages sufficed to procure peace and security for their Christian contemporaries."

"The analyses of individual German patients from the decades immediately preceding Hitlerian Germany throw some light on those problems of a national education and of a German psychology."

Discussing the search for whatever kind of defense mechanisms the Germans could find, Wittels adds: "Hindenburg himself was a pious churchgoer. But not so the generation of soldiers he commanded or their relatives in the hinterland. The lack of faith of his generation proved stronger and detached Eric [my patient] from the Augsburg confession. A strong religious faith supported and sustained by a faithful congregation can help a man struggling against the terror of his feminine component (castration fear) but Eric—and his entire generation with him—had to seek elsewhere for defense."[51]

Hitler has given enough of his emotional background in *Mein Kampf*[52] for us to understand that he suffered from repetition compulsions which could be shared by a great many Germans, and in a sense it could help his personal equilibrium if he could impose on others as cultural patterns the neurotic drives which animated him. What I mention above may be an answer to the following questions of Erikson:

"On the stage of German history, Hitler senses to what extent it is safe and expedient to let his own personality represent with hysterical abandon what lives in every German listener and reader."[53]

The new cultural patterns offered by Hitler brought to this unstable German generation a practical outlet for their aggression by the creation of scapegoats on a national scale (Jews, Communists, Pluto- democrats), a neutralization of their guilt by a complete submission and a brotherhood tie in criminal destruction, megalomaniacal hope in grandiose national ideas which were constantly propagated.

Such a culture may be called neurotic or psychotic in so far as it stimulates more infantile drives (sado-masochistic, anal, homosexual, etc.) than it offers sublimation opportunities; also, it forces the individuals by a strong social coercion to adjust themselves to those perverse patterns or to live in a constant dread of being killed. This civilization is neurotic because its individuals cannot grow without fear and cannot adjust themselves directly to reality.

---

[51] Fritz Wittels, Struggles of a Homosexual in pre-Hitler Germany. *Journ. of Psychopathology,* Vol. IV, 1943, pp. 420 f.

[52] See R. de Saussure, *L'Inconnu chez Hitler,* Oeuvres Libres. T. II, New York, 1943.

[53] Erikson, *op. cit.,* p. 476.

The outcome of these destructive periods has, of course, considerable economic consequences and forces a majority of families to start from scratch. The poor conditions of many families impose a great number of frustrations, increase the aggression within the family and lead back to a strong paternal authority and thus the country has to start with a new cycle of civilization.

The Nazi and similar totalitarian cultures are not the only neurotic types of culture. I do not want to sketch others here as our space is limited. I just want to recall the last phase of so many civilizations when the opportunities to gratify needs become so numerous and when the individual desires are so much stronger than the collective coercive force. The result is that people tend more and more to resolve their conflicts in changing the outside circumstances instead of adjusting and reinforcing their character. People of those civilizations belong to many social, professional, scientific, artistic societies and they have many more environments on which to project their early conflicts than is the case in less differentiated societies whose members project essentially on the political structure.

In a more liberal society the children have not been submitted to a strong discipline, their superego, and often their ego, is very weak. They have suffered rejection because of the many interests of the parents and they project this under the form of a rejection of the state and of society. Just as we frequently find a lack of ego structure in people of such cultures those civilizations have a lack of social cohesion which makes them especially vulnerable.

For proper evaluation I think that the method should also be the same, as I have pointed out on several occasions. One should try to describe the main types of families, then describe the kind of early conflicts they determine, and study the connections which exist between those conflicts and society structure on one side, cultural patterns on the other side.

Some authors have neglected to do so and in a certain measure arrived at a deadlock. One of the mistakes made by Brickner who characterized the German culture as paranoid or by Kecskemeti and Leites who characterized it as compulsive consists of making a diagnosis on the general ideology or some character trends, which does not give an idea of the underlying structure of the society.

Henry Lowenfeld has attacked the conclusions of the latter book[54]

---

[54] *Op. cit.*, p. 255.

in recalling that the State ideologies have a sublimation function and "that the rather narrow concept of clinical pathology is insufficient to describe the wealth and health of the cultural problems of a nation." This, I feel, is a question of terminology and such a diagnosis does not even describe on the individual level the richness of a personality. We all know how conscientious and interesting a man with a compulsion neurosis may be and we also know that in many ways he is adjusted and capable of cultural creations.[55] If a diagnosis is made of a group, there is no reason to see it in a more derogatory way. Failing to start their descriptions from the family structure, those authors give us a descriptive more than a psychodynamic diagnosis.

Lowenfeld also writes: "Even if the group has some general characteristics, we must not forget that every member did not react in the same way. This fact accounts for the lack of accuracy applied to politics." This objection is not valid. When one characterizes a group through a diagnosis it does not imply (1) that all the members of the group have this characteristic, (2) that beside the neurotic trend one may not find normal ones. A compulsive neurotic does not behave only with compulsion and nevertheless we do not question the diagnosis.

Further Lowenfeld writes: "The fight of the Nazis against the doubts of their followers when the war situation became more serious shows a rather realistic appraisal of the situation and is not indicative of compulsiveness."[56]

Such an opinion is most debatable. The Nazis were compelled to think they were right and this contributed to their policy much more than a realistic view. But when we say the Nazis we do not mean every one of them.

In all of us every idea is invested with more or less energy; it may be with sexual desire, with compulsive drives, with inhibitions, and so on. In a given culture, it happens that for many individuals an idea has the same dynamic charge. For instance, the idea of father will be differently invested according to the libidinal index of a civilization. Certainly, in the growing period of the Nazi militarism, the idea of victory had a different dynamic charge than it did during the last days of the regime.

---

[55] See Hartmann: Ich-Psychologie und Anpassungsproblem. *Internationale Zeitschrift für Psychoanalyse und Imago*, 1939.
[56] Lowenfeld, *op. cit.*, p. 256.

But as soon as the threat of defeat grew, the fear of the consequences blinded a certain number of Nazis who stuck more dogmatically to the idea of victory. Dogmatic belief in such cases is a defense mechanism, a form of reaction formation with a compulsive character.

Let us quote once more Lowenfeld.

"Freud was always of the opinion that the neurosis is a product of the great demands which civilization makes on man's instincts. However, civilization concomitantly offers ever changing aids for the mechanisms of defense and channels for sublimation. It is in view of this fact that the question becomes pertinent as to whether cultural development is not actually motivated by man's endless need for help in the struggle with his instincts. This question tends to be overlooked today, apparently because of the prevalent rebellious attitude toward civilization. Before attempting to answer such a question we must first try to further clarify the relationship between our culture and the sublimations and repressions it offers."[57]

Of course, in so far as a civilization succeeds in giving a maximum of gratification and new lines of sublimation, especially for the aggressive drives, it brings a cultural development. But many cultures fail to give those sublimation lines and drive their members to regressive abreactions. When Lowenfeld writes: "This question tends to be overlooked today, apparently because of the prevalent rebellious attitude towards civilization", he seems to imply that every culture brings a positive human development, which is certainly not the case. With a certain number of basic emotions a whole socio-cultural system can be built. In a chess game, one trick has a consequence on the whole system of defense or attack. Likewise if some of the basic emotions are changed, the whole socio-cultural system will change.

Collective Mental Hygiene

If we accept, as I did in the last paragraph, that neurotic cultures exist as well as cultures which are more suitable than others to facilitate a normal instinctual adjustment, then we must admit that a comparative study of cultures should show which one is the most efficient. If we can relate such a culture to a certain family structure and ego training, then we shall be able to improve the level and the strength of a civilization. A similar idea was expressed by Margaret Mead: "One of the problems

---

[57] Lowenfeld, *op. cit.*, p. 2.

of our emerging culture is to learn ways which have never been approximated yet, of blending the essence of permanent human preoccupations with the accidents of idiosyncratic, local, time limited experience."[58]

Of course, a culture cannot be handled like a single man, because many economic factors interfere; nor is a society isolated from others and modern life makes the interdependence of societies increasingly greater. But there is no doubt that a better knowledge of the causes of decay may help a culture to be more conscious of the dangers which threaten it and of the remedy which should be applied. If this knowledge is used at the right time, there is no reason why the human beings could not fight against what in the past seemed to be a historical fate.

In order to make such collective therapy successful, a much deeper study must be made about all the problems we just alluded to in the present paper.

Many a psychoanalyst or psycho-anthropologist has already made contributions along these lines. We cannot give a complete survey of their papers, but let us quote some of them.

In a general way, Money-Kyrle and Flugel have tried to give some standard of normalcy of a civilization. Money-Kyrle[59] discusses the problem from Melanie Klein's angle, stressing the importance of good introjection, while Flugel[60] has a more general approach. Both insist on the fact that the only ethical criterion which is acceptable is normalcy.

To outline such a program is of course much easier than to succeed in concrete realizations.

In our opinion, the only efficient way is to work on the family structure and to discuss how to change the interplay of groups. This will be possible only in changing at the same time some economic factors.

Current events very often impose discussions about one aspect of a civilization, just as the Nazi regime raised the question, "How to handle collective aggression." Of course, in no case does the repression or the suppression of a drive bring the solution of the problem and it is the whole dynamics of the culture which should be discussed.

---

[58] Margaret Mead, Art and Reality. *College Art Journal,* Vol. II, May 1943, p. 120.

[59] Money-Kyrle, Some Aspects of Political Ethics from the Psychoanalytic Point of View. *Internat. Journal of Psychoanalysis,* 1944, p. 166.

[60] Flugel, *Man, Morals and Society,* New York, Int. Univ. Press, 1947.

This has been clearly expressed by Zilboorg; he defends the idea that aggression is not only a pathological drive, bad from an ethical or cultural point of view; it is also a normal phenomenon. "Let us imagine aggression wholly eliminated from human nature. No matter how hungry we might be, we would then be unable to kill an animal for food,"[61] etc.

"A society whose aggressive drives are inhibited would theoretically be a very pacificatory and peaceful society; it would not be able to defend itself against other dangers; figuratively speaking, it would be self-centered, ready to make concessions to the very first demands of an aggressor. It would be an appeasing society, enthusiastic about peace in our time under the very pure barrels of the aggressor. Luckily, such a society fails to survive and stops being a factor in our civilization, or—still more luckily—it seldom remains in the state for very long; 'the worm turns' and the society averts the aggression and fights for survival."[62]

The great difficulty in changing any type of national behavior is caused by the fact that the children raised by parents with a neurotic national character will project in their adulthood the repressed tendencies of the childhood. It is only in giving a more normal environment to the child that something can be improved.

Douglas Haring saw that very clearly when he wrote:

"Democracy, therefore, cannot be created by fiat among a people whose deepest feelings run counter to democratic traditions. Only by changing the patterns of social experience in infancy can a society undergo permanent reform, either toward democracy or toward autocracy. Nazism and Nipponism are possible in the long run only in populations where a majority of homes are patriarchal microcosms."[63]

In training the child to repeat in a few years the experiences of thousands of preceding generations we quicken the mastery of the younger generation but at the same time we train the young brains to repeat. A study of the scientific production would be interesting from that point of view. Of course, it is a necessity in scientific research to be familiar with the work of others, but a great part of

---

[61] *The Treatment of Aggression.* Round Table 1943 Dynamics, by G. Zilboorg. *The American Journal of Orthopsychiatry.* Vol. XIII, 1943.
[62] Zilboorg, *op. cit.*
[63] Douglas J. Haring, *Aspects of Personal Character in Japan*, p. 16.

scientific production consists of repetition, in other words, of what others have discovered. The identification with the master or the genius plays a great part in this phenomenon, but also our methods of teaching which in so many cases are still too dogmatic. We should teach more methods of research, observation or experimentation and leave to every student a greater liberty of synthesis.

The repetition compulsion in education prevents us from preparing the student for his practical life at an age which would be nearer to his sexual and physical maturity. We teach too much knowledge and not enough methods of adjustment. This repetition compulsion in scientific work, due to a wrong educational training is responsible for the discrepancy between modern discoveries and our adjustment to them. Alexander has discussed similar problems:

Asking whether we have now reached the atomic age, Alexander says, "It is more likely that, paralyzed by mistrust and fear of one another, we shall regress into the darkest phase of human history."

"My conclusion is that we are the victims of a cultural lag inasmuch as we still live emotionally in the past and have not caught up with the new conditions brought about by science and its technical achievements. Following the inertia of habit, instead of making use of the labor-saving devices of industry for turning our creative capacities to other fields that lie outside the production of material goods, we are apt to follow traditional patterns, and as a result more people will want to earn their living from industrial production than will be needed. This incongruity between ideology and economy will with the further improvement of automatic tools, steadily increase in the future. The result will be that periodic unemployment will remain with us as a constant source of insecurity and a constant threat to self-esteem, arousing the feeling of having lost one's social usefulness. This insecurity and the frustration of having no opportunity to make use of one's productive capacities are the main source of emotional maladjustment in our times, taking the place of sexual repression which dominated the scene during the Victorian era."[64] The psychoanthropological school has also tried to apply the knowledge acquired about the national character of two countries to the problem of increasing a reciprocal understanding. This is a starting point toward

---

[64] F. Alexander, Mental Hygiene in the Atomic Age. Published by the National Committee for Mental Hygiene, New York, 1946. *Mental Hygiene,* Vol. XXX, pp. 530, 543.

improving international relations. As long as this research is isolated, it will not have a far-reaching success but the day will come when nations will be more conscious of their national character, and will accept their defects with less resistance; and from this day on we may hope for some improvement. In the course of fifty years it became obvious to a great many people of our civilization that we had an unconscious and that our early sexual experiences were playing a determining role on our later character. A better knowledge of the cultural structures and their psychodynamics could be of a great help in the future. As an example of this effort to come to a better international understanding by psychological means let us remember that Margaret Mead in her paper, "The Application of Anthropological Techniques in Cross-National Communication,"[65] has attempted to iron out some of the misunderstandings between American and British people in trying to find the roots of these difficulties in cultural patterns, namely in early educational influences. On this basis, she explained, for instance, why the American soldier was generally boasting, while the British was understating his accomplishments: a difference which led sometimes to deep misunderstandings.

Glover has understood that collective mental hygiene could be solved only by personal education, which makes it so difficult. He writes: "The analyst believes that the environmental influence brought to bear on the child could be fundamentally altered to the great advantage of infantile adaptation."[66] He is in favor of measures directed towards the elimination of sadism and sadistic inhibition from parental policies. He is even prepared to give his blessing to experimental research in these directions provided the research is not carried out by enthusiastic (biased) amateurs. On the other hand, although he believes that the phases of development responsible for war and peace reactions can be radically altered in this way, he cannot say definitely that comprehensive changes in environmental policies will prove an effective safeguard against war. Finally he says that the only radical approach to the most primitive phases is a prolonged individual analytical approach, adding that it may be impossible to bring about a deep change in the attitude of parents

---

[65] Margaret Mead, The Application of Anthropological Techniques in Cross-National Communication. *Transactions of the New York Academy of Sciences,* 1947. Series II, Vol. 9, pp. 133-152.

[66] Glover, *War, Sadism and Pacifism.* London, Allen and Unwin, 1933, p. 105.

toward their children until they too have been treated by the same process. Many other passages of Glover's essay (which has recently been enlarged in a new edition) should be quoted and discussed, but lack of space forces us to restrict ourselves and give just a sample of the different works which contributed to collective mental hygiene.

Should Analysis Be Practiced For Non-Therapeutic Purposes?

Psychoanalysis, as Glover and Hartmann have pointed out, discovers many sociological data but it is difficult to use it for sociological purposes. The physician is trained to help the patient to get better and his main interest will always tend toward the therapeutic side, no matter how many sociological problems may retain his attention.

On the other hand, we know that psychoanalysis is not only a therapy but also a method of research. For this reason, it should be questioned whether analysis should not also be practiced by well-trained sociologists who at the same time would receive a complete analytic training. They would practice more for sociologic investigations than for medical purposes.

With the few experiences he acquires in the course of his professional life, an analyst will never be able to answer such questions as: Does an oedipus complex have other and more or less typical forms in families with an only child, in families with several boys, in families where the boys have an older or a younger sister? Does a child who has neurotic trends make a better spontaneous adjustment to life if it has left the family early than if it has to stay longer in its pathological environment?

The physician has a hunch about such questions but he cannot prove his experience with statistical figures, while a sociologist could choose his cases according to the problems he wants to solve.

As soon as people would come for non-therapeutic purposes, they could be investigated in regard to special subjects. A group of scientists could be tested to observe the unconscious drives at stake and what emotional factors are still playing a role in their scientific research or writings; a group of artists could be investigated to know what helped their artistic dispositions to flourish or to be inhibited.

No doubt that our psychological and sociological knowledge would be greatly enriched if analysis would be practiced in those non-medical fields. But the general objection (besides the fact that right now the Institutes have not enough training analysts) is that it would be dangerous to let analysis slip out of medical hands. Many methods are dangerous when not in professional hands, but we cannot give them up for this reason. Psychoanalysis is today a necessary tool for the psychologist as well as for the sociologist and the medical psychoanalysts are too busy in their own field to pretend to solve the many problems of psychology and sociology which cannot be solved without analytic investigation. No doubt that some men will commit errors, will take the responsibility of cases which should go to the medical man, but serious men will always work conscientiously and after a time of abuses, the scientific standards will force only qualified people to use the method.

We know that the material is not the same when psychoanalysis is practiced by different schools. Karen Horney and her followers are not interested in infantile conflicts and their patients bring forth only few facts of their early childhood.

In a normal psychoanalysis the emotional changes are mainly due to transference processes and the patient as well as the analyst are not interested in the sociological implications of these processes, namely the family structure and the different social frames into which the patient has projected his affects before he transferred them onto his analyst. If analyst as well as analysand are interested in sociology, sociological material will also come to the fore.

CONCLUSION

I have tried to expose some aspects of the problem of applying analysis to history and of trying to improve the method of investigation. I am conscious that the field is overwhelming and that this approach is still very imperfect. My purpose was to attempt a synthesis which I hope will be a springboard for new research.

BIBLIOGRAPHY

Aron, Raymond: *Introduction à la philosophie de l'histoire*. Paris, Gallimard, 1938.

Alexander, Franz: *Our Age of Unreason*. Lippincott, 1942.

———Mental Hygiene in the Atomic Age. *Mental Hygiene*, Vol. XXX, 1946.

Bergler, Edmund: *Talleyrand, Napoléon, Stendhal, Grabbe*. Wien, Int.Psa.Verl., 1933.

Bonaparte, Marie: *Mythes de Guerre*. London, Imago Publ. Co., 1947.

Conant, James B.: *On Understanding Science*. New Haven, Yale Univ. Press, 1947.

de Saussure, Raymond: *Le Miracle Grec*. Paris, Denoël, 1939.

———: *L'Inconnu chez Hitler*. New York, Oeuvres Libres, I, II, 1943.

Dollard, John, et al: *Frustration and Aggression*. New Haven, Pub. for the Inst. of Human Relations. Yale Univ. Press, 1939.

Dumas, Jean: *Traité du suicide*. Amsterdam, 1773.

Eder, M. D.: Psychoanalysis in Relation to Politics. In: Jones, Ernest, ed. *Social Aspects of Psychoanalysis*. London, Williams & Norgate, 1924.

Erikson, Erik H.: Hitler's Imagery and German Youth. *Psychiatry*, Nov. 1942, Vol. 5.

———: Ego Development and Historical Change. *The Psychoanalytic Study of the Child*, II, New York, Int. Univ. Press, 1947.

Fenichel, Otto: In: Ernst Simmel (ed.) *Antisemitism*. New York, Int. Univ. Press, 1946.

Flugel, John C.: *The Psychoanalytic Study of the Family*. London, Int. Psa. Press, 1921.

———: *Man, Morals and Society*. New York, Int. Univ. Press, 1946.

Freud, Sigmund: *Beyond the Pleasure Principle*. London, Hogarth Press, 1922.

———: *Totem and Taboo*. New York, Dodd, Mead, 1918.

———: *Civilization and Its Discontents*. London, Hogarth Press, 1930.

Fromm, Erich: *Escape from Freedom*. New York, Farrar & Rinehart, 1942.

Glover, Edward: Man, the Individual. In: *Social Aspects of Psychoanalysis*. London, Williams & Norgate, 1924.

———: *War, Sadism and Pacifism*. London, Allen & Unwin, 1933.

Gorer, Geoffrey: Themes in Japanese Culture. *Transactions of the N. Y. Academy of Sciences*. Series II, Vol. 5.

Guiraux: *La Propriété foncière en Grèce*. Paris, 1893.

Haring, Douglas G.: Aspects of Personal Character in Japan. *The Far Eastern Quarterly*, 1946. The Method of Character Structure.

Hartmann, Heinz: Ich-Psychologie und Anpassungsproblem. *Int. Ztschr.f.Psa. and Imago*, 1939.

Jekels, Ludwig: Napoleon, *Imago*, 1914, I-IV.

Jones, Ernest: *Essays in Applied Psychoanalysis*. London, Hogarth Press. 1923.

Kardiner, A.: *The Psychological Frontiers of Society.* New York, Columbia Univ. Press, 1946.

Kris, Ernst: Notes on the Psychology of Prejudice. *The English Journal,* Vol. XXXV, No. 6, June 1946.

Laforgue, René: *La névrose familiale.* Paris, Ed. Denoël, 1936.
———: *Talleyrand.* Geneva, 1947.

Leuba, John: *La famille névrotique et les névroses familiales.* Paris. Ed. Denoël, 1936.

Lorand, Sandor, ed.: *Psychoanalysis Today.* New York, Int. Univ. Press, 1945.

Lowenfeld, Henry: Some Aspects of a Compulsion Neurosis in a Changing Civilization. *Psa. Quarterly,* XIII, 1944.

Mead, Margaret: Art and Reality. *College Art Journal,* II, May 1943.
———: Trends in Personal Life. *The New Republic,* Sept. 23, 1946. (The Family vs. the Group)
———: The Application of Anthropological Techniques in Cross-National Communication. *Transactions of the N. Y. Academy of Sciences,* Series II, Vol. 9, 1947.

Money-Kyrle, R.: Some Aspects of Political Ethics from the Psychoanalytic Point of View. *Int. J. of Psa.,* 1944.

Piaget, Jean: *The Moral Judgment of the Child.* London, K. Paul, Trench, Trubner & Co., 1932.

Rank, Otto: *Der Mythus von der Geburt des Helden.* Vienna, Deuticke, 1908.
———: *Das Inzestmotiv in Dichtung und Sage.* Vienna, Deuticke, 1926.

Richard, Abbé: *La Théorie des songes.* Paris, 1766.

Róheim, G.: *Origin and Function of Culture.* New York, Nerv. & Ment. Dis. Publ. Co., 1943.

Schilder, Paul: *Goals and Desires of Man.* New York, Columbia Univ. Press. 1942.

Simmel, Ernst, ed.: *Antisemitism.* New York, Int. Univ. Press, 1946.

Sorokin, Pitirim: *Society, Culture and Personality: Their Structure and Dynamics.* New York, Harper, 1947.

Wittels, Fritz: Struggles of a Homosexual in Pre-Hitler Germany. *J. of Psychopath.,* Vol. IV, 1943.
———: Collective Defense Mechanisms Against Homosexuality. *Psa.Rev.,* XXXI, 19, 1944.

Zilboorg, Gregory: Psychiatry as a Social Science. *Am. J. Psychiatry,* Vol. 49, Jan. 1943.
———: The Treatment of Aggression. (Round Table Disc.) *The Am. J. of Orthopsych.,* Vol. XIII, No. 7.

Part One

ANTHROPOLOGY

NOTES ON EXCISION
By Marie Bonaparte (Paris)

Explorers, travellers, missionaries and anthropologists have often told us about the custom of excision or clitoridectomy, which is practiced in many tribes. Montaigne quoted the "circumcision" of women amongst the most strange customs of mankind and wondered at it.

However, though this custom has often been described, its reasons, and even its rationalizations, have remained obscure, and its results in relation to the women's psychosexuality hardly seem to have interested the investigators.

It is known that sometime in the nineteenth century European surgeons themselves, encouraged by the harmlessness achieved in operating by asepsis, practiced clitoridectomy on little girls who masturbated excessively, in order to "cure" them. It is also known that, in general in such cases, these obstinate little girls were in no way cured and went on masturbating. Textbooks of surgery mention this fact incidentally, and it was confirmed by Professor Pinard, when I asked him about this matter. He could show me no woman who had undergone this mutilation, as clitoridectomy had not been practiced in Paris for a long time.

Once, in Vienna, Freud handed me a book published in Berlin: *Neger Eros*, by Felix Bryk, a traveller who had resided in East Africa. There he had studied the customs of the Nandi, a tribe living on the slopes of Mount Elgon. He described in his book how the Nandi girls were submitted to the operation that deprived them of their clitoris: when they had reached nubility, towards their seventeenth or eighteenth year, an old woman burnt their clitoris away with a red hot stone. Bryk tried to understand the reasons for this cruel custom. He assumed that Nandi men tried to feminize to the utmost their female companions in thus suppressing from their anatomy the last vestige of the penis which the clitoris is, and this, he added, ought to favor the transfer of the woman's sensitivity from the infantile erogenous zone, which is the clitoris, to the adult erogenous zone, which for women, at puberty, ought to become predominantly the vagina. Freud observed that Bryk no doubt was acquainted with his own theory of the transference at puberty, in girls, of the sensitivity from one zone to the other, and Bryk's hypothesis seemed to him worthy of examination and verification in the light that the observation of facts might throw upon it.

Anyhow, Freud told me, this operation probably does not suppress the erotic orgastic potentialities of the women, as the Nandi men would otherwise not have accepted, he thought, a custom liable to deprive them of sharing their voluptuous sensations with their female companions, a state of things which, in all countries, men value. I then tried to get information from some travellers or anthropologists who had had sexual relationships with such women, even with Somali women who had been subjected to the cruel custom of infibulation. They told me that these women seemed capable of sexual pleasure. But at such times men are not very apt to observe realistically and coldly; moreover it is known how often men of all colors can be deceived by women in this respect. A man's vanity helps him to be deceived, and also his laziness. Nandi men themselves could be liable to such illusions. This problem could not be tackled by the male partners who are and remain the worst and most unreliable observers on the psychosexuality of women.

The human material of observation was lacking, and even up to now whilst I am writing this, the material I have been able to collect is very scanty. However, as precise observations on this subject are scarce and as I do not know when I shall be able to collect some more, I thought that it might be useful to publish what I have gathered in the hope that other investigators may thus be led to complete my observations and to test on new cases the correctness of the hypothesis I have assumed.

Case 1. In the autumn of 1929, I had gone to Berlin with Freud. There I heard, through a Dr. Hupfer, a young woman doctor in Berlin, about a most interesting case she had seen at the Leipzig psychiatric clinic: a young German woman was suffering from compulsive masturbation; she had submitted to every surgical mutilation in order to get rid of it, but all this in vain. I then resolved, when I returned to Vienna with Freud, to stop on the way in Leipzig, in order to see this woman.

There, at the town's psychiatric clinic, Dr. Hupfer, and Dr. Herbert Weigel introduced the patient to me.

This woman was then thirty-six years of age. She was fair, rather pretty, distinguished looking, and belonged to the small bourgeoisie.

The patient herself revealed to me the following: the compulsion she suffered from drove her to masturbate up to fifteen times a day. This made her most unhappy, but she could not resist the compulsion; it seized her at the most inopportune moments, for instance whilst she was preparing the family meal. Then she had to stop her work and run in the next room, where, crouching on the ground, she masturbated. The act was short, afterwards she could return to her domestic work. She was then overcome by a terrible feeling of shame, but shortly afterwards the compulsion cropped up again.

In coitus with her husband, this woman remained entirely frigid, being of an exclusive clitoridic type. Perhaps once or twice, when slightly drunk, did she experience in coitus some sort of vaginal sensation.

In order to put an end to her painful and humiliating compulsion, she consulted doctors. One of them sent her to a surgeon.

I should have liked to read the surgical observations. Of course, I waited for them in vain. Dr. Weigel could not obtain them from the surgeon for me. All I could get were the following data which Dr. Weigel sent me in a letter that I translate here:

Leipzig, May 5, 1931

Madame,

I am pleased to be able to give you more exact data on Mrs. R. (born 1893). Since her tenth year she has suffered convulsions of the external genitalia and masturbation which gradually increased to eight, ten, twelve times a day. Married 1922. Prefers masturbation to coitus. In 1928, laparotomia with resection of the nerves. (Ablation of both tubes and ovaries.) All this without the least result. It seems that her husband is unskilled in coitus; he carries it out without any preliminaries. Alleged conscious masturbation fantasy: her husband manipulates her with his fingers.

After being analyzed for four weeks by Dr. Hupfer, she did not come any more. One clinic suggested to her a new operation, probably she followed this suggestion.

We have a meagre record of her past development. Illegitimate pregnancy in 1918. In 1927, she was delivered of a legitimate child who died after 3 days. Since then the desire to masturbate has increased. Her father has epilepsy. Two of his sisters are psychotic. Hoping you can use these meagre data, I remain. . . .

I had the opportunity, together with Dr. Hupfer, to examine this woman in the gynecological position. Two large, lateral cuts were visible at the place where the nerves had been resected. The clitoris had been entirely removed, down to its roots. The vestibular region as well as that of the vulva appeared quite flattened. Upon my request, the patient indicated to me her erotogenic zone which was located rather high up, about one inch from the mouth of the urethra, exactly upon the scar of the *glans clitoris*.

This very high-principled woman was obviously deeply unhappy. She had far-reaching work-inhibitions. She would have preferred losing all capacity of sexual gratification to remaining the way she was.

In June 1941, we were evacuated from Greece, which the Germans had conquered, to Egypt. I then thought that I might pursue my investigations on excision, as in Egypt most of the Moslem and Copt women are excised, generally between the ages of five and ten. I went to see Professor Mahfouz Pasha, the gynecologist of the Cairo Coptic hospital. He described precisely the operation, which consisted in the ablation of the glans clitoridis and of the labia minora.

It was believed—so he told me—that this custom had been brought to Egypt by the Moslems. It is known, however, that it was an immemorial North-East African custom: dating from the time of the Pharaohs, Egyptian mummies were excised.

At the Coptic hospital, Professor Mahfouz showed me two excised women whom he had just delivered. The two labia minora of one of these women were as if welded together on top of a stump of the clitoris which I could feel through the labia. Very little of the clitoris seemed to have been removed in these two cases.

He said that the erotic sensitivity of the women was in no way affected by the operation, in spite of the fact that the women were excised, so it was said, in order to calm them down. He had not observed more frigidity among Egyptian women than among European women. At the time he had two Frenchwomen and two other Europeans who came to him in order to be cured of frigidity. He treated them with extracts of hypophysis and of testicle. (Freud thought that the libido was in both sexes essentially male.) He said he sometimes achieved results. (Perhaps mostly due to transference?) Thus he would have brought back only the clitoris sensitivity. He agreed that other cases could only be influenced by psychotherapy.

Professor Mahfouz had not noticed if there were more women of the vaginal type among the excised women than among other women, and he could not answer my questions on that point.

He told me that it would be impossible for me to undertake a psychological investigation in his Cairo hospital, as I wished to, because it would give rise to a great scandal.

In order to undertake such an investigation, several conditions are required, and these are difficult to find together.
1. An excised woman has to be found.
2. This excised woman must be able to speak a language which is familiar to whoever conducts the research.
3. This excised woman must be intelligent and cultured enough to understand the scientific interest of the research.
4. This excised woman must thus consent to reveal her psycho-sexuality and the scenes of her erotic life with real sincerity. That is why a woman will probably be more successful than a man in this research. Women speak more readily to women.

How many obstacles on the road to the investigation have to be surmounted can be seen: of a material, linguistic, intellectual and above all a moral nature.

In two parts of Africa which for reasons of discretion I cannot name here, I could find two women fulfilling the conditions above mentioned.

Case 2. Mrs. A. is forty years old. She has been married for eight years, has three children, one son and two daughters.

She was excised when she was six years old. The operation took place in a village. The woman who performed it was a kind of wise woman, a fortune-teller.

Mrs. A. remembers the operation. She suffered intensely. Her four sisters, all older than herself, also were excised. They all are married. Mrs. A. tells me that her own daughters, now five and three years old, will not be excised! For the last twenty years, this custom has tended to be abandoned in the cultured classes. Mrs. A. thinks that girls are excised in order to diminish the women's sexuality in the warm climates. But it fails to do so!

At a second interview, I asked Mrs. A. about her response in sexual intercourse. She says that she is perfectly normal in this respect. She is satisfied each time. But time was needed until she got accustomed to the act. Moreover, at the beginning, her husband was impotent. This state of things lasted about three months. He then went to consult a doctor, who thought that it was because, until then, he had been too chaste. The doctor told him that he ought to advise his young wife to help him. She did so, and the same evening was deflowered. She bled and suffered much, and had to consult a doctor. She then had to abstain a week from sexual intercourse, which was then resumed. Her husband was then suffering from ejaculatio praecox. Little by little the sexual act grew longer and after three months she herself experienced orgasm. For her, it must be stronger towards the end.

Mrs. A. first menstruated when she was fourteen. She records masturbation in childhood (independently of her excision) and, later on, she took up masturbation again from her twentieth year onwards. (She married at 32.) Her masturbation was manual, external, without being specifically located at the clitoris.

Her mother used to threaten to punish her masturbation. The little girl did not give it up in spite of this!

Mrs. A. is a most maternal woman and lives surrounded by her children. She tries now in her turn to stop her little girls from masturbating. She thinks that in childhood it is bad for the health. I reassured her. Her little boy is already in the latency period.

Mrs. A. evidently belongs to a mixed clitorido-vaginal type. She masturbated externally in childhood and before her marriage, and this precocious and obstinate masturbation did not prevent her ultimately from having vaginal responses, and being perfectly well adapted to the normal sexual act.

Case 3. Mrs. B., whom I was able to see twice at length, is thirty years old, and is a most intelligent woman. Her father was a middle-class merchant, her mother a peasant's daughter. She was very young when she lost her father. When she was about eleven years of age, her mother and her maternal aunt decided, in spite of her paternal uncle's resistance, to have her excised: for otherwise, people said, when the woman gives birth to a child, the clitoris grows bigger, which would make a husband feel disgusted.

When she herself had just been born, her clitoris had been treated, as is customary, with very strong alcohol, in order, so they say, to prevent it from growing big, a big clitoris being considered as an ugly thing, and moreover, as the sign of an excessive sexual appetite. She said, either for this reason or perhaps constitutionally, she had a very small clitoris.

The woman who had excised her was a horrible black woman, from Central Africa. As the clitoris was so small, the black woman cut off more than was necessary: Mrs. B. does not know if something was cut off from the labia minora. Whatever the reason, she had a hemorrhage and an infected wound, with fever. She was in bed for several weeks. The memory she has kept from the operation is one of horror. She records her grudge against her mother for having handed her over to the operator. She resented the fact as though she had been deprived of something precious, she felt as if she had been subjected to some unjust and obscure damage.

She was twelve years old when she first menstruated; this was after her excision. When she first menstruated she did not suffer and did not get frightened at the sight of blood.

She does not remember ever having masturbated her clitoris, neither in childhood nor afterwards, neither before nor after her "circumcision". She only remembers some vague anal masturbation, which procured her something like the pleasure experienced at scratching some part of the body that itches: this she indulged in after her excision.

She married three years ago. She bled very little when she was deflowered. After three months, she experienced orgasm in normal intercourse, but she always has remained very slow and in general has an orgasm only once out of three times. The sexual act has always to be long for her: twenty minutes or half an hour rather than five minutes, but she never has looked at the watch.

Erogenous sensitivity has persisted on the scar of the clitoris. If her husband tickles her there, she experiences pleasure, but as though it were local, superficial, though liable to end in orgasm. But the whole of her being remains outside of it and she accuses her mutilation of causing this feeling of incompleteness in such cases.

On the other hand, through the vagina, in coitus, with the penis, she experiences full satisfaction. When she can attain orgasm, she feels perfectly happy afterwards; otherwise she remains grumpy and cannot have any more pleasure after the man has achieved his, neither through him nor through herself.

If, during coitus, her husband touches her clitoris or rather the clitoris' scar, this hinders the developing of her voluptuous sensations.

She prefers the normal posture (dorsal decubitus). She also likes lying on the man. The sitting posture, the riding on the man, does not give her any pleasure. She has read Van der Velde's book (*Ideal Marriage*) and has tried what he advises.

It is easy to see that Mrs. B. belongs constitutionally to the cloacal type (anal masturbation in childhood) with some weak phallic, clitoridic adjunct. Hence the small disturbance brought to bear upon her erotic possibilities by the mutilating excision, which does not in fact reach the internal, vaginal zone.

This case is comparable to the case of a European woman, not excised, whom I knew. This woman, who married when she was eighteen, remained entirely frigid with her husband. After a few years she divorced and remarried. With this second husband she long remained quite frigid. Then, suddenly, she experienced an exclusively vaginal orgasm. Her clitoris remained absolutely insensible. This continued until about her thirtieth year. Clitoridic sensitivity returned one day quite as suddenly. However, she could never experience full voluptuous gratification through the clitoris, because she belonged to the type which is predominantly vaginal and in such cases, the clinical picture is always this.

As she was not excised, this woman could not blame this incompleteness of hers on mutilation of the clitoris, which she might have done if she had been excised.

Freud's theory of the transference of the girl's erogenous sensitivity from the clitoris to the vagina is known. Freud thinks that all little girls masturbate on the clitoris; their sensuality manifests itself in a male mode. Only at puberty does the girl's sensitivity leave the clitoris and get transferred to the vagina. The more or less successful ultimate adaptation of a woman to her erotic function in coitus is conditioned through the more or less successful degree of this transference; physical transference can be inhibited by psychic factors. This evolution does not always progress favorably. Feminine frigidity is in most cases only a vaginal anaesthesia, the clitoris alone having retained the total libidinal cathexis of childhood.

Is this theory to be accepted categorically? Some authors, women pupils of Freud, have doubted it. For instance Karen Horney, Ruth Mack Brunswick and Melanie Klein think that some cases of vaginal masturbation are to be found among little girls. However, Freud believed that these were probably anal masturbations retrospectively attributed to the vagina, which, in his opinion, is not discovered in childhood, but only when the blood of the menses begins to pass through it.

Melanie Klein and also Ernest Jones think that, on the contrary, the presence of the vagina would be guessed at an early stage by the child and that the libidinal cathexis of the clitoris would be due to some reaction against the vagina, rather than to a persistent infantilism of the erogenous zones. It would be a defense mechanism against the anxiety roused by the female function, implying the fear of the retaliatory destruction of the little girl's body by the mother whom the child had wished to rip open in order to scoop out the treasures she imagined in the mother. This reaction mechanism thus seems to these authors to be of a psychogenetic nature and only secondarily brought to work.

I myself believe that, in cases of persistent clitoridism in women, the causation is much more primitive and constitutional. All living beings, including human beings, are bisexual. The human erogenous zones reflect every one's individual psychosexuality. Phallic active trends express the male element, cloacal passive trends the female element in everybody. The anxiety of penetration no doubt plays its part in the woman's refusal of her vaginal erotic function. But this "perforation complex" of the female, as I have called it in an essay[1]

---

[1] Marie Bonaparte: Paleobiological and biopsychic views. *International Journal of Psycho-Analysis*, London, 1937, translated from the French, *Vues paléobiologiques et biopsychiques, Revue française de psychanalyse*, Paris, 1937.

on this subject, expresses the virility complex of the girl or of the woman. Male sexuality's orientation is centrifugal, convex. Female sexuality's orientation is centripetal, concave. But it happens that the vital reluctance which all living beings—from the amoeba to the elephant—oppose to the penetration, to the wounding of their substance, is here in favor, from this vital point of view, of the male. Do children not howl when the doctor thrusts a spoon into their throat to look at it or when the anal penetration of an enema is forced upon them?

Feminine sexuality implies, in fact, more vital dangers than male sexuality. But for castration, to which the male external genitals are more exposed than the female internal genitals, and venereal diseases that threaten both sexes, woman is much more readily endangered by her sexuality. The real dangers of pregnancy and of childbirth have no counterpart in the sexuality of the male, even if we do not count the pain and sufferings accompanying most of the woman's sexual functions: menstruation, defloration, and again childbearing and birth.

So it naturally happens that women accept this virility complex better than men do their femininity complex. The convex, phallic, psychosexual engram of the libido is in general more accentuated and better tolerated in women than the concave, cloacal, psychosexual engram of the libido by men. Most very virile men are intolerant, not only of enemas and suppositories, but, when they have fever, of the medical thermometer if introduced in the anus.

On the contrary, for a woman to possess her full female erotic function, the erotization of her internal zones must be such that the vital anxiety awakened by the fear of penetration be neutralized and surpassed by it.

Do the two feminine types of adult women, the cloacal-vaginal and the phallic-clitoridic, reveal themselves at the outset of life, in childhood, through different modes of masturbation, one tending to be external, the other to be internal? And if cases of internal masturbation in childhood can be observed or inferred, to what degree and with what frequency does this form of masturbation occur and, in each case, is the masturbation anal or vaginal? Anyhow, it seems that masturbation which is simply anal, as in the case of Mrs. B. (our Case 3) must in itself suffice to predict a vaginal sensibility in adult life, the vagina, as Lou Andreas Salome once said so well, being only an annex hired from the anus, both deriving from the original and concave cloaca.

Does vaginal infantile masturbation really happen? How far is the natural barrier of the hymen an obstacle to this infantile sexual activity in each case? Is a very resistant hymen a male stigma? (Mrs. A., our Case 2, from Egypt, suffered much when she was deflowered, but was all the same of a vaginal type!) And amongst the women of this vaginal type, are there some who deflowered themselves in childhood, and not only, as sometimes happens, at adolescence, with carrots or candles?

I do not think, however, in contradiction to what is generally believed, that a prenuptial clitoridic masturbation in young girls conditions an ultimate vaginal anaesthesia in coitus. Persistent and exclusive clitoridic masturbation is rather conditioned than conditioning. For it seems to be the expression, less of a belated infantile sexuality, than of some marked degree of virility in the woman's sexuality. Lasting and exclusive clitoridism in a woman is rather the expression of something additional in excess, than of something lacking in her bisexual constitution. The male, as Marañon[2] probably rightly thinks, seems in fact to constitute a progress from the female; the woman, in whom all is smaller than in the man, would thus be a man inhibited, stopped in her evolution by the addition, the excrescence of the female annexes.

Accordingly, if a woman constitutionally belongs to the mixed vagino-clitoridic type (as Mrs. A., our Case 2) she can masturbate externally as much as she likes before her marriage: she will not become a woman of the clitoridic, of the exclusive external type for that reason. And her cloacal, vaginal erogenous zones will only be awakened when she is subjected to coitus.

This mixed type, cloacal and phallic at the same time, seems moreover to be the most frequent amongst women.

There are two sorts of frigidity amongst women: the total and the partial, which leaves out the type with the clitoris as the only erogenous zone.

The first kind of frigidity, which involves the vagina and the clitoris and makes them both anaesthetic, is of an hysterical nature, it is a psychogenetic, neurotic inhibition. It can give way all of a sudden, under the influence of life, or with a new sexual partner, or through successful psychoanalysis. What then appears underneath is generally a normal erotic function, of a feminine, vaginal type. Such

---

[2]La evolution de la sexualidad y los estados intersexuales.

was the case of the European woman whose case I summarily related. This is not surprising: femininity and hysteria are closely related; a certain fragility, lability of the libido is necessary in order to bring about quite as complete an inhibition of the libido, and this fragility, this lability is not of a male, but of a female nature. Such an inhibition can have been caused by brutal interdictions of sexuality in childhood, masturbation or sexual play with partners, is of a psychogenetic nature and psychic causes can also end it. The prognosis of total frigidity is in general hopeful.

Quite different are the cases of partial frigidity of a clitoridic type. These are almost always based on a constitutional, biological bisexuality, which resists psychic and other influences. The libido, in these cases, finds an outlet, tends to pass and repass through the same channel, as happens in various perversions where it finds full satisfaction all the same, although not through the normal channel.

And the woman of a clitoridic type remains unconsciously proud of her virility, in spite of the conscious, repeated and often intense suffering she experiences on account of her lack of satisfaction in normal coitus, which she resents as an infirmity. In the most extreme cases, the repugnance to penetration can go so far that the clitoris, otherwise so sensitive, becomes anaesthetic if a vaginal penetration accompanies its excitation, and this, whatever posture the male partner consents to adopt.

Surgical treatment, such as the Halban-Narjani operation which brings the clitoris quite near the opening of the vagina, does itself very little to change, in these extreme cases, sexual anaesthesia in coitus due to such a repugnance to penetration.

It would all the same be wrong to think that such women, so reluctant to being penetrated, are therefore necessarily homosexual. The object choice and the libido positions are independent facts. Exclusively clitoridic women are often very heterosexual; worshippers of the phallus, they could not love a being deprived of it. They desire the man, they try to get him with the activity of their own virile nature, but in coitus they display what could be called an unconscious psychology of sword swallowing: "See! See! I love him so much, my beloved, that I risk for his sake the terrible danger of penetration! But it does not do anything to me! I feel nothing! I remain intact!"

And these women, though longing for the man, are very often more or less reluctant to experience maternity.

Is it possible to suppress excessive clitoridism in women by cutting off their clitoris? The first case we have related, the case of the Leipzig woman, seems to answer this question negatively. But it could be objected that this was an exceptional case, on account of the intensity of the masturbatory urge, and of the fact that clitoridectomy was performed when the patient was already advanced in age: at such a time the nervous engrams are fixed and cannot be modified. Such is in fact the case with eunuchs castrated when adult. All the same, the testimony of Professor Pinard, which I described at the beginning of this essay, and also of other authors, all tend to contradict the possibility of inhibiting little girls' masturbation by cutting off their clitoris, as it was once tried in Europe. And our Case 2, the lady I was able to question, who was excised when she was six years old, tends to confirm the fact, this woman having indulged in masturbation of an external if not exclusively clitoridic type after her excision. This did not prevent her, as we already mentioned, from manifesting after her rather belated marriage, a normal vaginal sensitivity which her constitution kept in reserve ready to awaken in the normal sexual act.

I think that the ritual sexual mutilations imposed on women of some African tribes since time immemorial,—[Cleopatra herself must have been excised!]—constitute the exact physical counterpart of the psychic intimidations imposed in childhood on the sexuality of little girls of European races, and I think that from the point of view of the final sexuality of the women, they produce the same results. With the progressive introjection of the external persons of authority surrounding the child, with the corresponding strengthening of the superego or conscience, less physical coercion seems necessary than in more primitive times when the archaic instincts of humanity were stronger and more difficult to curb. The same results which were formerly obtained by physical violence are then secured by psychic intimidation. Our penal code no longer includes the tortures of former times, or those that one still meets with in primitive tribes. And the intimidation of juvenile sexuality follows the same law of decrease relatively to the repression's brutality as the penal code.

But if the mutilations affect psychosexuality in intimidating it more or less according to its degree of original strength, they do not seem any more able than the psychic intimidations imposed on our children to make it alter its orientation. The orientation seems derived from nervous centres which are constitutionally more or less bisexual, and this whatever happens from the outside.

Amongst the excised women, the clitoridic women whose libido is strongly oriented in a male convex fashion must retain the same erotization of the clitoris' scar as was the case with the Leipzig woman (Case 1). The vaginal women are naturally not perturbed in their orgastic possibilities by the excision of the clitoris. The women of a mixed type, vagino-clitoridic, keep their two erogenous zones, as did my two other cases (Cases 2 and 3).

Amongst these last cases, could some woman be found whose type is indecisive enough to be influenced by the excision? Would in this case the excision of the clitoris contribute to interiorize the erogenous zone, to reinforce in some degree the internal vaginal sensitivity? Freud, when I told him my objections to Felix Bryk's thesis, once expressed this moderate opinion. But I am inclined nevertheless to think that the physical intimidation of the girls' sexuality through the cruel excision is probably no more able to feminize them, to vaginalize them, than the psychic intimidation of clitoridic masturbation imposed on little European girls. The proportion of clitoridic women amongst Europeans or Americans is high enough, even amongst girls who were terrified in childhood by various threats on account of their masturbation, to doubt the success in this respect of excision itself.

I know it has been assumed that excessive clitoridism in European or American women would be due to the perturbing influence of civilization, which would tend to feminize men as well as masculinize women, to attenuate, in brief, the difference between the sexes.[3]

According to this thesis, primitive women would be normal to the highest degree! Of course, statistics on this very difficult object of investigation, the mysterious psychosexuality of woman, are not available. But the belief in the absolute normality of the primitive woman must be some offspring of the illusion "à la Rousseau" of man's perfection in the state of nature, who would have been corrupted through civilization—an utopia which has moreover in great part been revived in our times by the Communists in their attacks against society, this society that would be the cause of all evils. Anthropologists who have paid attention to this matter, as did Géza Róheim,

---

[3] Marañon has said the contrary and expressed the hope that in cultured races, through a continuous progress, men and women will become less and less bisexual or intersexual!

have found many cases of clitoridism amongst primitive women.[4] To doubt it would moreover be to doubt biological human bisexuality.

Yet amongst the African women belonging to the two last types, the vaginal and the mixed, some must be found whose libido, like the libido of certain Europeans, is not firm enough to resist intimidation, in this case the physical, cruel intimidation of excision. The women then probably lose all possibility of erotic gratification. Though I met none, there must be, among African as among European women, wholly frigid women, and these cases of total frigidity must be curable through the influences of life, being comparable to the European case I have related on parallel lines with my Case 2.

Are we to find again, amongst excised women, from the narrower biological point of view of the erotic function, the three great classes of women which Freud has so well distinguished and described from the more general point of view of the total feminine psychosexuality?

Freud, in one of his last essays,[5] has classified women in three great categories, following their reaction to the infantile discovery of the difference between the sexes and to the penis envy which ensues: the ones who *claim*, the ones who *accept*, and the ones who *renounce*.

Claimers, having seen the boys' penis, and wishing to possess it, claim it with such force that they can unconsciously imagine they have it. They seem to think their clitoris is a little penis and tend to assume in life all the masculine psychic and social attitudes. Here one should distinguish, as Abraham did, two sub-types: the revenge type (*Rachetypus*) and the wish type (*Wunschtypus*). In this last case, the illusion to possess all the same a penis can deny reality to such a degree that the woman loses the revenge urge.

The women who accept are those who are adapted to their biological functions as well as to their social role. They have duly replaced the penis envy by the wish for a child, and accepted the substitution of the vaginal feminine zone, whereby man and child will pass, to the male phallic one. Erotization of penetration succeeds in these cases, the woman has differentiated the penetration-wound in order to give pain and death and the penetration-caress in view of voluptuousness and life. A harmonious mixed type, vagino-clitoridic, is frequent in this group.

---

[4]Cf. G. Roheim, Psychoanalysis of Primitive Cultural Types. *International Journal of Psychoanalysis, XIII*.

[5]"Female Sexuality", *Int. J. Psa., XIII*, 1931.

The women who renounce are those whom the discovery of the difference between the sexes has discouraged and rebuffed to such an extent that they choose to renounce the exertion of their sexuality. They give up the rivalry with the man in these biologically disadvantageous conditions. The totally frigid women, who have all the same accepted the man belong to the "accepting" group, though temporarily inhibited. The true "renouncers" really renounce man's embrace, nor do they try to rival him in his domain. Rather do they constitute those armies of old maids devoted to social feminine functions of substitute maternity: children's or hospital nurses, teachers, social workers, often more or less desexualized. They seem to be a kind of counterpart, in the human species, of the workers among bees and ants. They probably occur much more rarely in primitive societies, where women can less easily shrink from their role of reproducer of the species than among us.

Here we must stress the fact that a girl's reaction to the discovery of the difference between the sexes must, primarily, be determined by the more or less bisexual constitution of the subject, taking into account a certain psychic moment due to the events of childhood.

Every child, when it has occasion to watch the intercourse of adults, reacts to this "primal scene" as a male or as a female, identifying itself more or less to the active male or to the passive female, following the greater or smaller degree of virility or femininity in its own constitution. The same must happen in view of the discovery of the difference between the sexes.

It is generally in the predominantly patriarchal primitive societies that ritual sexual mutilations are imposed on the children. The "fathers", the ancients of the tribe, these successors of the father of the prehistoric primal horde, seem to be the ones who try thereby to intimidate their children's sexuality, the sexuality of their sons, who are to be their rivals, the sexuality of their daughters, who are to be their companions.

But to what extent do the fathers of the tribe wish to feminize to the utmost their daughters, as well as to intimidate their sexuality, through the rite of excision? (Let us note incidentally that the execution of these mutilations on girls is delegated to old women, who must be happy to take revenge of their old age on the young whom they thus torture!)

That such a wish be present, as Bryk supposed, does not seem impossible. There appear to be in fact two kinds of men, as well in the most civilized as in the most primitive societies. They might be named the enemies or the friends of the clitoris.

When the Egyptian moslems shout, as the supreme insult to European women: "Mother of clitoris!" they express the first of these attitudes. Bryk also relates that the Nandi men speak with a profound repulsion of that which hangs between the legs of the woman, meaning the clitoris, and I have told what Mrs. B. said about the disgust which a husband would feel if, as one feared, the clitoris of his wife were to grow bigger after a confinement!

Very virile men seem in fact to shrink from all that is not feminine in woman, and this attitude is met with in many Europeans.

On the other hand, there are men who are more bisexual, more feminoid themselves, and who like to find in the woman something like the lacking complement of their own virility. Having remained fixed in the unconscious to the "phallic mother" of their infantile imagination, they institute what could be called the class of the friends of the clitoris. These men like women to possess this diminutive penis, they play with it and I have even heard of an extreme case: this man, a European, was fond of reversing the relations of the sexes and loved to introduce his partner's clitoris in the opening of his own urethra!

In this group of the worshippers of the phallic mother belong the men of those African tribes who, at the opposite of those performing excision, indulge, like the Bapedi of North Transvaal, in elongating the labia minora of the girls, which then simulate a penis.

Yet these diverse customs seem to satisfy only the imagination of those who impose them on the girls, the girls thereby are probably not much changed in regard to their more or less bisexual native constitution, to which external influences can only add light variations. Were the labia minora of the Bantu girls extended to a quarter of a yard, they all the same are not penes, and it is not enough to cut off a woman's clitoris to interiorize her sexuality, as we have seen from the example of the Leipzig case. Even in the case of Mrs. B., external masturbation was not abandoned in spite of the performed excision.

From the example of European women, who are subjected to a psychic intimidation of their sexuality in early childhood, and also of the African women who are subjected to such an intimidation of their sexuality through cruel ritual mutilations, it seems that women's sexuality is very reluctant to change its individual, natural orientation, which is in each case more or less constitutionally bisexual.

Educational influences can be decisive in inhibiting sexuality from a moral point of view; I have known a little girl who, in childhood, was subjected to a most excessive repression of masturbation; her hands were tied every night to the bars of her bed, for months and months. This was a real catastrophe for her sexuality, she became so totally, so tenaciously frigid that nothing, neither a new lover, nor even psychoanalytic treatment, could bring back her erotic sensitivity. But the degree of erotic virility in a woman does not seem as easy to modify. Were one to forbid a girl clitoridic masturbation under the worst threats, were one even to cut her clitoris off, it seems impossible thereby to change the degree of her constitutional bisexuality.

In the conflict between social morality and human instinct, education and re-education often prove most powerful. But in the conflict which rages in the interior of the instinct between the male and the female which dwell in each of us, the power of education or re-education remains rather small. Here nature has the last word.

HETEROSEXUAL BEHAVIOR OF THE MOHAVE INDIANS*

By George Devereux, Ph. D. (Topeka)

INTRODUCTION

The sexual life of the Mohave Indians, which unfolds itself in a society which encourages the attainment of genitality, as well as its spontaneous manifestation in overt behavior, is perfectly characterized by Freud's description of Greek sexuality (33): "The most pronounced difference between the love life of antiquity and ours lies in the fact that the ancients placed the emphasis on the impulse itself, while we put it on its object. The ancients extolled the impulse and were ready to ennoble through it even an inferior object, while we disparage the activity of the impulse as such and only countenance it on account of the merits of the object." Since society and the individual alike valued sexual activity as such, even in aboriginal times Mohave promiscuousness was only slightly curbed by the institution of marriage (5, 28, 34, 38).

On the one hand, the Mohave were lenient toward those who failed to attain psychosexual maturity, and interfered only slightly with relatively unsublimated pregenital strivings (10). On the other hand, they neither tolerated nor condoned wanton aggressivity, and other inadequately sublimated, or distorted, manifestations of pregenital strivings unless, as in warfare, they happened to serve a socially 'useful' purpose. Malice, witchcraft (11), quarrelsomeness and objectionable narcissism were severely penalized (12). Two concrete examples will serve to illustrate this point.

(a) *Orality*. The Mohave were free to eat voraciously and to engage in fellatio, whereas erotic biting, oral sadism and oral-dependent behavior were condemned (12, 18).

---

*From the Musée de l'Homme, Paris. Copyright by George Devereux and Librairie Gallimard, Paris.

(b) *Anality*. The Mohave were permitted to enjoy excretion and to erotize the anal region (10), while greedy, stingy, fussy, or paranoid individuals were mercilessly ostracized (12).

In brief, the Mohave valued the object-directed manifestations of Eros, but condemned excessive narcissism and destructiveness, regardless of whether aggression was directed at others or at one's own self. The tendency to oppose Eros to Thanatos being one of the major cultural themes of the Mohave, aggressiveness could manifest itself only in highly sublimated and devious ways.

Mohave genitality does not satisfy, however, every criterion of genital maturity, as defined by certain authorities. This discrepancy is probably due to the fact that some existing theories of genitality mistakenly imply that Eros and the reality principle are contrasting, or even mutually hostile, factors in the psychic economy of man. Yet it seems self-evident that man cannot satisfy his sexual and affective needs without an awareness and acceptance of reality, since an external love object is, by definition, a part of reality, and reality acceptance alone can enable the individual to win the full sexual and affective cooperation of the love object. Hence the reality principle is hostile only to grossly narcissistic and distorted pregenital strivings, precisely because it is the very foundation and the essential condition of genitality. Attempts to contrast Eros with reality therefore indicate an unconscious inability to differentiate between mature genital love and the object-alien, dereistic and narcissistic pseudo-love obtaining between mother and child, which is incompatible both with genitality and with the reality principle (3). Even if genital love were historically connected with this type of reality-alien and object-alien pseudo-love, we would still be entitled to think of genital love in terms of the functional autonomy of motives (2) and to question any attempt to predicate a *functionally meaningful* nexus between the two in genital characters. Hence attempts (48) to salvage "romantic" love must be repudiated as psychoanalytically unsound ethnocentrism.

Freud's own writings are instructive in this context. Even where an ethnocentric bias caused him to define specifically Euro-American phenomena as typically human, his dynamic analyses usually contain every requisite element for a correct interpretation of exceptions to these reputedly "universal" aspects of "human nature". This implies that the applicability of Freud's dynamic analyses to tendencies contrary to what he believed to be "human nature" is a proof of the universal validity of psychoanalysis, which attained its rightful position in the comity of sciences when it began to test its *conclusions* in terms of its own methods (17), in the crucible of anthropological data.

Restrictions

The paucity of heterosexual restrictions provides us with a rather adequate measure of the degree of sexual freedom enjoyed by the Mohave Indians. Several types of restrictions exist:

I. *Restrictions on the Choice of a Partner*

(1) Incest taboos prohibit sexual relations between members of a gens and all descendants of one's eight great-grandparents. It was possible, however, to marry a second cousin, provided only that a ceremony, purporting to dissolve kinship bonds between bride and groom, was performed. Incestuous relations occurred, however, even in aboriginal times, and the contemporary Mohave are becoming rather careless in their observance of the rule of gentile exogamy (13).

(2) Sexual relations between the very young and the elderly, while not prohibited, tend to be ridiculed, especially when the woman is considerably older than the man (Case 10). Certain men are known, however, to "get the young girls first".

II. *Temporary Continence*

(1) Parents must refrain from intercourse for a period of four days following the death of one of their children, lest the woman should become barren (22). Some couples were known to have violated this rule.

(2) "Feather-singers" who participate in funeral rites must be continent until they have been ritually purified. A "feather-singer", who violated this rule, became paralyzed.

(3) Mourners must be continent until the end of the funeral rites "because they are weak from having cried so much". One mourner at least attempted to violate this rule (18).

(4) It is not quite certain whether or not the ritual protagonists in the scalp ceremony are expected to be temporarily continent (38). Several persons are known to have violated this alleged rule.

(5) Hunters should refrain from intercourse for several days before going to hunt deer (56).

(6) Anyone handling certain magically "lucky" objects should be temporarily continent. Several persons have fallen ill after violating this rule.

Rules pertaining to temporary continence clearly reflect the Mohave tendency to contrast sexuality with death. Five of the six rules pertain to death, and killing, while the sixth concerns dangerous and aggressively "lucky" substances.

III. *The Reality Situation*

The reality situation, as distinct from social and ritual taboos, puts few restraints on sexual activities.

(1) Reprisals against adulterers were relatively harmless, as well as exceedingly rare. Hence the fear of reprisals did not haunt persons planning to commit adultery.

(2) Promiscuous women were punitively raped and clitoridectomized only if they made themselves obnoxious through vulgar and aggressive sexual, as well as non-sexual, behavior (21).

(3) The fear of pregnancy was negligible, since the Mohave did not penalize either abortion and infanticide, or unmarried motherhood (20).

(4) Venereal diseases are so common among the Mohave Indians that a legitimate spouse is almost as likely to be a source of infection as a casual partner. Furthermore, since venereal diseases are not surrounded by an aura of moral condemnation, the fear of contamination does not seem to inhibit the manifestations of the sexual urge. An informant specifically stated that his alleged fear of venereal disease was primarily a means of repelling the unwelcome advances of a woman (Case 1).

IV. *Subjective Inhibitions*

(1) Virginal boys and girls are believed to be afraid of intercourse.

(2) The only allegedly chaste adult member of the Mohave tribe was a half-Cocopa man. (See below.)

(3) The average Mohave Indian avoids sexual relations with old or repulsive persons.

(4) Persons "in love" are usually monogamous.

Only a small and conservative minority observes *every* restriction listed herein above, since the Mohave superego is a typical example of the "patchy" and non-pervasive primitive superego described by Roheim (50). On the whole, the sexual life of many Mohave Indians was limited only by personal handicaps, a fear of awkward situations and, occasionally, also by a lack of opportunity.

ECONOMIC CONSIDERATIONS

Economic obstacles do not impede, as a rule, the satisfaction of the sexual urge. Payment for sexual favors was neither expected nor proffered, although men frequently gave their sweethearts a silk handkerchief or some groceries. These gifts were tendered, and accepted, simply as tokens of one's affection, and were not thought of as payments. True economic motivation in sexual behavior came into being only with the arrival of white men (21). In general, Mohave women granted sexual favors rather freely, since sexual activity was viewed simply as a means of "having a good time," and was encouraged by the old, who often warned the young that they had but a little time to enjoy themselves (39). Yet there were definite limits to promiscuousness. "We are not like the Whites. If a girl likes you, you can have her without paying her," the old half-Cocopa man explained. "If, however, a girl decides to reserve herself for a certain man, she will refuse to have intercourse with anyone else, regardless of any offers or gifts."

THE PHYSIOLOGY OF SEXUALITY

Since the Mohave think of intercourse as a form of amusement, their physiological theories of sexual behavior are far simpler than are their beliefs concerning the physiology of the actual reproductive process (22).

"Castration suppresses the sexual urge." "Castrated animals cannot copulate because their seed has been removed." (23) "Unlike male animals, men cannot survive castration. A man died as a result of a therapeutic gonadectomy performed by the Reservation Physician."

(M.A.I. Nettle, M.D., after checking her records, informed me that no gonadectomy was ever performed at the Agency Hospital.)

The Mohave do not spay female animals, and hence know nothing about the ovaries.

The idea of castration appears to elicit only a moderate amount of guilt and anxiety, since when people gather to watch the gelding of a stallion, only their curiosity and laughter suggest a certain amount of empathy, anxiety, and guilt feelings (23).

"Erections are a manifestation of sexual desire." "The penis stands up because it longs for the vagina." "When the penis is erect, the anal sphincter is tightly closed." (The latter remark reveals a considerable interest in sexual sensations.) "Erections are due to the hardening of the penis. That is why old men, whose muscles are weak, have such weak penes." "Even babies can have erections. This is quite noticeable, since the genitals of cradled infants are always exposed. It is very funny that babies too should have erections." (Infantile erections were also observed by Dr. Nettle.) Five- and six-year-old boys are known to wake up with an erection. The Mohave seem unaware of the fact that a full bladder, prolonged travel, extreme fatigue and sleepless nights can produce reactive erections.

The Mohave do not know at what age the sexual drive reaches its peak. "Our ancestors could copulate until they died." (In aboriginal times the life expectancy of the Mohave Indian male was probably somewhat lower than it is today.) "We are less potent and less fertile and have smaller penes than our ancestors. This is due partly to the disappearance of ceremonies which formerly safeguarded our health, and partly also to our licentiousness."

While we are obviously dealing here with the well-known "small penis fantasy" (26), this fantasy has some basis in reality, since, according to Dr. Nettle, the Mohave's penis is smaller than that of the average American, Negro or Mexican, and seems especially small in contrast with the Mohave woman's large vagina. Mohave men joke quite freely about the "huge" penes of aliens, while Mohave women pretend to be afraid of the large sexual organs of White, Negro and Mexican males (21). As a matter of fact, the Mohave fear all close contact with other races, whose "stronger" blood "hits" their own, relatively "weak" blood, and infects them with the ahwe: hahnok (foreign disease) ailment (9, 21). No decent Mohave comments, however, on the contrast between the smallness of the *average* Mohave penis and the largeness of the *average* Mohave women's vagina. "Only a worthless kamalo:y makes derogatory remarks about her lover's penis" (21). Such remarks are fiercely resented.

The realism of the Mohave regarding the penes of other races, combined with their inter-sexual "tact" in this respect, is significant, especially since, despite their craving for large phalli (Case 4), Mohave women pretend to be frightened by the "huge" penes of alien men. These reactions to the large penes of aliens are probably rooted in the oedipal situation, since, according to Freud, the small boy is humiliated and intimidated by the size of the paternal penis, whereas the small girl is both frightened and excited by it. When the Mohave outgrow their conscious incestuous wishes and fears, they apparently project fantasies about the paternal penis, or about the phallic father, on alien races.

Evidence tends to support the hypothesis that the Mohave unconsciously identify alien men with paternal ogres. Only aliens, the immediate forebears of the Mohave, and certain evil mythical giants, who are sometimes slain by boy heroes (24, 49), are credited with huge phalli. In addition, the Mohave also have culturally standardized fantasies that the unborn child can be harmed by the paternal penis (22, 49). Some mythical giants likewise use their penes either as clubs or else as weapons of genital or anal aggression (13). Last of all "the strong blood of the alien races hits the weaker blood of the Mohave Indians" (9, 21). It is hence probable that the small boy's conscious fears of castration and the little girl's incestuous wishes are overcome only when they begin to differentiate between the "good" and the "bad" (or "tempting") father, and identify the latter (and, presumably, also the "bad" phallic mother) with alien men with huge penes. This partial identification of the "bad" parents with threatening aliens enables the child to love the "good" parents in a relatively unambiguous manner.[1]

---

[1] This hypothesis has certain paradoxical implications concerning the unconscious motivation and meaning of exogamy (30) and endogamy, both of which appear to be reaction formations against incestuous wishes, although they are by no means identically motivated. Exogamy is probably a reaction formation against incestuous desires centering about the "good parent" of the opposite sex, whereas the system of endogamy may be a reaction formation against incestuous wishes involving the "bad parent" of the opposite sex. A systematic psychoanalytical exploration of the dynamics of various marriage systems is, however, beyond the scope of this study.

The Mohave have no theories concerning the ejaculatory mechanism, although they know that the sperm is "stored" in the testicles. "The orgasm of adult males culminates in ejaculation, whereas that of boys less than fifteen years of age does not."

The sexual excitement of women, less obvious than that of men, is described as a diffuse sensation involving the entire body, but centering about the genitals. Informants seemed to be unaware of the erectility of the nipple and of the clitoris. No reference was made to an "itching" of the clitoris, perhaps because, according to ample, though indirect, evidence, Mohave men do not titillate the clitoris before intercourse, although a folk-tale reports that a young man, while courting a runaway girl, nudged her, patted her knees, and said, "havalik ma havalik-lik-lik-lik" (clitoris, thy clitoris, -ris, -ris, -ris) (24). The absence of any reference to an increase of vaginal secretions during pre-copulatory excitement, and several specific references to the preparatory lubrication of the penis suggest that Mohave women sometimes engage in copulation without an adequate amount of foreplay.

Mohave women, like Mohave men, are believed to be sexually inferior to their ancestors. "In aboriginal times Mohave women copulated until the age of sixty."

The generalized signs of sexual tension in either sex are well known. "We judge the sexual eagerness of people by their eyes. They have restless eyes, behave restlessly, and laugh noisily." "They strut like peacocks." Appearances can be quite misleading, however. "Not the noisy and flirtatious ones, but the little 'white-winged' shy ones are the easiest to get."

Aphrodisiaca are unknown, since, although alcohol is said to increase sexual desires, "when a man is drunk it is hard for him to get an erection" (Case 12).

Impotency is extremely rare. Congenital impotency is thought to be incurable, while impotency due to the paralyzing effects of contact with a rattle-snake could be cured by shamans specializing in this now forgotten art. The nexus between the phallic snake and impotency may be due to the belief that the paternal penis can harm the unborn child (22, 49), and to the notion that if an "unborn child's parents kill a snake, the child will be born a monster." No bonafide case of impotency has been recorded. The old half-Mohave and half-Cocopa man never had had either a wife or a known sweetheart, because "he had to work hard to support his large family of relatives." Actually the sexual isolation of this man was probably due to the fact that one of his parents belonged to the enemy Cocopa tribe. His continence, industriousness and unselfishness suggest that he had to validate his uncertain status, and overcome the Mohave fear of alien contacts, by being a conspicuously loyal kinsman.

Frigidity, stricto sensu appears to be unknown. Mohave informants of either sex laughed at the idea that a woman could be frigid, since, like the local Whites, they were convinced that Mohave women are more passionate than men. Nonetheless, one or two female informants asserted that "a woman may leave a husband cruel enough to copulate too frequently". Since these informants knew no woman who had deserted her husband because of his excessive sexual demands, one suspects that they were merely indulging in wishful thinking comparable to their alleged fear of "huge alien penes". Imaginary situations of this type are rather obvious variations on the theme of rape fantasies.

Impotency, frigidity and sterility are invariably due either to natural causes, or else to the violation of certain taboos, and cannot be induced by means of witchcraft.

Erotic Preliminaries

Since Mohave society is a sexually permissive and gratifying one, the individual is not expected to flee temptation, but to seek it. Hence the Mohave can overcome his rather lenient superego without intense stimulation, and without a prolonged aim-inhibited courtship. On the other hand the Mohave cannot engage in Stendhalian "crystallizations" (54) since ready sexual gratification makes it almost impossible to overvalue either a love object, or love itself. Hence he seems to remember actual coitus rather than erotic preliminaries. Several Mohave provided vivid and authentic descriptions of coital experiences which contrasted rather sharply with the relatively dry and psychologically shallow narrative of events which led to sexual intimacies. Time and again one felt that informants were anxious to dispose of preliminary events as quickly as possible, in order to settle down to a leisurely discussion of the details of actual coitus. This narrative technique is the very opposite of the one characteristic of Euro-American novelists, pornographers, Don Juans and analysands, whose incisive and vivid accounts of erotic preliminaries contrast with their repression-blanketed or else turgid descriptions of the sexual act itself. This culturally determined difference in experiential and mnemic emphasis may have influenced our theories concerning the dynamics of fore-play, and the structure and function of the superego.

In view of the above considerations the listing of stimuli which, according to the Mohave, produce sexual tension, is a psychologically rather unproductive undertaking, since whenever the threshold of stimulation is an exceptionally low one, stimuli tend to lose their individuality and meaning, and seem to be dynamically neutral. Few of the sexual stimuli listed by the Mohave are of any interest to the student of sexual psychology. The stimuli listed fall mostly into three groups:

(1) Grossly obvious stimuli.

(2) Conventional signs or signals, notifying either a certain individual or else all and sundry, of one's willingness to engage in sexual ventures.

(3) Social situations, such as dances, in which sexual activities are more or less expected.

Since the principal sexual stimuli seem to be the structure of Mohave society and the nature of Mohave sexual ethics, it seems inexpedient to differentiate too sharply between a stimulus and an opportunity.[2]

Imagination plays a comparatively negligible role, and is said to be of a rather innocent character. The thought of being with the opposite sex, ideas of companionship, of travel with a woman, and the like, may induce young people "to marry before they reach the end of a journey". (The Mohave were great travellers.) (38, 43). This may explain why only spouses and close relatives of the opposite sex may share the same seat of a wagon, without appearing immodest (19).

The rare instances of romantic love are differentiated from sexual desire, as well as from affection, perhaps because they tend to cause "strange matches" and "trouble".

A very important sexual stimulus is humor, which, since the Mohave are not hostile to genitality, has two functions. It enabled them to neutralize the superego's disapproval of the *pre-genital* and

---

[2] An analysis of the function of stimuli in Mohave sexuality suggests that sexual stimuli are frequently mere "magical" conventions, regardless of whether the stimulus is the American's box of candy, or the Australian native's raping technique. Compare in this context Rotter's analysis (53) of the magical significance of inducing sexual tensions in others, and Agoston's observations (1) on the "reassuring" function of courtship.

oedipal components of sexual acts, and effected an integration of id impulses with ego functions. The entire fabric of Mohave sexuality—with the exception of the purely procreative functions—is so richly colored by humor, that informants were almost unable to discuss sexuality in a serious manner. At any rate, sexual humor appeals so greatly to the Mohave, that they are always willing to try out a new or absurd way of engaging in coitus. There is, however, nothing complicated and neurotically "obscene" about their humoristic attitude, rooted in the fundamental exuberance of a nation, "half child, half warrior" (38), since it manages to transform even the most ribald incidents into "good 'clean' fun". Sexual humor is probably also a marginal manifestation of the Mohave Indian's "exploratory reflex", whose conventional expressions were adventurous travel, warfare which was almost a kind of sport (38, 43), and, perhaps, also the psychic adventures of shamans (11, 38).

Another important stimulus is the tendency of friends and relatives, and more especially of the old, to encourage sexual activities (39). "Sex appeal" which straddles the spheres of endopsychic and visual stimuli, is today a household word among the Mohave, who explain that this quality is independent of youthfulness and beauty. "Many a lovely girl gets only a homely old husband, whereas a girl without beauty is often much courted and sought after." Like the term "love", the term "sex appeal" is used mostly in order to "explain" matches which seem puzzling or odd to the casual observer.

Love tokens are not, properly speaking, sexual stimuli. Mohave Indians of either sex, especially the unmarried, often carry on their person an object—usually a silk handkerchief—belonging to their current sweethearts. Love tokens are not permeated with the sweat or perfume of the donor, and are not brought into contact with the skin of the recipient. Adulterous women, if found to possess such love tokens, are usually ordered to discard them. As a rule they comply with such requests, since a refusal might lead to a divorce, which, in some cases, is not desired. Love tokens are never used as fetishes and hardly ever function as true sexual stimuli.

Sexual humor and opportunity always excepted, none of the above-mentioned stimuli seems to produce much sexual tension. The principal sexual stimuli are certain sense impressions, especially when they occur in a propitious setting which permits an immediate gratification of the impulse. In fact, propitious occasions, as such, frequently act as specific sexual stimuli. Thus, many Mohave men and women, who found no occasion to copulate at a dance, may feel that they have been more or less "cheated out of a good time". This does not mean of course that everyone does, in fact, copulate at dances, just as the almost mandatory Saturday night date of American college girls does not mean that every girl does actually have a Saturday evening date.

Impressions

Visual stimuli play a major role in arousing the sexual urge. The sight of a person of the opposite sex is probably the fundamental stimulus, especially if that person enhances his or her attractiveness by means of ornaments, or by provocative behavior. "People in search of a love-affair, as well as those who wish to get married, paint themselves beautifully. People flirt by eyeing one another. They also make faces, strut about like cocks, or swing their hips. But the most exciting thing is the sight of the genitals." The aboriginal loose fiber skirt facilitated the "accidental" exposure of the vulva. "Men who see the female genitals between the tassels of the fiber skirt have erections, but do not ejaculate." (This answer was obtained in reply to a question concerning skirt-fetishism.) A woman may deliberately expose her genitals, in order to seduce a man, or else may permit him to examine her vulva, as a proof of her affection (Case 1). Even a married man may sometimes examine the vulva of his wife "just to see what it is like, since every vagina is different". (Cf. the personal name Hithpan Kunyamehv, different kinds of vaginas.) A man may, however, also examine the genitals of a wife suspected of adultery, allegedly in order to detect traces of sperm or an excess of vaginal moisture, but in reality chiefly in order to humiliate her. It was asserted that vaginal examinations of the latter type do not lead to intercourse, but this is open to doubt. The old Mohave adage: "Never interfere with quarrelling spouses. Eventually they will sneak out and have intercourse, and then you will have two enemies instead of one," suggests that some vindictive vaginal examinations may lead to intercourse followed by a reconciliation.

Genital examinations during fore-play sometimes enable one to detect in time the presence of chancroids (Case 1).

Men, too, expose themselves now and then. Some men boastfully display their penes stained with blood from a ruptured hymen or from the catamenial flow of their wives or mistresses. Exhibitions of this type are "neither funny nor even in good taste", perhaps because, in

Mohave belief, menstruation is intimately connected with the entire reproductive process (9, 22).

The following case history, which describes the visual excitation of sexual tension, was obtained on two separate occasions. Though the informant did not specify that he was repeating himself, the names and dates prove that both accounts refer to the same incident. The two versions have, therefore, been blended into a single narrative.

Case 1. In the 1880's a combined dance and gambling party was held at your interpreter's grandparents' camp, somewhere between Ehrenberg and La Paz. I was between fifteen and eighteen years old at that time, and attended this gathering in the company of two other boys, ten or eleven years old, one of whom was still inexperienced sexually. A thirty-year-old woman from Needles also attended the dance. We paid quite a bit of attention to her, trying to approach and touch her, or to slip an arm around her waist. She hit one of us, but she did it only in fun.

After a while I recalled that a singer lived near the place where a wire fence now divides our reservation from the State of Arizona, and suggested to this woman that the four of us should visit him and listen to his songs. She readily agreed to come with us, and even offered to carry me there on her back. I refused, however, (jokingly?) asserting that she had hiku:pk (syphilis) which might give me sores on the belly. She insisted so much, however, that I finally consented to let her carry me. She also kept on denying that she had syphilis, and offered to let me "feel" her, and "examine" her for syphilitic lesions. "There is a wash," I finally said. "I'll strike a match and look you over." She agreed at once, and lay down to be examined. I looked her over rather carefully and discovered that she had a sore on her vulva. Instead of telling her of my discovery, I avoided further arguments by promising to have intercourse with her on the way back. She agreed to this postponement, whereupon we proceeded to the house of the singer, who readily consented to sing for us.

After listening to the singer for a while, we decided to return to the main gathering. On our way back we lay down and slept for a while in the bushes. The woman was trying so hard to persuade me to have intercourse with her, that she even presumed to put her leg on top of me! (Mohave women are not permitted to be on top during coitus. Violations of this rule are ridiculed in the personal name "Copulates (actively) with her husband".) She did not succeed in seducing me, however.

When we reached camp next morning, people teased me about having gotten myself a wife, and laughed about it, because the woman said that it was true. "Do you know what to do with her?" an old man asked. "Make her lie down, and examine her all over. If she lets you do that, you may be certain that she loves you." I believed

the old man, and decided to follow his advice as soon as practicable.
Early in the morning people urged the singer to sing some more. "All right," the singer replied, "I will sing some more toward noon. I surely will." Toward three in the afternoon the four of us went down to swim in a pond near the Colorado River. After we swam for a while, the woman again asked me to have intercourse with her. "I know that you are diseased," I said. "Where did you get the disease? Do you have any sores?" "I have no sores. Go ahead and feel me," she replied. Yet, even though she did all sorts of tricks, like floating on her back, with her skirts pulled up, and displaying her legs and her belly, I refused to touch her, saying, "If I 'felt' you, which I won't do, my fingers might rot away and fall off. I am going to look you over, however. Lie down and spread your legs, so that I can examine you." When she lay down, I found that she had one sore each on her labium maius, her vagina, and her clitoris. I was wondering whether or not to have intercourse with her, because, despite her sores, the sight of her vulva excited me when, all of a sudden, I saw the head of the old man, who had advised me to examine her, pop up between the bushes. Since I knew that he was spying on us for fun, I decided not to copulate. At the same time a funny idea, which made me laugh, struck me. I knew that one of the boys was still inexperienced, and, like other chaste boys, would probably cry when he copulated for the first time. I called him and said: "Go and hug her! Feel how she feels." He hugged her immediately, and the woman let him do it. Then I asked the other boy to hug her too, which he did. Another Mohave boy, called "Ball-headed Nigger", was also loafing nearby, but was so scared that the other boys told him to go away. The woman still wanted to have intercourse with me, but, being afraid of getting sick, I merely lay in the pond, and watched the others from the corner of my eye. The boy who had been inexperienced was in front of her, and the other one was behind her, copulating with her vaginally and rectally at the same time.

You know that Indians are supposed to be unemotional, and that only immodest women show their excitement. This woman didn't care about proprieties, however, and hugged the boy who stood in front of her as hard as she could. When this boy became very excited, he began to cry like a fox or like a coyote, making sounds like "ah-ah-ah". That is what boys do when they copulate for the first time (Case 7). Girls, however, don't cry when they are being deflowered, because people would laugh at them. They just groan quietly. Well, after a while I stopped watching them, and went off somewhere. That was the last time I had anything to do with that girl. Another fellow, who had had intercourse with her, got hiku:pk (syphilis?) from her. This girl has died since.

(Other instances of group copulation are described in Cases 10, 11, 12 and 13.)

The above case-history illustrates the stimulus value of visual impressions, as well as of humor.

Conditions of illumination do not seem to stimulate the Mohave who, in reply to a direct question, told me that moonlight, semi-darkness and the like do not arouse them sexually.

Auditory stimuli are, generally speaking, of a sublimated type. Music, especially singing, plays a relatively important role in Mohave eroticism, even though they have no songs of a sexual or amorous character. Many Mohave have their favorite songs which, when sung under the proper circumstances, put them in a mood for amorous ventures. Some persons are considerably affected by certain songs. Boys especially tend to become "brilliant and talkative" while listening to songs, although girls too are affected by music. "A girl might go to a dance or to a gathering, listen to the songs, and end up getting herself a boy." During one of my visits to the Agency school a group of girls sang "Bird" and "Turtle" songs for me, and afterwards seemed less shy and more talkative than usual.

Mohave legends record that men play their flutes in order to attract women (38), and even at present the flute is played primarily by boys in search of amorous adventures (6). Yuma girls are also said to play the jew's-harp in order to attract the men (6). Mohave girls, on the other hand, do not seem to play either the jew's-harp or the flute for erotic purposes.

Olfactory stimuli repel rather than arouse Mohave Indians. "Only harlots use perfumes." "The smell of the vulva and of its secretions nauseates us." This statement seems to be substantially correct.

Case 2. B. B. used to say that the cunnus smelled like fish. When people teased him for being a bachelor, he usually replied that he was unworthy of being chosen, and that no woman wanted him. People knew, however, that L. H.'s wife cared a great deal for him, and laughed at his mock humility. When B. B. finally found a wife, he was for a while somewhat shy of appearing in public, since he feared that people might remind him of his remarks about the smell of the female genitalia, and about his own worthlessness.

Kuwal claimed that he married transvestites because the foul smell of the vulva repelled him. Once, when a woman entered the house in which he was living, he exclaimed, "Hyuh! They smell!" Another time, while living with one of his relatives, he used to exclaim at breakfast, "Hyuh! What is the matter with you women? You smell bad." Finally he said it once too often, and a woman told him off properly: "If you don't like our smell, then get out of here!" She was so angry that she even threw some dirt at him. Kuwal had to run away, and people laughed at him (10).

Normal men also dislike the odor of the vulva. A man vomited when, during a mass copulation, his face was pushed against the vulva of the drunken woman, while another man was allegedly blinded (gonococci?) as a result of a similar practical joke (Cases 11 and 12). The dynamics of this nausea reaction, which may explain why both male and female informants denied the occurrence of cunnilingus, were discussed elsewhere (18). Informants frequently spoke of sexual intercourse as a "smelly business". Since the vulva is never cleansed, remarks about its odor may have some basis in reality, although the fully clothed Mohave woman does not have an unpleasant odor. The smell of the female genitals does not, of course, prevent the Mohave from copulating a great deal. "People will have intercourse any time, day or night," the unmarried, blind half-Cocopa man remarked with contempt. "They will do it even though it may 'smell up' the bed clothes."

The odor of blood in general, and that of menstrual blood in particular, is greatly disliked, and even feared. This may explain why many Mohave voluntarily refrain from intercourse with a menstruating woman. On the whole, "only people with a perverted sense of humor copulate with menstruating women," although coitus during the menses is not prohibited.

Male organs, on the other hand, are not believed to have a repulsive smell. Hence men and women alike admitted that fellatio occurs quite frequently.

Gustatory stimuli seem to play only a minor role. The Mohave did not kiss in aboriginal times, and some of the older people still feel that kissing is rather ridiculous. Amorous biting is thought to be a sign of undue jealousy, characteristic of white immorality (18). Fellatio is, however, common, and one infers that the semen is often swallowed (18).

Tactile stimuli, other than the direct stimulation of the sexual organs and of the rest of the body, seem to be non-existent. All informants denied that contact with certain materials, such as silk or velvet, or with love tokens, would elicit sexual tension.

The mechanical stimulation of the genital organs, and of the breasts is both rudimentary and direct. It is, in general, of short duration and leads, whenever possible, to immediate intercourse.

Sexual stimulation is, apparently, welcome at any time, since it is usually possible to satisfy the urge at once. Excessive sexual desires are believed, however, to cause convulsive "fits" (21, 58).

The sexually offensive. The rule that the woman should wait until the man takes the initiative, is frequently violated. Hence the older Mohave allege that "the young are running wild and pay little attention to the rules of decency, which demand that the man should take the initiative. In the past, people courted only when they wanted to get married." The last remark is probably a rationalization, since the sexual mores of the Mohave do not seem to have undergone a qualitative change in recent times. On the other hand the often repeated statement that the women are so "improper as to do *all* the courting" fails to differentiate between courtship and the initiation of intercourse on the one hand, and, on the other hand, between marriage and casual copulation.

Formal and planned courtship leading to marriage was, and still is, usually initiated by the man, though exceptions to this rule occurred even in aboriginal times. Casual and adulterous affairs, on the other hand, which may or may not lead to marriage, are usually initiated by women.

Marital intercourse tends to be initiated by the husband, the wife being expected to comply with the demands of her spouse. The same is probably true also of protracted extramarital affairs. Casual copulation, on the other hand, is so frequently initiated by women that even Americans living on, or near, the reservation are aware of it. "The women do all the courting. That is why one never hears of rape," Dr. Nettle remarked. The Mohave themselves were unable to mention any *bona fide* cases of rape,[3] as we understand it, since the Mohave conception of rape excludes three similar acts:

(1) Attempted public rape, undertaken in mock anger, as a practical joke.

(2) The punitive serial rape of harlots and of notoriously lewd wives (21).

(3) The serial rape of intoxicated women, who were not, as a rule, deliberately plied with liquor beforehand, but were simply discovered in a state of severe intoxication. It is significant that these women do not seem to resent afterwards the fact that they had been sexually abused.

---

[3] Compare, however, a dubious case, allegedly involving incest and robbery (13).

The Mohave do claim, however, that some women not merely initiate intercourse, but may even "rape" a recalcitrant man. In fact, according to the Mohave, the only case of "rape" took place when A. W. allegedly "raped" a boy who refused to marry her. "One day, at dusk, she simply went to that boy's house and, after 'raping' him in his own bed, succeeded in becoming his wife." Although no longer married to A. W., the man is still quite touchy about this incident, and, though known to me personally, could not be questioned. The incident itself is well known, and was reported to me both by Dr. Nettle and by the Mohave.

Men usually initiate a formal, old-fashioned courtship, leading to marriage. "The boy goes straight to the girl's house and sleeps with her in the other room." (Sic! Mohave houses usually have only one room.) "Courting couples sometimes share a pallet outdoors." "The parents of the girl seldom mind." Courtship of this type resembled "bundling", and did not necessarily culminate in coitus. According to some informants, courting couples did not even engage in intimate caresses.

"A man lying with his woman, will take her whenever he feels like it, and in whatever position he prefers to do it. He will get hold of whichever orifice of her body is most handy, regardless of whether it is the vagina, the anus or the mouth.[4] The woman will not think of refusing him, lest he desert her, although she may desert him if he forces her to copulate too frequently, regardless of whether he is her husband or her lover. No one would talk about this. It is nobody's business." (The latter assertion is probably a gratuitous one, since sex is an important topic of conversation.) Although male and female Mohave informants, as well as a Yuma woman, repeatedly asserted that excessive sexual demands on the part of the male were a form of cruelty, they were unable to cite an actual divorce or desertion caused by excessive sexual demands. Hence, in view of the notoriously strong sexual urge of Mohave women, we may be dealing here with an ideal pattern, rather than with an actual one.

At this juncture it is necessary to distinguish between forepleasure and atypical forms of coitus.

---

[4] This obviously oversimplified statement is, nonetheless, not a wholly implausible one. An Indochinese Moï informed me that an intoxicated man had oral intercourse with his wife, by mistake.

Forepleasure: Actual coitus, be it vaginal, anal or oral, is preceded by very little foreplay. Women may manipulate a man's penis either at his request, or upon their own initiative, although they may not presume, however, to "push back" the foreskin (Case 13), since such an act would resemble infantile masturbation (18). Genital manipulations are not supposed to produce an orgasm, but merely to arouse desire. Fellatio, is, however, usually an end in itself. Hence, like anal coitus, it must be discussed separately.

Men, in turn, play with the woman's breasts, "and get her all excited", even though "this is not a decent sort of behavior". Men do not kiss, or suck, the breasts or nipples of their mistresses, nor does a woman ask a man to kiss her breasts, since foreplay of this kind would be "suggestive of mother-son incest", and would also imply that the man needed someone to mother him, because his own mother was dead (18). Coitus between the breasts is likewise unknown. "We are not that civilized!" a well educated female informant said with contempt. "No man would play with the breasts of a woman long enough to induce an orgasm. He does it only long enough to excite her." The absence of cunnilingus is due primarily to the fact that the smell of the vagina is repulsive to the Mohave.[5] For the same reason the Mohave generally refrain from manipulating the clitoris or the vagina. "It is, however, usual to excite a woman until she groans. A man may rub his penis against the clitoris until the girl groans and pants, 'Hyeh! Hyeh!' (aspired) and begs him to insert it into her vagina. Men overstimulate girls in this manner only for fun, and afterwards tell the story to people who will laugh and joke about it. Only bad men do such things." Intralabial intercourse is not prolonged, however, until orgasm ensues. "There is a normal place for the penis. Hence there is no reason why one should perform interfemoral or intralabial coitus." (But cf. Case 6.)

Summing up, coitus is frequently preceded by a certain amount of "hugging" and caressing. The European oral, as well as the Mongolic nasal kiss were unknown in aboriginal times. Erotic biting was rare, and was believed to be a sign of jealousy (18).

---

[5] The average Mohave does not even understand what cunnilingus means. In reply to a query regarding its occurrence an informant related that some practical jokers pushed a man's face against the vulva of the drunken woman, when his turn came to copulate with her (Case 11).

Normal Coital Behavior

The Mohave have few coital positions. The usual position is the ventro-ventral one, in which the man assumes the top position. No part of the woman's body is supposed to be on top of the man, since it would imply that *she* was the active partner in intercourse. The woman either stretches out her legs, or else bends them at the knees. Sometimes she further elevates and spreads her thighs by placing her hands behind her bent knees. A "decent" woman never entwines her legs around the man, since in this position her calves and feet would have rested on top of the man's body.

The lateral (ventro-ventral or ventro-dorsal) position was resorted to very rarely, since in this position one of the woman's legs usually rests on the man's body.

Naturally there were some exceptions to these rules. Case 1. records that the woman put her legs on top of the man. Women may also "rape" a drunken man by squatting on top of him. The male personal name Itcuy kunyen (Coitizes her husband) describes the behavior of women who "have to do all the work, because their husbands are no good".

Coitus in a standing position is rare, and is sometimes resorted to by couples standing in shallow water. Vaginal and anal intercourse both may take place in this position either simultaneously (Case 1) or consecutively. Coitus a tergo, in which the woman, who supports herself on her hands and knees, or else bends forward and rests her palms on, e.g., a toilet seat, is approached from behind, is relatively rare. An instance is recorded further below. Drunken women may lie, or be laid, face downward, and be approached vaginally from the rear. The Somali position (49), i.e., a man kneeling in front of a woman who lies prone on her back, was mentioned only once, in connection with the serial abuse of a drunken woman (Case 12). The Trobriand (44) or Australian (49) squatting position is unknown.

Women are expected to be passive during coitus, and should not wriggle. "A woman must take no part in the hip work. We think it is awful for a woman to do that. We don't like it." Although this statement was made by a female informant, it probably reflects also the male view.

It is not customary to change position during any single copulation. When further intercourse is desired, new positions may be assumed.

In theory it is not the woman but the man who guides and inserts the penis. The "rape" of drunken men forms an exception to this rule. In a case of rectal intercourse, it was likewise specified that the insertion of the penis was guided by the woman (Case 4).

Previous to its insertion into the vagina or into the anus the penis is sometimes wetted either with spittle (18), or else with moist clay. One informant stated that the lubricant was applied to the vulva or to the rectum. The most reliable informants stated, however, that it was applied to the penis itself (Case 6).

During intercourse "the partners hug each other, but as a rule do not talk to each other", especially when there are other people in the vicinity. When nocturnal intercourse takes place in a house inhabited by several people, the spouses sometimes try to disguise it by ostentatiously carrying on a conversation. However, when people are alone, they tend to converse a little, especially during foreplay. Terms of endearment are not in general use among the Mohave. "If I call a Mohave 'honey' they laugh at me", a woman informant stated. This is not a hard and fast rule, however, although it is considered indecorous to chatter and "to make little purring noises" during intercourse. "People are not inclined to talk during intercourse. They are too excited, waiting for the orgasm. Therefore the better they feel, the quieter they are," a woman informant declared.

The above statements make it quite clear that the sole conscious goal of intercourse is orgasm. Coitus interruptus is unknown. A woman may, either on her own initiative, or at the request of the man, strain the muscles of her thighs, in order to tighten her vagina. Spontaneous contractions were not mentioned, however. Even though the Mohave prefer a violent climax to lingering pre-orgastic excitement, they do not like intercourse to last less than fifteen minutes. (Although it is notoriously difficult to form accurate estimates of the duration of coitus (4), this estimate, given by a woman, is probably correct, since the Mohave are, in general, good at estimating time elapsed.) Although women too enjoy the prolongation of the act, the slowing down of the coital movements is, generally speaking, initiated by the man. According to the Mohave, their coitus lasts appreciably longer than that of White men. "Whites get soft too quickly." Hence, despite the fact that the large sexual organs of Whites, and especially of Mexicans, were supposed to cause the women some pain (21), Mohave prostitutes often boasted that they were making "easy money". According to Dr. Nettle, "For a long time neither the lady-teachers of the Indian Agency, nor myself could get any washing done, as the only available washer-woman sent us word that she had an easier way of making two dollars than hanging all day over the washtub." (46)

Some women were subject to flatulence during intercourse. "When the bald-headed Chinaman pokes W. in the vagina, she lets out all sorts of gases by the rectum." Several instances of flatulence are on record. In other instances—apparently because of an intermittent lack of tonus—the vagina emitted gurgling sounds either during or after intercourse.

Case 3. A young couple, aged twenty and twenty-one respectively, lived with one of the husband's relatives. My interpreter remarked that this man had tattooed her, and that Dr. Nettle had saved the life of the woman who, despite the ministrations of a certain shaman, almost died in childbirth (46). Since they lived with relatives, they copulated in the bushes behind the house. One day, early in the afternoon, the man took his wife to the bush. He had lowered his trousers, and his wife had pulled up her skirts, when an elderly man, who lived in the same house, came out, and interfered with them. "What are you doing anyway? I just came up and found you acting like that!" The husband promptly pulled up his trousers and ran away as fast as he could, leaving his wife, who was too embarrassed to flee, in the bushes.

Later on in the day, when the husband, who had gone to attend a game of shinny played on the overflow of the Colorado River, came home, he could not find his wife, who had remained hidden in the bushes. Not until twilight did she finally go back to the house, walking so slowly and appearing so bashful, that people began to ask questions. When she refused to speak, her husband explained that they had been surprised while attempting to copulate, and that his wife had been too bashful to come home before suppertime.

A few days later, when this couple—which, like many Mohave, slept outdoors in the summer—went to bed behind the house, the husband asked his wife to perform fellatio. The woman promptly assumed a suitable position and was just about to begin, when the same man emerged from the house and saw them. This time he did not say anything, however, and went past them, to the outhouse. After looking around carefully, the couple was just about to resume fellatio when, on his way back to the house, the man stopped by their bed and said "Why don't you two behave yourselves? Now you act as though you were quarrelling."[6] Although the husband kept on wishing that the man would mind his own business and leave, so as to enable them to resume intercourse, the couple remained silent.

---

[6] Quarrelling couples usually sleep with their heads pointing in opposite directions, except when the woman is pregnant, since this sleeping position might cause the child to be born feet first and die (22). This taboo might perhaps prevent some married couples from going to bed unreconciled.

One (cold?) night, this couple went to bed in the house. Since the fire was burning, the same old man, whose bed happened to be facing that of the couple, saw that they were engaging in anal intercourse. The young woman had eaten too much, however, and had gas in her intestines. Hence, she was suddenly compelled to break wind, whereupon both she and her husband began to giggle. Once more the old man interfered. "My heavens, what did you two let loose?" This remark awakened the rest of the household, and everyone began to bait the couple: "What are you two doing there in that corner?" When they did not reply, the old man remarked, "They turned loose something." These incidents were related to the main informant by the husband, after he had left his wife.

Ejaculatio praecox is unknown. If the woman reached the climax first, the man continued until he too achieved orgasm. On the other hand one infers that, if the man reached the climax first, he did not prolong intercourse until the woman too had achieved an orgasm, since it was repeatedly stated that the man withdrew his penis immediately after ejaculation. Apparently the penis was never left in the vagina between two acts.

Intercourse comes to an end when the penis is withdrawn after ejaculation. Since vaginismus and penis captivus are unknown, the technique of relaxing the cramp by inserting a finger into the woman's anus was likewise unknown. The withdrawal of the penis is sometimes accompanied by a "snorting" vaginal sound, rendered as "khe, khe". The personal name Holukumk'ok (pulls it out with a click) also refers to this phenomenon.

The Mohave believe that women can neither produce nor suppress at will these noises, whose real causes are unknown to them.

Medically speaking, these frequently described sounds may have several causes.

(1) The most important factor is probably the disparity in the size of the male and female organs, since the Mohave specified that sexually experienced women produced sounds far more frequently than did relatively inexperienced ones. Hence, these sounds may be due to coital and post-coital spasms, followed by a gradual relaxation of the vagina. Since vaginal spasms are closely linked with orgastic potency (37, 47), and since Mohave women are known to be orgastically potent, the above interpretation seems to be a plausible one, despite the fact that the Mohave did not mention spontaneous vaginal contraction.

(2) Copious vaginal secretion may facilitate the production of a vacuum, and hence the production of coital and post-coital vaginal sounds. The following data suggest that Mohave women have copious coital and orgastic secretions:

(a) The Mohave Indian's awareness of the woman's orgastic secretions (called "the female seed") suggests that these secretions are copious ones.

(b) The Mohave believe that recent intercourse can be detected by the presence of excessive vaginal moisture.

(c) A man allegedly contracted (gonorrheic?) blindness, when his face was pushed against the wet vulva of a serially raped woman.

(d) The Mohave refer quite often to the unpleasant smell of the vagina. Such odors are usually due to a deterioration of excess vaginal secretions.

A case history describes the occurrence of such vaginal sounds in some detail:

Case 4. (Obtained from Hivsu: Tupo:ma) "In my youth an old man told me that our forebears had such huge penes—some of them eight inches long—that is was very difficult to insert them into the vagina. (Informant's fingers imitated a difficult insertion.) Of course people who are only 'two inches' long have no such difficulties!"[7] At present only Lavur Modhar (Burro's penis) has a large penis, although even his is smaller than the penes of our forebears. However, I want to tell you what this old man told me. A man met at a dance a married woman, who agreed to have intercourse with him, whereupon they went off and hid in the bushes, at some distance from the gathering. This man had a very large penis. "Put it into my vagina," the woman said. When the man replied: "allright", the woman lay down on her back, bent her knees, and pulled up her thighs with her hands, whereupon the man began to insert his penis. "Gee; you sure have a big one!" the woman exclaimed, "I sure like it." The man then thrust his penis so deep into her vagina that it bumped into her cervix. The woman groaned and said, "I do like it!" "Well, feel

---

[7] The history of this colloquialism may be of interest to students of linguistic acculturation. In 1932 the Mohave took a liking to a limerick about a bishop whose penis was two inches shorter than that of the vicar, and pinned copies of this limerick on their walls. Henceforth "two inches" began to be used as an English equivalent of modhar pikapi:k (stubby penis) so consistently that any reference to "two inches" automatically elicited laughter.

it then!" the man replied. "Pull it out a little bit, so I can feel it," the woman begged, whereupon the man partly withdrew his penis, but did not interrupt his coital motions. The woman touched his penis and said, "How I love it! It feels so nice! My husband's penis is so small that one can hardly feel it." She kept on talking this way until the man had an orgasm and withdrew. "I'd like to know how it feels in my rectum", the woman said. The man replied: "I'll do it to you rectally after a while," but the woman kept urging him, until he inserted his penis into her rectum. "Push it in little by little," the woman exclaimed, seizing the penis by its root and inserting it gently into her rectum. "And don't pull it out entirely, as you move. I am afraid I might have a bowel movement." The man tried to be careful, but when he became very much excited, he accidentally withdrew his penis entirely, before beginning the downward stroke. He promptly felt that his thighs had gotten very wet, but gave the matter no further thought, and the couple remained in the bushes until morning.

At dawn the man suddenly exclaimed, "You know, something sure stinks! Is it my breechcloth, or your skirt?" He touched his penis and, after feeling it all over, realized that it was covered with some messy substance. (The name "Yellow Thigh" mentioned by Kroeber (39) may perhaps refer to this incident, or to a similar one.) He tried to make the woman smell his finger, but she withdrew, saying "No—leave it alone." "But it is all over us," the man insisted. It is probable that when his penis slipped out of her rectum, the woman had had a bowel movement, though neither of them realized it at the time. Maybe that smell put them to sleep. (The audience received this remark with shouts of laughter, since it seemed probable to them that the old man, who had told this story to informant, must have been the hero of this adventure. Indeed, interpreter remarked rather cryptically that the Mohave seem unable to keep a story to themselves.) At any rate, the woman found her experience so satisfactory that she deserted her husband and married her lover.

After the new couple had been living together for a little while, one night, when they both left the house to defecate, the man asked his wife whether she wanted to do something she had never done before, and the woman replied "Yes, I do." After they had defecated the man said: "Go down on your knees and bend forward, until your breasts touch the ground. I want to insert my penis into your vagina from the rear." While they were copulating in this position the woman's vagina suddenly began to make strange noises that sounded like 'Kha'-Khouk'-Kha'-Khe', and made her giggle. The husband tried to ask: "What's wrong?" But by then both of them were guffawing so loudly that the people who lived in the same house began to wonder what was happening. Despite the noises the couple completed the act. When the noises, which sounded as though air were coming out of the vagina, did not cease after she got up, the woman became disturbed. "What is the matter with me?" she asked her husband, who had to reply that he did not know. Eventually the woman started to walk toward the house, but the continuous vaginal noises began to worry her. "I don't know what to do!" she complained. "Maybe you busted something inside of me." She started for the house once more, but stopped again, because the noise could be heard at every step. "I can't go back like this to the house," the woman said, and both of them began to giggle once more. "Hold your breath", the husband advised. "Maybe it will stop then." The woman held her breath, but the noises continued, and both of them kept on giggling. Finally they went back into the house, but, just as the woman sat down, her vagina once more emitted these sounds, which one could reproduce by snorting like this: kho khoook.

Since vaginal noises are "very funny things", the telling of this story was constantly interrupted by merriment.

The genitalia are not cleaned after intercourse.

The frequency of intercourse. A honeymooning couple copulates once a night, and, later on, "while affection still lasts", about once a week. Three copulations a night are believed to be a good performance, and many persons said that four acts were the maximum. Others asserted that six times a night would be a thing to boast of in public. If a newly wed girl lost weight, people said that her husband was wearing her out. "If a man uses his wife too often, they say that he is like a dog, which is just about the lowest possible epithet" (23). "His wife might run away if he insists on having intercourse too often." (As stated above, informants were unable to cite any desertions due to excessive sexual demands.)

When I cite evidence (36, 41) indicating that middle-class Americans copulated somewhat more frequently than they did, the Mohave gratuitously nicknamed a certain White "Copulates all night." (*Real names of this type usually ridicule not the person's own characteristics, but the odd or objectionable behavior of another person.*)

The Mohave Indian's sex-act lasts longer, however, than that of the White man, "who gets soft almost at once". Hence despite the "hugeness" of the White men's penis, and despite the fact that many customers repeated the act, Mohave prostitutes boasted that their trade was not a strenuous one (21).

Special Types of Coitus

Virginity. Neither the Mohave girl herself, nor anyone else, took pride in, or valued her virginity, nor, despite the smallness of the Mohave penis, expressed a preference for the virginal vagina. Nor did anyone view defloration as a degradation of the girl, or as an infringement of property rights. Hence the American attitude toward chastity, and accounts of the Omaha (45) or Somali (49) obsession with virginity, struck them as simply preposterous. Whatever trace of anxiety the Mohave may have experienced, because of the unavoidable shedding of blood, and because of the psychological "taboo of virginity" (32, 35, 60), was adequately neutralized by their tendency to view defloration as a humorous exploit, or as "a kind of sport". Hence some women boasted of having had virgin lovers, while some men were known to remark about a former mistress: "I got her in shape for you fellows." On the other hand "only a bad man would boast of having deflowered his present wife". This specification probably reflects a desire for privacy, rather than a concern for morality.

Girls are deflowered unceremonially and always by means of the penis. An account of the Tongareva type of finger-defloration (57) caused interpreter—who likes to exaggerate—to exclaim: "The relatives of the girl would beat a man to death (?), if he thought of doing such a thing either at birth, or at puberty or at any other time." Some informants stated that the average girl was deflowered at the age of eleven or less. Older people alleged, however, that in aboriginal times defloration occurred at a somewhat later age. This statement completely ignores aboriginal child-marriages (14). It is also probable that many eleven year old "virgins" no longer have a hymen, partly because of previous masturbatory practices, and perhaps also because of infantile sex-play.

"When a girl is deflowered she bleeds. The noise made by the tearing of the hymen can be reproduced as "chrrr", or "prrr". (Obviously a purely imaginary sound.) "It is indecent for a girl to 'holler' during defloration, or when giving birth. Should she cry out, people will tease her for being unable to bear pain. The man who deflowered her would tell it to other men, and she would be ridiculed in public." Sometimes, instead of deflowering them, men merely copulate anally with young girls, "because the rectum of a girl ten to fourteen years of age is larger than her vagina." (This is the custom also among the Patwin (40), and among some of the Moi of Indochina.) Some female informants claimed, however, that it is more difficult "to slip into the rectum, than to slip into the vagina, even when one is very careful and patient". It is probable that my woman informants referred primarily to patience on the part of an adult woman, since a young girl's colon is, in fact, larger than her vaginal tract. Defloration, as well as anal intercourse, frequently involved the use of the above mentioned lubricants. Men and boys alike deflowered young girls. Some adult humorists almost specialized in the seduction of young girls, whereas more sedate men usually chose women nearer their own age.

Case 5. Humar kunyamasav (white baby) used to go around with two other men, one of whom was Saukmuhan (look at things *at* dawn, or *in* the dawn), the father of T. R. These three men were gay, ne'er-do-well fellows, much addicted to jokes. Up to the age of thirty, Humar kunyamasav always (sic!) managed to get himself some virgin. Once he attempted to have anal intercourse with a thirteen year old virgin on the roof of her own house. Even though the girl was quite willing, the insertion hurt her so much that, after lamenting and groaning for a while in a subdued voice, she finally cried out. Her grandparents, who were in the house, heard the noise, and came out to investigate. When the frightened man quickly withdrew his penis the girl accidentally soiled him, so that, 'covered with faeces', he had to run 'for sweet life' (?), pursued by the girl's irate grandparents. When this incident became known people nicknamed him Amaykatcerktce (defecated upon). After the age of thirty he married several times, but never lived with his wives for any length of time. (In 1932, when he was about sixty years old, he was still "conservative" enough to wrap his long hair in a bandanna, and, at the same time, "progressive" enough to drive his rickety Model T Ford recklessly on the wrong side of the road. During the time when Americans of Japanese ancestry were interned on the Mohave reservation, this man was killed when an internee's car hit his own at an intersection. "This created a great deal of bitterness among the Mohave.")

Case 6. Another of the 'Three Musketeers' (sic!), Saukmuhan, managed to marry a virgin, who, for quite some time, refused to be deflowered by her husband, and successfully foiled his stealthy attempts to penetrate her during intralabial coitus. At last Saukmuhan asked her to lie down on her stomach, 'spat resolutely in his hand', lubricated his penis, and performed anal intercourse. However, when he withdrew his penis, he found it covered with soft faeces. Because of this incident Saukmuhan acquired the nickname Porkupork, which supposedly reproduces the sound of defecation.

Boys cared even less for their chastity than girls did since, if they remained continent, they were ridiculed for being unable to get a girl. The first sexual partner of a young boy was usually a girl his own age (Case 7), since normal women usually preferred experienced lovers. However, since some lewd women liked to boast of having seduced a previously chaste boy, some youngsters had their first experience with a dissolute adult woman (Case 1).

Case 7. T. D. obtained his first sexual experience when he went to swim with the daughter of P. N. and with his younger brother E. D. Coitus excited him so much that tears were rolling down his cheeks. When T. D. had finished, he told his younger brother, who stood by looking at them, "Now go ahead and do your part!" E. D. refused, however, saying "I saw that you were crying. I don't want to cry."

Generally speaking, the Mohave do not approve of too early intercourse, although a girl may have intercourse immediately after reaching puberty, including even the very first day of her menses (sic!), without damaging her health. Boys were urged, however, not to marry or have intercourse too early. "Watch out for women," the old warned them, "They will sap your strength". (Compare also the Hopi belief that castration increases a horse's strength.) "Everything they do will go wrong and turn against them, if they start their sexual life too early. It makes them highstrung and unable to conceal their emotions." (The Mohave imagine that they resemble the stolid Plain Indians depicted in "Wild West" films and magazines.) The Mohave are so convinced that *only* early sex relations produce a highstrung personality-type, that a certain White was credited with early sexual experiences merely because he was upset when he crumpled up the fender of a friend's car. Although at present the *average* adolescent first copulates at the age of twelve or thirteen, sexual relations—sometimes involving even the transmission of venereal diseases—occur even between children less than seven or eight years old. "In aboriginal times people had their first sexual experiences at a much later date. That is why our young people do not remain potent until they die."

Since there is no latency period among the Mohave, continuous prepubertal genital activities of all kinds are the rule, rather than the exception.[8]

---

[8] Primitive data do not support the theory that the oedipus complex and castration anxiety *automatically* lead to a latency period, especially since Róheim (52) has shown that the oedipus complex and castration anxiety are present also among tribes without a latency period. It is therefore not the absence, but the presence of the latency period which stands in need of an explanation, which must include a re-appraisal of the thesis that education and civilization presuppose genital frustration.

Anal intercourse deviates from the standards of sexual behavior instituted by the dying God Matavilye, who ordained that people should copulate for reproductive purposes. A woman of about thirty-five remarked however, that "anal intercourse seems to have been popular among the older generation", even though it allegedly causes "loose bowels" (diarrhea) and hemorrhoids. (According to Dr. Nettle, the hemorrhoids of Mohave women are due to their fatness, and to numerous childbirths.) Passive male homosexuals (10), and children born to women who, while pregnant, engaged in anal intercourse, also have "loose bowels".[9]

Several men, and all female informants, asserted that women enjoyed anal intercourse, even though some of them liked to play coy. Even the few men who thought that women did not enjoy anal intercourse admitted that most of them consent to it quite readily. While only a few women are known to be adverse to anal intercourse, no woman is so much addicted to it that she practices it to the exclusion of vaginal coitus. The Mohave consciously profess to engage in anal intercourse either because it is a "painless" way of copulating with virgins, or else because it appeals to them as an unusual and humorous sexual exploit (Cases 1, 3, 5, 6, 10). It is never thought of either as mere foreplay, or as a means of contraception. Anal fondling and masturbation are unknown.

Although Mohave anal eroticism cannot be discussed at this juncture, the leniency of Mohave toilet-training, combined with the fact that the anal stage overlaps both with the end of the long lactation period, and with the beginnings of the phallic-oedipal stage (18), may perhaps explain why the adult woman's anal erotism is so easily coordinated with her genital sexuality. (The colon is stimulated even during vaginal intercourse, since the penis is constantly thrust against the wall separating the vagina from the rectum.) The intensity of anal sensations may make rectal intercourse attractive to young virgins, who have not, as yet, attained full genitality.

The anal zone is erotized also in the normal male (Case 8), as well as in homosexuals. (10)

Fellatio was described even by the austere, blind, half-Cocopa man

---

[9] Diarrhea is an important symptom in many of the ailments known to Mohave shamans, and occurs both in male and in female patients. Constipation, on the other hand, is quite exceptional. The self-induced constipation of passive male homosexuals is definitely linked with anal birth fantasies (10).

as a common form of sex-behavior. Although men think that women do not enjoy fellatio, all female informants stated that women enjoyed it so much that some women actually prefer it to anal coitus.

Case 8. was reported by the main woman informant. "An old man told me that he frequently had oral intercourse with his wife. When he became excited he pushed in his penis as deeply as he could, and his wife sucked it in even further. When he ejaculated, his rectum went in so deeply between the buttocks that it looked like a hole. It seemed to him as though his anus were being pulled forward by the suction applied to his penis."

An almost identical statement, made by a male informant, enables us to localize the sensation in the collicular prostatic-anal region, which is erotized only by a limited number of men (25).

Case 9. Tcukah anyay had the power to sing the Tuma:np'a Utaut cycle. Once, when he sang for a group, a woman deserted her husband and married him. One day, when he asked her to perform fellatio, she played coy, and refused to do it. They were quibbling and tossing about in bed, until the man got up and went outside to urinate. When he came back his wife said: "Where did you go?" but feeling sulky, he did not bother to answer. "What is the matter with you? Why are you cross?" the woman insisted, but he did not answer her and just kept on sulking. "You can do it between my legs in the cunnus, and you may also use my rectum—what more do you want?" she protested, but since he continued to ignore her, she finally performed fellatio, and had such an intensely pleasurable oral sensation that his sperm bubbled from between her lips. When this incident became known, the man received the name Nyamasava takavekva—white spills from the mouth." (18)

Fellatio is prohibited during pregnancy, lest the child be born without a "throatcap" (epiglottis?) and be mute (22).
The psychodynamics of fellatio were discussed elsewhere (18). Cunnilingus was unknown (18).
Intrafemoral coitus was denied, although there is some reference to it in Case 9, and perhaps also in Case 6.
Intramammal coitus was likewise denied. The Mohave expressed surprise when told that both men and women may achieve an orgasm in that manner.
Group promiscuousness consists, as a rule, in the serial abuse of a drunken woman by a group which may include the woman's own hus-

band (Case 10), as well as friends of the participants summoned by messenger (Case 11). As a rule the men "take turns" on the woman, no attempt being made to rape the woman simultaneously vaginally, anally and orally. Vaginal coitus is the rule, although anal coitus may also be attempted (Case 10). Incidents of this type should not be confused with the punitive rape of kamalo:y-s (21). The serial abuse of drunken men by women is rare, and seems to be retaliatory in character.

Case 10. (Told in the presence of a former husband of Mah, "on whom several men, including her own divorced husband, used to take turns when she was drunk". The case of Mah will be reported elsewhere.) "E., an alcoholic, is ten or twelve years older than her husband, who cried when he was sexually initiated (Case 7). One day, when E. was drunk, a group of young men, including her own husband, and even some schoolboys, were 'taking turns' on her, some place near the old jail and the old pool-hall. Her husband, who was also drunk, watched the proceedings quite dispassionately. 'I know she is my wife', he mumbled, 'yet I don't mind you fellows taking turns on her, and getting your fill. She's drunk again and she has it coming to her.' Only when the men grew tired of vaginal intercourse, and turned her over, intending to perform anal intercourse, did he protest: 'I don't want you to have rectal intercourse with her—her rectum is for me alone.' (This, of course, was not a traditional restriction, but merely the fancy of a drunken man.) When the men paid no heed to him, he struggled to his feet and surprised the men by trying to fight them off. (According both to Dr. Nettle, and the native policeman, a drunken Mohave does not fight, but merely passes out.) Since the men had had enough of the fun anyway, they let the couple, walking hand in hand, stagger down the slope of the mesa, and go home. The husband was not angry, nor was either of them ashamed, when they sobered up." At this juncture informant repeated, with an indulgent and knowing smile, that E. was older than her husband.

Case 11. "Three elderly men from Needles, Papelahmaly (paperbag), Aovahwat (tobacco-red) and Tinyamuhvec (a term which describes sudden nightfall) found a pretty, but notoriously alcoholic, Walapai woman lying in the bushes, while her husband, equally drunk, was 'sleeping it off' somewhere else. The men carried her to a house near the Colorado River, which belonged to Kunyoor (beef on top), who has the power to take visitors to the land of the dead. When they found their prospective host absent, two of them said to the third one 'Kunyoor is our friend. Go and get him!' and, as soon as the messenger departed, began to 'take turns' on the girl.

When Kunyoor arrived, and knelt down between the woman's legs, a practical joker pushed his face against the girl's wet vulva and thighs. Since the girl had just started to urinate, Kunyoor fell into her urine. Fearful of being blinded, Kunyoor rose at once and staggered about with closed eyes, until he fell into the Colorado River. It must have been quite a drop, since the water level is usually way below the bank on which the house is built."

Older men often resort to such abuses, because they cannot get young girls otherwise.

Case 12. "A woman, who, after several years of marriage had separated from her husband, asked a man to persuade him to return to her. The intermediary, wishing to seduce her, did not deliver her message, however, and pretended that her husband had refused to be reconciled with her. Then, under the pretense of wanting to comfort her, he sent for some whisky, and plied her with drink until she passed out, whereupon several men 'took turns' on her during the rest of the night. Eventually the seducer himself and one or two of his personal friends turned up toward dawn, decided that the girl was still not drunk enough to suit them, and gave her some more whisky. After a while one of them slipped his hand into the woman's vagina—and a big vagina it must have been!—and said: 'There is something inside —try it'. Another man then spat on his hand 'to lubricate it' and slipped it into the vagina. 'Leave her alone!' a third man said, 'You might bust something inside. She and her husband will get together again. So let us just take turns on her and let us not hurt her.' The man promptly withdrew his hand and said 'Pooh', because the woman was all wet between the thighs. 'Come on, you have intercourse with her first,' someone said to one of the men. Two men, seizing the woman's legs, spread them, and lifted them up, so that the woman was entirely exposed. The man chosen was, however, too drunk to copulate, and knelt down very slowly. 'Come on!' the other two urged him. 'I can't,' the man said, very much abashed, 'I can't get an erection.' 'Get nearer then,' the other two said, and pushed him forward, whereupon he lost his balance and fell face downward on her vulva. 'The poor fellow' (sic!) was so nauseated that he vomited. When this incident became known her husband refused to take her back. As to the woman, she later on contracted a (venereal?) disease and died."

This narrative is atypical in several respects. Premeditated scheming, cheating and lying are contrary to Mohave character structure, as well as to Mohave ethics. Nor do the Mohave intoxicate a woman for the purpose of "taking turns" on her, although they feel free to copulate serially with women found in a state of intoxication. The insertion of the hand into the vagina is likewise unusual, because of the Mohave Indian's notorious dislike of vaginal odors. Last, but not least, it is psychologically implausible that the seducer would intoxicate a woman, leave her to some unnamed men appearing from nowhere, stay away until dawn, and then decide that she still wasn't drunk enough to suit him. It is far more likely that, after delivering his false message, the seducer gave her some whisky, and then left the depressed woman to get drunk by herself, if she chose to do so. All in all, I suspect that the story was either badly told, or else badly interpreted. The present version of the story is a wholly improbable one.

Case 13. (Told by Hivsu: Tupo:ma) One or two years after the Needles railroad was built, a white man took fifteen shinney-players, and two women who were to be the team's concubines, to Los Angeles, and lodged them in a Pullman car shunted on a side-track. As soon as they reached Greater Los Angeles, their manager went to wire to Los Angeles and El Monte, that the game was to take place at Long Beach. In the meantime he gave the Mohave a day off, and advised them to see the town and the ocean. Instead of visiting the town, as they started out to do, the Mohave stopped at the first saloon, where someone presented them with a case of hard liquor. The men carried the liquor back to their Pullman, and proceeded to get drunk with the women. By the time I got back, one of the women was so drunk that some of the men were "taking turns" on her, while the rest were either plying the second girl with drinks, or else tussling and arguing among themselves as to whose turn would come next. When the second girl also passed out, the men took turns on both women, until they had enough of it. Then they deposited the girls side by side near the Pullman, and, after raising their skirts and exposing them "in full view", began to laugh and to throw dirt at them. Toward eight or ten o'clock that night one of the men finally wiped the dirt from between the girls' legs with his handkerchief, and said: "Leave those girls alone!" The men quieted down, but, just as he was lifting them up to carry them to their Pullman berths, semen began to drip from their vaginas, and the men burst out laughing once more. Eventually the girls were laid on their berths and fell asleep. People had quieted down in the meantime, and everyone, except me and four other men, was "sleeping it off," when one of the men said "How about having some fun? Let us set fire to the pubic hair of these girls." "Don't you do it! It might blister them and they will be unable to walk tomorrow," I protested. Then another man said: "Let us rub sand into their pubic hair first. That way their skin won't burn, and the fire will merely singe off their pubic hair." One of the men got some sand or dirt and rubbed it into the girls' pubic hair. These girls had nice pubic hair, and one of the men tried to set it on fire. I did not like the joke, and fought them off for awhile, trying to protect the girls, but I was outnumbered and had to stand by, while they singed off the hair of one of the girls. The hair burned well, but the girl was not entirely unconscious, as yet, and, after rolling over, cussed out the men. Once more I pleaded with them to leave the girls alone, but the others paid no attention to me, and proceeded to singe off also the pubic hair of the second girl. Her pubic hair too burned a little, until she also rolled over. Eventually I rubbed out the fire with my bare hands, while one of the men jeered: "Your hands are ruined. Don't eat tomorrow and don't touch anything!"

Next morning I asked the girls if they knew that they had been burned, and when the girls replied that they had noticed it, I told them who had done it. The girls said nothing, however, at that time, even though one of the guilty men was related to one of them.

Sometime after our return to Needles, two of the guilty men got drunk and passed out near the iceplant. The two girls, who happened to come by just then, exposed the penes of the men, pulled back their foreskins, tied them back with pieces of string, applied red paint to their exposed glans, and painted the shafts with yellow and black stripes. Then they left the men lying in plain sight. (The baring of the glans penis, which is a severe insult (18), especially when done to a relative (13), was further aggravated by the use of red paint, which is used only by women.)

It was obvious that whereas Hivsu: Tupo:ma had enjoyed his share of the intercourse, he strongly disapproved of the subsequent "practical joke" which was not a regular part of the treatment which any intoxicated woman must expect. From the psychological point of view it is interesting that several Americans deemed the sexual abuse more grievous an offense than the burnings, whereas my informant who, despite the obligatory "devilishness" of the shaman, was a very good fellow, felt that only the burning was cruel. The cultural pattern traces here a boundary-line between custom and cruelty, which does not coincide with Western ideas.

The deliberately brutal serial abuse of prostitutes and of promiscuous wives was reported elsewhere (21).

The after-effects of coitus are aching knees and hips, general weakness and drowsiness, and a darkening of the sex organs (18). At the same time, "one notices at once people who had intercourse the night before. They are proud and sparkling". The characterological effects of precocious sexual experience were described above.

The Aftermath

Freud (31) believed that mankind's tendency to perform sexual acts in secret is due to the desocialization of mating couples, who temporarily withdraw their libidinal cathexes from the community at large. It is hence desirable to analyze the role and function of sexual acts in Mohave society in terms of the publicity accorded to any amusing or deviant sexual incident.

Indiscretion. The Mohave readily admit that they are "unable to keep a good story to themselves", although they add that "thoughtful people watch their tongues", and do not boast of their sexual adventures. I am yet to meet any of these "discreet" individuals, however. Yet boasting is known to be a double-edged sword, "since a man may make some remark which, later on, under altered circumstances, he would prefer not to have uttered". (Cf. the case of B.B., above.)

With the exception of the notoriously indiscreet kamalo:y (21) women are usually somewhat more discreet than men are. "When a woman asks a man to have intercourse with her she sometimes warns him that if he discussed their intimacy with anyone, he need not come back for further favors." Yet there is little evidence to suggest that the fear of publicity inhibited the sexual spontaneity of an appreciable number of individuals.

Eyewitnesses. Mohave housing conditions do not provide any privacy, since almost every one-room house is full of relatives and friends, some of whom are homeless because their houses were cremated when a person past cradling age had died in them, while others are temporarily single or widowed adults, homeless children, or young couples who do not, as yet, have a home of their own. There is usually also a contingent of happy-go-lucky or, more rarely, of frankly parasitical individuals, who drift from one friendly household to another and, depending on their personality make-up, either lend a helping hand, or else sit back and ask to be waited upon. Several of our case-histories illustrate the lack of privacy which results from overcrowding.

Children as well as adults are in a position to witness intercourse. One infers from the often repeated remark that "children are supposed to keep their eyes open", and to learn about sex through direct observation, that no odium was attached either to attempts to observe coitus, or to being seen in the act. (I propose to describe elsewhere an incident known to have been observed by a child.) The Mohave do not share, however, the Yuma belief (49) that children become smart through witnessing parental intercourse.

Co-wives in aboriginal polygynous households seldom witnessed sexual relations between their husband and another co-wife. One informant asserted that each wife had a house of her own, and cited the myth of Halyec Matcoo:ta (24) in support of this allegation. Most informants believed, however, that all members of a polygynous family lived in the same house, but specified that intercourse occurred only in the absence of the rest of the wives.

Coitus may be observed by accidental eyewitnesses (Cases 3, 15) as well as by practical jokers, who deliberately spy on copulating couples (Cases 1, 14). Yet, even though a crowd of boys may gather to watch another boy engage in bestiality (23), no Mohave can be described as a voyeur. Conversely, while one or both partners may, now and then, invite observation, true exhibitionism is likewise absent, since neither this pseudo-exhibitionism, nor this pseudo-voyeurism appears to be a genuine neurotic symptom.

Case 14. "My uncle happened to be hunting one day, when he noticed a couple swimming in the Colorado. He paid no attention to them, however, until he saw them take shelter under the river bank, whereupon he decided to stalk them. He came too close, however, and fell in the river, when the overhanging bank collapsed under his weight. My uncle's shout of surprise brought his presence to the attention of the couple who asked him what he was doing there with a gun. My uncle, very much abashed, could only mumble something about having come to hunt ducks."

Case 15. L. H. was a pillar of the church while he was living with his first wife and, being one of the righteous, felt entitled to be critical of others. One day this couple's niece—who, with her husband called "His bad luck" (20), also lived in L. H.'s house— became ill and had to be hospitalized. While she was in the hospital "His bad luck" went to swim with a girl in an irrigation ditch. They were enjoying their swim when L. H. and his wife happened to come by. The man promptly drew a deep breath and submerged himself, but when he came up for air he saw that his uncle and aunt by marriage were still standing on the bridge. He promptly took another deep breath and submerged himself again, but when he came up for the second time, his eyes met once more the stern gaze of his wife's relatives. L. H. then left and reported "His bad luck's" conduct to his ailing niece. L. H. had changed a lot since that time! He left his wife, eloped with the wife of the Mohave Sunday School teacher, and is less holy now, but we still don't think much of him. An ordinary Mohave might have watched the couple and might even have gossiped about it, but no decent person would go to the hospital and upset a sick woman with tales of her husband's affairs. Of course L. H. belongs to that small group of Christians (?), who are a credit neither to their tribe, nor to their adopted faith. (The two "practicing Christian" Mohave known to me seemed to be ethically inferior to the unconverted ones.) There was a great deal of resentment against L. H., and when he finally eloped with the wife of another man the notoriously good-natured Mohave openly rejoiced about his sudden loss of dignity.

In contradistinction to unwelcome "snoopers", two types of witnesses may be present by special invitation.

(1) During the early reservation days Mohave prostitutes were frequently accompanied by men or boys, who acted as witnesses to the transaction, saw to it that the woman was neither abused, nor cheated of her pay, and were usually paid a small fee for their services (21).

(2) Couples who do not wish to be surprised while copulating during a dance or a gathering, sometimes ask a friend to act as an unpaid sentinel.

"A girl, who had a steady lover, told her girl friend just before the dance started, that she wished to have intercourse with a man whom she had just met. The girl friend did not merely approve of her plan, but even offered to be on the lookout for the girl's accredited lover. The two thereupon disappeared in the bushes, while the girl friend kept watch over them."

Yet, even though they are usually not particularly upset if they happen to be discovered in the act, the Mohave prefer to copulate in private, and resent compulsory public intercourse.

"While the Parker, Arizona, bridge was being built, a white worker forced his Mohave mistress to have intercourse with him by the worker's campfire. Even though this woman was probably little more than a prostitute, she felt humiliated by this incident (21)."

Even humorists, who openly announce their intention to copulate with their wives, generally perform the act in more or less decorous semi-privacy. In general, the Mohave try not to attract attention even when they engage in ordinary and legitimate intercourse. Hence even spouses try to camouflage the sex act by ostentatiously pretending to be merely conversing with each other. "Yet the Mohave are so bad at present, that they will copulate even when there are other people in the house," an old informant remarked. Swimming couples do not attempt to conceal sexual activities by partly submerging themselves, because, "should water seep into the vagina, the woman would contract the kumadhi: hikwi:r disease." (The hikwi:r are mythical aquatic snake-monsters.)

Publicity. The Mohave Indian is passionately interested in his own sexual adventures, as well as in those of others. Hence, partly because of the impulsive indiscretions of the participants, and partly because of over-crowding, no sexual escapade can remain a secret forever. The Mohave accept this situation rather casually, and their gossip is humorously tolerant rather than vicious.

The lack of sexual privacy has its advantages, however. Since the real details of actual incidents circulate in the form of official versions, which various informants, consulted six years apart, could repeat in an almost identical form, it is almost impossible to broadcast untrue, or viciously distorted, rumors about anyone. Even the few informants who believed that some people did invent imaginary anecdotes, were unable to quote a sample of wholly fictitious gossip. Apparently the Mohave are too interested in discussing real incidents to have time for imaginary ones. "People would soon find out that a certain story is not based on fact. If it is funny enough, one or two might repeat it, but would specify that it is a purely imaginary one. They might say: 'Have you heard the funny story X is telling about Y? We know, of course, that it isn't true, but it is funny enough to be repeated'." The attitude toward a kamalo:y's malicious stories is somewhat different, and those repeating them would emphasize the character-defects of the liar, rather than the humorous nature of the story. "They would say: 'That kamalo:y X is a worthless person, and a liar as well. One of her latest lies is that Y has done thus and so. I feel sorry for Y—he is a decent person. Why does that kamalo:y have to pick on him?'" (21) Unlike Whites, the Mohave do not imagine that where there is smoke there is necessarily fire as well, and "always investigate and consider the source of a rumor". Hence the sympathy accorded to the victim of a kamalo:y's lies is not an empty pretence.

Only one type of distorted rumor appears to gain a wide circulation. Two friends, jointly involved in an escapade, may later on mystify everyone by accusing each other of having been the real hero, or the true victim thereof. These humoristic mutual "accusations" are propounded so tenaciously, and repudiated so fervently, that in the end none but the participants themselves know precisely what role each of them played in the actual incident. Distorted stories of this kind are rather popular, because the mystification of the audience eventually becomes one of the comical aspects of the incident. Yet even in stories of this type the actual events are not, apparently, either distorted, or embroidered upon. An example of such mutual "accusations" was cited elsewhere (21).

Thus, paradoxically enough, the publicity given to sexual exploits actually protects the individual against malicious gossip. Furthermore, since such rumors are freely mentioned in the presence of those whom they allegedly concern, no Mohave is denied the opportunity to disculpate himself if he can, and if he chooses to do so. (One wonders whether a Mohave, erroneously believed to have participated in some disreputable but comical adventure, would care to deny such rumors, unless external circumstances made it seem desirable for him to do so.) Last of all, the knowledge that everyone's sexual behavior is also openly discussed, tends to make the Mohave rather tolerant of his fellow man. "Before you talk of him, think of what he might be saying of you", is a well known Mohave adage. All in all, since Mohave gossip is seldom malicious, no Mohave need develop paranoid ideas about secret rumors and conspiracies. In this respect the Mohave Indian's ego security is distinctly better protected by reality than is that of persons who live under the terror of public opinion so eloquently castigated by Stendhal (55).

Gossip turns into condemnation, however, whenever basic tribal ethics are violated. Public opinion condemns incest and stinginess so mercilessly that it can, now and then, bring about the termination of some highly irregular relationship. Yet even this is not an absolute rule. An incestuous couple, surprised *in flagrante delicto*, brazenly refused to interrupt the act, and told the intruder to go away, and leave them to their pleasure (13). Similarly, when, because of verbal pressure from the family, a woman broke off an adulterous and incestuous relationship, the man was believed to have killed himself not because of the gossip, but because of the termination of the affair (13). On the other hand the patient husband of an adulterous wife killed himself when his father heckled him about his leniency (7).

Summing up, boasts about sexual exploits seem to have taken over the social and psychological functions of boasts about warlike exploits.

The Mohave Indian's relative indifference to the presence of witnesses during the sexual act, which is partly rooted in a realistic acceptance of crowded living conditions, can be profitably interpreted in terms of Freud's dynamic analysis of patterns of object cathexes (31). The Mohave Indian is apparently not conditioned to invest large amounts of libido in any single object at any time, since most of his libido is usually homogeneously distributed over a considerable segment of his tribe (13, 15). Only incestuous relations seem to be over-libidinized, witness the fact that an incestuous woman brazenly refused to interrupt the sex act, when an indignant relative burst into her room (13).

The absence of intense object relationships does not entitle us, however, to affirm that the average Mohave is not a genital character, since already A. Balint has questioned the thesis that intense object-relations are a *sine qua non* component of mature genitality (3). The average Mohave must be described as a genitally mature individual, partly because his sexuality is, on the whole, not a neurotic and guilt-laden one, and partly also because he is capable of forming numerous, socially meaningful, object relationships (12, 13, 14).

The Mohave Indian's capacity to perform affectively meaningful sexual acts even where privacy is lacking, contradicts Freud's thesis that only affectively meaningless coitus can take place in public. On the other hand Freud's dynamic analysis (31) of this allegedly universal need of privacy enables us to understand the Mohave situation in terms of a characteristically wide distribution of libidinal cathexes, which is fully compatible with a properly formulated conception of genitality.

Supernatural Coitus

With the exception of minor semi-legendary characters (24), Frog, daughter of the God Matavilye (5), is the only supernatural said to have had sexual relations with human beings (23). Dream-intercourse with the dead is defined as a genuine experience of the soul (8), which usually culminates in an orgasm without ejaculation (27), and causes the dreamer to contract weylak nyevedhi: (anus-pain, ghost disease). Witches, who dream of intercourse with their victims, become so obsessed with the desire to join them in the land of the dead, that they deliberately bait the victim's surviving relatives, until the latter decide to kill them (11, 38).

The eschatology of sexual intercourse consists simply in the belief that the souls of persons engaged in sexual relations also copulate with each other (8).

Conclusion

Sexual intercourse in Mohave society appears to be a pleasurable and humorous activity, singularly free of neurotic trends, especially if one avoids the fallacy of generalizing exclusively from case histories, which record primarily unusual incidents. The routine sexual life of the average Mohave Indian, while considerably less inhibited than that of Western man, is probably a rather simple one, precisely because it carries a smaller load of anxiety, and is therefore less likely to become a stage for the testing, or acting out, of various neurotic fantasies. Hence, though certain escapades approximate the behavior of neurotics and perverts, they are not necessarily symptoms of perversion or of neurosis, but merely illustrate Freud's thesis that "the fore-pleasure gained by the technique of wit is utilized for the purpose of setting free a greater pleasure by the removal of inner inhibitions" (29), through a successful defense against anxiety.

Roheim's (49, 51) realistic and flexible analysis of Australian genitality shows that existing definitions of genitality must be revised in the light of anthropological findings. The data and interpretations presented herein above merely broaden the scope of Roheim's reevaluation of the problem of genitality, through a systematic consideration of the libidinal economy characteristic of the society in which the psychosexual development of the individual unfolds itself (15, 16).

The amount of libido which can be invested in a mature sexual relationship is probably determined by the relative emphasis which a culture puts on "conjugal" as contrasted with the "consanguine" family (42). This emphasis is determined in turn by the extent to which a given society approximates the ideal types of *"Gesellschaft"*, respectively of *"Gemeinschaft"*, as defined by Tönnies (59).

A further elaboration of this hypothesis would be both inopportune and speculative in the present state of our knowledge.

BIBLIOGRAPHY

1. Agoston, T. Some Psychological Aspects of Prostitution: The Pseudo-Personality. *International Journal of Psycho-Analysis,* 26:62-67, 1945, and 27:59, 1946
2. Allport, G. W. *Personality: A Psychological Interpretation.* New York, 1937
3. Bálint, A. Liebe zur Mutter und Mutterliebe. *Internationale Zeitschrift für Psychoanalyse und Imago,* 24:33-48, 1939
4. Bergler, E. and Róheim, G. Psychology of Time Perception. *Psychoanalytic Quarterly,* 15:190-206, 1946

5. Bourke, J. G. Notes on the Cosmogony and Theogony of the Mojave Indians of the Rio Colorado. *Journal of American Folklore,* 2:169-189, 1889
6. Densmore, F. Yuman and Yaqui Music. *Bureau of American Ethnology, Bulletin,* 110, 1932
7. Devereux, G. *Mohave Suicide.* Typescript. Committee for the Study of Suicide, Inc. New York, 1936
8. Devereux, G. Mohave Soul Concepts. *American Anthropologist, n. s.,* 39:417-422, 1937
9. Devereux, G. Der Begriff der Vaterschaft bei den Mohave Indianern. *Zeitschrift für Ethnologie,* 69:72-78, 1937
10. Devereux, G. Institutionalized Homosexuality of the Mohave Indians. *Human Biology,* 9:498-527, 1937
11. Devereux, G. L'Envoûtement chez les Indiens Mohave. *Journal de la Société des Américanistes de Paris, n.s.,* 29:405-412, 1938.
12. Devereux, G. Mohave Culture and Personality. *Character and Personality,* 8:91-109, 1939
13. Devereux, G. The Social and Cultural Implications of Incest Among the Mohave Indians. *Psychoanalytic Quarterly,* 8:510-533, 1939
14. Devereux, G. Primitive Psychiatry (Part 1). *Bulletin of the History of Medicine,* 8:1194-1213, 1940
15. Devereux, G. Social Structure and the Economy of Affective Bonds. *Psychoanalytic Review,* 29:303-314, 1942
16. Devereux, G. *Human Relations and the Social Structure.* (A Course of Lectures Given in the Graduate Division of the Department of Anthropology of Columbia University.) New York, 1944
17. Devereux, G. The Logical Foundations of Culture and Personality Studies. *Transactions of the New York Academy of Sciences,* Series II, 7:110-130, 1945
18. Devereux, G. Mohave Orality: An Analysis of Nursing and Weaning Customs. *Psychoanalytic Quarterly,* 16:519-546, 1947
19. Devereux, G. Mohave Etiquette. *Southwest Museum Leaflet,* 22, 1948
20. Devereux, G. Mohave Indian Infanticide. *Psychoanalytic Review,* 35:126-139, 1948
21. Devereux, G. The Mohave Indian Kamalo:y. *Journal of Clinical Psychopathology,* 9:433-457, 1948.
22. Devereux, G. Mohave Pregnancy. *Acta Americana,* 6:89-116, 1948.
23. Devereux, G. Mohave Zoophilia. *Samiksā. Journal of the Indian Psycho-Analytical Society,* 2:227-245, 1948.
24. Devereux, G. Mohave Coyote Tales. *Journal of American Folklore,* 61:233-255, 1948.
25. Fenichel, O. *The Psychoanalytic Theory of Neurosis.* New York, 1945
26. Ferenczi, S. *Sex in Psychoanalysis.* Boston, 1916
27. Ferenczi, S. *Further Contributions to the Theory and Technique of Psycho-Analysis.* New York, 1927
28. Forde, C. D. Ethnography of the Yuma Indians. *University of California Publications in American Archaeology and Ethnology,* 28:83-278, 1931
29. Freud, S. *Wit and Its Relation to the Unconscious.* New York, 1917
30. Freud, S. *Totem and Taboo.* New York, 1918
31. Freud, S. *Group Psychology and the Analysis of the Ego.* London, 1922.
32. Freud, S. The Taboo of Virginity. *Collected Papers* IV, London, 1925
33. Freud, S. *Three Contributions to the Theory of Sex,* New York, 1930

34. Gifford, E. W. The Kamia of Imperial Valley. *Bureau of American Ethnology, Bulletin,* 97, 1931
35. Gordon, P. *L'Initiation Sexuelle et l'Evolution Religieuse.* Paris, 1946
36. Harvey, O. L. A Note on the Frequency of Human Coitus. *American Journal of Sociology,* 38 :64-70, 1932
37. Hitschmann, E. and Bergler, E. *Frigidity in Women.* Washington, 1936
38. Kroeber, A. L. Handbook of the Indians of California. *Bureau of American Ethnology, Bulletin,* 78, 1925
39. Kroeber, A. L. Earth-Tongue, a Mohave. (in) Parsons, E. C. (ed.) *American Indian Life.* New York, 1925
40. Kroeber, A. L. The Patwin and their Neighbors. *University of California Publications in American Archaeology and Ethnology,* 29 :253-423, 1932
41. Landis, P. H. *Population Problems.* New York, 1943
42. Linton, R. *The Study of Man.* New York, 1936
43. McNichols, C. L. *Crazy Weather.* New York, 1944
44. Malinowski, B. *The Sexual Life of Savages in North Western Melanesia.* London, 1932
45. Mead, M. *The Changing Culture of an Indian Tribe.* New York, 1932
46. Nettle, M. A. I. *Mohave Women.* (MS. of a Lecture Delivered Before a Women's Civic Club.) Parker, Arizona, n.d.
47. Reich, W. *The Function of the Orgasm.* New York, 1942
48. Reik, T. *A Psychologist Looks at Love.* New York, 1944
49. Róheim, G. Psycho-Analysis of Primitive Cultural Types. *International Journal of Psycho-Analysis,* 13 :1-224, 1932
50. Róheim, G. A Primitive Ember (in) Magyarországi Pszichoanalitikai Egyesület Tagjai: *Lélekelemzési Tanulmányok.* Budapest, 1933
51. Roheim, G. Women and Their Lives in Central Australia. *Journal of the Royal Anthropological Institute of Great Britain and Ireland,* 53 :207-265, 1933
52. Roheim, G. The Oedipus Complex and Infantile Sexuality. *Psychoanalytic Quarterly,* 15 :503-508, 1946
53. Rotter, L. K. A Nöi Genitalitás Pszichológiájáról. (in) Magyarországi Pszichoanalitikai Egyesület Tagjai: *Lélekelemzési Tanulmányok.* Budapest, 1933
54. Stendhal. *De l'Amour.* (H. Martineau edition). Paris n.d.
55. Stendhal. *Le Rouge et le Noir,* Paris, 1831
56. Stewart, K. M. Mohave Hunting. *The Masterkey,* 21 :80-84, 1947
57. Te Rangi Hiroa. Ethnology of Tongareva. *Bernice P. Bishop Museum Bulletin,* 92, 1932
58. Toffelmier, G. and Luomala, K. Dreams and Dream Interpretation of the Diegueño Indians of Southern California. *Psychoanalytic Quarterly,* 5 :195-225, 1936
59. Tönnies, F. *Gemeinschaft und Gesellschaft.* Leipzig, 1887.
60. Yates, S. L. An Investigation of the Psychological Factors in Virginity and Ritual Defloration. *International Journal of Psycho-Analysis,* 11 :167-184, 1930

ORAL TRAUMA AND TABOO
A PSYCHOANALYTIC STUDY OF AN INDONESIAN TRIBE*

By Warner Muensterberger, Ph.D. (New York)

I ANTHROPOLOGICAL INTRODUCTION

Off the West Coast of Sumatra, at the periphery of the Malay Archipelago, is a chain of small islands, some of them very small indeed. Now, the Malay Archipelago proper, has been, and is still being, traversed by streams of migrating peoples, and the cultural configurations have changed continually due to their influence. But the afore-mentioned group of small islands does not favor contact with foreign elements, since it does not lie in the path of these wanderers.

Nias, the largest of this group of islands to the West of Sumatra, has become more or less renowned because of its characteristic and highly developed megalithic art and culture. But the islands of Batu, the *Mentawei* archipelago, and Engano more to the South are much less known and have received hardly any scientific attention.

We will deal in this paper with some cultural trends of the aborigines of the Mentawei group of islands: Sabirut (or Siberut), Sipora, North Pagai and South Pagai. The Mentaweians are a comparatively pure remnant of an old Indonesian population with Veddoid characteristics while the inhabitants of the other islands, Nias and Batu, are culturally as well as physically related to a number of tribes in the mountains of Further India, especially with the Nagas of Assam.

But the social, economic and religious customs of the Mentaweians have been maintained and have developed comparatively independent

---

*This treatise was written in Holland during the occupation, in 1944-1945, under the auspices of the Royal Institution for the Indies, Amsterdam. Owing to the postwar conditions in Europe it could not be published earlier. The author is greatly indebted to Dr. Géza Róheim for his invaluable suggestions.

of their neighbors—customs which disappeared long ago from the life of the other peoples of Indonesia or, at most, left sporadic traces here and there. In spite of their proximity to the more highly civilized Nias and Sumatra, one searches in vain among the Mentaweians for clear traces of some relationship with neighboring peoples.

The peculiar characteristics of Mentaweian culture may be traced, in a large part, to the isolated position of these islands. The heavy groundswell off the coast makes it almost impossible to land on any of the islands with unstable, unseaworthy vessels. That is why, to be sure, this group of four habitable islands has remained so isolated for many centuries.

However, we find a surprising but obvious connection with some cultures of Melanesia. For instance, one peculiarity of the Mentaweians is that they still use bows and arrows for hunting, whereas most of the other Indonesian tribes have replaced these missiles with the blowpipe or even the gun. And as in the Pacific area, taro is the staple food of the Mentaweians. The social organization shows typical traces of age groups. So, too, we find remnants of initiation ceremonies.

But the Mentaweian native society has a still more primitive aspect than does the Melanesian. It lacks stone implements and the people know nothing of pottery, whereas both these cultural achievements are found among the inhabitants of Melanesia. It would seem, then, that while the Papuans and Melanesians have already reached the neolithic age, the Mentaweians still live in the "period" of wooden implements.

On the other hand, zoological research shows that although the animal world of Nias bears unmistakable signs of relationship with the Sumatran fauna, that the Mentawei is more Javanese in character.[1] These facts lead me to conclude that the Mentaweians' connection with Java, the islands of the Sunda Strait and finally the territory east of Indonesia, has been of a more lasting kind than has been their contact with Sumatra or even with the island of Nias.

Certain anthropological data agree with the zoological discoveries. At least Rassers points out, in a convincing manner, very striking likenesses between anthropological data from ancient Java and the Mentawei group on the one hand and New Guinea, the Banks Islands and the Solomon archipelago on the other—notably in connection with the longhouses for men. Furthermore, I see obvious correspondences

---

[1] H. H. Karny, Auf den Glücksinseln, *Die Natur,* 1925, pp. 17 ff.

between the old Balinese village republic of Tnganan Pagrinsingan and Mentawei.[2]

We are especially concerned with certain peculiar traits in the social structure and the religious life of the Mentaweian population, particularly the North Pagaians—the people best known to us and the most thoroughly described. We have assumed the task of investigating the typical features of the social structure of these people more in detail than has heretofore been done, with a view to gaining a better understanding. For we are faced here with psychological phenomena the fundamental idea of which has so far remained a riddle that science has been unable to explain.

II Some Mentaweian Myths of Origin

The myths of any people are important keys to the basic meaning underlying their particular social structures and trends of behavior. I shall present some Mentawei legends without immediate commentary, so that they may be freely referred to in interpreting the material which follows.

The Mentawei legends are remarkable because they do not include, as far as we know, a single creation myth. But there are a number of stories and fragments of myths telling of the far-distant past, including the slaying of man's first ancestor and of his transformation into an animal.

1. *Siakau and the First Human Beings*

The earth was a dreary waste and there were no human beings on it. There were only powerful and evil spirits, who fought with each other and lived in darkness. The most powerful of these spirits was Siakau. He was in search of a weapon with which to protect himself against his enemies and he wanted to get himself a thick, sharp-pointed bamboo stick. So he selected a strong tree-trunk, but when he split it with his ax, out came four human beings who, no sooner had they set eyes on the spirit, fled and hid in the depth of the forest. There they built a hut to live in and cleared a plot of land to till. They worked from sunrise till the moon came out, but no crop flourished and they were hungry. In this condition they were discovered by Siakau. Once again they wanted to flee from him, but the evil spirit pitied them and he promised to help them.

---

[2] W. H. Rassers, Over den oorsprong van het Javaansche tooneel, *Bijdragen Koninklijk Instituut voor de Taal-, Land-en Volkenkunde van Nederlandsch-Indië*, (B.K.I.), Vol. 88, pp. 435 ff.

From then on matters improved and the four would have had no cause for complaint, had not the field-mice and monkeys ravaged their fields and stolen their fruit. So they decided to go hunting and try their luck once more, and Siakau promised to guard their fields.

As soon as the four had gone, Siakau transformed himself into an iguana, so that he might be better able to keep an eye on the animals prowling about and, as he had promised, he remained near the fields and plantations.

A new day dawned and an enormous number of monkeys emerged from the forest and scattered themselves about the fields. The spirit was just about to change himself hurriedly into a tiger, but it was too late. Monkeys pressed upon him from all sides and hindered his every movement. In the meantime, the others destroyed the crops and stole the fruit, after which they disappeared with the loot, leaving the iguana where he was.

The four returned from the chase, found their fields in ruins, their fruit stolen. They took it for granted that no other than the iguana was the culprit. And without recognizing the animal as the spirit, Siakau, two of them threw themselves upon him and consumed his flesh. Very shortly afterwards they died in great pain and fear, as if they had been poisoned.

The other two, fearing contamination, fled in haste. In another part of the country they became the first parents of the Mentawei race.[3]

2. *The Deer and the Crocodile*

Once there lived a father and mother (who had not yet been married according to the sacred rites) and two children, a girl, and a little boy, several years younger than his sister.

One day the man came home and gave his wife some fish he had caught, to cook for their dinner. The woman put the creatures in a pan made of bamboo, and filled another pan with bananas. Before putting the pots on the fire, however, she left the hut for a moment. Her little son took advantage of her absence to meddle with the contents of the cooking vessels. He threw out the fish and put snakes and other animals in their place and for the bananas he substituted banana skins. On her return, his unsuspecting mother put the pans on the fire and let them boil until their contents were done.

When the family was about to begin the meal and the lids were taken off the pots, a quarrel arose between the man and woman. The man accused his wife of wanting to feed him on banana skins, and the wife insisted that her husband had given her snakes to cook instead of fish. Naturally each felt innocent of any effort to deceive the other,

---

[3] Cf. H. A. Mess, De Mentawei-Eilanden, *Tijdschrift van het Bataviaasch Genootschap,* (T.B.G.), vol. 26, p. 76; and C. M. Pleyte, Die Mentawei-Inseln und ihre Bewohner, *Globus,* vol. 79, pp. 1 ff.

consequently their anger rose to fury, and finally the husband got up and left the place.

Not long after this incident, the mother went down to the river with her sister to fish, and instead of going back home to her children she stayed by the river and consumed her large spoon-shaped fishing-net. Her sister in great alarm tried to prevent her from swallowing it, but in vain. "This is my revenge," said the mother. "I am not going back to the village, and the handles of this net will be turned into a pair of antlers."

The next day the children went out to look for their mother. It was a long time before they found her, but finally the three of them sat down together somewhere in the forest. The mother nursed the little boy and both children fell asleep. Then the mother got up and left them to their fate.

When the brother and sister awoke, they once more went in search of their mother. They called her and wandered through the forest in every direction, but to no avail. At long last they found her, but this time in the form of a deer. Terrified, they asked her what she had done, and she answered that this was her revenge.

The children wanted to go back to their village, but they didn't know how to get there. They lost their way completely, and finally found themselves in a meadow, where a man named Gulubena lived. This man liked the girl and decided to take her as his wife. So they observed punen, that is, offered the prescribed sacrifice followed by a period of taboo, partook of a common meal and thus became man and wife.

After a considerable time a son was born to this couple. Gulubena's wife went to the upper reaches of the river one day with her brother and there they encountered their father, whom they did not at first recognize. Nor did the father know his children, but after a while the brother and the sister realized that this man was their tete'u.[4]

The father then took his children to the river to bathe. They swam and ducked down under water; first the children dived, remaining below the surface while the father counted: one, two, three and so on up to nine, at which point they emerged, breathless. Their father laughed at them and asked them to count while he stayed under water. This they did: twenty, thirty, and on to one hundred. Then they heard a rushing of water and a voice which said: "Now I am a crocodile. I am going away."

Since then the crocodile is an object of worship among the people of the Mentawei Islands, who offer sacrifices to it and pay honor to it in various ways.

---

[4] Among the Mentaweians *tete'u* is the usual word by which to address a widowed father or grandfather.

There are several versions of this story. But they all concur, however, on the essential points. One of these recounts how the woman was changed into a deer, which her husband proceeds to hunt and kill. The legend continues:

"When the man had slain and consumed the deer, which was his wife, he went down to the riverside with his two sons. On reaching the water's edge he said to the elder: "I will dive; you count." The boy counted ten, and then his father came to the surface, but no change had apparently taken place in him yet. Then the younger boy was made to count, while his father remained under water, and when he had reached twenty, the man emerged with a tail. The older boy was so frightened at the sight, that he ran away. Then the father addressed his younger child: "You must bring me food every day." And the boy carried out the command faithfully. Every time he came to the water's edge with the meal, the crocodile appeared, making a great deal of noise, to get what his son had brought to him. One day the other boy wished to take part in the work of supplying the animal with its food, but his brother tried to dissuade him. He insisted, however, and taking a small bowl made of sago leaf fibres, filled it with food and proceeded down to the bank of the river. But when the horrible beast emerged from the river with a great noise, the boy was so frightened that he threw down the bowl of food and fled. And the crocodile cursed his sons saying, 'Now that you have behaved in this manner, I will eat you and your descendants, whenever you are guilty of any misconduct.'
This is why crocodiles even now, eat human beings."[5]

3. *The Legend of Women Without Men*

The following story will serve as an introduction to another of the ideas of ancient times and quite clearly belongs to the same cycle of myths as do the above.

Long, long ago there was a village called Sabe'u Sinanalep. No one knows where it was located. Certainly it was not on the Pagai islands; perhaps it was in the ancestral home-land of the Mentaweians on the island of Sabirut. In any case in that village lived no men— only women. These women all wanted a child and with this object in view sat with their legs spread far apart so that the East wind could blow between them. Consequently they all became pregnant, but their children were not all born at the same time. Whenever a child was born, the women fought for possession of it. Each wanted to claim it as her own, and the little creature soon died as a result of the rough treatment it had received. None of the children survived long. This is

---

[5] J. F. K. Hansen, De groep Noord- en Zuid-Pageh, *B.K.I.*, vol. 70, pp. 184 ff.

why, when a woman is about to bring into the world a child, whose father's name is unknown, the Mentaweians say: she has followed the example of the women of Sabe'u Sinanalep.[6]

Morris seems to refer to this same idea in the following short sentences:

"There are only women there. The East wind is their bridegroom. When he blows on their sex organs, children appear."[7]

Here, as in the legend quoted above masculine creative powers are ascribed to the wind.

III The Structure of Mentawei Society

The Mentaweians are deeply impressed with the story of the first ancestor being slain by his children. If they were not, the myths and legends which refer to the incident so openly and clearly would not have survived until now. The importance of this idea is represented not only in their stories, but also in their manners and customs, and in fact, in the whole Mentaweian social structure. Freud's concept of primitive society is largely confirmed by the life of the Mentaweians today.

A striking aspect of this society is the social organization. It is an almost leaderless society, a clan in which is found equal rights for all men, a series of sacred obligations, the right of property for women, sanctity of animals, clan exogamy, such as Freud pictured.

The village or *kampong*, as such, in some strange way misses being a social unit. It is apparently composed of a number of clans, called umas, between which there is no other bond than that their members intermarry, and which are quite independent of one another, except economically.

The clan community is strictly exogamous, therefore a number of umas in the village is necessary to enable intermarriage within an economic unit. The village is usually endogamous. The uma arrangement functions to prevent any possible incest between mother and son or brother and sister, in the following way:

If the man belongs to uma A, his wife through ritual marriage becomes a member of that same clan-community, together *with her children*. Hence the children also belong to clan A. As long as the

---

[6] A. C. Kruijt, De Mentaweiers, *T.B.G.*, vol. 62, p. 102 and pp. 35 f.
[7] M. Morris, *Die Mentawei-Sprache*, Berlin, 1900, p. 129.

man and woman remain at the *rusuk* stage (a long period of free love which precedes marriage), the mother and children remain members of uma B, that is, of the mother's father's clan. And since the clan-connection is matrilinear, incestuous relations between a son and his mother (or a brother with his sister) is made impossible.

The father, who belongs to clan A, is, theoretically at least, according to this arrangement, permitted sexual intercourse with his daughters, or the daughters of his mistress, during the rusuk period. According to the direct patrilinear system, the children of a father belonging to clan A would also belong to clan A. This being the case, the father could not maintain sexual relations with his daughters, but the son could do so with his mother, as these two would belong to different clans. This is prevented by the rules laid down for the rusuk stage, from which we may conclude that the interdiction of incest between mother and son is older than the ban on sexual relations between father and daughter, just as succession along the female line belongs to an earlier epoch than does that along the male line. We have, therefore, every reason to assume that incest interdictions are especially directed against the incestuous desires of the son. Of course, there are exceptions, particularly in the small number of cases, where the influence of colonization and missions is felt (1939). Yet to marry a girl from one's own uma is never permitted. To do so would be to go counter to all the traditional conceptions of decency and suitability as well as being contrary to religion. It would be incest. The uma prevents its men by means of the above rules, from having sexual relations with the women of their clan, including the mother and sisters and also the sisters in a classificatory sense. It is this regulation which guarantees the clan security and order, and in the last instance its very existence.

In most cases a man follows the old custom of choosing a partner for life from his own village. However, he is not legally bound to do so. On the other hand, economic considerations forbid the woman's leaving her native place to take up her residence elsewhere. For she has property and is the one responsible for the care of the taro fields, which pass from generation to generation in the female line. This means that it is the woman, and not her husband, who guarantees the family its food. For although the husband fishes, hunts or tends his banana-groves, he merely contributes supplementary elements to the nourishment necessary for his wife and children. If the woman were to move to the kampong of her husband, the family would be solely dependent on his exertions, as she herself would own no fields or plantations and hence would not be in a position to provide for her dependents. Consequently it comes about quite naturally that a Mentaweian selects a wife from among his fellow-villagers and this woman, after being married according to the usual rites, becomes a member of her husband's clan-community. Being transferred from one uma to another does not affect her rights as a land-owner.

The unitary nature of the clan only really becomes manifest on special communal or religious occasions. The community house, also called the *uma*, is the center of the clan. It is the point around which the life of the joint family circles and, as with all primitive peoples that have a building of this kind, it serves many purposes. It is at one and the same time the community or assembly house, the sacred home of religion, the dancing hall, the place where hunting trophies are kept, the dwelling-place of the rimata (clan priest), the sleeping chamber of young men. Women are not actually forbidden to stay in this building, but in general they are supposed to occupy a room separate from that of the men. Years ago (and sometimes even now in exceptional cases), it was also the house in which the whole group lived.

Gradually, in the course of evolution on the four Mentawei islands, each *lalep* or small household family, consisting of father, mother, children, and sometimes grand-children, began building itself a separate hut within the village, which little dwelling also went by the name of lalep. The father is the *ukui* or priest of his household, as the *rimata* is the priest of the whole clan.

Now before a man is ready to found a lalep of his own, many years elapse. In the course of these he grows into a fully developed, recognized member of the men's group, at which time he is no longer involved with receiving instruction and promotion, but with the assumption of a number of duties and cares which involve a sacred responsibility for his own household and even for the whole clan, vis-à-vis the spirits and demons. Upon reaching the lalep stage an adult male becomes a member of the group of those holding the franchise in the circle of "brothers" among whom a successor is chosen when the rimata dies. The man who has attained the rank of ukui must repress his elemental drives. He must renounce many privileges and loose habits which were permitted him during the rusuk period.

The life of young people during the rusuk stage appeals to every Mentaweian, for it is a carefree time, and to give it up is not easy, especially for the young man.

As long as the adolescent youth has not yet found the girl of his choice he is supposed to spend his nights in the community home, not in the parental hut. Presumably this is a measure calculated to prevent incestuous practices. But the youth does not sleep in the community for long. Sexual relations begin fairly early, during puberty, and in this informal manner the rusuk period of the young people begins. It is true that during these years the teeth are filed, but although this does not appear to have any formal religious significance, and is rather regarded as an aspect of beauty culture, the fact that a man is obliged to have his teeth filed sometime before his ritual marriage, points to this custom being rooted not merely in aesthetic but also in some religio-magic conceptions.

When a young man from the Pagai islands has definitely chosen a girl, the two agree to go and keep house together in a rusuk. This rusuk is a small, lightly built hut, situated outside the actual village area. The young man gives the girl little presents and takes pleasure in playing the part of attentive admirer, in the hope that by so doing he may bind her to himself. It is a remarkable fact that the girl's mother seems to some extent to influence her daughter's choice.[8] In Siberut young women often take up their abode in deserted houses and receive their lovers there. A common sleeping hut corresponding to the rusuk is not found here, however.

For meals the two go to their respective parental laleps: the man to his father's, the woman with her children to her father's. Food is therefore connected with the life of the lalep or with that of the clan, a fact which Freud has set forth in detail theoretically.[9]

As compared with the ritually married man, the youth living in the rusuk condition has very many privileges. He is much freer to do as he likes and, if the girl becomes pregnant he does not have to regard this as a serious matter. Nor is he obliged to go through a period of couvade, such as we find among the ritually married Mentaweians. The father of the expectant mother does this in his stead, seeing that the child which is to be born will belong not to his

---

[8] Kruijt, *op. cit.*, pp. 8 f.
[9] Cf. Sigmund Freud, *Totem und Tabu*, Gesammelte Werke, Vol. 9, London 1940, p. 164.

father's clan, but to that of its maternal grandfather. In view of this fact it is the latter who must submit to a whole series of deprivations and who performs many acts of self-denial in order to establish paternity.

One is tempted to see in this custom a relic of the period in which the father wielded full authority and possessed absolute power over the women of his clan or tribe, including the right to complete freedom in sexual matters. Another, more apparent remnant of that era is the *jus primae noctis*. And among the Mentaweians the girl's father is supposed to behave toward his daughter during and after her pregnancy as if he were her rightful spouse.

The girl leads an almost promiscuous life during the rusuk period, for the relations between young people are then in no sense binding. It is by no means rare for a young girl to have two or three children by different men and then once again to take a new lover. And the young man often leaves his chosen love in the lurch without taking further notice of the children. While the lalep stage is strictly monogamous and divorce is practically impossible then, the rusuk man has the right to maintain sexual relations with those sisters in his wife's family, who are not already ceremonially married and who, hence, belong to another clan.[10] This custom seems to bear the mark of group-marriage. Here and there sexual excesses occur, which in the case of lalep men would bring down the wrath of the spirits. For instance, Kruijt heard of seven young men in Sibaibai in North Pagai who are all said to have ravished the same young girl.

It is doubtful that this social organization and these sex regulations are based on any rational grounds. Speaking from a psychoanalytic point of view, we assume that they are the result of a constellation of drives and wishes as they were channelled during early childhood.

IV   FRUSTRATION IN INFANCY AND EARLY CHILDHOOD

Many areas of the Mentaweian social life become clearer to us when we direct our attention to the position of the little child. The peculiar marriage system and the unusual, yet socially sanctioned relationship between father and mother must have its effects on the infant.

---

[10] E. M. Loeb, Mentawei Social Organization, *American Anthropologist*, vol. 30, p. 428.

After the first few months, the child plays a minor role as a recipient of his mother's attention. She leaves him in the care of others. She does not attend to his personal needs. She is little concerned with his comings and goings. It is easy for this child to interpret his mother's rejection as a result of the attention she is paying to her lover.

It is a stranger who is keeping the child from his mother—a stranger, since the lover has comparatively little contact with the child. As long as a man and woman are not officially married, the child's father does not live with the family. He belongs to another uma and has no right to take an active part in the upbringing of his spouse's children, whether or not they are his own. (Psychologically, the maternal grandfather takes over the father's position.)

Since the mother changes lovers several times, even the mother-lover relationship appears unstable to the child.

The instability of the maternal care and love is seen as a result of the instability of the sex relationships. And the reverse is certainly true since the instability of the sex relationships stems from the instability of their mother's love and attention.

To some extent one can understand this attitude of the Mentaweian mother as a reaction formation against severe taboo. It is a fundamental custom that the mother remain with her newborn in seclusion for some months. During this period she has to perform certain rituals. This forced isolation is a sacrifice for the young mother and disturbing for the older children. Until the taboo period is terminated, she is supposed to mingle as little as possible with other people. After the punen, however, she is free. As Kruijt told me, there have been several cases of a mother running away, taking a new spouse and leaving her little baby to one of her sisters or an older daughter.

There is always somebody around who will pay attention to him, and so the infant is given a kind of outer security but not having a consistent object relationship, provokes at the same time anxiety, frustration and hostility directed against the mother as well as against the man or men who deprive him of protection and mother's breast.

The anxiety which the child feels about food, appears in so many stories. In the second tale, we learn about the mother who runs away from her son. His sister automatically takes care of him, and when they together find the mother she must be induced to give her little son the breast. While the children are asleep the mother leaves them again.

Taken together with the behavior toward their small children, we understand that this story merely reflects the insecurity of the Mentaweians, in their basic anxiety about mother's care and love. However, not only the mother but the father, too, runs away. He reappears in the form of a crocodile (tete'u), asking his children for a sacrifice in the form of food. It seems clear that the child experiences mother's lover as the man who not only takes mother away, but with mother, food.

The other version of the same legend, however, gives us an even deeper insight in the child's reactions. Here we are told that the father slays the deer and consumes it. In this case the rape of the woman (deer-food-breast-mother) is described as a murderous and cannibalistic act, while on the other hand the father changes into a crocodile, "a horrible beast", which not only killed and ate mother but which threatened his son with the same punishment, with the words: "I will eat you . . . whenever you are guilty of any misconduct."

In the third story we learn about the women without men. The lack of men can be considered as a form of hostility against mother's lover. But the legend discloses even more than that. It reflects an anxiety which seems to threaten all Mentaweians, concerning mother's aggression and unkindness. The women become pregnant without having husbands. And when they fight for the possession of the first baby born, the child dies because of their harsh treatment. The story is a projection of the deep-rooted insecurity to which the Mentaweians are subject, as a result of their fear of the lack of mother's love. And incidentally, this undercurrent of the fear of mother's unkindness is another reason for the late legal marriage, which is such a striking institution in this society.

We can now better understand the meaning of the first legend. While the murder of Siakau, their benefactor, reveals to us the hostile feelings toward a father image, we find at the same time that a lack of food, caused by the destruction of the fields, is the immediate reason for his death. Again: the fear of hunger leads to an aggressive deed. As in a dream we discover a displacement from the ghost, Siakau, to the monkeys and back to the ghost in the shape of an iguana. But it is still Siakau who is killed by the children since they believe him to have destroyed their precious crops. It is he who deprived them of food or mother. As such he is no longer a benefactor but his role has basically changed to that of an enemy who is a competitor and who has to atone for his malevolence with his life.

The stories mirror a phase of severe oral frustration with an accompanying image of a selfish mother and a dangerous father.

V The Meaning of the Sacrifice

The conflict which is aroused in the child as a result of the food deprivation is partially resolved in the sacrifice of pigs and chickens which is an integral part of every taboo period.

In order to understand the relationship between the sacrifice and the unconscious drives of the Mentaweian it is necessary fully to describe the sacrificial ceremony.

The pigs and chickens are willingly contributed by the families, each of which possesses one or more of them. The animals are killed in a ceremonial way. Pigs have to be stabbed in such a manner that no blood falls on the ground and so that they bleed to death inwardly. According to accounts, to spill blood would be considered a gross insult to the spirits of the earth. In such a case a new punen might be required. From the liver of the animals mixed with taro, staple food of the island, the rimata prepares a sacrificial meal which he divides into as many portions as there are families. Each family-head receives his share to offer to the household gods.

When a sacred animal is brought home by the hunters, punen has to be observed. The following is a fairly detailed account of such an occurrence:

"When a deer has been shot, the fortunate hunters, the hounds and the victim are all decorated with leaves and flowers. A cheerful procession then enters the uma or the village. The dead deer is laid on the ghost-stairs. The gong sounds and all the men assemble in an exalted mood. Then the priest (rimata) comes with a grated coconut and he calls the soul of the deer, which has remained in the forest. Meanwhile the creature is taken into the community-house by the young (unmarried) men. The antlers are detached, the animal is flayed and cut into pieces which find their way into the pots and dishes. Meanwhile the men play the *tudukat,* a kind of wooden instrument which produces tones that are sometimes trumpet-like and then again soft and plaintive.

While this is going on, the meal is cooked or otherwise prepared for consumption. When it is ready, the priest takes a small piece of the heart and one from the back of the animal to offer as a sacrifice. Only men who have been ceremonially married may be present when this rite is performed. Finally the priest repeats a number of ritual sayings and the young men, who crowd about the entrance to the place of sacrifice, fill in the pauses with drum beating."[11]

After this the meat is *equally* divided. Only when this food has

---
[11] Cf. Hansen, *op. cit.,* p. 190.

been consumed to the very last bit may the men resume their ordinary occupations.

The punen is brought to a close when the young men go coconut gathering and the ceremonially married men go fishing. On their return the coconuts as well as the fish are again equally divided.

On the island of Siberut a similar ritual is held. When anyone has caught or has killed a big game animal, his entire uma undergoes taboo for a number of days. No stranger is allowed to enter the clan's domain. Here, as in the Pagai Islands, the punen continues until the last piece of the meat has been consumed. In Siberut, the sacrificial feast and all the regulations connected with it are called *keikei* (*ma-keikei*—it is forbidden). The skulls of the pigs are elaborately decorated, in which ornamented condition they somewhat resemble the heads of deer or birds.[12]

In both the Mentawei and Siberut ceremonies of sacrifice and the sacrificial feasts, every animal that has been killed and each pig that is to be offered for sacrifice is taken to the clan-house and there is divided among the clansmen after the ceremonial blessing and the haruspication. Should anyone hold back a small portion of the meat or an animal to keep for himself—even a little monkey—he would inevitably sicken and perhaps die. As a rule, the men are required to remain in the clan-house for a while, in order to partake of a *common* meal there; each is allowed to put away part of his allotted portion of meat to consume later at his own home with his wife and children.

A feast of this kind is usually accompanied by dancing. "Originally these dances were performed in the uma on the occasion of a punen," writes Wirz (l.c.). The men always dance in couples, stick twigs in their belts and ornament themselves with leaves and flowers. They imitate the characteristic movements of animals and birds. The chief of the clan himself gives a representation of a bat and a seaeagle. The latter, although not exactly a sacred animal, is pictured in almost all clan-houses. Furthermore, there are chicken dances, pig dances, heron dances and monkey dances. The characteristic movements of these animals, particularly those typical of the rutting and mating season, and the movements involved in searching for food and

---

[12] Cf. Loeb, *Sumatra*, Vienna, 1935, p. 206. Also *Mentawei Religious Cult.*, p. 209. P. Wirz, Het eiland Sabiroet en zijn bewoners, *Nederlandsch-Indië, Oud en Niew,* 1929, pp. 234ff. Compare this with the corresponding customs of the island of Nias and other territories of the "megalithic" area of South-East Asia and Oceania.

eating are imitated. With very rare exceptions the animals chosen are those which are found together with human figures on the walls of the uma.

Now it is not the animals per se, which are killed when the pigs and chickens are sacrificed. These creatures represent substitutes for humans, as is customary among so many tribes. Such a substitution satisfies an unconscious need and functions at the same time as an adaptation to reality, in the sense of a social and psychological claim.

It is for instance a rule among the Mentaweians that anyone leaving the clan for good shall offer a pig to the spirits of the uma "in order to have his soul removed from the list of the uma."[13]

An interesting account of how pigs came into this world, which shows their close relationship with humans, was told to Loeb:

"This was the origin of pigs, according to the story of our forefathers. It happened in this manner. Formerly there lived a small girl whose father and mother were dead. The people said that the little girl was lost because, since she had no relatives, there was no one to care for her. So the little girl did nothing but run around and cry, thinking all the time of her dead father and mother. Finally an old woman who loved the little girl said to her, 'Oh, little girl, do not always be crying. Come here and eat the yams that I have for you.' But the little girl replied, 'I do not wish them, mother.' Then the old woman offered the little girl bananas, pounded taro, and sago. But the little girl refused them all. Finally she had offered every kind of food she had, but there was none that the little girl would accept. Then the old woman became angry, and spoke thusly, 'If, then, you do not wish other kinds of food, eat this human excrement!'

"When the old woman spoke in this manner, the girl went on her knees to the ground, and ate the excrement. When she had finished, a tail, the hair of an animal, a long snout, and four feet came out of her body. Her speech now was only a grunt.

"This was the manner in which pigs originated, according to the story of the people of Mentawei."[14]

This short tale reaffirms a fact which is well known from other data collected in various parts of Indonesia, namely, that certain animals are descendants of man or are transformed human beings and therefore intimately related to man.

These facts having been established, we cannot regard the killing of the pigs as anything but some kind of substitute sacrifice. In every case these creatures take the place of a human being.

[13] Loeb, *Sumatra*, p. 266. Compare also *Mentawei Religious Cult*, p. 209.
[14] Loeb, Mentawei Myths, *B.K.I.*, vol. 85, pp. 69 f.

Analytically seen, it would not be surprising if other animals had analogous significance in the cultural life and inner experience of the Mentaweian. There are various versions of the second legend in which mother, in a revengeful mood, takes the shape of a deer and in that form deserts her children, her daughter and her little son who is still being nursed. Although she is urged by her sister and daughter to take care of the infant's feeding, she disappears in the woods.

As we see here the mother is identified with the deer, the animal which is the chief game in Mentawei. The fact that deer are symbolically related to the mother is also corroborated by the strange form of the coffins on the island of Siberut which represent deer. The soul of the deceased is thought to re-enter a deer. The dead one returns to the deer, as it might to the body or womb from whence it came. Now, pigs seem to be a substitute for deer.

Universally, the mother is identified with food and protection. The connection between food and mother is even stronger among Mentaweians than elsewhere, since taro, the staple food, is in the hands of the woman. The fields are the property of women, and the men must depend upon them for their basic nutritional needs. The situation in Alor, as DuBois describes it, can be applied to Mentawei. The Alorese woman actually can dominate over the male by the threat of the withdrawal of food,[15] which creates a constant ambivalence on the part of the man toward the woman, since he has a need for love and resents at the same time her dominating power.

The love and the aggression which the Mentaweian feels toward his mother, he cannot express openly. So he identifies animals—the deer, the pig and even the chicken—with the food-giving mother. In this manner, he is able to realize the fulfillment of his unconscious desires. The animal is mother. The incorporation of mother symbolizes an act of aggression against father from whom she is recaptured. Thus we can explain the resulting passivity and self-restraint as a socially approved modification of self-punishment.

A similar development is often clinically observed. We see how early denial and deprivation imposed by the parents arouse aggression in the child against parent images. Since this aggression is soon suppressed, the child is forced to abandon it. He usually turns it against

---

[15] Cf. Abram Kardiner and others, *The Psychological Frontiers of Society*, New York, 1945, pp. 157 ff. There are several striking similarities between the Alorese and the Mentaweian behavior structures.

himself by punishing himself for every satisfaction with anxiety, guilt-feelings, passivity, and so forth.

We find in the legends almost no traces of feelings of sibling rivalry which is so much more emphasized in many other Indonesian tribes. In Mentawei, there is merely reciprocity and mutual help of the siblings which, too, is reflected in the social organization. The equality of men in Mentawei culture is evident in the obligatory division of the meat of a pig, the huntsmen's prey, the coconuts. Killing the animal under such strictly prescribed conditions and then compulsively dividing the meat into equal parts, shows merely the suppression of a hidden wish of these people, the hostile self-interest to keep mother (breast, food) for himself. His thought process is as follows: "If my clansmen were not compelled to divide the meat in such a way, there might not be any left for me." The many restrictions which follow the consumption of the meat serve to control the unconscious and unexpressed desires and fears of the individual. The general solidarity of the siblings is the reflection of these desires and fears, since a competitive disagreement would only lead to retaliation within the tribe and would disturb its existence.

To the Mentaweians the crocodile is a symbol of father. In the first myth the father takes the form of this animal. (We may assume that the Mentaweians do not distinguish between iguanas and crocodiles. Both animals belong to the same family, the *iguanidae*, and essentially resemble one another.)

In the second myth, this animal is addressed as tete'u, a (widowed) father or a grandfather. A very severe taboo follows the killing of crocodiles. Only as a matter of dire necessity may one be permitted to lay violent hands upon these creatures. Even then an unusually severe period of taboo follows the act.

Much the same attitude toward the crocodile has been noted among the Punan, the most primitive of the indigenous tribes of Borneo, among the Dayak of Borneo, the Toraja of Celebes and a number of other peoples in the Pacific area. In the Eastern part of the Malay archipelago many legends are current according to which the first crocodile was born of a human mother. This again shows how closely related the Oceanic feels himself to animals of this kind.

Again in the initiation ceremonies of Melanesia, mainly in New Guinea, the crocodile plays a significant part. It is this animal which devours the boy who is to be initiated. There, the candidates are swallowed by, or rather thrown into, the mouth of a monster made in the image of a crocodile (a basket-work affair), from which they again emerge as "one newly born". This is a symbolic act representing second birth. Here, too, the crocodile performs a double task: it destroys and it gives birth—perhaps a projection of the inimical and affectionate feelings of maturing youth towards their fathers. The crocodile again appears in the ceremonies of the tribes inhabiting the Purari Delta in South Eastern New Guinea,[16] where it is called the *Kaiemunu*. Graphic representations of this animal are found in the men's house of this district and it is regarded by the natives as a creature emerging from the water, hence a crocodile or giant fish. In related ceremonies, fertility rites and ancestor worship come very much to the fore. Here the totemistic animal *par excellence* is the crocodile or snake.

Typical of all tribes belonging to the Indonesian culture area is the following description of conditions in Banka, an island off the East coast of Sumatra: "The reverence paid the crocodile is so deep that the natives think the weal or woe of their families depends upon this animal. No one would venture to do it any harm, and if in self-defence a man wounded one of these creatures he was in greater danger than if he had committed the most terrible murder... To be changed into a crocodile is the thought these people most delight to dwell upon in connection with immortality. The natives honor it with all sorts of titles of respect, speak of it always with devotion and regard it as the peer of kings."[17]

A number of other tribes worship the crocodile in like manner, but fear it at the same time because it brings about earthquakes if not treated with the necessary respect.

The passages in the Mentaweian myths which deal with father (iguana), invariably refer to him as one who is pressing his children for food, or depriving them of it.

In the first legend Siakau, the great spirit (in the form of a crocodile) is accused of permitting the destruction of the crops.

The second gives various versions of how the father changes into a crocodile and asks for a daily meal. He wants food and, it would appear, the same food as his children eat. I should like to quote another variation on this theme heard by Loeb. Here, too, we find the parents separating. After a considerable interval the children find

---

[16] F. E. Williams, *The Natives of the Purari Delta*, Port Moresby, 1924, pp. 131 ff.

[17] T. Epp, *Schilderungen aus Holländisch Ostindien*, Heidelberg, 1852, pp. 152 f.

their father. His daughter refuses to give him his food cooked, and insists on providing it raw. The father accepts it in this state but decides to become a crocodile.

"When the father and his son arrived at the mouth of the river, the boy remained on the beach and his father went fishing. The father threw the net into the water, djarat! Then he dove for the fish. It was nine o'clock (the time that chickens lay eggs) when he came up to the surface. He had one net-load of fish. Then the father threw the net again, djarat! He dove and arose to the surface again at midday. He again had one load of fish. He asked his boy: 'How well did I do it, child? Did I stay under the water for a long time?' 'Yes, tete'u, it was a long time,' said the boy. The father then said, 'Go, child, to the village and take this fish with you. Also take these fire tools. Such is the manner of my body that I will never return again. See how I have changed into a crocodile!' The boy said, 'Oh, how sorry I am that you have changed into a crocodile! My mother has changed into a deer and you have changed into a crocodile. Why are you angry at my elder sister? Tell me, so I may know the reason.' 'Yes, child, I am angry with your elder sister. I said to her, Oh child! If you are tired of giving me food, do not give it to me, even if I go hungry. But I do not wish to be given raw food. But she did not obey my words. That is why I am changed into a crocodile. And now child, listen to my teachings. Do not cut your possessions with a knife. If you do, the spirits of the things which are cut will call for me, and I will come and eat you. Do not cut up your food on the fields, do not throw your taro around, do not cut up your bananas. No matter what kind of things you own, do not cut it up. Otherwise the things that are cut will call for me, and most certainly I will come and eat you. Do not throw refuse into the rivers, lest I come and eat your pigs. These are my instructions for you. Do not forget them. Tell them to your elder sister. I have finished my speech to you, child, and I am going. Do not wait for me. Look at me! I have changed to a crocodile.' "[18]

In the first place he commands them to be sparing in the use of knives, an injunction which the Mentaweians obey even to this day. The meaning of this peculiar interdiction seems quite evident. Its object is to forbid aggressiveness, of which cutting with a knife is a symbol. The other interdictions, however, are connected with food and eating and show us again the interdependence of feeding and parental relationship. The father is not given the proper food and he becomes angry. And when he speaks to his son, it is as if he were saying, "If you do wrong, I will eat what is rightfully yours" (you, your pig). Again, a threat to deprive the child of food.

---
[18] Loeb, *op. cit.*, pp. 204 f.

We know that food represents mother, and so we have a picture of father insisting upon the right to share mother with the child. The mythological father is described as a two-sided character which is an indication of the ambivalence which the Mentaweians feel toward him. He regards the paternal parent as a kind protector, but at the same time as a hateful, exacting rival for the mother's food and attention. These hostile images which are aroused gain the upper hand and bring about a longing to destroy the father. In the myths we find this veiled wish to eliminate the father. Two of the first four primeval human beings kill and eat, in supposed ignorance of his identity, their benefactor (father) in animal form, but they die in great agony as a result of their heinous sin.

Our third legend, though doubtless a mere fragment, recounts the greater part of the main theme. It appears, on closer examination, to tell the same story as do the other two. We must endeavor to identify ourselves with the narrator: apart from the symbolical substitution of the wind for this *vis virilis*, men are ignored. They are entirely absent. What can this more or less conscious repudiation of fathers and fatherhood mean but an indulgence in the false hope of their non-existence? Absolutely no notice is taken of the man, which as we know from countless instances, is tantamount to a magic hostility. According to the narrator, then, the children of Sabe'u Sinanalep have only mothers and no father, which amounts to a mythologically successful realization of the oedipus wish.

VI Taboo and Social Organization

In observing such oedipal tendencies in Mentaweian personality we reach a more thorough understanding of the way in which this emotional attitude toward the father is expressed. In the first myth, the great spirit Siakau is eaten by two people, after being transformed into an animal. What we see here is the expression of the oral-sadistic wish.

The significance of the act of consuming the body becomes amply clear from a consideration of the child's early psychical sufferings. We find, besides the obviously hostile desires, a certain measure of affection which, too, is expressed in the incorporation of the object. The feeding frustrations of the Mentaweian child pave the way for a greedy love and a greedy destruction, and it is not at all surprising that the destructive fantasies appear as an oral aggression.

This ambivalent attitude is again found among the hill tribes of the island of Solor. There it is customary to cut out the heart of a slain enemy, cook it and divide it among those who won the fight. Among the Pakpak Bataks of Sumatra only an adult man, whose teeth had already been filed down and who was then considered a mature and competent member of the community, could serve an anthropophagous sacrifice. The skulls of the victims were preserved in the community house (*balé*) as were the bones. All adult men were duty bound to participate in this meal; these included even the sons of the man who was to be eaten, and a father had to join in the cannibal orgy at which the victim was his son. Two independent observers— Raffles and Leyden—report that the Batak (exactly which sub-tribe of these is meant, is not clear) often ate their own relatives when they became old and useless, not from motives of greed or self-indulgence, but because they considered this a worthy act. A somewhat later statement by de Boudijck Bastiaanse corroborates the observations of Raffles and Leyden. He asked the Batak why they ate their parents, and was told that this was done simply in token of love and respect. The children wish in this way to become as intimately connected as possible with persons who have been near and dear to them.[19]

It is reported that the Langa, Rokka and Wogo of the island of Flores also kill their relatives when they get old and sickly and then eat the dead bodies. Light is thrown upon the basic attitude accompanying such action in a description given by Steinmetz, who tells us that a son is glad to have a father who is large of stature and heavily built. For it is thought by these people that by consuming the raw heart of a brother-tribesman his strength and power are absorbed.[20]

Although other Indonesian tribes actually performed patrophagy, we have no immediate proof of a similar background among the Mentaweians. The legends and a number of the ceremonies, however, show a more or less conscious intention of "cannibalistic" gratifications.

It is true that the oral-sadistic tendencies toward the mother and toward the father point to two different kinds of relationship, yet both are connected. The longing of the infant for mother's breast is basically of a narcissistic-loving nature, expressing the desire for food and

---

[19] Cf. E. Volhard, *Kannibalismus*, Stuttgart 1939, pp. 279 ff. G. A. Wilken, *Handleiding voor de vergelijkende volkenkunde van Nederlandsch-Indië*, Leiden 1893, pp. 21 ff. J. H. de Boudijck Bastiaanse, *Voyage dans les Moluques...*, Paris 1845, pp. 66 f.

[20] R. S. Steinmetz, Endokannibalismus, *Mitteilungen der Anthropologischen Gesellschaft Wien*, vol. 26, pp. 8 f.

attachment. In consequence, the father (i.e. mother's lover) is inevitably a rival. As such the little child must, by defeating him, identify with that man who is closer to mother than to himself. Since the frustration starts during the oral phase, the infant tries to defeat him by oral means: by embodying the rival, he is unified with him. Thus, the infant identifies himself with father who is already identified with mother. In this way the infant attempts to solve the problem of his oedipal tensions.

Our presumption that such cases are instances of the ambivalent or bipolar attitude is fully corroborated by psychoanalytic observations. The results of probing the depths of human consciousness have brought to light the fact that a man's attitude toward both the living and the dead is ambivalent in nature. There co-exist in one mind two mutually contradictory feelings, the roots of which are unconscious. So too, the common expression "loving a person to death" does not express only love, but implies an active, aggressive, cannibalistic element, the original meaning of which has been repressed and forgotten and now finds expression only in this symbolic phrase. Our terms "sweetheart", "cookie", "honey", "sweetie-pie", "sugar", also have an oral significance. Many symptomatic actions and many a dream reveal this underlying meaning.

These anthropological counterparts of analytic views obtained clinically and confirmed time and again, preclude the necessity of asking whether or not they are merely unproven hypotheses. Even the few examples cited from a comparatively very small area in Indonesia indicate the world-wide significance of this essential drive in man.

The founding of a new uma or clan will further enlighten us on the prevailing attitude toward the father because the main religious activities are composed of the sacrifices made to *Tete'u*, a very much dreaded spirit of earthquakes, a power which inspires in the Mentaweians both fear and reverence.

A new uma originates in a way almost analogous to biological processes. A part of the old community detaches itself to form a fresh unit under the leadership of a new, pre-determined head.

Generally a group of this kind settles in the same river basin as the parent-clan. Very elaborate ceremonies precede the choosing of the location, the clearing of the ground and the building of the new houses. First a provisional hut is erected to serve as general dwelling house and sacred place of worship at the same time. Pigs and chickens are taken there and killed according to an established ritual, the pigs having their gullets cut and the chickens their necks wrung. This is the only occasion on which it is permissible to let blood fall on the earth. As far as I have been able to discover every other ceremony requires the pigs to be stabbed by the unmarried men in such a way that they bleed to death internally. But when a new uma is founded, the confines of the village are marked out with blood, the idea probably being to indicate blood community with the spirits of the soil and at the same time to ward off evil, foreign influences by magic means. This one time the strong blood-tie which binds man to the spirits under the earth is openly admitted; for once the blood which unites man to the earth must be allowed to flow unimpeded. This ceremony is accompanied by a prayer in which the rimata says: "Here are our sacrifices for you, spirits of the earth. *You that stay under the earth are the owners of our village.* If any blood from our food should fall upon the ground, be not angry." The belly of the animal is then cut open and the liver offered to Tete'u, the rimata saying: "This is for you alone! Help us! Take us under your protection!"

Another point becomes clear with regard to Tete'u. He evidently occupies a higher position than all the other spirits. According to Loeb's conclusion he was the first and most powerful sorcerer or magician. The people envied him his magic powers and decided to kill him. When they were busy building the clan-house, they asked Tete'u to dig under the main pillar. Tete'u descended into the hole and when he reached the bottom his companions let a heavy tree-trunk fall on his head. This is the reason—so the story goes—why formerly *a human sacrifice* was always made when a new uma was being established. For by way of avenging the attempt upon his life Tete'u made the earthquake and destroyed the village and all belonging to it.[21] Only a sacrifice could satisfy his desire for vengeance.

A second sacrifice is made to Tete'u at a later stage of the erection of the clan-house. This time he is offered a few chickens and some chicken sauce, while the rimata prays: "We give thee sauce, Tete'u, so that we may be allowed to live."[22]

We may safely assume that at an earlier period not animals but human victims, perhaps of head-hunting expeditions, had to be supplied for this sacrifice. The victim was buried under the main pile of the clan-house, on the very spot where long, long ago the great

---

[21] Loeb, *Mentawei Religious Cult*, pp. 193 f.
[22] *Ibid.*, p. 196.

magician Tete'u was imprisoned. In former times the marriageable youths were tatooed on their return from such head-huntings.

Today in the place of a human being, a pig or several chickens are sacrificed. We know that the pigs and chickens have replaced mother. Now we can paraphrase the prayer of the priest. "We offer to let you share mother with us so that we may be allowed to live." And in the other invocation addressed to Tete'u it is only necessary to add the name, the real meaning of which is father or widowed father. The prayer then becomes: "Help us! Take us under thy protection, father!" And this brings us a step nearer the essential meaning of the sacrifice to the old magician or to the father transformed into a crocodile.

Tete'u, the devourer of mother's food, the man who took mother away, was made to descend into the hole meant for the chief pile on which the building was to rest, in an attempt to murder him. Thereafter this man developed into a dangerous earth-spirit who, from time to time, made the earth quake and thus prevented his fellow-clansmen from living in peace.

The real object of the sacrificial ceremony brought out in the invocations uttered is to appease and propitiate the earth-spirit for the hostile deed against the father. The offerings, first in the shape of human victims and more recently in that of animals, are regarded as substitutes for mother.

The interpretation of the father-child relationship which we have gleaned from the myths and the sacrificial ceremonies is borne out in reality by Mentaweian life. Father's position can be vividly demonstrated by comparing his life with the life of his son.

Apart from the taboo restrictions relating to his clan and his father's household, the youth suffers from no restrictions through *punen* or *lia*. These are taboos which play an enormous and decisive part in the life of the married Mentaweian and drive him in some strange way to a far-reaching passivity, and which affect the unmarried man much less. The latter may enjoy almost every pleasure, may hunt and fish as much as he likes, may till the land and make plantations, go off on expeditions, he has certain privileges in his clan which we shall consider in detail later.

When a young man has lived in this fashion with one or more women for a number of years, sometimes for over a decade and has begotten several children, some of whom have in this time reached late puberty, he decides, often not without inner conflict, to contract a ritual marriage, and to found a lalep of his own. With the help of his wife's relations he makes the necessary preparations. He plants banana groves and builds his hut in the village. When everything has been arranged as tradition demands, the man has to ask the parents of his future wife for her hand. This step is not taken by the young man himself, but by the bridegroom's father or some other male relative. It appears that the urge to enter on this new stage of life does not in most cases originate with the young couple but rather with some of the older relatives on one or the other side.

The marriage ceremony merely consists of the significant act of a meal taken together by the man and his wife. With this the woman is transferred from her father's clan or uma to that of her husband. After this ritual meal the two may take their food together in their own hut. Exceptions to this rule are the sacred sacrificial meals in the uma, in which the husband is obliged to participate.[23]

After the marriage the newly established family enters upon a considerable period of taboo.

As soon as the couple have become man and wife, the children born to the woman during the period of free love, including those resulting from other premarital relations on her part, are re-adopted by her husband. Thus they all pass from the clan of their maternal grandfather to that of their mother's husband, just as she has done —a custom which, again, reminds us of the transition from polygamy to monogamy.

We spoke of the great emotional restraint and the repression of elemental instincts to which a married man must subject himself. All this sets a deep mark on the life he has led so far. Let us consider the most important of these restrictions. The father of the family is not permitted to dig in the earth or plant anything. He may not kill animals such as swine, deer, monkeys. (For animals are frequently, as the myths bring out, images of ancestors.) He may join a hunting party, but he may not shoot the game. He may not beat snails to death, nor hunt frogs. Furthermore he may not eat "bad" food, in which category are included squirrels, black monkeys, land or water turtles. He must not fell trees or touch corpses. He must eat nothing which may not also serve as ritual food. Among the forbidden foods are swine and hens that have died a natural death. All foodstuffs imported from foreign areas are also regarded as "bad". The pun-

---

[23] Loeb, "Mentawei Social Organization," *A.A.*, vol. 30, p. 428.

ishment for any transgression of these rules would be the magic death, or at least the sickness of his children. Another result of such careless conduct on his part in these matters is that the wife of the offending man might remain childless or have a still-born baby.

Enterprises which rusuk men may undertake without preliminary formalities, an ukui may only initiate after observing a period of taboo, long or short as the case may be. Laying out taro fields or planting banana groves belong to this class of undertaking.

The most stringent prohibition is that which forbids unfaithfulness to one's spouse—a sin which would result in the death of both parents and children.

During the punen period of the whole clan, the heads of families are obliged to spend their nights in the community house, as they are permitted no sexual intercourse while the taboo lasts. On the island of Sabirut they have to sleep in the community house always, as there no sexual intercourse is allowed in a man's own dwelling. Finally, married men are not allowed to enter a cemetery, and consequently care of the dead and burial belong to the duties performed exclusively by the unmarried men.[24]

There are still other taboos to which an ukui must subject himself under certain conditions. We said that Mentaweians recognize certain duties resembling more or less pre- and postnatal couvades. The additional restrictions connected with this custom are laid upon the husband of the pregnant woman or mother, or, in case the woman is still at the rusuk stage, upon her father.

The ukui must give up all work in the fields—all heavy labor in fact. The meaning of this prohibition is not hard to ascertain. Labor, as such, is, to a certain extent, of a sublimated sexual character. It must be remembered that, with very few exceptions, psychophysical components lose in significance as the degree of sublimation rises. Restrictions such as those just mentioned are considered necessary to counteract unconscious desires. For instance, the married man among the Mentawei natives is forbidden to tie knots or go fishing. He is forbidden to perform certain tasks in the fields and plantations. He may not whole-heartedly participate in the joys of the chase. He is made economically dependent. Furthermore he is obliged to observe certain taboos in connection with his food and to abstain from all sexual intercourse during his wife's or his unmarried daughter's pregnancy.

---

[24] Kruijt, *op. cit.*, pp. 14 ff. Loeb, *Mentawei Religious Cult*, pp. 234 ff.

He must continue this abstinence for six or eight months after the birth of his child or grandchild. He may not gather wood or sago. Parents are not allowed to hurry or to quarrel in the house. When they go into the fields to work for the first time after the birth of the child, they must protect themselves against sunburn by means of a sun-hat, otherwise the child may suffer as well as they themselves.

We might multiply instances indefinitely. Not all restrictions are equally well known to us. There are other taboos connected with building a house, with one's behavior on the death of a fellow-clansman, while hunting, when making a boat, when resting on the river's bank or at the seashore.

But this is still an incomplete impression of the lives of married men in the Mentawei islands. Really to grasp the degree to which the married man's activity is repressed and his sexual life inhibited, one must picture to oneself the humdrum and monotonous daily round in these isolated villages, which are mostly in the interior of these islands. Besides, I have only mentioned the most important and striking taboos. Hansen, an officer in the Netherlands army, who was obliged to spend several months on the islands, states in his report that of the twelve months of the year an average of ten are taken up by taboo periods. (From this he draws a conclusion which does not do credit to his insight, namely, that the indigenous population of these islands is lazy.) As a result of many of these taboos the Mentaweian is not able to support himself and, to a large extent, is dependent upon his wife and his children. This puts the woman in a position of ascendancy which is further maintained by her right of property and the influence she exerts over her daughter's final choice of a husband.

In most primitive societies young men are impatient to become legitimate husbands. As such they achieve a status whereby they have special privileges and rights denied to others. It is the married man who has the enviable position and the youth who strives toward it.

But the Mentaweian youth hesitates and postpones the decisive step for as long as he possibly can. And no wonder. As a youth he is free to go as he pleases. He may sleep with the young girl who catches his fancy. His life with her can be an idyllic one, free from care and petty responsibilities. When difficulties arise he is able to seek a new mate. He is given free rein to express his masculinity both sexually and otherwise.

When he marries, he has assumed an unbreakable bond, not only to one woman for better or worse, but to a life which compels him to suppress his sexual energy, and denies him the means of engaging in most substitute gratifications. A great number of restrictions or taboos are placed on him. All taboos are directed toward making the married man a passive and ineffective creature.

The same motives which prevent the Mentaweian from marrying willingly prevent him from accepting the position of head of the clan, or rimata, with a light heart.

The equality among men of position—the men married according to sacred rites—bears a distinctly collectivistic stamp. The collectivism which we find in the Malay archipelago and among the Mentaweians is unusually clear. They will have nothing to do with any definite leader or chief, recognizing only as a religious head or clan priest, the rimata. The rimata is chosen from among the group of householders or ukui, and as this group almost always consists of brothers or sons of brothers, the chief naturally belongs to the joint family. In most cases he is a son or brother of the deceased head by whom he has, as a rule, already been made acquainted with his tasks and duties and installed in his new office. "When a rimata is beginning to age," says Kruijt, "it is fairly well known who is to take his place. A little while after the death of the old rimata, the village fathers meet in the uma. One of the elder among them then takes the floor and proposes that a certain person, the choice of which has been predetermined, shall be appointed rimata. The suggestion is unanimously accepted. The bearer of this new dignity may be a young man. The requirements are that he shall be a man, married according to the sacred rites and thoroughly familiar with the punen regulations."[25] His office affords him no special rights or privileges, but only added responsibilities and furthermore requires of him the most stringent repression of elemental instincts. Nor is this rimata the village chief, as is the priest so often in other parts of Indonesia, but merely dean of the clan or joint family. The number of rimata depends entirely on the number of umas of which the village consists.

The head of the family is responsible for the house, the lalep; the rimata for the whole clan. And in the latter case, being responsible means stimulating the vigor of the clan, sacrificing to the spirits, settling quarrels and disputes. What strikes us most forcibly is that

[25] Kruijt, *op. cit.*, p. 83.

this tribal chief is enmeshed in a still closer network of taboos and regulations than the one which envelops other householders.

Naturally the rimata in his capacity of father of a family has to observe the appropriate taboos as does every other ukui in his clan. But in addition to these there are the other restrictions that bind him. A rimata may not hold any burning thing in his hand. For instance, the unmarried men must light cigarettes for him. It is feared that the burning thing might fall from him upon his fellow-clansmen and spread fever, just as the sunburn of the parents may be transferred to the children. Nor may the rimata carry water or feed chickens or pigs. During a taboo period he must not accompany the other men when they go out to hunt (according to the sacred rites) or go fishing, but must remain in the village. The only action he may perform is sacrifice. He must not begin his meal until the other clansmen have finished theirs. Owing to these restrictions he is entirely dependent on the industry and work of his children and his wife, and if he has no family of his own, he adopts nephews to help him.[26] Djagomandri, the most advanced head of an uma in Sila-oinan, repeatedly asserted that a priest, as soon as he has entered upon his function, is forbidden all sexual intercourse. If he should indulge in this contrary to the age-old rules, he would endanger the existence of the whole clan.[27]

Besides these special taboos there are many professional duties which bind the rimata to all sorts of forms and regulations and make his life anything but easy. Because of the intimate relationship existing between the social, economic and religious aspects of life, his presence is required on all ceremonial occasions affecting the clan or its members. Whether a fellow-clansman has died, or a new taro field is being planted, or the huntsmen's booty is to be divided and the appropriate sacrifice made when a new taboo period is to be inaugurated, or an initiation ceremony has to be performed in honor of the newly established community house—whatever the event, the head of the clan must be present in person to take the lead in the festivities and perform the ritual acts. These mainly concern the sacrifices, the preparation of the sacrificial food, the dismembering of the sacrificial animals, vatication and pantomimic dances in imitation of the various sacred animals such as bats, sea-eagles or swine.

Apart from all this the head of the clan has little or no authority

[26] Loeb, *op. cit.,* pp. 235 f.
[27] Kruijt, *op. cit.,* p. 84.

of any importance. Hansen even speaks of the "anarchistically inclined Mentaweian" who has practically no respect for his rimata. On another occasion he remarks: "The power of this Mentaweian rimata does not mean much. By nature the Mentaweian prefers complete anarchy. Often the chiefs enter upon their functions unwillingly."[28] If we take into consideration how mercilessly the rimata has to suppress his instincts and his desires, if we remember what personal sacrifices are expected of him and how little thanks he gets for all his pains and care, it is understandable that not always the most capable offer themselves for this post. The rimata is at best *primus inter pares*, at least in regard to the rights and privileges of his position.

VII Funeral Rites

After the death of an adult male and especially of a rimata the unconscious aggressions of the Mentaweian come forth in a most revealing manner.

There are variations from the funeral rites which shall be described below, due to the local coloring in different places. However, the discrepancies are minor ones and so cannot disprove the main points with which we shall deal.

When a death has occurred, the village is regarded as unclean and the dangers which may ensue are sought to be evaded by a punen. The corpse is carried about in the hut several times or is taken out by the back-door of the building. The spirit of the dead man is revengeful and secretive and must in this way be taken on a false track. If, in spite of all this, he manages to find his way back to the village, he will make his presence known by knocking and rattling at the back-door of the hut. The best way to drive him away under such circumstances is to make a sacrificial offering and wave fans of dry leaves and twigs.[29] As soon as the corpse of an ukui or rimata has been taken away, the *katsaila*, a magic bundle of leaves found in the house or in the uma, as the case may be, is picked to pieces and thrown under the building, where, until the Netherlands Government authorities interfered, all rubbish heaps were located. This bundle of leaves is always taken care of by the father of the family, or by the rimata

---

[28] Hansen, *op. cit.*, p. 130.
[29] Hansen, *op. cit.*, p. 177.

in the case of the whole clan, and it is supposed to be the bearer of the life-forces of the family or of the clan.[30]

Another custom connected with mourning is that of cutting the hair. This ceremony is performed in the fields or groves of the deceased. A child's hair is shorn when his father or mother dies; a married person's upon the death of a child or of a spouse. In the village of Silabu it is customary to shave the heads of the widow and children when the husband and father passes away. In Sa'umangania, only boys and men have the hair cut off the back of their heads when their fathers die.

Almost everywhere in the Mentawei Islands it is customary to destroy a few trees and bushes on a man's property after his funeral, the rational idea being that the plants thus killed are meant for his use. It is explained as a kind of sacrifice to the dead, called *usud*. A pig and several chickens, also belonging to the deceased, are ceremonially killed on these occasions. But one is inclined to regard this ceremony as an expression of hostility as well as grief, as it is the animals which the dead man particularly liked that are especially selected for this purpose.

After the funeral the young men who attended to the burial generally take a bath, but only after having devastated and destroyed some of the possessions of the deceased. Next morning punen begins for the whole clan. In the village of Taikako, a funeral festival is held about ten days after the death of a socially important fellow-clansman. On this occasion, too, pigs and chickens are killed.

In Sabirut, where the foreign influence, mainly of Malays, Chinese and Arabs, has been felt longer than in the other Mentawei Islands, the local Chief of Police happened to discover a custom reminiscent of the one described above. While exploring a wild part of the country, he came upon the burial ground of the little village of Simatalu. There he found a number of wooden coffins, each with a stag's head carved at the head-end and a tail at the foot-end. According to the accounts given by the natives a coffin of this kind was placed there for every dead body. The local funeral rites, it appeared, demanded that the relatives of the deceased should remain watching the corpse until all the flesh was off the bones. During this wake, the body of the dead man must be flushed with water and then brushed

---

[30] The *katsaila* consists mainly of kroton leaves which hang on the chief pillar of every sacred house, hence of the uma and the lalep. This bunch of leaves corresponds essentially to the *tjurunga* of the Australians.

with a sort of broom, until all the bones are clean, after which the latter are collected and put away.[31] There can be no doubt that the somewhat divergent customs of both Pagai and Sabirut Islands spring from the same mental source, and in both cases we are dealing with an obviously ambivalent attitude toward the dead.

When the old rimata dies, the young men—the married men are not allowed to touch a dead body or to bury it—carry him to his boat. When he is dead, his widow calls to the vital force of his fellow-clansmen, saying: "Come, come, ye spirits of our souls (*kinasima-gere*)." And she continues: "Do not leave us alone, do not follow him. We fear his ghost." When the young men arrive at the burial place with the corpse, *they cut the dead man's fingers to the bone at the knuckles*. They do the same at the thighs and the toes. Now except for a dead chief of a clan, only a condemned and beheaded witch is treated in this way. According to the natives, this is done in order to prevent, if possible, the return of the dead man, or rather the return of his ghost to the village. This treatment is necessary, because the rimata is in possession of the souls of his fellow-clansmen and the latter might wish to follow him into the grave. If the souls say: "We follow you, father!" the dead man must answer: "Go hence, young men! Go hence, young women! Ye cannot accompany me. My hands and feet are wounded and my thighs are injured. I cannot take you with me or take you on my knee. Go back to the uma. There you will find your mothers. There you will find your fathers."[32] The usual punen is held after which there follows another period of strict taboo known as the *panogad punen*.[33]

Kruijt's report of the treatment accorded the rimata's corpse is somewhat different. But the difference is important only if we confine ourselves to superficialities and do not take into consideration the inner meaning of this extraordinary ceremony. The underlying reason for these measures is always the same. It is really the power of the dead priest or chief over the life forces of his clan that gives rise to this remarkable and at the same time significant custom. The palms and the soles of the feet of the corpse are blackened with soot, and during the ceremonial wailing the dead man is addressed in these words: "Take my vital spirit, father." But the deceased is supposed to answer: "I cannot take you with me. My hands and feet are dirty." After that

---

[31] Kruijt, *op. cit.*, p. 173.
[32] Loeb, *op. cit.*, pp. 218 ff.
[33] Kruijt, *op. cit.*, pp. 175 ff.

the body is disposed of in the customary way, but this burial is followed by a long taboo, a much longer one than that which succeeds the death of ordinary persons. [34]

Since the head of the clan is able to hold and bind the vital power (*ketsat*) of his people by magical means, his person is obviously gifted with special force and it is therefore not inconceivable that he might prove a source of danger. He is not head by divine right. He is merely an executive appointed by the clan, a representative, and as such, a person who wields a power which accumulates in the vital strength of the uma. This quality in him is not suggested by the everyday attitude of his people toward him. It does come out on festive occasions, however, and as we see particularly after his death. It is then that the ambivalence of the attitude toward him is really fully manifested by means of these special measures—measures not taken in the case of an ordinary death. His demise seems to increase the importance of the head of the clan.

The difference between the treatment of a dead rimata and the treatment of other corpses reflects the attitude held by the rimata during life toward his fellow-clansmen, in spite of the very small power he possesses. The general attitude toward the person of the rimata is a surprising one: during his life-time the man is hemmed in on all sides, to an extraordinary degree, by restrictions upon his freedom—almost all activity is forbidden him. He may not have sexual intercourse and is obliged to attend to a whole series of duties and social obligations which others like to avoid if possible. He becomes a slave to his dignity, as it were. Finally, the dead body of the priest-chief is mutilated as is that of a witch or sorcerer, who is dangerous to the community. That the ghost or soul of the dead man is feared is given evidence in the formula uttered by the widow, by way of exorcism: "We fear his ghost!"

There must be some vehemently aggressive element at work, when men allow themselves to become guilty of such an act of violation and at the same time to show such fear.

Now the careful restrictions of the chief's initiative during his life-time become much more comprehensible. The many taboos which he has to observe, the numerous prohibitions which hem him in, all these can be nothing but so many chains by which the community binds its leader.

---

[34] Kruijt, *op. cit.*, pp. 84 f.

But the strong ambivalence is seen in the ceremonial wailing and mourning for the dead. The element of self-chastisement is present in the mourning rites which demand that the nearest of kin—once probably only the nearest masculine relatives—have their hair cut off. The general anthropological background for this custom is convincing enough to prove that it is a remnant of self-mutilation. Among other peoples in similar circumstances, the survivors often give themselves flesh wounds or cut off their fingers, toes and even their hands and feet. To appease his remorse, primitive man adopted the habit of inflicting such wounds on himself, according to the formula *pars pro toto*. The survivor applies the method of sympathetic magic on himself in the belief that his sacrificing a portion of himself will please the deceased. It is a balancing reaction of the superego, to compensate for the unconscious aggressions. On the one hand the Mentaweian would prefer to dispense with all authority, but on the other he feels the need of it.

And so no matter how minor his authority compared to similar functionaries in other tribes, in a certain sense the rimata is more than the titular head of the community. For in questionable cases the final decision as to whether a taboo should be declared or not rests with him. Viewed from this standpoint he appears as enmeshed in a network of combined independence and coercion which well represents the inner relation between the head of the clan and the community itself.

This peculiar solution is satisfactory in two ways: It satisfies the clan's longing for a father and at the same time it allows free play to the feeling of hatred against the old autocratic chief, the symbolic representative of the father.

VIII Taboo and Guilt Feelings

Just as the other "peculiarities" of Mentaweian life can be understood from a psychoanalytic point of view, so can the taboo. We have observed the infant's libidinal fixation to the breast of his mother which in itself develops ambivalent feelings in the baby. The rejection which the little child experiences so early makes it feel that mother is a bad woman. He only can get hold of her (breast, food) by killing her, i.e. her substitute. Then he internalizes this substitute in the form of meat. This kind of reaction reminds us of manic fantasies.

Since the mother image is split into a food-giving, loving one and a withholding one, a depressive reaction follows after having absorbed the normally forbidden meat. In order to overcome his distress and guilt at having behaved in such a manner, the Mentaweian takes refuge in mourning and remorse, i.e. in an extreme passivity.

This whole cycle explains to us the seemingly strange institution of taboo in Mentawei society. It usually starts with a festive elation and is later followed by the contrasting inertia. The Mentaweians call it *punen*, when it applies to the whole clan, and *lia* when it affects only the household. For the sake of simplifying matters, I will only use the term punen and include the lia under this head. Punen has been mentioned repeatedly in this paper and has occasionally been defined as "taboo period" or "taboo". This definition does not always quite cover the entire meaning of the word.

A punen begins with a ceremonial washing of the hair, after which the participant decks himself for the event in a very charming combination of flowers, leaves, paint and feathers. No work is done in the fields and gardens and strangers are forbidden to enter the domain of the uma. The chief punen activities are the ceremonial slaughter of pigs and chickens, the sacrifice of the liver of these animals, and soothsaying. During the succeeding nights sacred dances are performed in which the sacred animals are represented. Later on there is a ceremonial hunting of monkeys and deer. If members of the uma wish to arrange a feast, they make all kinds of preparations. They carefully lay in a stock of food, dress in holiday fashion after a ceremonial bath, kill several domestic animals, spend many hours in dancing, refrain from all work and particularly from sexual contact. Sexual intercourse is forbidden. The men do not sleep in their own huts but spend the night in the community house. No special ceremony is held to mark the close of the taboo period. The women simply go back to their work in the fields and the men once more go fishing.[35] The restrictions on sex are especially striking because in other parts of the Southwest Pacific and Africa the regularly recurring festivals involve a complete relaxation of all the restrictive measures which at other times are attended to with great vigilance and are most strictly obeyed.

A punen is held on numerous occasions. To enumerate them all

---

[35] Loeb, *Mentawai Religious Cult*, p. 189.

is not feasible, because there are so many and probably not all of them have as yet been determined. We will, therefore, limit ourselves to the most obvious and important, which are: the founding of a new village; the establishment of a new community-house; the death of the old chief and the choice and installation of his successor; the return of a ghost to the village; the outbreak of an epidemic; the mischance of blood touching the (sacred) soil of the village; the slaughter of sacred animals such as monkeys, tortoises or deer; the murder of a clan-mate or the death of a man or woman attacked by a crocodile; the birth of a child and the consecration of a ceremonial marriage.

How drastically the punen and the accompanying regulations effect the rhythm of tribal life has been described by Duyvendak in detailing the erection of a new clan-house. First of all the women lay in a considerable stock of sago, which cannot be gathered while the punen lasts. This done, a three days' punen is held. Then a shed is built on the beach for the fishermen and next day is punen again. The shed is then opened for use—another day's punen. The men now go fishing for the purpose of laying in a stock of food. This takes some time and meanwhile no hard labor is permitted, as the rest of the village is observing punen. Next, the fish is dried and smoked and again a day's punen follows. Now the real building commences, but there are so many rules, and so many precautionary measures have to be taken that this work cannot proceed either without being hampered in all sorts of ways. Omens play a prominent role here. The most important event is the erection of the main pillars of the clan-house. Then follows another day's punen. The next day the men go hunting monkeys, and this involves several successive days of punen.[36]

These punen rules have remained in force from one generation to another and the one who knows the rules and regulations best is chosen from among the older ceremonially married men to assume the function of the head and priest. So these taboos have held their place with the Mentaweian man for many generations as *one* of the expressions of his inherent conservatism, and he will pass them on to his children and grandchildren. Each clansman keeps an eye on his fellows to see whether or not they obey the rules.

---

[36] J. Ph. Duyvendek, *Inleiding tot de Ethnologie van de Indische Archipel*, Groningen, 1940, pp. 37 ff.

Anyone familiar with the Mentaweian culture naturally wonders about the many taboos or, more accurately speaking, the many occasions which demand a taboo period. But in his description of Mentaweian culture Duyvendak finds little to say that is really enlightening in regard to the taboo regulations, and finally is forced to conclude: "Among the Mentaweians we are unable to discover the main outlines of this system."

There are superficial explanations of the overwhelming number of taboo periods and regulations observed by these people. Conceptions from the phenomenology of religion such as "mysterium tremendum", "belief in demons", "fear", "awe", do not touch the core of this matter, and if one accepts such descriptions as explanations, the customs remain incomprehensible, and can be seen merely as a unique phenomenon in the psychology of homo sapiens.

We must recognize motivations of the unconscious with its wealth of data providing supplementary indications concerning the mechanism of and reactions to *repression, displacement* and *condensation.*

Unconscious displacement, for instance, comes into play here, just as in biblical times when use was made of the proverbial scapegoat. Another example is the vicarious sacrifice found in Borneo, where a slave may take the place of a fellow-tribesman, a buffalo that of the slave, a goat that of a buffalo, and finally a hen that of the goat. The Mentaweians also use such obvious mechanisms of displacement in the same way when they substitute animals for humans. If one tries to obtain an explanation of all this from the natives themselves, not much is gained. Their explanations are not spontaneous, but are rather studied rationalizations. However, this is not surprising when we remember the clinical experience of the psychoanalyst whose patients produce the most extraordinary rationalizations when explaining their dreams, impulses or fantasies with apparent logic.

The many interruptions to the construction of a new community house, the restrictions following the fall of a tree, the return of a ghost, the death of a clansman or a successful monkey-hunt may all be called as illogical and dark as the actions of a compulsion neurotic. What was originally fear, becomes simple observance; awe is formalized. But these are meaningless words—labels which don't explain anything, unless we discover what is at the base of all formalized fear and awe. Only comparison with the unmotivated actions of a mania, a compulsion neurotic or—sometimes—a child, suggests our seeking an age-old, no longer comprehensible, logical basis for these taboos. These restrictions must refer to acts and customs which were originally strongly effective and played a considerable part in the early life of the individual or of the community.

In the course of many centuries these taboos have acquired a superego quality for the Mentaweian. It has become an unquestioned habit, which he takes for granted, to lay down his implements as soon as his wife, or, in the case of one who is not ceremonially married, his daughter, knows herself to be pregnant, or to temporarily renounce sexual intercourse during the period of community work in the fields. He does not regard these prohibitions as restrictions nor does he consciously resent them for interfering with his freedom.

Our own civilization furnishes us with an example of the development of a taboo which has acquired superego quality. Four hundred years ago, in 1530, Erasmus of Rotterdam thought it appropriate in his *De civilitate morum puerilium,* to point out to his students that the genitals should be exposed only when really necessary. We must remember that in those days these matters were discussed quite openly and without self-consciousness. Such instruction in our day, fifteen generations later would be regarded by every member of a civilized community as quite superfluous. If any of our contemporaries is unable to adapt his conduct to this view, he is regarded as a pervert.

It is quite permissible to assume that the same is true in respect to the Mentaweian taboos and mores, namely, that they were fully justified at the time they were formulated and under the circumstances prevailing then, and that they serve an unconscious function now. We could add that in the Mentaweian society, aggression against the dead rimata is normal from this point of view; not to join the others in the violent act would be "neurotic" behavior not adapted to the exigencies of Mentaweian reality.

But these unconscious aggressions, in turn, cause other unconscious reactions. If an individual is aggressive, he feels guilty and tries to ease his guilt by one or another means. He must maintain a balance, so that he and his society can survive. But balance through sublimation has not been highly developed by primitive man. He must resort to a system of compulsive rules so that the balance is forcibly maintained. And so in the literature dealing with Indonesian tribes we often come across the idea of cosmic unity, of the ritual regulation of the whole life-pattern of the group and its magic balance. For primitive people life does not begin at conception or at birth, nor does it end with death; neither are death and birth the only caesuras in the external cycle of being on earth and being elsewhere. Buying and selling are not merely commercial matters but they possess a magic aspect as well. They suggest an exchange of powers. Marriage does not concern merely a man and a woman, but two members of two groups, which also become more closely bound, metaphysically, because of the union. The murder of a man affects not only his relatives, but the whole clan, the magic power of which has been reduced by what has happened. Vengeance must be taken for this death on one of the members of the guilty clan, so that the balance may be restored. No one will, of course, deny that in this connection there are many differentiations, many shades of distinction, but these are of little moment when we consider the matter from a general standpoint.

Membership in the clan involves rights and duties which a man must fulfill, or else he will jeopardize the cosmic order, the magic balance. This kind of danger is nothing but a derangement of the orderly life of the community, and if we want to trace the producer of this derangement, we find it is brought about at intervals by the ghosts of forebears, the dead who wish to exert their influence even from beyond the grave. Any resistance, any obstinacy brings punishment, and this punishment in some way or other always involves a diminution of the life-energy of the community or of the individual.

It appears that the violation or transgression of a compelling order always produces trouble, as primitive man, children, and compulsion neurotics fear. Resistance to the traditional order of things may produce fatal results.

Even the apparently most commonplace things may fall under these rules. For instance, when sago is being gathered and a drop of liquid falls on the ground, a punen has to be held, otherwise misfortune will befall the village. When the young men are at work tilling the fields, little children and the mothers of laborers must remain at a distance, otherwise the youths will take sick. If a man should eat a deer, a monkey or a turtle by himself, he would bring down some disease upon his uma. On the day of a fellow-clansman's funeral, a number of taboos have to be observed. Among other things, sago for chicken feed may not be prepared in the village or in the fields. No fire may be lighted on the banks of the river. No one may fish in the sea or fetch taro from the fields. If one should disobey one of these rules, the ghosts of the dead might appear and say: "You are not keeping your village holy. Do you wish the dead to return?" Then the ghost would come home and bring disease and destruction into the village and the people would come to a bad end.[37]

When we compare regulations of this kind, which are not enforced by outside means, but which quite obviously arise from within, with the ceremonial compulsions so frequently observed in children, we discover a strong parallel. Everyone has at some time noticed "children counting steps or paving-stones as they go along or playing a game that they take very seriously, of stepping on each slab without touching the lines which divide them, or hitting, say, every fifth bar while walking along railings."[38] If their plan is upset, they draw one or another conclusion from this fact. Naturally there is no trace of any causal connection or logic in all this. Nor have the children any idea of the meaning which lurks in the ritual of this game and the expectations which accompany it. The preconditions which lead to compulsive games of this sort or to the symptomatic actions of sufferers from compulsion neuroses, must be unconscious. Ernest Jones cites the fine example of Lady Macbeth: she has acquired the habitual gesture of rubbing her hands as if washing them. Shakespeare gives us the solution of the riddle when he expresses her inmost thoughts: "What! will these hands ne'er be clean? . . . Here's the smell of blood still; all the perfumes of Arabia will not sweeten this little hand." We have here an example of symptomatic action; a wish referring to a distinctly unpleasant conception is transferred to a neutral area and there finds satisfaction.[39]

The displacement of stress and the distortions, i.e. the dynamic processes which form a compulsion and produce the appearance of a taboo have appeared in all possible areas. Such rules as not allowing moisture to fall upon the ground when sago is being beaten, not per-

---

[37] Loeb, *op. cit.*, pp. 234 ff.
[38] Heinrich Meng, "Zwangsneurosen und ihre Behandlung," in: Federn-Meng, *Das psychoanalytische Volksbuch,* 3rd impression, Bern, 1939, p. 246. Cf. also Jean Piaget, *La représentation du monde chez l'enfant,* Paris, 1939, pp. 121 ff.
[39] Ernest Jones, *Essays in Applied Psychoanalysis,* p. 288.

mitting blood to touch the earth, can be explained. They suggest that "Mother Earth" should not be soiled or besmirched. But what can be the original meaning of the *mos* that parents must wear sun-hats when working in the fields in order to protect their children from sun-burn? Or the original meaning of the rule that a man preparing poison for arrows may not lie down to sleep until his work is finished? It is surely useless to look for the meaning of isolated punen regulations and to try to trace them to their source. One would lose oneself in fanciful speculations spun of air. On the other hand it is always possible without much trouble, to recognize the general purpose which would explain the illogical taboos, namely, the tendency, also found among neurotics, to be continually passing from object to object by way of free association.

If we then assume that the real motive driving a man to obey a given taboo is more or less hidden, the fundamental structure of this extraordinary system of taboos gradually becomes clear. The function is essentially a double one: to check and suppress, as much as possible, the unconscious desires and wishes in which an unsocial motive predominates; to protect the life of the community against danger and harm, and furthermore to bring about a peaceful condition of things— the desire of a passive, infantile stage.

Conclusion

The Mentawei culture is explained in many respects by the unsatisfactory maternal care which is given the child, and which gives rise to an early hostility against mother, as well as against the man who deprives the child of mother's care. The hostility felt toward the man is given expression through the many restrictions placed upon him. These aggressive feelings once having been released create a conflict, and as a result the Mentaweian punishes himself by forcing himself to become entirely passive. This series of emotional reactions to early deprivation gives us a key to an understanding of the mechanisms in Mentawei culture.

It seems likely that the animal sacrifice is an expression of the child's struggle with mother's lover to be fed by mother. There is a regular cyclic repetition and fulfillment of this unconscious longing for mother's breast; a rhythmic return of similars. Tete'u, the crocodile, represents then the man who took mother away from the infant;

who, perhaps symbolizes the despotic father and enemy. Later, the rebellious children join forces and slay Siakau or Tete'u as the myths and the sacrificial ceremonies reveal. We find a trace of the mythological event in the attitude toward the rimata. He cannot escape the wrath of the disappointed children, even after his death, when they maltreat his corpse like that of a criminal.

But there is the inner struggle between these feelings of hatred and the conflicting feelings of love, so that after the dead body is violated and the property destroyed, a period of great self-condemnation and deep remorse follows. They abstain from sexual intercourse. They exaggerate their grief to the point of reacting to every aggressive act with a feeling of guilt and passivity.

The multitude of punens gives us a clear proof of the profound ambivalence of the Mentaweians: every sacrifice is a reminder of the antagonism between child and father; every punen is a repetition of the subsequent self-reproach and remorse. The sadistic tendencies, expressed in the slaughter of the animal, turn afterwards into the masochistic form of self-restraint. Passivity becomes the law.

However, much of what the infant once was denied and of what had to be repressed, is permitted to the young man. They are allowed free erotic relations with the unmarried girls and their sisters which nearly approaches the desired incestuous condition. They are permitted to express much of their hostility toward the symbolic father, the rimata. They may perform the sacrificial slaughter and in that way give rein to their infantile desires of getting mother (i.e. food). It is they who are in the real sense of the word the usufructuaries of the oedipal situation, not, as with many other tribes, the old men. (This seems to me a remnant of matriarchy, for the father evades the conflict with the son.)

It would seem, then, that the basic traumatic event of the Mentaweian originates in an excessive frustration already as early as in the oral phase. It is rooted in the experience of the child who is deprived of mother's breast.

It does not matter whether one has really expressed one's aggression against mother's lover, i.e. father. The only point of significance is the unconscious hostile impulse—the eternal struggle between love and hatred, between Eros and the desire to destroy.

In summary it can be stated that the fundamental conflict is an ambivalence against both, father and mother. The Mentaweian resents the mother who left him unsatisfied as he hates the father who stole mother. So mother as "the provider of narcissistic supplies" (Cf. Fenichel) should be loved and incorporated. As such the pigs and chickens are a symbol for the ambivalent introjection. But after the deed follows the depression and remorse as an obsessive attempt to receive forgiveness for the oral destruction; to show obedience since one fears revenge. These trends remind us in more than one respect of the characteristics which appear in depressive neuroses as a result of early frustration and lack of affection in the oral phase. Moreover we see that the oedipal conflict does not appear as sexual rivalry but as an ultimate consequence of the oral needs of the infant.

THE OEDIPUS COMPLEX, MAGIC AND CULTURE

By Géza Róheim, Ph.D. (New York)

CULTURE AND INTERPRETATION

The interpretation of the data of anthropology with the aid of psychoanalytic insight is what I mean by psychoanalytic anthropology. Most psychoanalysts are not aware of the fact that there is any problem at all in this field. The situation is very different from what it was when Freud wrote *Totem and Taboo*. In those days psychoanalysis and anthropology were separate worlds. What Freud wrote made but little impression upon the anthropological world and psychoanalysts did not really care very much what official anthropology thought about their interpretations.

Today we have a different situation. The majority of anthropologists admit that interpretation of a kind is possible. At the same time, however, it has become practically axiomatic in anthropology to claim that interpretations are valid only within limits of one culture.

Margaret Mead expresses prevailing opinion in the following sentence:

"As America has a moral culture—that is a culture which accepts right and wrong as important—any discussion of America must simply bristle with words like good and bad. Any discussion of Samoa would bristle with terms for awkward and graceful, for illbred and 'becoming to those bred as the daughters of chiefs'."[1]

Kluckhohn has six paragraphs in which he tells psychoanalysts what to do about anthropology, and tells us that:

"Cultures must be regarded as wholes having organization as well as content. Data must not be too cavalierly torn from their configurational context."[2]

---

[1] M. Mead, *And Keep Your Powder Dry*. New York, W. Morrow, 1942. pp. 10, 11.
[2] Clyde Kluckhohn, Psychiatry and Anthropology, in: *One Hundred Years of American Psychiatry*, New York Columbia Univ. Press, 1944, p. 615.

Henceforth, as Mead tells us, we are to be interested in differences only.[3] In a recent publication Mead goes even further and decrees:

"To convert these stereotypes it will be necessary for psychology gradually to assimilate and reduce to useful form the more recent findings of ethnologists which stress that a fully acculturated member of a living culture differs in every respect and systematically from members of any other culture."[4]

If this is true there is nothing more to be done about it. Research in anthropology ends here, there is no point in teaching anthropology any more—*finis Poloniae!* Since the anthropologist is presumably American, English or French and his informants are Navaho or Azande or Pitjentara and since the two, viz., the anthropologist and the informant, belong to different cultures they have nothing in common and they cannot understand each other. *"Du gleichst dem Geist, den Du begreifst."*[5]

What is the origin of these curious distortions? It cannot be a matter of indifference to the psychoanalyst to know what is going on here, as all the dissident schools of psychoanalysis have their root in this very same problem. Fromm declared that the oedipus complex was the result of patriarchal institutions.[6] The only basis for such a statement is Malinowski[7] and I have shown several times how absolutely wrong and untenable Malinowski's conclusions are. The fact that I have proved the existence of the oedipus complex in a society even more matrilineal than the one studied by Malinowski has not made the least impression on the majority of anthropologists.[8]

With regard to Malinowski's famous "refutation" this is how matters really stand.

---

[3] M. Mead, The Use of Primitive Material in the Study of Personality. *Character and Personality.* III. pp. 1-10.
[4] M. Mead, in L. Carmichael, *Manual of Child Psychology,* New York, John Wylie & Sons, 1946, p. 669.
[5] Goethe, *Faust.* First part, first act.
[6] E. Fromm. *Autoritaet und Familie.* Paris, 1936, pp. 80-110.
[7] Br. Malinowski, Mutterrechtliche Familie und Oedipuskomplex, *Imago X,* 1924.
[8] Cf. G. Róheim, Psychoanalysis of Primitive Cultural Types, *International Journal of Psychoanalysis,* XIII. Idem, Dream Analysis and Field Anthropology, in: *Psychoanalysis and the Social Sciences I.* p. 87, and a forthcoming book on: *Psychoanalysis and Anthropology.*

"What does the word tama (father) express to the native?" "Husband of my mother", would be the answer given by an intelligent informant.[9] He would go on to say that this *tama* is the man in whose loving and protecting company he has grown up. The father is a close companion of his children, he takes an active part in the cares which are lavished upon them and later has a share in their education. Socially it denotes the man who is in an intimate relationship to the mother and who is master of the household. "So far *tama* does not differ essentially from father in our sense. But as soon as the child begins to grow up and take an interest in things outside the affairs of the household and its own immediate needs, certain complications arise and change the meaning of *tama* for him. He learns that he is not of the same clan, that his totemic appellation is different and that it is identical with that of his mother."[10]

The young boy goes to his uncle about the age of eight or ten. Till then he lives in the same type of family environment as our own children. So what is he doing in the meanwhile? Just waiting to develop an *avuncular complex?* What about myths? Momovala goes into the garden with his daughter and has intercourse with her. The girl goes to the seashore and sings to a shark to come and eat her up. At home Momovala has such violent intercourse with his wife that he kills her with his penis. Then he cuts his own penis off and dies.[11]

There was a woman who had five clitorises and there was a stingaree. He rapes her again and again and each time he cuts off one of her clitorises. She has as many sons as clitorises and now only one son and one clitoris is left.

"The youngest son prepares a number of spears made of strong, hard wood and places them all along the road which the stingaree has to cross. The stingaree comes and sings 'One only, a solitary one clitoris remains, I have come, I shall finish it off. It will be over with her clitorises, she will die.' One after another he pierces the stingaree with the spears till he kills him."[12]

---

[9] This is also the nucleus of what any child in our own society thinks about his father.
[10] Br. Malinowski, *The Sexual Life of Savages*. London, G. Routledge, 1929, p. 5.
[11] Malinowski, *op. cit.*, p. 346.
[12] Malinowski, *op. cit.*, pp. 343, 344.

The point in this story is that the erogenous zones of the woman are identified with the sons. On the other hand the motive of the hidden spears connects this story with the *ogre against son* myth of these areas, the oedipal origin of which I discussed in the *Riddle of the Sphinx*. I would also interpret the myth of Inuvaylau[13] as an oedipal myth modified by the matrilineal setting, but I would not quote this to prove my viewpoint, since this is just the kind of myth the opposite viewpoint is based on.

But the story of the woman who gave birth to a white cockatoo is clearly an incest myth.

"A woman gave birth to a white cockatoo who then flew away into the bush. One day she went into the garden, telling her *kasesa* (clitoris) to look after the earth baking oven. The clitoris replied confidently *kekekeke!* The cockatoo had observed all this from the bush and next day it just swooped down and struck the clitoris and ate all the food that was in the oven. This was repeated several times till the woman and the clitoris died of hunger."[14]

The clitoris is the guardian of the oven, the oven is the vulva. The bird swoops down repeatedly on its mother's genital organ.

Anthropologists claim that in a different society there need not be an oedipus complex.[15] I claim that anthropologists, although they cannot deny any more that the oedipus complex exists in our society, take refuge in various "happy isles" untainted by these wicked things.

Before we come to the conclusion that there may be societies in which, as there is no strong parental authority, there is also no oedipus complex let us look at our own patients.

Each family we investigate through the microscope of our own patients is a society in a nutshell. It is by no means true that in "Western Culture" every family is organized on a patriarchal basis and we know of many cases in which the father is every bit as lenient and

---

[13] Malinowski, *op. cit.*, pp. 348-356.
[14] Malinowski, *op. cit.*, pp. 344, 345.
[15] Kroeber also accepts Malinowski's statement on the absence of the oedipus. A. L. Kroeber, *Totem and Taboo* in Retrospect, *American Journal of Sociology*, XLV. The only explanation I can find for the acceptance of such a view is that it was published in thick volumes. Cf. also Melville J. Herskovits, *Man and his Works*, New York, A.A. Knopf, 1948, p. 48.

probably far more henpecked than any Trobriand father could be. In one case I analyzed, the father was very meek and always subservient to the mother. Yet in the dreams of his eighteen-year-old son he appeared in the guise of giants or monsters who attacked the mother. Moreover this theory forgets completely that the oedipus complex is not limited to the boy, but there is also a female oedipus complex. How could this be made dependent on a strong or weak paternal authority?

The attitude of modern anthropology is best exemplified by an excerpt from an excellent field monograph by Cora du Bois.

"I set down three dolls on my verandah floor. A boy, about ten years old, immediately said 'It is a man, his wife and child.' I suggested," the ethnographer writes, "that it was a woman and two children. The four or five children accepted this for a time, although L. asked: 'Have you a man, too?' When I said, that I had no male doll, B. commented: 'They are divorced.' B. then sent the mother off to work in the fields and left the other sibling in charge of the infant. B. immediately picked up the larger doll, laid it in the mother's lap and said: 'She nurses her older child too.' Then he said: 'No, that isn't good,' and stood the larger doll between the legs of the seated mother. A. then placed the infant doll in the same position, saying: 'It is being born.' Whereupon L. chimed in with a single word: 'Copulation.' This suggests that the role of the larger doll had reverted to that of husband."[16]

Really and truly it does suggest just that. But it also suggests something else. *The child in Alor thinks that fathers are necessary, whereas the lady ethnographer things they are not.* She was evidently ready to investigate sibling rivalry but was not interested in the oedipus complex. The modified version of the Thematic Apperception Test in anthropological field work contains a picture that directly suggests sibling rivalry. But there is nothing that corresponds with the same degree of obvious meaning to the oedipus complex.[17]

---

[16] Cora du Bois, *The People of Alor*. University of Minnesota Press, 1944. p. 71.
[17] William E. Henry, *The Thematic Apperception Technique in the Study of Culture-Personality Relations*. Genetic Psychology Monographs, 1947, pp. 3-135. All this is influenced by David M. Levy, *Studies in Sibling Rivalry*, Research Monographs No. 2, American Orthopsychiatric Association, 1937.

The Navaho are probably the best studied primitive tribe of the whole world. I do not intend to refer here to my own short period of field work in 1947 or rather to the results I gathered from that field work. What I want to point out is the central importance of the oedipus complex in their religion. The remarkable fact is that some of the many anthropologists who have an extensive first hand knowledge of this tribe al o know quite a lot about psychoanalysis. Yet in their published work they do not seem to notice that the whole religion of these people with its extensive ritualism is based on the oedipus complex.

The Oedipus Complex of the Navaho

It is generally admitted that curing rites form the core of Navaho religion. A number of the afflictions cured are due to contact with alien enemies or ghosts and these are all dealt with by Monster Way or Enemy Way.

"The entire Monster Way legend is devoted to Monster Slayer and his campaigns. In Enemy Way he serves as a pattern by order of Black God who is the author of the rite. The patient should therefore reproduce Monster Slayer even in his appearance. He should rub himself with charcoal and red ochre as Monster Slayer had done. He should wear a shoulder band, wristlets and head-plume to imitate his exemplar. The figure of the bow and queue which Monster Slayer and his brother drew on their bodies were ordered by Black God to be a prominent feature of the future rite."[18] According to another version, Slayer of Monsters and Child of Water were themselves the first patients to undergo the rite. When they had killed the big giant Yeitso they carried his scalp as a trophy and hung it on a tree, reporting to their mother. While relating the encounter to her they swooned and lay unconscious whereupon she prepared a concoction of herbs struck by lightning, sprinkled them with it and shot a spruce and pine arrow over their bodies, thus reviving them.

"Accordingly to-day this ceremony is conducted in cases of swooning, or weakness and indisposition attributed to the sight of blood or of a violent death of man or beast especially if this has occurred to

---

[18] Father Bernard Haile, *Origin Legend of the Navaho Enemy Way.* Yale University Publications in Anthropology. No. 17, 1938, p. 53.

a pregnant woman, or even to a husband or father during the period of her pregnancy."[19]

According to the Coolidges "after the Slayer and his brother, the Scalper had killed the giant Yeitso, they took his scalp and his war clubs and took them back to their mother. But soon they became sick and began to have bad dreams about Yeitso and the medicine men could do nothing for them, so Changing Woman, their mother, sent for the Flint People who sang over them and cured them of their dreams."[20] After killing further monsters another set of bad dreams came, necessitating more ceremonies.

One of these is the killing of the scalp. This is not such a simple matter because the man who kills the scalp is given but a year or two to live. Therefore they pick some old man who is poor and has nothing to live for. "The patient and an assistant, painted black like him and representing the Slayer and the Scalper, now come out and march toward the scalp, the patient carrying a crow's head in his hand while the following song is sung:

"The Slayer walks
"He is painted all black
"He carries a bow
"And everybody looks at him
"The Scalper jogs along
"He is painted all black
"He carries a bow
"And everybody looks at him.

"Two pinches of earth from the gopher mound are put into the moccasins of the patient which thereby become the moccasins of the Slayer. This is the song.

"Put on moccasins, put on moccasins, put on moccasins.
"The Slayer's moccasins put on.
"He is lucky with the bow.
"Everlasting moccasins you put on.
"The Scalper is lucky in killing his enemies.
"His moccasins you put on,
"Everlasting moccasins you put on.[21]

---

[19] Franciscan Fathers, *An Ethnologic Dictionary of the Navaho Language.* Saint Michael's, Arizona, 1929, p. 366.
[20] D. Coolidge and M. R. Coolidge, *The Navaho Indians,* Boston, Houghton Mifflin, 1930, p. 168.
[21] Coolidge and Coolidge, *op. cit.,* pp. 180-182.

"When Nayenesgani, the War God, became sick from killing so many enemies, the Holy Wind told him to blacken his body from the feet up and drive out the evil spirits of the dead. He did so and recovered and this procedure is still followed in practically all the Navaho ceremonies."[22] "The Hero Twins, Monster Slayer and Child of the Water, are invoked in almost every Navaho ceremonial. Their adventures establish many of the Navaho ideals for young manhood. They serve especially as models of conduct in war and can almost be called the Navaho war gods."[23]

What is the mythical background of the rite?

Changing Woman (or Turquoise Woman) gives birth to twins, the Sun being their father. The older boy was Nayenesgani, the Slayer, and the younger was called Child of the Water. The Sun warned his wife Changing Woman to hide her sons from the giant Yeitso. She dug a hole in the floor and every time she heard Yeitso coming she put them in it and covered the hole with a flat stone. The great giant came often *for he was in love with her* and jealous of the Sun, but she kept the little ones hid. The children grow up quickly and go to seek their father, the Sun. He had a wonderful palace in the east where White Shell Woman[24] was his wife. *He cruelly attempts to kill his own offspring.* Finally when he fails to kill them the Sun gives them the straight lightning and the crooked lightning. Then they kill Yeitso the Giant who was the Sun's eldest child.[25] The gigantic stature of Yeitso and the diminutive size of his antagonist are emphasized. But it is really the Sun who kills the giant and when the elder brother rushes at him he does so with his father's stone sword.[26]

In a far more detailed version of the story we have the typical "ogre" situation. The Sun's wife hides the children. The Sun unrolls the "darkness curtain". "He lassoed the boys, where they sat, raising them with it and dashed them down against the jutting flints. But the pair of live plumes floated upward with them and landed them against

---

[22] Coolidge and Coolidge, *op. cit.,* p. 162.
[23] Clyde Kluckhohn and Dorothea Leighton, *The Navaho.* Harvard University Press, 1946, p. 124.
[24] The same as Changing Woman under another name.
[25] Coolidge, *op. cit.,* pp. 127-129.
[26] Coolidge, *op. cit.,* pp. 129-130.

where they had been seated before." Then the usual attempt is made to kill them in the sweat bath. The dawn children rub them with dawn pollen and make them look exactly like themselves.[27] There is another attempt to kill them with burning rock crystals. Finally they tell him that they came to get the zigzag lightning arrow and the straight lightning arrow to kill the big ye-i. "Lonely traveling big ye-i has devoured us all! Horned Monster has devoured all of us and Monster Eagle and those that kill with their eyes!" The Sun nevertheless reproaches them for wanting to kill the big giant, their elder brother. But finally the Sun himself is the first to shoot according to the myth because of the "perfect disc agate" on the giant's head.[28]

Before discussing similar and parallel myths we note

(a) that the sun tries to kill his own children,

(b) that the children kill the giant who had made amorous advances to their mother, i.e., the giant is a father substitute,

(c) that it is really the Sun (or Monster Slayer with the Sun's sword) who kills his own child, the giant.

If there ever was an obvious oedipal myth, surely this is it. Note moreover that the first patients to be cured were the two brothers who were made sick by the ghosts of the giant or the monsters they had killed. Navaho religion being mainly a curative practice based on this myth, and the Navaho needing these rites for bad dreams and all sorts of "bad" events (for instance lightning kills sheep), we may say that the spiritual life of the tribe is based on oedipal guilt feelings.

The myth of the dual heroes of course is not limited to the Navaho. In the Chiricahua Apache version, Changing Woman is called White Painted Woman and the two heroes are Killer of Enemies and Child of the Water. The father is a drop of water or lightning. All the other children of White Painted Woman had been destroyed by the Giant.

"Killer of Enemies went on hunting. He killed a deer and built a fire. He started to cook his meat. When the meat was done, he broke

---

[27] The dawn children are also children of the Sun.
[28] Father Bernard Haile, *Origin Legend of the Navaho Enemy Way*. Yale Univ. Publ. Anthr. No. 17, 1938, pp. 91-111.

off a little brush and stuck it in the ground, then he took the meat and put it on the brush to cool off so he could eat it. But every time just when Killer of Enemies thought he was going to eat the meat the giant would come." The Giant took all the meat and left Killer of Enemies crying. There were only these three human beings, White Painted Woman, Killer of Enemies and Giant, i.e., Mother, Son—and Father. The other child—Child of the Water[29]—was about to be born. This child was hidden under a hole in the fireplace. When he was old enough to hold a bow and arrow, he killed the Giant. The Giant was after the baby, his mother kept hiding him. While Killer of Enemies just cried like a baby, the little one, Child of the Water, killed the Giant. Child of the Water was first tested by his father, Lightning, who hurled lightnings of various kinds at him (like above with the Sun).[30]

Further details to prove the same point may be omitted here. The question I ask is simply this: how is it possible to overlook the oedipal significance of this myth?

However, let us take a very *deviant* people with a childhood situation that is quite different from our own. It is well known that Kardiner believes he has proved that these people can have no oedipus complex.[31] Instead of monogamy we have polyandry, the mothers stimulate the children sexually and reject them when they would still need breast feeding.[32]

I will quote several myths to show that whatever the social organization may be, we still have the oedipus complex.

Marquesas Culture

It has become a commonplace now, carried over to handbooks, that the people of the Marquesas Islands have no oedipus complex. "From the arrangement of institutions we can safely rule out the element of father hatred."[33]

---

[29] The roles of the two heroes are inverted.
[30] M. E. Opler, *Myths and Tales of the Chiricahua Apache Indians.* Memoirs of the American Folk-Lore Society, Vol. XXXVII, 1942, pp. 1-14.
[31] A. Kardiner, *The Individual and his Society,* New York Columbia University Press, 1939, Chapter VI.
[32] Linton, in *Kardiner,* pp. 164-166.
[33] Kardiner, *op. cit.,* p. 218.

"The oedipus complex is nowhere in evidence except in one tale, that of the hero Toke-Tika. Here one could with some stretch of imagination say that it is a fantasy of killing the uncles, who can conveniently be made into father substitutes, and then impregnating the mother so that she should give birth to successive children which the hero then makes part of himself."[34]

This is the myth of Tiki contained in Handy's Marquesan Legends.

Tiki's wife was called Hina-mataone. (Heap of sand accumulated by the sea.) He went to lie down on a heap of sand and a girl came out of it. This was Tiki's daughter. His wife said: "Do not bring in my daughter because you will mate with her!"

When she grew up, he built her a house in the depths of a valley and said:

"Go up to the mountains! There you will find a house and a man who resembles me in every way. You will believe that it is I but you will be mistaken."

The girl paired with Tiki and had children by him.

For this reason the natives say: Tiki is the god of the *kaiakaia*, a word meaning one who is cruel, a cannibal, or who cohabits with his relatives. Tiki had another wife Hina-totoho-nui.[35] She was said to have been the wife of the good looking Tiki while Hina-mataone was the wife of the Tiki with the ugly body.[36]

Tiki asked his women-relatives to make him a loin-cloth. They presented him one full of slits and holes. He put it on backside foremost so that the tail hung down in front. With eyes and nose streaming with mucus and breaking wind he made his way up the valley. The people who saw him said with one voice "Kill him!" When they tried to catch him, he disappeared to reappear again as a handsome man. It is said that Tiki kept all his evil features concealed *in his anus*. (My italics.) Tiki appeared again in the valley in his evil form. The people caught him and they tried to knock his eyes out but they could not do it. They pulled out his tongue and tied a knot in it but he

---

[34] Kardiner, *op. cit.,* p. 247.
[35] Is she identical with the Hina-nui-te-po of the Mani myths?
[36] E. S. Craighill, *Handy's Marquesan Legends.* Bernice P. Bishop Museum, Bulletin 69, Honolulu, 1930, p. 123.

untied it. They tried to knock his teeth out but could not. They attempted to strangle him but he eluded their grasp. They cut off his ears but Tiki picked them up again and stuck them on the side of his head. His feet and arms were cut off but he stuck them back again. At last they cut open his stomach. Tiki wept and fled to the seashore. He slept there for a long time and then returned to the valley. The people caught him again and made preparations to roast him. Suddenly while they were abusing him, his disgusting form vanished and he assumed the appearance of a very handsome man (poea). Instantly all the women were struck with a passionate desire for him and implored the men to leave him alone and let the women have him, and then he suddenly became ugly again. This time they seized him and broke his body all to pieces but every time they did it he was restored.

He escaped again and slept in the sand. A great eel seized him by the foot. He cried out to his wife to bring him his knife. His wife said: "I am tired of sleeping with a demon" (vahine hae). However, she pulled at one end while the eel was pulling his feet.[37]

Once he went to sleep in the mud of the taro patch. They filled his eyes with mud. Hoaani came and cut off one of his fingers and stuck it into the mud. A taro leaf grew where the finger had been planted and the finger grew back on Tiki's hand. Two of his fingers were cut off and planted and the same thing occurred again. They tried to cut off the penis but Tiki escaped and ran away.[38]

Now if ever there was a "primal horde" myth, surely this is it.

We have:

(a) The god who commits incest with his daughter and becomes the prototype of criminals (incest and cannibalism).

(b) The multitude against the one criminal or supernatural being.

(c) The ambivalent attitude regarding the Primal Sire (beautiful and ugly shape).

(d) The attempt to castrate the Primal Father. (By the way, according to Kardiner, they have no castration complex.)

---

[37] Handy, *op. cit.*, p. 123.
[38] Handy, *op. cit.*, p. 124.

(e) All sorts of symbolic derivatives of castration (eyes, fingers, etc.) that fail to be effective. The god is the restitution fantasy mobilized against castration anxiety.

Perhaps somebody will observe here, why do I call him a god, why a Primal Father?

Tiki is the creator god of Nukuhiva. He dwelt in the lower region called Hawaii. He was the leader of the spirits and he had the power to create other beings. Feeling lonesome he created a child in the sand and went away. Three days later it was a full grown woman who immediately became his wife. They had children and the boy married his sister. He decided to make a place for his children to live upon. The land (-fenua) of Nukuhiva arose out of the water.[39] After a time the wise men realized that Tiki would vanish and never be seen again, so his likeness was made in stone. He taught them all the things they knew, both good and bad, and then he vanished.[40] We see therefore that Tiki is really,

(a) the creator god;

(b) source of both good and evil;

(c) his vanishing is his death. Idols reproduce the image of the primal father.

Someone might object that this is not an oedipal myth at all. Just a mild case of measles, I mean Electra complex. However, we are told that Tiki's father was Tiki-tapa (i.e., Tiki the Holy) and his mother Kahu-one (pile of sand)[41]—and that is also the name of his wife.

Tiki said that in Hawaii there is death while on earth there is life. He made a pile of sand which he named Hina, with the face of sand (Hina-mataone). He slept with her and a girl child was born. He planted a banyan tree for his daughter, when he did this the red feathered bird (manukua) came.[42]

According to Tregear, Tiki was a general name for the gods in the Marquesas but the first Tiki is again born of a father-daughter incest

---

[39] Handy, *op. cit.*, p. 122.
[40] Handy, *op. cit.*, p. 122.
[41] Handy, *op. cit.*, p. 123.
[42] Handy, *op. cit.*, p. 123.

between Dawn and Daylight. At various other places we find him as creator or first man.[43] In Hawaii Kiki, the first human being, seduces Lailai, the wife of his brother Kane, the god.[44] At Mangaia a chasm, supposed to be the road to the other world, is called Tiki's hole.[45]

In New Zealand we have Tiki as the first human being. But in the same role we have frequently Maui or Mauitiki. Maui is also identified with Tangaroa. Maui wishes to have intercourse with his sister. Hina tells her that she will meet a man called Tiimaaratai who is again himself in another form. Their son is Tii.[46] We have here the New Zealand form of the Marquesas story—first human beings, incest. "Children of Tiki" means mankind in general, especially the nobility. Schirren recognizes clearly the identity of Maui and Tiki,[47] Maui-potiki, the Fisher of Islands, is another New Zealand story.[48]

According to a Marquesas myth, Maui obtains fire by overcoming his ancestor or great-grandfather Mahuike.[49] In the Samoan version Tiitii, the son of Talanga, followed his father and watched where he entered the underworld. He pretends to be his father Talanga and then we have the usual struggle with the god of the underworld for fire.[50] A Tongan version of the same story has a Maui-Kisikisi in it and Maui Motua. Maui Kisikisi (Maui Tikitiki) tore off a piece of the loin-cloth of Maui Motua that had a fire smouldering in it (fire and genital organ) and told the fire to run into different trees. Maui Kisikisi ran and Maui Motua chased him to the underworld.[51] The following is the story in Niue. There was a father Maui and a son Maui. The son was also called Titikilaga, it was he who lifted up the

---

[43] E. Tregear, *The Maori Polynesian Comparative Dictionary*, Wellington, Whitcombe and Tombs Ltd., n.d. pp. 510, 511.
[44] A. Bastian, *Die heilige Sage der Polynesier*. Leipzig, E. A. Brockhaus, 1881, p. 74.
[45] W. W. Gill, *Myths and Songs from the South Pacific*, London, Henry S. King and Co., 1876, p. 18.
[46] C. Schirren, *Die Wandersagen der Neuseelaender*, Riga, 1856, pp. 64, 65.
[47] Schirren, *loc. cit.*, p. 70.
[48] Schirren, *loc. cit.*, p. 71.
[49] M. Radiguet, *Les derniers sauvages*, Paris, Duchartre, 1929, p. 163. Handy, *ob. cit.*, p. 12.
[50] G. Turner, *Samoa, a Hundred Years Ago*, L. Macmillan, 1884, pp. 210, 211.
[51] E. W. Gifford, *Tongan Myths and Tales*, Bernice P. Bishop Museum, Bulletin 8, 1924, pp. 22, 23.

heavens.[52] The son finds out that his father keeps the fire in the underworld and follows him.

"The boy came down from the tree and the father rushed at him. Then they struggled, the father swinging the boy off his feet and throwing him onto the ground. The boy arose and wrestled with his father once more. The boy felt that his body was hurt and when his father again rushed at him he thought he was about to be killed. Then he gathered all his strength in order to conquer his parent and when they wrestled he seized his father and threw him to the ground. Immediately the child rushed forward and seizing the fire he returned to the earth above."[53] Now this is the Niue version, not the Marquesas. But can it make much difference that in the Marquesas version the older Maui is a grandfather?

This is the first myth I find in the collection of Karl von den Steinen: Hatanea Motua kills the son of Apekua as a sacrifice to the gods and is then captured by Eetie, the brother of Taketa. Eetie kills Taketa's wife. Dying she gives birth to Vaka Uhi. Vaka Uhi is brought up by two grandmothers while the nephew lives with Taketa. Nephew and son are rivals. Taketa refuses to eat the fish offered him by his own son because they come from a man whose mother has been sacrificed.

The son is offended and wants his axe; it is thrown into the toilet for him.

Taketa's wife tells him that his father has fallen into a seven days' sleep.

Son and nephew are now rivals in boat building. Each time the son tries to fell a tree it jumps back into its place. This is manipulated by the two grandmothers. Finally they tell him how to catch the divine boatmaker who is doing this by his incantation and make him build a boat for him.

Nephew and son set out on two boats. The father is with his nephew. The son breaks his boat to pieces, he is going to commit suicide. But he swims to a place owned by the chief Tuhakana.

---

[52] Edwin M. Loeb, *History and Tradition of Niue*. Bernice P. Bishop Museum, Bulletin 32, 1926, p. 211.
[53] Loeb, *op. cit.*, p. 213.

Nephew and father set out in search of the son who has disappeared. He appears to them in two shapes, tattooed and untattooed, so as to confuse them. Finally Taketa arrives at the place owned by Tuhakana (host and friend of Vaka Uhi).

They fight and Taketa kills Tuhakana. After this he sleeps for seven days. His son burns the house and Taketa is burnt to death.[54]

Here we have an indubitable Marquesan case of a son who kills his father. The objection might be that the case is not the oedipus motive, because the reason for the parricide is rejected love. However, if we look closer we see that the son is really the avenger of his mother. It is through his mother having been sacrificed that he is defiled and rejected. According to K. von den Steinen, Eetie and Taketa are really the same person, i.e., the son kills the father who has killed his mother. He is enabled to do so because Taketa's wife (duplicate of his mother), like Delila, tells him about the seven days' sleep, which is the hero's weakness.

This interpretation is borne out by another version of the story reported by Handy.

Taketa went to war and killed the wife of an enemy chief named Hitapu. At home he found a child Vakauhi whom he gave to an old woman to raise. Follows the motive of the rivalry with Ohatu, here the old woman's grandson. Finally looking down to the underworld he saw Hitapu who was his father and whose wife Taketa had killed. We find the same motive of Taketa seeking Vakauhi and of the attempt of the latter to burn the house but in this version the father escapes.[55] The father of version A is the killer of the mother in B, which makes the revenge motive quite clear.

The son-father-in-law antagonism, is surely simply the son-father antagonism displaced. The father-in-law wants to keep his daughter.

Kena's father-in-law wants to kill him because the younger man is more successful in "fishing" (i.e., coitus). The father-in-law injures his head but he was healed and fled to the mountain.[56] In the myth of

---

[54] Karl von den Steinen, Marquesanische Mythen. *Zeitschrift für Ethnologie*, LXV, 1933.
[55] Handy, *l. c.*, p. 135.
[56] Handy, *op. cit.*, p. 117. (The rest of the story does not concern us here.)

Toke-Tika, mentioned by Kardiner as the one story where somebody—who would be wrong of course—might think of an oedipal interpretation, this is the sequel that Kardiner does not mention or notice. Toke-Tika took to wife the daughter of Tu-Fiti. He asked his son-in-law to dive for a net and when he came up, his father-in-law struck him with the spear. A large shark bit off his head while the lifeless body floated in the current. The sharks took the head directly to his mother's house. The head was recognized and placed in a small house at the rear of the dwelling. Through the great power of Toke-Tika his mother conceived and in one month and a half gave birth to a male child.[57] He makes his mother conceive, his father (in-law) kills him, the sharks bite his head off (castration)—if all this is not enough "oedipal" for anyone, I think it ought to be.[58]

But the anthropologists would say to all this: "If you assume the universality of the oedipus complex, you are also assuming that the oedipus complex of the individual is phylogenetically inherited, an assumption that cannot be reconciled with the findings of biology."

In the early days of psychoanalysis, when Freud wrote *Totem and Taboo*, he was impressed by certain analogies that presented themselves in the animal phobias of children and the totemism or religion of primitive people.

Totem and Taboo is famous for the Primal Horde hypothesis but we have all overlooked the fact that it also contains another explanation of totemism.

"If the totem animal is the father, then the two main commandments of totemism, the two taboo rules which constitute its nucleus—not to kill the totem animal and not to use a woman belonging to the same totem for sexual purposes—agree in content with the two crimes of Oedipus, who slew his father and took his mother for a wife and also with the child's two primal wishes whose insufficient repression or re-awakening forms the nucleus of perhaps all neuroses. If this similarity is more than a deceptive play of accident it would perhaps make it possible for us to shed light upon the origin of totemism in prehistoric times. In other words, we should make it probable that the

---

[57] Handy, *loc. cit.*, p. 108.
[58] The sections on the Navaho and the Marquesas will be discussed in detail in my forthcoming book.

totemic system resulted from conditions underlying the oedipus complex just as the animal phobia of 'Little Hans' and the poultry perversion of 'little Arpad' originated from it."[59]

In other words, people who have beliefs or customs comparable to those of these children (and of others observed later in clinical analysis) have an oedipus complex.

But why must Freud go further and conclude that what we have in the child is a reverberation of what happened in the evolution of the human race? This has little to do with the findings of clinical analysis. Freud is here applying Haeckel's famous biogenetic law. Modern biology does not accept this law, at least in its original form.

Garstang writes: "Ontogeny does not recapitulate phylogeny, it creates it."[60]

Freud regarded this hypothesis as indispensable in order to explain the parallelisms in content in children, neurotics, normals and primitives. In *Moses and Monotheism* he speaks about the evolution of the individual as an abbreviated repetition of the evolution of the race.[61] He also thinks it necessary to assume that the psychological precipitate of those events had become inherited by successive generations.[62]

In other words the Primal Horde theory implies the inheritance of acquired characters (Lamarckism). This is where anthropologists have made a firm stand against psychoanalysis and with the Primal Horde theory rejected also the assumption of the universality of the oedipus complex.[63]

Biologists who uphold the Lamarckian position are an infinitesimal minority. Huxley writes:

"It is, however, necessary to realize that important indirect objections can be made to the Lamarckian view. In the first place, there is

---

[59] S. Freud, *Totem and Taboo*. London, G. Routledge and Sons, 1919, pp. 219, 220.
[60] W. Garstang. The Theory of Recapitulation: a Critical Restatement of the Biogenetic Law. *The Journal of the Linnaean Society* (Zoology), London, Vol. XXXV, 1922-1924. The meaning of this will be clear from what we have to say about Bolk's theory.
[61] S. Freud, *Moses and Monotheism*, New York, W. W. Norton & Co., 1939, p. 211.
[62] S. Freud, *loc. cit.*, p. 233.
[63] Cf. recently D. Bidney, On the Concept of Culture and some Cultural Fallacies, *American Anthropologist*. 1944, XLVI.

OEDIPUS COMPLEX, MAGIC AND CULTURE 191

the fact of Mendelian recessivity. A recessive character can be rendered latent indefinitely by keeping the gene concerned in the heterozygous condition; yet when the recessive gene is allowed to unite with another like itself the resultant character is identical with that of pure bred recessives in which it has been manifested and therefore exposed to recessive stimuli throughout." Specifically on higher mammals Huxley writes:[64]

"These have their internal environment regulated to an extraordinary degree of constancy. The temperature of the blood, and to a still higher degree its salt composition and its acidity, are kept constant by elaborate special mechanisms. The reproductive cells like all other cells in the body are exposed to the internal environment supplied by the blood stream. How then can changes in the external environment be submitted to them? The regulation of the internal environment provides an effective shock absorber for all the more obvious alterations which could occur in the external environment."[65]

But even if the neo-Lamarckian view in its Soviet form proved to be correct—and that is hardly likely—this would prove that adaptation to environmental conditions, alterations in the food or conditions of climate could be inherited,[66] but how would this support the theory of an inherited guilt? And how could guilt be inherited unless it is there in the first place? Freud writes:

"In order to find these results acceptable, quite aside from our supposition we need only assume that the group of brothers banded together were dominated by the same contradictory feelings towards the father which we can demonstrate as the content of ambivalence in the father complex in all our children and neurotics. They hated the father who stood so powerfully in the way of the sexual demands and their desire for power but they also loved and admired him."[67]

In other words they had an oedipus complex. Why should we then base our claim to the universality of the oedipus complex on the

---

[64] Experiments on insects and food habits are not relevant for the reasons mentioned by Huxley above. Cf. Sladden and Hewer. Transference of Induced Food Habits from Parent to Offspring. *Proceedings of the Royal Society of London.* (B) 126, 30, X.

[65] J. Huxley, *Evolution,* New York, Harper and Brothers, 1942, pp. 460, 461.

[66] Cf. Trofim Lysenko. *The Science of Biology Today,* New York, International Publishers Co., Inc., 1948.

[67] S. Freud, *Totem and Taboo,* p. 237.

Primal Horde and racial unconscious when in order to make the Primal Horde theory work, we first have to assume that the hypothetical ancestors had an oedipus complex?

In a paper that has been often quoted in psychoanalytic literature, I elaborated Freud's theory of the Primal Horde. But even then, as early as 1923, I wrote that the assumed eating of the father must really have been a repetition of the oral stage, that is of the infant nourished by the mother.[68] Here we have already in a nutshell what later became "ontogenesis instead of phylogenesis".

But what about the Primal Horde myths? I myself have enumerated a number of myths that seem to say exactly the same thing that Freud says in *Totem and Taboo*.

This is the Fan version of the Primal Horde:

A giant crocodile demanded tribute from the people. Every day he ate a human being and at full moon he received a new wife, one of the virgins of the tribe. After cohabiting with the new wife he would eat her. The Fan attempt to escape but fail and now the crocodile doubles the tribute. Finally he does not eat the chief's beautiful daughter and she is delivered of Ngurangurane, the Son of the Crocodile.

The human son of the crocodile is eager to avenge the death of his grandfather. He invents palm wine and the giant crocodile is now drunk and asleep. When it is asleep, the Son of the Crocodile orders Lightning to strike his father. Lightning refuses horrified at the idea of parricide. But compelled by the magic of the mother of Ngurangurane, he finally strikes and kills the sleeping monster. They then danced the Fanki, the funeral dance that is now customary when a chief dies. This was to appease the spirit of Ombure. The Son of the Crocodile then took the stone knife still in use for funerals, sacrifices, and for circumcision, and cut the corpse into little bits. Everybody ate of the flesh of the crocodile. Thus the angry spirit could do nothing because wherever it went it found its own flesh and blood. A huge statue of Ombure was erected and the same sacrifices were dedicated to it which he had enacted in his lifetime.[69]

---

[68] G. Róheim, Nach dem Tode des Urvaters, *Imago,* IX.
[69] R. P. H. Trilles. *Le totemisme chez les Fân.* Bibliothèque Anthropos. I. 4. Fasc. Muenster. C. W. 1912, pp. 183-205. Interpreted previously as Primal Horde myth in *The Riddle of the Sphinx,* London, Hogarth Press, 1934. pp. 191, 192.

The two supreme "totems" or cult objects of the tribe are the crocodile and the elephant. This is the myth of the origin of the elephant totem.

In old times each human village lived under the rule of a family of elephants. Animals come to the elephant to complain that human beings are killing them. The elephant summons them to defend themselves against this charge. But seeing that they refuse to come, Father Elephant decides to go to their village and see for himself. The Chief of Men has enormous traps made on the way. Father Elephant falls into these traps and each time this happens he thinks he is dead. The Chief of Men sees what has happened and each time expresses his astonishment and indignation. Who could have done such a thing to let Father Elephant fall in the trap? He helps Father Elephant to climb out but when he is just about to come quite out, the Chief of Men and his followers run away. This is repeated several times. Finally, however, Father Elephant is there and the Chief of Men confesses his guilt. After having given presents to all the animals to atone for killing them, he enters into a blood covenant with each species, and finally with the elephant himself. When a chief dies, his soul is temporarily incarnated in an elephant. These elephants can be recognized because their skin is lighter than that of the other elephants. In dreams they reveal to men, that is to their children, where to go to hunt elephants but they must be careful not to kill the ancestral elephant, that would mean killing the tribe.[70]

Comparing these two myths we see that in one case we have the *father as criminal*. The crocodile father eats human beings and owns all the women. The sympathy of the narrator is evidently on the side of the son who kills the Crocodile Father, while in the elephant myth we have the same story revised from the point of view of the superego. Mankind is the criminal, they confess their crime. Father Elephant represents justice yet human beings try to kill him, but hypocritically pretend to be concerned about him.

Without going into all the ramifications of the myth in present day ritual we can see here how the myth reflects the oedipus complex of today with the paternal ogre whom every son has to overcome.

I once discussed the myths of the Andaman Islanders, interpreting

---

[70] Trilles, *l. c.*, pp. 202-212.

them as survivals of the Primal Horde. But we should not forget that *myth always represents as projected into the past whatever conflicts exist in the present.*

Puluga forbade the ancestors to make use of a certain tree for fuel when cooking turtle or pigs. The men would have their throats cut as a penalty and the women were to be deprived of their breasts by Mother Sun or by Sir Moon. They violated the taboo and the deluge came.[71] Usually the taboo in these stories is against eating certain foods reserved for Puluga (Biliku) or killing the cicada. Mite is Puluga's wife, she is identified either with the bronze-winged dove or the cicada.

Bilika lived with his wife Mite. They had a child. The ancestors ate Bilika's food, loito and kata and other plants. Bilika was angry. He smelled their throats to see whether they had eaten his food and then would cut their throats. Finally they came together and killed Bilika and his wife Mite.[72] In another version Bilika cuts the men's throats and the breasts of the women.[73]

According to another version certain ancestors failed to observe the taboos for neophytes as they exist today, therefore they were turned to stone.[74]

If we do not believe that the mneme can preserve traces of events that took place in prehistoric times it is simple enough to explain the structure of these myths. Incest or incestuous desires provoke the wrath of the Father God. Thunder is his voice or weapon. This is the way it was in the beginning, *whatever exists today goes back to a mythical prototype.* The Puluga of the Andamanese corresponds to the Karei of the Semang and the supreme sin against Karei is incest. Karei punishes also intercourse during daytime. He is appeased by the blood sacrifice, that is an incision into the leg and blood thrown skyward. If somebody has committed murder and Thunder is not

---

[71] E. A. Man. On the Aboriginal Inhabitants of the Andaman Islands, *Journal of the Royal Anthropological Institute,* XII. pp. 173, 472. G. Róheim, Primitive High Gods, *Psychoanalytic Quarterly,* III, Supplement 1934, p. 20.
[72] G. Róheim, *op. cit.,* quoting A. R. Brown, *The Andaman Islanders,* London, Cambridge University Press, 1922, p. 200.
[73] *Ibid.,* p. 20.
[74] Róheim, *op. cit.,* p. 16.

OEDIPUS COMPLEX, MAGIC AND CULTURE 195

appeased by the flowing blood, the murderer's *body is cut open* (body destruction) and then the blood is thrown to the sky. Parents may not sleep in close bodily contact with their children of the opposite sex.[75] We notice also that the women are the ones who first perform the sacrifice of blood and that Karei has a mother, grandmother or wife, Manoid, who lives in the earth and has also to be appeased by pouring blood.

Without going into further details it seems possible that in this mythology we have two superimposed strata, one oedipal and genital and the other pre-oedipal and oral. There are always two deities, a father- and a mother-imago. Puluga in the Andaman Islands is really the spider—*and the spider sucks blood*.[76] The sky beings do not eat. When they feel hunger *they pick fruit from the tree in the sky and suck it*.[77]

The Baiga in Central India tell another typical Primal Horde myth.

In those days Nanga Baiga was living in Nanga Pakar. Bhagavan (Creator) gave him this boon.

"From your left side will flow black blood, from your right side red blood."

Those who drink of the black blood become witches, those who drink the red blood magicians.[78] But the Creator became jealous of Naga Baiga, and sent a snake to bite him. The ancestor thought it was a stick and scratched his back with it. It bit him and he died.

He told his sons that they were to cook his flesh in twelve pots and eat it. His sons would inherit his magic.

But the Creator did not want this to happen, so he told the sons what a great sin it would be if they ate their father. Only one of them got a whiff of the steam of the cooking pot and he became the first medicine man.[79]

---

[75] P. P. Schebesta, Religioese Anschauungen der Semang. *Archiv fuer Religionswissenschaft*, XXIV.
[76] Róheim, *op. cit.*, p. 30. The lizard, of course, symbolizes the penis.
[77] Schebesta, *op. cit.*, p. 228.
[78] I. e., healers.
[79] V. Elwin, *The Baiga*, London, John Murray, 1939, pp. 340, 341.

The sons eat the Primal Father. But the Primal Father himself has a superego in the person of the Creator. The latter plans his death which takes place in the form of an involuntary suicide.[80]

But this idea of "magic only partially acquired" is a common feature of present day Baiga life. Initiation consists of taking the master's leavings. The older man takes liquor into his mouth, spits it back into a leaf cup and gives it to his disciple to drink. One of the most common complaints of the younger generation of medicine men is that their parents have not told them everything. Mithu darkly suspects his father of holding back vital information.[81]

Therefore it would seem that we have difficulty in learning from the father, i.e., in identifying with the father. The difficulty is the superego appearing in the narrative as the Creator. The oral element is again conspicuous.

In other versions we find other indications of a fusion of the parental *imagos*.

The Mungarai have a tradition about the origin of their bullroarers. In the mythical period there was a big man called Kunapippi who gave them their totem names and classes. He belonged to no special class or totem himself and he was a very big man with a very big foot. He existed before the present generation of human beings. He had plenty of spirit children in his bag, all boys and no girls. He sang out, like men do now when they perform ceremonies, quivering his hand in front of his mouth.

He showed them the ceremonies, gave them their totem names and classes and then ate all the boys except two who managed to escape. These two brought reinforcements in, killed Kunapippi and cut out two boys who were alive in his inside.[82]

This certainly looks like a Primal Horde myth with the brothers united against the Primal Sire who has the big toe (phallos).

---

[80] G. Róheim, The Oedipus Complex and Infantile Sexuality, *Psychoanalytic Quarterly*, XV.

[81] Elwin, *op. cit.*, p. 43.

[82] B. Spencer, *Native Tribes of the Northern Territory of Australia*, New York, Macmillan, 1914, pp. 216, 217.

However, if we look at it more closely it is a projection of the initiation ritual into the past. In the ritual the individual receives his totem name and gets initiated into the ritual. The eating and disgorging of the boys is the typical narrative told to the non-initiated while the final killing of the father-imago is the wish of all young men.[83] The Murngin myth of the Great Father Snake whose pool is contaminated by the menstrual blood of the two Wawilak sisters, whereupon he swallows their sons who are about to be circumcised, looks like one of these Primal Father myths. However, the boys who are about to be circumcised are told: "The Great Father Snake smells your foreskin. He is calling for it", and they run to their mothers for protection.[84] I have discussed the interpretation of this myth previously[85] and all I want to do now is to emphasize the *ambisexual* nature of the snake; in its erect position it is a phallic symbol and in swallowing its victims it has a female significance.

But then there are situations that look very much like the Primal Horde as a contemporary or nearly contemporary institution.

An old Aranda, named Renana, at Hermannsburg, told me about an Aranda who lived at Ellery Creek and was a contemporary of his grandmother (i.e., about 1880-1890). He had intercourse with all women, even his own classificatory mothers, his younger sisters, both real and classificatory, his real daughter, his father's sister and niece. He was a very strong man and people were afraid of him. He would rape any woman he caught in the bush. Beside his wife who was "straight" (in the sense of the Aranda class system) he had three real daughters living with him as his wives. Finally public opinion was transformed into action, they united against him and killed him.[86]

In the first volume of this annual Dr. Feldman comments on the Primal Horde.

At the harvest festival of the Tabernacles Jewish boys who live in

---

[83] A female version of the Kunapippi story is given by Ronald M. and Catherine H. Berndt, The Eternal Ones of the Dream, *Oceania*, XVII.
[84] W. Lloyd Warner, *A Black Civilization*, New York, Harper and Brothers, 1937, p. 261.
[85] G. Róheim, *The Eternal Ones of the Dream*. New York, Int. Univ. Press, 1945, p. 179.
[86] G. Róheim, The Primal Horde and Incest in Central Australia. *Journal of Criminal Psychopathology*, III, 1942.

an orthodox Jewish environment play a game called the *firstborn game*.

The boys are all under thirteen, that is children according to the Jewish ritual law. Each boy stakes, let us say, five nuts and places them in a straight line on the ground. The biggest nut is placed at the left end of the line. This one is called the "firstborn". Each boy throws a nut at the whole line. He wins all the nuts to the right of the one he has knocked out of line. He who dares to aim at the "firstborn" wins the whole line of nuts at a blow. In this case each player has to put nuts on the line again and the game continues with the next boy.

Usually one boy gets very heated and aims all the time at the firstborn, no matter how often he loses. Feldman explains the game on basis of the present day situation. "The father is absolute master of the house and in this he is supported by a host of different laws, orders of the Bible, customs, etc. The first born son has a prominent position in the family circle, gives the youngsters orders and in general represents the father. The younger ones try to gang up against him and to make him feel ridiculous. If the age difference between the firstborn and the other boys is not great, the enmity between him and all the other boys is replaced by the enmity between the father and the boys and the firstborn nut becomes a symbol of the father . . . " "From the clinical point of view," Feldman writes, "there is no need to assume that the boys carry with them memory traces of the ancient struggles of their ancestors. Everything is there *in statu nascendi*, the father, the females, the firstborn and the other sons. The conflicts are the same as in the hypothetical brother-horde."[87]

In the same volume we have also a very interesting instance of "Primal Horde" myths or rites by Bunker. Oxen were driven round the altar of Zeus Polieus, on which were laid cakes of barley mixed with honey. One ox went up to the altar and ate the cakes. This one would be the chosen victim of the sacrifice. The sacrifice was performed by two men, one felled the ox with an axe, the other cut its throat with a knife. All those who afterwards flayed the ox tasted its flesh. Both the murderers threw down their weapons and fled. The weapons were brought to trial, declared guilty of the crime of oxmurder and thrown into the sea. Then they sewed up the hide of the ox and stuffed it with clay after which they set it up just as it was

---

[87] Sándor S. Feldman, Notes on the Primal Horde, *this annual*, I, pp. 175, 176.

OEDIPUS COMPLEX, MAGIC AND CULTURE 199

when it was still alive. Then they yoked it to a plough as if it were still ploughing.

The ox deserved to die because it had eaten of the cake of Zeus Polieus. But slaying the ox was a crime, therefore

(a) two men share in the crime,
(b) the whole community shares in the crime by devouring the slain animal,
(c) the actual murderer flees,
(d) the axe and the knife are declared guilty,
(e) restitution of the ox in the act of ploughing.

According to the myth, Sopratos or Dromos, a stranger outraged by the sacrilege, was the first to kill the ox. He fled, was discovered and then relieved of the pollution he had incurred by "all doing the act in common." Sopatros became a citizen and thus all made themselves sharers in the murder. The etymology of the word is important. Sopatros means Savior of the State, really of the πατρα, the paternal clan. The one who is most guilty, the leader of the brother-horde in the fight against the father, is also the savior.[88]

If we do not assume the unconscious survival of primeval events, the myth can be explained quite simply on an id and superego basis.

The ox is really quite justified in eating the cake on the altar, for the ox or bull symbolizes Zeus himself.[89] We suspect that the honey-cake is a female symbol and what follows is a series of attempts to shift the guilt inherent in all sexual situations. First the bull (father symbol) has intercourse and then it is killed by the two sons. Bunker's rendering omits the female element. The axe and the knife with which the beast was slain had been previously wetted with water brought by maidens called "water carriers." When the stuffed ox had been re-erected and yoked to a plough, a trial took place presided over by a so-called king, to decide who had murdered the ox. The maidens who had brought the water accused the men who had sharpened the axe and knife, and the men who had sharpened the axe and knife blamed the men who had handed these implements to the butchers; the men who had handed these implements to the butchers blamed the butchers

---
[88] For these data and references, cf. Henry A. Bunker, Bouphonia or Ox-Murder, *this annual*, I, pp. 165-169.
[89] Cf. A. B. Cook, *Zeus,* Cambridge University Press, 1914, I-III.

and the butchers laid the blame on the axe and knife which were accordingly found guilty and condemned and cast into the sea.[90]

The whole myth is an attempt to get rid of the guilt of parricide. It is the ox, it is the two killers, the whole community, the maidens, finally the weapons, i.e., the penis who is guilty. Without a superego mechanism this myth could not exist. The mythical *technique* of regarding the ritual as a repetition of something that happened in primeval days does not prove that the myth really represents an event.

What it does show is that the myth and the ritual represent the oedipus complex and a series of superego-dictated defense mechanisms, to get rid of the guilt:
(a) The guilt is shared by two hero murderers;
(b) there is a series of attempts at projection ending up with blaming and rightly so—the sexual impulse itself;
(c) the guilt is shared by the whole community which is also perfectly true since the desires that underlie the guilt are common property.

If we re-examine all these myths and rituals that look as if they might be based on events similar to those that Freud assumes in his Primal Horde hypothesis, we find that they are all attempts to deal with the problem of guilt, i.e., they presuppose the existence of the superego.

They can be summarized in varying formulae:
(1) The father is the tragic hero.[91]
(2) The son is the hero, abetted by his mother.
(3) The hero (son or father) is a criminal.
(4) The group is the hero.
(5) The group is guilty.
(6) Woman is the criminal.[92]

In the Mentawei myth we find clear indications that an ontogenetic situation is projected into the past—the phallic father (iguana) deprives the son of his mother in the oral stage.

In the days when Freud wrote *Totem and Taboo*, we knew very little about the oral stage of evolution. Without endorsing all the

---

[90] I. G. Frazer, *Spirits of the Corn and of the Wild*, London, Macmillan, 1912 (quoting Pausanias, Porphyry, Aelian, etc.).
[91] Not enumerated this time but compare: *The Eternal Ones of the Dream*, pp. 16, 17.
[92] Reserved for another publication.

hypothetical conclusions Melanie Klein and some of her followers arrive at, we may safely assume that, since the maternal object is both frustrating and gratifying, the infant will have the imago of a "bad" and a "good" mother. A remark made by Winnicott is significant in this connection.

"We try to reduce everything to instinct and the analytic psychologists (Jungians) reduce everything to this part of the primitive self which looks like environment but which arises out of instinct (archtypes). We ought to modify our view and to see if it is true that in the earliest theoretical primitive state the self has its own environment which is as much self as the instinct which produces it."[93]

In all child's play we see a rapid *to* and *fro*, an oscillation of object-directed and self-directed aggression.

A very simple instance from the Pilaga play material published by the Henry couple will show what I mean. A little boy of four makes the turtle doll bite the mother doll, then sister doll; then he makes the turtle doll bite the self-doll over and over again. He picks up a knife to cut sister doll's throat, saying, "I kill her." Then he passes the knife over her feet, saying "I kill her vulva." Then he picks up the self-doll and repeats the movements over the throat and penis of the self-doll, saying "I cut off my penis."[94]

Similar sequences I have observed wherever I carried out doll play with the children of the Central Australians, the Normanby Islanders, or the Navaho.

The child discovers the non-self in a frustration situation and then it discovers the same object as relieving this frustration. Since the infant is still in a stage of dual unity, that is it oscillates between regarding itself part of a mother and as an independent human being, the very aggression by which it separates itself from the mother also rebounds in the form of talio anxiety against the child.[95] The father

---

[93] D. W. Winnicott, Primitive Emotional Development, *International Journal of Psycho-Analysis*, XXVI, 1945.
[94] Jules and Zunia Henry, *Doll Play of Pilaga Indian Children,* American Orthopsychiatric Association, 1944, pp. 91, 92.
[95] Cf. G. Róheim, *War, Crime and the Covenant,* Journal of Clinical Psychopathology Monograph Series, I, 1945, pp. 1-6 Cf. "Each new experience must either integrate with earlier experiences—or must partly displace the effects of earlier experiences so as to dominate them." "The old is for the most part dominant over the new." G. Murphy and L. B. Murphy and Th. W. Newcomb, *Experimental Social Psychology,* New York, Harper and Brothers, 1937, p. 167.

first steps into this dual unity situation as a stranger (this is the position to which all matrilineal societies regress) and then the introjection process is repeated. We will now call the Primal Horde myths quoted above simply oedipal myths and then it becomes all human why the "brothers" in these myths "eat" the father: because all human beings begin life in a symbiotic situation, that is they "eat" the mother.

If we re-think carefully what Freud himself has taught us about the sequence of anxieties in human beings, we must come to the same conclusion.

Freud regards separation anxiety, that is the state of being without the mother, as the primal form of all anxieties. Anxiety is a signal given by the ego to indicate helplessness with regard to inner needs.[96] At the next phase of development we have again a separation anxiety, for that is what castration anxiety means: the organ of reunion with the mother is in danger.[97] Since Freud, Bergler and Eidelberg have studied this phase in detail, their opinion is that the boy carries over libidinal cathexis from the maternal nipple to the penis.[98] After being separated from the maternal nipple the second danger is that of being separated from the penis, or castration.

It follows therefore that the oedipus complex is not created by society. It is evolved by the child itself. The separation anxiety of course corresponds to the preoedipal stage while the phallic or castration anxiety is the oedipal stage proper. We assume that the human psyche goes through a series of stages. After all the soma and the psyche cannot be completely separated from each other and if we are all first infants, then children, etc., till we grow to middle age and then decline, why should we not assume in the manner of Gesell and Ilg that the psyche goes through a similar series of unfolding and decaying?

I am quite aware of the fact that the soma and the psyche are not quite comparable. The psyche is much more dependent on external

---

[96] S. Freud, *Hemmung, Symptom und Angst,* Vienna, Int. Psa. Verlag, 1926, p. 82.

[97] Idem, *ibid.,* pp. 84, 85. Cf. also F. Alexander, The Castration Complex in the Formation of Character, *International Journal of Psycho-Analysis,* VI, 1923, and O. Fenichel, *The Psychoanalytic Theory of Neurosis,* New York, W. W. Norton, 1945, pp. 77, 276.

[98] E. Bergler and L. Eidelberg, Der Mammacomplex des Mannes. *Internationale Zeitschrift fuer Psychoanalyse,* XIX, 1933.

conditioning without which it would not develop at all and the many forms of which can, when viewed from a certain point of view, give us the *illusion of an infinite variability*. But this variability is not infinite, conditioning itself is not independent of the kind of animal we are and in the depths of the psyche, its growth course must somewhere converge with that of the body.

I have analyzed a patient who had a very dim memory of her father. The father died when the child was about two or three years old and he had been suffering from a brain tumor previously. Her mother and grandmother took care of her, and her mother did not have either another husband or another lover after the father's death. She had an elder brother who, however, was sickly and very neurotic so that the sister played the leading part in the family. Her brother became the prototype of her husband. So now you may ask, where is the oedipus complex? Among her cousins there were two, a brother and a sister about ten to fifteen years older than herself. These two were very close to each other and in her analyzed dreams they always played the role of a married couple. The female cousin whom we shall call Mary was the ideal. She had to grow up to be like Mary. But at the same time she hated Mary because Mary took John away from her. John was the man with whom she was in love. In conscious life this love took the form of a teacher-pupil relationship on a purely intellectual level. But unconsciously, as the analysis revealed, it was the real thing. She also had the typical oedipal transference relationship to the analyst and his wife.

What are the games that children play? One group in which they exercise motor skills; that is the functional pleasure of the skills mastered by the developing ego. The second group, the formalized games, are abreactions of the trauma of separation.[99] The third group, also practically universal, is "playing grown up". Little boys call each other "men" and they call the little girls they play with "women". The range of these imitative activities may vary from actual attempts at coitus to play-imitations of useful or ritual activities.

Psychoanalysis calls this process *introjection*. The young of our species grow up by a partial identification with adults which gradually becomes a complete identification. It is also the mechanism

---

[99] Cf. G. Róheim, Children's Games and Rhymes in Duau, *American Anthropologist*, XLV, 1943.

of transition from passivity to activity. A little girl who is afraid of the dentist has a doll and plays at being the dentist and pulling the doll's teeth. The mere fact that she has a doll is surely universal and indicates her play identification with the mother. The boys' activity games develop more on the phallic line, riding imaginary horses or throwing spears.

Now it is clear that in all these games the ideal for the girl is the mother. It is she whom the little girl wants to replace and the father is the most admirable of all men. Conversely the boy could never grow up if he did not pattern himself on an adult and the person whom he sees most frequently and who serves as an ego-ideal is the father.[100] This is the reason why I regard the oedipus complex as far more important for human development than sibling rivalry. Both have this feature in common that the father and the younger sibling break the chain of imaginary or real unity, the dual-unity of mother and child. But the difference is that the oedipus complex is the vehicle through which we grow up.

We do not need the Lamarckian hypothesis of the Primal Horde to explain the universality of the oedipus complex. Bolk's views on the retarded evolution or foetalization of mankind give us far more reliable biological background. As I have emphasized so often, the point that Bolk makes is not only that human childhood is prolonged but that it is never completely left behind.[101]

Huxley summarizes the views of Bolk and others as follows: "Judged by the law (which applies to most other mammals so far investigated) which regulates the amount of food consumed before the adult phase is reached, *man's immaturity has been lengthened some sevenfold*. This could not have occurred in a polytocous form. It was only after man's ancestors had ceased to have litters and bring forth a single young at a birth that the further evolution of man became possible.

"The typical adult human condition of hair on the head but almost complete absence of hair on the body is passed through as a temporary condition at about the time of birth by the anthropoid ape. The hymen of the human female has been stated to represent the

---

[100] It makes absolutely no difference whether this "father" is the real progenitor or not. The same is valid for the mother concept.
[101] L. Bolk, *Das Problem der Menschwerdung*, Jena, G. Fischer, 1926.

persistence of what in the lower mammals is an embryonic stage in the development of the urino-genital system. Most striking, the general form of the human face and skull with its absence of snout and of the bony ridges of the cranium is quite similar to the foetal or newborn ape but quite dissimilar to that of the adult."[102]

Later Huxley modifies this view with regard to the shape of the human skull and face. Quoting Weidenreich he comes to the conclusion that the transformation of the skull is a secondary feature depending upon brain growth. The brain's relative growth rate is high in early embryonic life, in most mammals it later slows down markedly and the high allometry of the face later comes into play. The shape of man's skull is due to the *persistence into later stages of the brain's early high relative growth rate.*[103] (My italics)

In other words we have according to this modification of the theory another and most important aspect of human nature: the size of the human brain, *explained on basis of a conservation of embryonic or early traits.*

Haldane, commenting on the time of action in genes in animal life, writes:

"Another common tendency has been retardation of certain characters relative to the life cycle so that originally embryonic characters persist in the adult. This is known as neoteny or sometimes as paedogenesis. In a neotenic animal such as man, many adult ancestral characters, e.g. the straightening out of the cranial flexure, do not occur."[104]

Neoteny, according to Haldane, can be due to accelerated maturity in some cases and general retardation of structural development *in relation to maturity* in others (e.g. man).[105] The words I have italicized contain the whole problem in a nutshell; man is relatively retarded, or putting the same thing in a different way, sexually precocious.

---

[102] Julian Huxley, *Evolution*, New York, Harper and Brothers, 1942, p. 526.
[103] F. Weidenreich, The Brain and its Role in the Phylogenetic Transformation of the Human Skull, *Transaction of the American Philosophical Society*, XXXI.
[104] I. B. S. Haldane, The Time Action of Genes and its Bearing on Some Evolutionary Problems, *The American Naturalist*, LXVI, 1932.
[105] Haldane, *op. cit.*, p. 19.

Since we have ample proof for maintaining Bolk's thesis that in mankind we have a species that has made certain infantile traits permanent we can also see that the human family is a consequence of this biological fact.

The adult male, being still a child, desires permanent dual unity with a new mother, i.e., the wife. Balint in a paper on "Eros und Aphrodite" suggested that object love in adult sex relationship is derived from the child-mother situation.[106] Miller writes in the *Journal of Mammalogy*: "Human-like association of male and female together with the psychological conditions which accompany it, seems to occur mostly in mammals whose young are born in a state which places difficulties in the way of their care by the female alone."[107]

While the biologist explains the co-existence of male, female and offspring purely on the basis of utility (Ferenczi called it *Nutzbiologie*), we may add the emotional point of view: in the human species the male stays with the female because of a tendency to conserve infantile traits.[108] Biologically the child is symbiotic with another human being, the mother. The adult in desiring a union of some duration with a woman is holding on to the infantile stage. The oral symbolism of the marriage tie shows that it is a repetition of a phase of life in which the oral communion is not symbolic, i.e., the child-mother situation.

The Kubu eat rice together, bride and groom mutually stuff a few morsels of rice into each other's mouth.[109] Milk and butter are first gifts by the young girl among the Va-nyenka.[110] Several monographs have been written about the role of commensality in the marriage ritual.[111] In Normandie they have a cake with a little Cupid figure

---

[106] A. Balint, Eros und Aphrodite, *Internationale Zeitschrift fuer Psychoanalyse*, XXII.

[107] Gerrit S. Miller, Some Elements of Sexual Behavior in Primates, *Journal of Mammalogy*, IX, 1928.

[108] Cf. H. Hartmann, Psychoanalytic Theory of Instinctual Drives, *Psychoanalytic Quarterly*, XVII, 1948.

[109] B. Hagen, *Die Orang Kubu auf Sumatra*, Veroeffentl. d. Staedt. Voelkermuseums Frankfurt a/M., II. 1908, p. 131.

[110] A. Lang and C. Tastevin, *La Tribu des Va-Nyaneka*, Mission Rohan Chabot V, 1938, p. 33.

[111] Cf. Hanns Baechtold, Die Gebraeuche bei Verlobung und Hochzeit, *Schriften der schweizerischen Gesellschaft fuer Volkskunde*, 11, 1914, pp. 105, 106. E. Westermarck, *Marriage Ceremonies in Morocco*, London, Macmillan, 1914, and literature quoted in P. Sartori, *Sitte und Brauch*. Handbuecher zur Volkskunde, Leipzig, Heims, 1911.

and a doll that represents the bride. In Languedoc the figures on the cake represent bride and groom.[112] Crawley is right when he asserts that eating together as a marriage ceremony means union, i.e., the two are to be one. In France:

"Boire, manger et coucher ensemble
C'est marriage ce me semble."[113]

At Santa Cruz a man calls his wife mother and she calls him son.[114] Fantan at Alor says:

"Wives are like our mothers. When we were small, our mothers fed us. When we are grown, our wives cook for us. If there is something good, they keep it in the pot until we come home. When we were small, we slept with our mothers, when we are grown up, we sleep with our wives. Sometimes when we are grown up, we wake at night and call our wives 'mother'."[115]

Sararerea, "eating together", is the Normanby Island name of a marriage ceremony and food presents and counter-presents between the two clans go on as long as the marriage continues. (Field notes.) In Hungarian the word for wife (feleseg) originally means "dear mother".[116] It seems that the ideal of the durability of marriage and the prolongation of infancy go together.[117] It follows that our delayed infancy or rather permanent infancy (neotenia, foetalization) must inevitably lead to a clash between the father and the offspring. From the child's point of view the father appears as an intruder, a stranger. Matrilineal societies like Normanby Island in which the father is called a stranger should be interpreted as having regressed to this phase of development.

In a case I noted while working on Normanby Island, a woman

---

[112] Arnold van Genep, *Manuel de Folklore Français Contemporain*, II, Paris, Picard et Cie., 1946, pp. 528, 529.

[113] E. Crawley, *The Mystic Rose*, London, Methuen and Co., 1927, II, p. 125. Quotes C. Di Fresne du Cange, *Glossarium mediae at infimae Latinitatis*, 1883-1887, under: Potare.

[114] W. H. H. Rivers, *History of Melanesian Society*, Cambridge University Press, 1914, I, p. 223.

[115] Cora du Bois, *The People of Alor*. Minneapolis, University of Minnesota Press, 1944, p. 96.

[116] Karjalainen, Wie "Ego" im Ostjakischen die Verwandten benennt, *Finnisch-Ugrische Forschungen*, XII, 1912.

[117] G. Róheim, Wandlungen und Urformen der Ehe, in M. Marcuse, *Die Ehe*, Berlin, Marcus und Webers Verlag, 1927.

was attacked by her husband because she gave too much attention to her baby. He burnt her vagina with a torch and she left him. A Japanese mother will turn to her husband and say to the child, "I like your father better than you. He is a nice man." The child gives full expression to his jealousy and tries to break in between father and mother.[118]

So far in discussing the oedipus complex we have regarded it simply as produced by the child itself as a growth phenomenon.

But marriage rites have shown that there is an "outside" aspect of the picture. Already in the preoedipal stage the "bad mother" is not purely the projection of the child's own aggression. Mothers are not as good as they are supposed to be.

In all the cases I have analyzed there were strong counter-currents to maternal love. I am not saying that these mothers did not love their children but what I mean is that they both loved and hated them. The sources for this ambivalence were manifold. First we have to consider the fact that we are never quite grown-up ourselves. In other words, every mother wants *to be* the baby. Next in order, if the baby is a girl, is the not unfounded notion that the little girl is a rival for her husband's love. Finally, as our life consists in a series of repetitions of childhood situations, the little girl represents the mother's mother and all the hatred she felt against her own mother now rebounds against her own child.

If the child is a boy the situation is different. The mother has now symbolically gratified her own desire to have a penis and has also a young lover plus a reincarnation of her father. The hostile currents in this case are mainly to be attributed to guilt feelings and of course to the factor mentioned above; the infant is still an infant and monopolizes much of the attention the adult would like to have.

With the father the situation is even less favorable for the offspring. There is no "paternal instinct" and the unconscious hatred is very strong. The father sees in the child a rival for his wife's love and a representative of his own oedipal guilt.

In the dreams of pregnant women I collected in Central Australia

---

[118] R. Benedict, *The Chrysanthemum and the Sword,* Boston, Houghton Mifflin, 1946, p. 262.

the child to be born would appear in the shape of the dreamer's mother or of a demon or a combination of both.[119]

The demons that threaten the child are projections either of the aggressive impulses of the mother or of those of the father. In connection with the mother-child relationship it is interesting that what we find in the demon-lore is exactly the *body-destruction fantasy* discovered by M. Klein as the archaic form of infantile aggression.

The Atharva Veda envokes Agni against the witch who is trying to kill the newborn infant.

The cursing sorceress: "Mayest thou burn, thou of the black footprint.

"She who cursed, cursing perpetrating evil deception. She who gets hold of our child to take its juices away.

"May her own child eat her."

In Austrian Silesia the nightmare demon sits on the child's breast, so that the breasts swell. The fluid that exudes from the breast in these cases is called "witches' milk".

The composite nature of this belief is interesting, for the infant who is attacked is really placed in the role of the mother. On the other hand in Masuria we are told that the steel put into the cradle is there to protect the child against the *"Erdmaennlein"*. These dwarves whose height is one span and who have a long beard are obviously phallic (paternal) symbols. They take the children out of the cradle and hide them in subterranean caves.

In Lotharingia the *Erdmaennlein* (earth-mannikin) sucks the child's breasts. Lillith, the typical "bad mother" of Jewish lore, *sucks* the child's blood and the marrow out of its bones. The Batak believe in a half-human, half-animal shaped being that kills children —but at the same time it cries like a child at night. The male and female beings in the clouds who according to the Papuans of Geelwinkbay kill children out of love clearly reflect the ambivalent emotions of the parents.[120] Various physical proceedings that are done to the children to improve their looks or for other rationalized purposes also indicate the hostility of the adults.[121]

---

[119] G. Róheim. Women and their Life in Central Australia, *Journal of the Royal Anthropological Institute,* 1934.
[120] Cf. H. Ploss and B. Renz, *Das Kind in Brauch und Sitte der Voelker.* Leipzig, Grieben, 1911, I. pp. 100-144.
[121] Ploss-Renz, *op. cit.,* Vol. II, Chapter XXXVII.

With regard to the famous couvade-customs there are three outstanding features: (a) the pretence that the father is the mother; (b) the pretence that the father is the infant; (c) the taboo against handling weapons or tools which might kill the child.[122]

It all amounts to one thing: fathers are dangerous, a pretence has to be made to deny their existence because they want to kill their children. In other words the oedipal or preoedipal ambivalence of the child is based not only on the aggressive impulses of the child but also on those of the parents.

The contrasting interests of the offspring and the male spouse are a biological reality. Levy writes: "The cleavage between sexual and maternal behavior is sharply demarcated in animals."[123]

Briffault writes: "There is thus opposition between the maternal and the sexual instinct." "The invariable tendency of the female is to segregate herself and form an isolated group with her offspring. The more prolonged the immaturity of the offspring the longer and more complete will be the segregation of the maternal group."[124]

Yerkes tells us about the chimpanzee mother: "As soon as the infant has emerged from her body the experienced mother . . . . gives her attention chiefly to it. She places it on her abdomen and breast and lets it cling to her. From time to time she handles it gently and freely moves it about . . . . By contrast the inexperienced mother isolated from adult companions at the time of parturition may act as if afraid of her firstborn and refuse to touch or allow it to cling to her.

"The role of the chimpanzee father in reproduction appears to be limited to mating. He has no part in the process of birth, nor is he permitted to care for the infant during its dependent stage of development . . . . It has been reported to certain observers that sexual intercourse may occur during pregnancy. This seems to be contradicted by reliable observations which definitely indicate that sexual receptivity and oestrus ordinarily do not occur during pregnancy and

---

[122] Ploss-Renz, *op. cit.*, Vol. I, Chapter X.
[123] D. M. Levy, *Maternal Overprotection*, New York, Columbia University Press, 1943, p. 139.
[124] R. Briffault, *The Mothers*, London, G. Allen and Unwin, 1927, I, p. 187.

that if the female accepts the male it is either in self-defence or to guard against injury.[125]

"The primate father apparently has little to do with his children beyond the occasional help that he may extend to any infant or juvenile of the group which may be in difficulty or danger. Savage males may indeed be an active menace to infants closely associated with their mothers, when the male makes a sexual attack upon the oestrous female. Zuckerman records instances in which baboon males have killed infants under such circumstances, whether their own or not . . . . ordinarily it has been the practice in zoological gardens to separate the male from the pregnant female or to remove the father after the birth."[126]

Pregnant women whom I have analyzed have always withdrawn their libido from their husband and concentrated all interest in a narcissistic cathexis of their own body.

Helene Deutsch writes: "Even in pregnancy women psychically prepare for motherhood by giving up all their emotional interests for the sake of the idea of the child and thus create the soil for instinctive, altruistic devotion to the real child."[127]

The taboos on intercourse in the pregnancy period or after pregnancy among primitive people are well known. At Lesu intercourse is taboo during pregnancy and the nursing period. One man said he did not want his wife to have children because of the restraint it put on his sexual life.[128] That a man should not have intercourse with his wife during her pregnancy is a rather widespread taboo, but in Celebes we find even tribes where he is forbidden to have intercourse with other women.[129]

---

[125] Robert M. Yerkes, *Chimpanzees, a Laboratory Colony*, Yale University Press, 1943, pp. 67, 68.

[126] Ernest Horton, *Man's Poor Relations*, New York, Doubleday Doran, 1942, pp. 330, 331.

[127] H. Deutsch, *The Psychology of Women*, New York, Grune & Stratton, 1945, II, p. 153.

[128] H. Powdermaker, *Life in Lesu*, New York, W. W. Norton, 1933, p. 243.

[129] H. Ploss and M. Bartels, *Das Weib*, Leipzig, Grieben, 1908, I, p. 929. Cl. St. Ford, *A Comparative Study of Human Reproduction*, Yale University Press, 1945, pp. 80, 81. A more detailed discussion of the whole subject cannot be given in this context.

Another reason for assuming the universality of the oedipus complex is the preoedipal background.[130] Nobody will deny that ambivalence is a factor in the child-mother situation. The role of the "bad mother" is taken over by the father who invades the dual-unity situation.[131] *The dual unity of the mother and child and the dual unity of the father and mother in the primal scene tend to overlap in myth and fantasy.*

A patient reports his reaction to seeing cats cohabiting on the street. "I felt revolted and afraid. I could not look. I imagined the tom-cat was tearing the female into two pieces. But I also thought it was like eating one's own mucus." Note the *separation* in the first fantasy and the cancelling of the separation or *reunion* in the second. The fantasies follow closely the well-nigh universal pattern of ritual[132] and are not dependent on any kind of social conditioning. Another patient tells me that between the age of one and two she held on tightly to her mother even while father and mother were actually having intercourse.[133] In mythologies that start with the *separation* motive I assume that these two meanings are condensed in one scene.

The Matuntara say the Waura (a kind of lizard called Mangurkunjerkunja by the Aranda) formed the first human beings who were "stuck together" (ngaluru-punguta). These beings defecated through the pores of their hand and wiped the faeces with their eye. Anus, urethra, and mouth were closed. Waura made the penis pulling it out of the human body and put a kunu (pointing bone) into it and made also the hole for urinating. He opened the woman with a stone knife but only in so far as to make her able to urinate. Then he said to the man, you have intercourse with her and make it bigger. The Pindupi and other groups around Ilpila call this lizard Pupula and say he made the first tukutitas out of the *ngaluru-punguta*, i.e., stuck together beings. Their body was quite smooth and flat, he cut the fingers, made the joints, etc. He told them how to split wood to make a fire and gave them their marriage laws.

The phallic lizard is acting so far as the principle that sep-

---

[130] Discussed already from a clinical point of view above.
[131] L. Rotter Kertesz, Der tiefenpsychologische Hintergrund der incestuösen Fixierung, *Internationale Zeitschrift fuer Psychoanalyse*, XXII, 1936.
[132] G. Róheim, Transition Rites, *Psychoanalytic Quarterly*, XI.
[133] This is according to what her parents told her.

OEDIPUS COMPLEX, MAGIC AND CULTURE 213

arates.[134] He must have been also the one to separate sky and earth because according to a fragmentary Aranda belief if anyone were to kill this lizard the sky would fall down on the earth.[135] World separation myths and myths of an individual who starts by being one and is then cleft in twain are essentially identical.

This is the Maori version of things primeval:

Rangi and Rapa were the source from which all things originated. Darkness then rested upon the heaven and upon the earth and they still both cleave together for they had not been rent apart. Their sons decide to rend them apart, so there should be light. "Lo he pauses, his head is now firmly planted on his mother, the earth, his feet he raises up and rests against his father, the sky, he strains his back and limbs with mighty effort. Now are rent apart Rangi and Rapa and with cries and groans of woe they shriek aloud.

"Wherefore slay you thus your parents? Why commit you so dreadful a crime as to slay us, as to rend your parents apart?"[136]

In Hawaii the myth is told as follows. Maui came to a woman and said:

"Give me a drink from your gourd calabash and I will push the heavens higher."[137]

The hero-son who separates father and mother can accomplish this deed when reinforced by the drink his mother gives him.

The oral and the visual appear in all these myths because the object is found through the eye and the mouth and it is through these same organs that the object is also re-introjected. In another Polynesian origin myth the beginning is explained through the fission of one being (instead of through the separation of two) and the result of the separation is Light.

In the depths of Avaiki lives a woman demon called "the Very-beginning". Such is the narrowness of her territory that her knees and chin touch, no other position is possible. She was anxious for progeny and she therefore plucked off a bit of her right side and it

---

[134] Cf. for further ramifications of the lizard theme G. Róheim, *The Eternal Ones of the Dream*, pp. 200, 201.
[135] W. Planert, Aranda Grammatik, *Zeitschrift fuer Ethnologie*, 1907.
[136] G. Grey, *Polynesian Mythology and Ancient Traditional History of the New Zealand Race*, 1858, pp. 3, 4.
[137] W. D. Westervelt, *Legends of Maui, a Demi God of Polynesia*, Honolulu, 1910, p. 32.

came a human being, Avatea, a word that means *noon*. He was half fish and half man.[138]

The original being is of great interest since the Great Mother is also—judging from the position—the embryo in the womb. The following description of fission is therefore simply the cosmic projection of birth.

When born, man sees the light, therefore the first being is Noon. *Avatea* in Maori is broad daylight, in Samoan *atatea* is wide, spacious and *oatea* is noon.[139] From this birth myth the transition to the oedipus myth is quite direct. Vatea dreams of a woman whom he finally finds and she becomes his wife. Her name is Papa[140], i.e., the Mother Earth of the Maori myth.

In the Greek myth of Hesiod, Kronos, after having separated Heaven and Earth by castrating his father Uranos, eats all his sons to prevent them from ousting him from his kingdom till finally he is tricked into swallowing a stone and Zeus survives to take his place.[141] The child who "eats" the mother becomes the father who eats the child.

The point I am trying to make is that the oedipal situation develops inevitably, not as a repetition of a phylogenetic pattern but from the preoedipal situation, as a reaction of the child to the intervening stranger. In the Platonic myth quoted by Freud the idea of three sexes, male, female and androgynous might be interpreted as the child in the primal scene situation between father and mother (androgynous) while the idea of a separation that follows represents both the son's desire to separate father and mother and the involuntary separation of the son from the mother.

An overdetermination of the myth is assumed or added to the hypothesis in *Beyond the Pleasure Principle*.[142]

In Marduk's Struggle with Tiamat the body of Tiamat who is a woman is cleft asunder forming Heaven and Earth. This act of the slaying of Tiamat is also conceived as the consummation of Marduk's

---

[138] W. W. Gill, *Myths and Songs from the South Pacific,* London, Henry S. King and Co., 1876, pp. 3, 4.
[139] E. Tregear, *The Maori Polynesian Comparative Dictionary,* Wellington, Whitcombe and Tombs, n.d.
[140] W. W. Gill, *op. cit.,* pp. 7, 8.
[141] *Roschers Lexikon,* article "Kronos."
[142] S. Freud, *Beyond the Pleasure Principle,* London, Hogarth, 1948.

marriage with the dragon-woman.[143] He splits her into two parts and with half of her he makes the heavens.[144] In the Sumerian version the abduction of a woman takes place after Heaven and Earth have been separated.[145]

From the child's point of view the myth is both a trauma and a wish. A trauma because Marduk, i.e. father, separates the child from the mother. A wish because the son Marduk separates father from mother.

In the mythology of the Lengua Indians (Gran Chace) the beetle as creator first forms supernatural beings who rule the earth. Then he forms man and woman, but joined together like Siamese twins. The spirits persecuted them so the beetle separated them that they might have the power to propagate their species and multiply.[146] In this myth it is really son and mother who are first united and then liberated to have intercourse against the will of the father.

Separation, coitus and the origin of light are interlocked in these myths. As I have pointed out many times the oedipus complex is really focused around the primal scene—or fantasies of the primal scene.[147] Fenichel writes:

"First the child perceives the primal scene, then it identifies with father or perhaps the two mean the same thing since seeing is originally libidinal.[148] The point is that seeing and eating carry over from the preoedipal to the oedipal phase. The all-seeing eye of the superego is first the eye of the child who has been observing the parent[149]", i.e., the oedipal superego is the introjection of the primal scene.[150] From one point of view we might therefore say that the

---

[143] W. A. Heidel, *The Day of Yahweh*, American Historical Association, 1929, pp. 413, 414.

[144] St. H. Langdon, Semitic, in: *Mythology of All Races*, Boston, 1931, p. 303.

[145] S. N. Kramer, *Sumerian Mythology*, American Philosophical Society, 1944, p. 79.

[146] W. Barbrooke Grubb, *An Unknown People in an Unknown Land*, London, Leeley and Co., 1911, pp. 114, 115.

[147] Cf. especially G. Róheim, *The Riddle of the Sphinx*, London, Hogarth, 1934.

[148] O. Fenichel, Schautrieb und Identifizierung. *Int. Zeitschrift fuer Psychoanalyse*, XXI.

[149] Fenichel, *loc. cit.* The primal scene is interpreted as a mutual act of suckling. Cf. Ruth Mac Brunswick, The Praeoedipal Phase of the Libido Development, *Psychoanalytic Quarterly*, IX.

[150] G. Róheim, *The Riddle of the Sphinx*, 1934, p. 283.

clash between the child and the father is inevitable because the adult is still a child. From another point of view we might add that the clash is inevitable because the child is already an adult. On the primate level sexuality has become non-functional, that is it appears long before its biological function can be fulfilled. Infantile, or as the zoologists say non-functional, sexuality is one of Freud's great discoveries. Zuckerman and others have shown extensive sexual play of juvenile primates.[151] Bolk emphasizes that while man develops slowly as far as the body is concerned the germ plasm develops too quickly, that is we have a premature incidence of sexuality.[152] The premature incidence of sexuality[153] like the prolongation of infancy[154] is also not new in the course of evolution but both these traits are more marked in man than in any other species. Bingham observes in apes that like with human infants copulatory action starts with mouthing behavior.[155] Human beings have an oedipus complex simply because we want to be adults when we are children and want to be children when we are adults.[156] Mankind, as Horace would say, is both *cupidus rerum novarum* and *laudator temporis acti.*

Fenichel writes: "It was no innate mystical oedipus complex that created the family as a place where it might be satisfied: *it was the family that created the oedipus complex.* (My italics.) In the second place the answer depends on the definition of the oedipus complex. The human infant is biologically more helpless than other mammalian children. He needs care and love. Therefore he will always ask for love from nursing and protecting adults around him and develop hate and jealousy of persons who take this love away from him. If this is called oedipus complex, the oedipus complex is biologically founded.

"However, Freud uses this term in a stricter sense: it signifies

---

[151] S. Zuckerman, *The Social Life of the Monkeys and Apes,* New York, Harcourt Brace, 1932.
[152] L. Bolk, *Das Problem der Menschwerdung,* 1926, pp. 23-25.
[153] Cf. G. H. Seward, *Sex and the Social Order,* New York, McGraw Hill, 1946, pp. 69, 70.
[154] R. Briffault, *The Mothers,* London, Allen and Unwin, 1926, I, p. 96.
[155] H. Bingham, *Sex Development in Apes,* Baltimore, Comparative Psychology Monographs, V, p. 100. Cf. p. 114, Non-reproductive Sexual Behavior.
[156] Cf. G. Róheim. The Divine Child, *Journal of Clinical Psychology.* IX.

the combination of genital love for the parent of the opposite sex and jealous death wishes for the parent of the same sex, a highly integrated combination of emotional attitudes which is the climax of the long development of infantile sexuality. In this sense the oedipus complex is undoubtedly the product of family influence. If the institution of the family were to change, the pattern of the oedipus complex would necessarily change also. It has been shown that societies with family configurations different from our own actually have different oedipus complexes. Efforts to explain different family configurations as 'repressions of the oedipus complex' seem to have failed."[157]

There are of course *specific preconscious reasons that explain why Fenichel comes to such a conclusion.* Malinowski has not shown that the Trobriand Islanders have a different family configuration; if we look closely at what he says, it is quite clear that the situation is the same. Moreover the substitution of the uncle for the father can only be accepted if we do not distinguish the conscious from the unconscious. How is it that a psychoanalyst accepts Malinowski's naive assumptions and fails to make this distinction? Is it the fond hope of mankind that like the famous Baron Muenchhausen it can pull itself out of a swamp by its own pigtail, that it can create a totally different kind of mankind by decreeing a different society? It is difficult to renounce this survival of infantile omnipotence.

The anthropologist Marvin K. Opler is less cautious than the psychoanalyst. He is very pleased that Malinowski has exorcised the demon for us all.

"If the oedipus complex were found universally then indeed a constant was found in society which acted regularly throughout history and was perhaps basic to its processes. Fortunately (sic!!) for history and social science this hegemony of the psychological was never proven. In one of the best full-length accounts of a society, Malinowski found that human nature did not conform to the dead level uniformity suggested by Freud in his *Totem and Taboo*. For one thing, the social organization of the Trobriands which Malinowski investigated made oedipus impossible because the father in this

---

[157] O. Fenichel, *The Psychoanalytic Theory of Neurosis*, 1945, p. 97. Fenichel quotes Malinowski's paper (quoted above) and Ernest Jones, Mother Right and the Sexual Ignorance of the Savages, *International Journal of Psycho-Analysis*, VI, 1924.

society occupied a place quite different from the authoritarian role of the male parent in western European households."[158]

The existence of the oedipus complex has nothing to do with the question of mild or harsh fathers. What Fenichel really means by different oedipus complexes is simply this: The life of one adult is not the same as the life of another—and neither is the life of one child the same as the life of the other. This pressure of reality combined with the fantasy systems of the child results in various techniques for dealing with the oedipus complex. In other words, everybody has a face but we are justified in saying that no two faces are exactly the same.

The human psyche is a continuous process. If psychoanalysis has discovered anything, it has discovered that the child is still present in the man. We have never quite outgrown our delayed infancy. How Fromm and Kardiner and other anti-Freudians[159] can continue to assert in the face of everyday analytic experience that the "harsh father" is the basic cause of the oedipus complex, is more than I can understand. I have analyzed many cases in which the father was a very mild person who never interfered with what his son did—and even cases in which there was free sex play with other children—and that made no difference whatever as far as the oedipus complex was concerned. As Klein observed in the discussion of my paper, these authors are behaving exactly like our patients who are trying to repress their oedipal guilt regarding their libidinal desire for their mother and blame it all on the severity of the father.

However, it is possible that we have here a question in semantics. Maybe some authors regard an oedipus complex only as such when it is *pathogenic*, others only when it manifests itself in social form, i.e., when it is *sociological*. But what I am talking about is *psychological*, the oedipus complex as a necessary phase of our growing up. Lest those ardent believers in differences be again shocked I hasten to add that this does not mean that all human beings are the same. There are many ways of dealing with the oedipus complex. In some societies we find an almost open avowal of oedipal rivalry (Mundu gumor)[160]; others deal with it by denying male aggression, or by

---

[158] M. E. Opler, The Psychoanalytic Treatment of Culture. *Psychoanalytic Review*, XXII, 1935.
[159] The appellation neo-Freudians is misplaced.
[160] M. Mead, *Sex and Temperament in Three Primitive Societies*, New York, William Morrow, 1935, Part II.

denying the connection with the father, or by projection in war and in many other ways. As we have said before, the human psyche is a continuous process. Our delayed infancy is caused by certain biological factors. In the psyche it manifests itself in the make-believe or play phase of our life which is the human way of preparing for adult adjustment to reality. Karl Groos in his two volumes on play writes about the imitative and the preparatory function of playing.[161] In this sense we can clearly see the inevitable teleological function of the oedipus complex: in the mother we have the forerunner of all the goals we wish to achieve, in the father the prototype of all the opponents that will face us in adult life.

Magic and the Primary Process

In a book I have had in preparation now for several years I define magic as based on three trends.

(1) Libido (and aggression) is primarily mobilized against the superego (cf. masturbation in anxiety situations, too frequent coitus). If the difference between the introject and the external world is disregarded *this is magic* (intrapsychic efficacity projected to environment).

(2) The subject forms an introject and plays the role of some other person (Shaman and the god who possesses him). This is the inevitable process of growing up, the "magical" aim is to influence environment by a modification in personality. Magic in this case is more or less valid.

(3) Every change that takes place in the subject is followed by a corresponding change in the world outside.

(4) The severed part is regarded as still connected with the whole, i.e., the child with the mother, and the symbol is equal to whatever it symbolizes.

Frazer who in my opinion is still the "Keeper of the Golden Bough", after discussing the great differences that separate one human group from the other, writes: "Yet, when we have penetrated these differences which affect mainly the intelligent and thoughtful part of the community, we shall find underlying them all a solid stratum of intellectual agreement among the dull, the weak, the ignorant, and

---

[161] K. Groos, *Die Spiele der Menschen*, Jena, G. Fischer, 1899. Idem, *Die Spiele der Tiere*, Jena, G. Fischer, 1907.

the superstitious who constitute unfortunately the vast majority of mankind. One of the great achievements of the nineteenth century was to run shafts down into this low mental stratum in many parts of the world and thus to discover the substantial identity everywhere. It is beneath our feet—and not very far beneath them—here in Europe at the present day and it crops up on the surface in the heart of the Australian wilderness and wherever the advent of a higher civilization has not crushed it under ground. This universal faith, this truly catholic creed, is a belief in the efficacy of magic. While religious systems differ not only in different countries but in the same country in different ages, the system of sympathetic magic remains everywhere and at all times substantially alike in its principles and practice. . . . If the test of truth lay in a show of hands or a counting of heads the system of magic might appeal with far more reason than the Catholic church to the proud motto, *Quod semper, quod ubique, quod ab omnibus*, as the sure and certain credential of its own infallibility."[162]

Frazer underestimates the extent of his realm of magic, it extends not only to every country but also to each and every individual, *it is that which we are made of.*

A patient tells me that he is astonished at his bank balance. He has much more than he thought he had. When he is depressed he always believes that he has very little money in the bank or none and when elated he is a millionaire. He also acts according to these moods without confronting them with reality.

Another patient tells me that her cousins, a boy and a girl in their twenties, will ask their parents from time to time to have intercourse. They have noticed that after this event there are always more customers in the store—a clear case of the sacred marriage of god and goddess (father and mother) to promote the fertility of the fields. Thus sleeps the great Kronides with his divine consort Hera on the peak of Trojan Ide.

> So Kronos son, and clasped his bride to his breast
> Beneath them Earth divine made grass to grow
> New-nurtured and the dewy lotus-bloom
> Crocus and hyacinth thick and soft withal
> Which raised them from the ground thereon they lay

---

[162] J. G. Frazer, *The Magic Art and the Evolution of Kings*, London, Macmillan, 1911, I. pp. 235, 236.

And o'er them spread a cloud magnificent
And golden, glittering dew drops from it fell
Thus slumbered still the Sire on Gargaros height
Vanquished by sleep and love, his wife in his arms.[163]

N. N. comes to be analyzed because of an anxiety symptom. Especially at night he gets the idea that he will not be able to breathe and must die. So he draws a very deep breath, but the more he does this, the more he gets the feeling that he cannot go on with it and he must die. One thing aggravates the symptom and one thing relieves it. If he has gastric troubles after drinking a lot of beer it is worse. He feels a pressure from the inside and a pressure from the outside. The symptom is relieved if he gets up. He feels still better if he runs about in the room and finally if that does not help he leaves the house.

In professional circles and among his friends he is known as an extreme perfectionist. Everything connected with him has to be absolutely perfect. First his work; as a medical administrator he is as near to perfection as is humanly possible. He is an obsessional chief and the employees in his department make fun of his dictatorship. Another characteristic feature of his personality amounts to an addiction. If he is not buying a new car (most of the time he is or at least talking about it) he is adding some small technical device to the car he has. If by the time he gets the gadgets a new gadget of the same category (which may be an improvement on his or not) is on the market, he feels hopelessly gypped. The same applies to his radio, his camera, the vacuum cleaner and everything else. Moreover, whatever he orders must be brand new. If there is a scratch on the surface of any object he receives from the factory, or on the cover or lid or a box or a button, he returns the whole thing. If the store compels him to accept with any of these drawbacks he gets a depression.

The third sphere of his perfectionism is his son, a nice and very intelligent little boy of three. The father loves him very much and the child is attached to his father. Yet there is always trouble. The father is always pushing him on and expecting him to accomplish things that are far beyond his age level. He is deeply depressed if the boy promises to do something and then is too afraid to do it (for

---

[163] *Iliad,* XIV, pp. 346 ff. A. B. Cook, *Zeus, a Study in Ancient Religion,* Cambridge University Press, 1914, I p. 154. III, 1940, pp. 1025-1066, Hieros Gamos.

instance, riding a bicycle). No son of his should break his promise or be afraid of anything. Like his work, his car and his son are symbols of his perfectionism.

The fourth symbol of perfection should be his wife, but there things went really badly. She wears the wrong dresses, gives him the wrong kind of food, even uses the wrong expressions. All these trifles are sufficient reasons for him to fly into a terrific rage and threaten instant divorce. He upholds his patriarchal superiority in the family circle in a manner that is sometimes positively medieval.

His father and mother came to this country when he was two years old. The father had been a cavalry officer in his native land. Here he went into business, made a lot of money, and gave his son the best possible education. The patient himself was a brilliant student, always successful in his work, in his social contacts and in his love affairs. His sex life evolved normally. First prostitutes, then girl friends of his own social class. At the age of twenty-two he fell in love with a girl who refused to become his mistress but consented to be his wife. The parents would not hear of the marriage. He was ready to break with them and earn his own living. However, she unexpectedly changed her mind and married another man. The result was a complete breakdown; he could not bear failure. He failed in his profession. Thereupon the father refused to send him his monthly allowance and he refused to go home. He worked through university, made good what he had lost in his profession and regained his standing with his father. At this period his personality underwent a change—the object-seeking genital trend was weakened and anal-sadistic traits were reinforced. He had mistresses but was not in love with them. He became meticulously exact in his work and about all the details in life.

Love came back into his life a few years later. This was an affair with a widow who was nearly his mother's age. This affair lasted a long time and left nothing but happy memories. Finally they separated because he had to go to another city and because marriage would have been impossible anyway—the difference in age was too great. But she always remained the great love of his life and was always held up as the ideal woman to all her successors.

The analysis revolved around the castration complex. This perfectionism was a gigantic and mostly successful attempt to deny his castration anxiety. His car or camera or radio represented his penis and getting always the best and latest model meant that there was nothing wrong with his penis. The usual expression in describing case material *is that something meant something.* But if we look at it more closely we see that the expression is inadequate. *If his car is perfect his penis will be perfect.* By buying always better cars he is performing magic to maintain his penis in perpetual erection. Therefore if some minor detail on the car is not of the very best, if there is a scratch on the surface of any of his gadgets the magic must fail since it is being performed with a castrated penis symbol.

Symbolism and magic go together and we suspect that in every symptom, perhaps in every personality development there is a significant element of magic.[164]

The penis symbolism was quite clearly the decisive factor as far as the patient's son was concerned. After the child's circumcision he imagined that there was a minute scar on the surface of the penis. Something had gone wrong with the operation. Well, now his whole pleasure in his son was spoiled. The son might as well be dead. This lasted for a short time, then he returned to his usual attitude. If a daughter had been born instead of a son that would have been an inconceivable catastrophe. In the course of the analysis this catastrophe actually happened and the result was a series of vivid castration dreams.

Finally there was the situation with his wife. He chose a woman of masculine type and spent most of his time protesting against her masculinity. All the details he objected to, however, meant the exact opposite. He was afraid because she had a vagina and this meant castration anxiety. The qualities he missed in her really meant that she had no penis and therefore did not help him in his magical system of warding off impotence and castration anxiety.

To say that he was performing magic all the time is only one side of the picture. The other was his father. He declares that the reason why he had to be so perfect was because only by winning scholarships and distinguishing himself in his profession he could exercise a moral pressure on his father to send him money. The real reason, however, was that all this perfection or magic was a shield to protect his penis and the person who was threatening his penis was his father. A dream in which he was doing a flying stunt like Super-Man to win the love of a girl who, however, unaccountably preferred a rather in-

---

[164] Cf. also Ch. Odier, *L'angoisse et la pensée magique,* Neuchâtel et Paris, Delachaux et Niestlé, 1947.

significant looking old man, tells the whole story: the old man is his father and the superego, the flying his erection magic. Some of his dreams will give us further insight into this war between the superego and the id.

Dream 1

Suddenly he finds that he has a new creditor or rather an old creditor whom he had completely forgotten. This is a watch-maker in New Orleans who had given him some jewelry.

Associations

He is expecting the check from his father to pay for the analysis. It ought to have arrived that day. Moreover, the watch-maker reminds him of his father's profession and of time. This means the date for payment in the analysis and reminds him of Kronos who eats his children. The jewels remind him of the Mother of the Gracchi, her jewels are her children. What he owes his father is his life, the fact that he did not kill him like Kronos, and he also owes him the jewels, the faculty to procreate children.

He has the breathing trouble again because he was getting worried about the check. Stretching his arms helps him against the breathing trouble. Stretching his arms reminds him of prayer and the breathing symptom originated when he was about four or five and had to say his prayers. He had to say a short prayer in the presence of his mother every evening. He did not understand the Hebrew text and used to recite it in a great hurry. While doing this he would get the breathing symptom and start turning blue in his face. Mother would be alarmed, stop the praying ritual, rush him out of the house and give him an ice-cream soda.

Why the anxiety when he was praying? Analysis reveals that he must have felt guilty about masturbation. When he is praying, that is, talking to God, he is taking a great risk. God, who is supposed to know and see everything, will cut his penis off for having masturbated.

The next dream bears on the subject of perfection.

Dream 2

(1) Two R.C.A. record players in the back of a Sedan; he sees them through a window and thinks they are not up to much.

(2) Two Gerard players (better quality) and a beautiful woman showing them in a room.

(3) One record player, Gerard, with seven or eight records and one single unit. It is in a cabinet which does not open on the top, but on the side like a vagina. It is a woman with brown hair parted in the middle and she shows it to him with an all-knowing air.

Inside, there is a kind of hook that holds the records and brings a new record down when one is played out.

Associations

The arrangement with the seven or eight records and the single unit would be perfect because intervals would be cut out and he would have to do the changing only after seven or eight records and while he is doing it a single unit plays. The main thing in this is *that the music is perpetual* and he does not have to touch it.

The hook or peg reminds him of the boast of his youth—*the sun never sets on the British flag*—meaning that his penis is in perpetual erection. Each record or music means a new woman. The woman with the brown hair he associates with the memory of the black vagina. Somewhere he saw a woman urinating, what he actually remembers is something black, the pubic hair. He must have been between three and five and he remembers both fear, desire and curiosity. The brown-haired woman also reminds him of his mother.

The two record players of inferior quality in the first scene above the seat, are the breast. He plays with his wife's breasts and this way he can cause uterine contractions. This gives him great pleasure, a proof of his omnipotence.

Interpretation

In his unconscious the woman whose vagina he saw and his own mother are one person. Mother shows him her vagina, he is not afraid. His penis (the hook) is in her vagina and keeps playing new records. The seven or eight players with one unit means a continuous pleasure (*Dauerlust*) without having to use his hands, that is, evading the masturbation taboo.

The inside of the cabinet is the inside of the womb, the perpetual pleasure is both a perpetual erection and the intrauterine situation. When I say this, he reacts with a fit of anxiety and increased difficulty in breathing. He had fantasies of drowning. Next day he declares that his wife is masturbating and he is convinced of the old belief that whatever she touches whithers.

The erection magic is a defense against castration anxiety.

Dream 3

He is on trial with a huge erect penis. His mother is there and two men of his own age.

The two men of his own age are the sons of his former mistress.

He is again on trial, there are candles, a garden, and a funeral.

Associations

The garden is like his home, the candles remind him of Catholicism, it is probably the funeral of Father Coughlin whom he has killed and that is why he is on trial.

He talks about a Negro nurse who took him to a Catholic church, made the sign of the cross on him with holy water and dealt in Voodoo, and hung some charms on his neck. He identifies this colored nurse with the image of the black vagina that frightened him. Other associations lead to the topic of masturbation and to the nurse doing something to him that the parents were not supposed to know. I conjecture that she must have masturbated him, her magic was that she could make him have an erection. Now he has the same power, he can erect his penis whenever he wants to. Father Coughlin in the dream, of course, represents his own father. The two dreams are fragments of one picture, i.e., he is on trial for his oedipal desires (erection, mother, father's death).

Dream 4

He and some other doctors are experimenting in the magical control of savages.

Dr. N. has a magical gold plate on his arm. This is the source of his magical power.

Associations

Dr. N. is his senior (equals father). The gold plate equals the Holy Grail, a dish full of rubies. His wife is menstruating. Another chain of associations leads to his mother's name.

Father owns mother's vagina, hence his power, the source of the power is the vagina.

The perfectionism was consciously organized with reference to his father. As long as he was eminent in his profession, his father could never deny him money. But if he failed his father had the upper hand. The whole perfectionalism was phallic "erection magic" extended to life and personality in general. An ever erect penis means the defeat of the superego, he is not castrated.

We might add that all this does not explain the claustrophobic aspect of the symptom. Perhaps it is not only the fact that mother rushed him out of the room when he developed the breathing symptom that conditions the rushing out later. He is alone in a room with his mother and he is talking to God, i.e. to father. God must know that he masturbates but also the unconscious oedipal content of his masturbation fantasy. Being in a room alone with mother means having intercourse with mother. But here we are reminded of some other facts and theories. A room in dreams symbolizes the womb—and we might say with Ferenczi that coitus with mother also means a return to the womb.[165] We are then reminded of another assumption made by Ferenczi viz., that the basic element of our omnipotence fantasies is the omnipotence of the embryo.[166]

Let us here translate omnipotence into something easier to comprehend, i.e., the absence of frustration. But here we will not follow Ferenczi any further in the thalassal theory but substitute something more tangible for it. Haldane assumes that "whenever the embryo is well adapted to its surroundings and can go on growing with relatively slight danger, there will be a tendency to prolong the embryonic phase." Examples may be found in the human embryo which rarely suffers from twin competition and "in a savage country may well be safer than the newborn baby."[167] As Huxley remarks, the prolonged intra-uterine period is one of the features that determine the uniqueness of man; it could never have occurred in a species that produced many young at a time because intra-uterine competition would have promoted the opposite tendency.[168] We know that mankind really tends to recreate the intra-uterine situation in many forms, both psychological and factual (introjection, house, town, country). Fundamentally we are all intolerant of suspense and expect an im-

---

[165] S. Ferenczi, *Versuch einer Genitaltheorie*, 1922. On Claustrophobia and the Womb. Bertram D. Lewin, Claustrophobia. *Psychoanalytic Quarterly*, IV. S. Feldman, On the Fear of Being Buried Alive, *Psychoanalytic Quarterly*, 1942.

[166] S. Ferenczi, Entwicklungsstufen des Wirklichkeitssinnes, *Int. Zeitschrift fuer Psychoanalyse* I, 1913.

[167] J. B. S. Haldane, The Time of Action of Genes, *The American Naturalist*, LXVI, 1932.

[168] J. Huxley, *The Uniqueness of Man*, London, Chatto and Windus, 1941, p. 14.

mediate fulfillment of our wishes. This slowing down of the stages of existence in which we are protected (intra-uterine and childhood) explains why man is eternally disillusioned and also why he never loses his faith in himself, the alpha and omega of magic and personality. Neurosis is frequently the magic of crying, i.e. when a child cries the mother will come to the rescue. The magical principle of the severed part as equal to the whole is also based on the original dual-unity situation, the child is still part of the mother.

In all other cases it can be shown that we act according to the *magical principle* that is the never quite outgrown belief that the external world is subject to our moods. The magical principle that I postulate is a transition from the pleasure principle pure and simple to the reality principle. Since we live in a society and our moods influence our immediate environment the magical principle is only partly unrealistic. Now of course it is perfectly justified to ask why in one culture the idea of magic is out in the open and why in the other it is latent. We can also try to find out the exact sociological significance of magic and many other questions relating to differences can be asked in this connection. But to say that this and only this is anthropology *is to make anthropology subservient to certain emotional and cultural trends of our times.* A similar situation was openly expressed in the Middle Ages: *Philosophia ancilla theologiae.*

The postulate of modern anthropology that a culture should be explained in its own terms is the same thing as saying that the patients' rationalizations should be accepted and no further interpretation should be attempted. There are still some people who believe that the *"proper study of mankind is man"*, and not only national differences. In this paper I intended to show: that modern anthropologists have a definite scotomization of the oedipus complex; that the assumption of the universality of the oedipus complex does not necessarily imply the theory of the inheritance of acquired characters (Primal Horde theory); that Bolk's views on human foetalization definitely imply the universality of the oedipus complex; that the assumption of a universal oedipus complex does not mean that all human beings go through the same childhood experience and does not mean the denial of differences that are characteristic of certain groups; that the principle of magic as a transition phase from the primary process to the reality principle is universal in mankind and does not depend on external conditioning.

Part Two

ESTHETICS

THE VALUES OF ORDER AND VITALITY IN ART*

BY HARRY B. LEE, M.D. (Chicago)

The traditional reference of the literatures of esthetics and art criticism to the mysteriousness of artistic beauty stems from our indoctrination by culture with a philosophical and theocentric esthetic that describes beauty as "an unanalysable mystery". Artistic beauty becomes an unanalysable ultimate only if one brackets it with natural beauty, views it as a universal that exhibits the Beauty of God, spells it with a capital B, and then speculates upon it according to the deductive method of philosophy.

Descriptive science can lead us out of mystery-mongering about artistic beauty, in the same way as it has about other mental processes, but only if we no longer misconceive the problem in accordance with an erroneous philosophical directive; for the attempts of such widely varied scientific approaches as those of psychology, experimental esthetics, and psychoanalysis, have all foundered upon the errors of this theocentric directive.[1]

The culturally given views about the nature of artistic experience have always adhered to certain principles deduced by philosophers from their assumptions about the nature of the universe, which principles I now question. These are (1) that artistic experiences, whether of making or appreciating, all result from the same kind of mental process, differing only in intensity; (2) that the appreciation of beauty results from becoming excited by an outer stimulus, i.e. our perception of the beauty in nature or in art; and (3) that artistic beauty and natural beauty are the same, a form of knowledge, each revealing in its particular way the universal Beauty of God, the perception of which arouses

---

* Read in condensed form before the Annual Meeting of The American Society for Aesthetics at Cambridge, Massachusetts, September 4, 1948.
[1] Lee, Harry B.: The Cultural Lag in Aesthetics. *J. of Aesthetics and Art Criticism*, VI, 1947, pp. 120-138.

pleasure that is spiritual in quality. Ergo, the confused meaning and poor repute of the words most frequently used to describe what happens when one beholds a work of art: "beauty," "spirituality", and "vitality". My object is to inform these vague words with some scientific understanding. I propose that the mental processes in making and in appreciating are of different kinds, that different kinds of mental processes occur in the various modes of making, and that different kinds of mental processes occur in the various modes of appreciating; that our significant experiences of artistic beauty are not excited by an outer stimulus, but arise from, and answer, inner spiritual needs; and that the beauty of art is not expressive of the Beauty of God. These propositions are based upon an intensive study of creative artists and sensitive appreciators who cooperated over long periods for observation according to the psychoanalytic method.

My theories about artistic experience are based upon facts collected from the observation of those who come to be treated for emotional illness. Some will say: "Well, these four-footed notions might explain the artistic experiences of your patients, and even of my best friends; but it does not explain mine or the experiences of other healthy people." I would reply that what medicine knows today about normal function is what it has learned from studies of minds and bodies sick with disordered function. I direct attention also to the fact that the biographies and autobiographies of artists and of the art-sensitive impress us with their neuroticism and not with their emotional balance. Those who are so touchy about their art as to find offense in this, and those who are quite comfortable with the philosopher's view that the leading features of artistic experience are unanalysable ultimates, will read no further here; for science rejects not only the philosopher's view that the beauty and vitality of art are "unanalysable mysteries", but also his concepts of the will and reason as autonomous functions.

Men find it difficult to relax their beliefs in the freedom of the will, and in reason as a realization of the divinity in man. These beliefs maintain a reliance upon the supernatural in order to avoid accepting a fuller responsibility for one's judgements and behavior. They are held so tenaciously because they comfort man against the anxiety aroused in him when confronted with the acceptance of a true mental freedom, one that is more mature and self-reliant, and that does not require the belief that he is the center of the universe. For example, man's need to disclaim his instinctual tendencies leads him to overlook Freud's view of the unconscious as the matrix of all creative experience, and to reject Freud's concept of the unconscious since it is one that associates our instinctive life and emotions with the imagination. Thus, he frequently prefers the philosopher's view of the unconscious as "unconscious *intellect*", and one that does not acknowledge determinism within the sphere of mental life. Since it overlooks his underworld of passions, it disturbs less his usual methods of dealing with these passions by excessive repression. Some rationalize this position, with Croce, in objecting to the passivity implied by the idea that the essential mental processes concerned in artistic activity are unconscious:

> "But it is well to note here, that those who claim unconsciousness as the chief quality of an artistic genius, hurl him from an eminence far above humanity to a position far below it. Intuitive or artistic genius, like every form of human activity, is always conscious; otherwise it would be blind mechanism."[2]

Others protect themselves against being reminded of the blood and baseness in man's nature with a protest against searching among "the crocodiles of the unconscious" for the source of that Beauty which, they say, is a manifestation of God. They must disclaim the underworld of passions and irrationality unmasked by Freud in the unconscious part of the same human mind that was recently called soul, not because it threatens the actual dignity of man, but because it disturbs their own repressive forces. The more man is indoctrinated with philosophical esthetics the more he needs to protest that it threatens human dignity to acknowledge an unconscious which harbors beasts, and the more unwilling he is to let Caliban be found also in the artist. The humanism of Dostoevski, who testified that "there cannot be any art without the collaboration of the devil" was more courageous. A truly humanistic view of the dignity of man cannot accept fuller responsibility for his instinctual tendencies while it clings to the belief that he is the center of the universe, and while it relies upon such dubious concepts as those of original sin, the autonomy of reason, and the freedom of the will. Instead, it should acknowledge the frailties of human nature, the essential unconsciousness of these frailties, their powerful but unwitting influence upon reason and judgement, and also their contributions to the noblest expressions of the human mind.

---

[2] Croce, Benedetto: *Aesthetic*. London, Macmillan and Co., 1922, p. 15.

Many who object to Freud's dynamic and deterministic concept of the unconscious neglect to remember that, besides crocodiles, the unconscious accommodates also the power to transmute "animal passions" into the crowning triumphs of the creative imagination. I quote two statements by Robert Louis Stevenson:

> "There is nothing more disenchanting to man than to be shown the springs and mechanism of any art. All our arts and occupations lie wholly on the surface; it is on the surface that we perceive their beauty, fitness, and significance; and to pry below is to be appalled by their emptiness and shocked by the coarseness of the strings and pulleys."[3]
>
> "Those disclosures which seem fatal to the dignity of art seem so perhaps only in the proportion of our ignorance; and those conscious and unconscious artifices which it seems unworthy of the serious artist to employ were yet, if we had the power to trace them to their springs, indications of a delicacy of the sense finer than we conceive, and hints of ancient harmonies in nature."[4]

Others will object that we have already had a surfeit of attempts to apply psychoanalytic theory to artists' works and artists' biographies in order to demonstrate the ubiquity of the oedipus complex. I sympathize fully with this objection, and agree that these pseudo-scientific applications of theory do little to illuminate the problems of creativeness and appreciation. I can add that I have been persistently critical of this kind of unscientific speculation.[5,6,7] I do not offer to apply psychoanalysis to works of art, but to report the results of applying the psychoanalytic method of observation to the mental processes of art-sensitive persons, to "the live creature in the environment" and not to his works or his biography.

It has become a tradition to estimate the literature of esthetics as a chaos. Conflict has always existed among these theories, since each new philosophy stretched its metaphysics to explain also the values of art. However, a critical reading of the literature of esthetics cultivates an

---

[3] Quoted by Spearman, C.: *Creative Mind.* New York: D. Appleton and Co., 1931, p. 4.

[4] Cf. footnote 3, p. 5.

[5] Lee, Harry B.: A Critique of the Theory of Sublimation. *Psychiatry,* II, 1939, pp. 239-271.

[6] Lee, Harry B.: The Creative Imagination as a Psychoanalytical Problem. *Psychoanalytic Quarterly,* 1948.

[7] Lee, Harry B.: A Theory Concerning Free Creation in the Inventive Arts. *Psychiatry,* III, 1940, pp. 229-294.

increasing appreciation of the intuititive wisdom of the men who contributed the many nuggets of truth it contains in subjectively distorted form. It is possible that this reputed chaos is only an apparent one, made up of theories deduced from different philosophies, and so reflecting their differences; and even that this surface chaos contains more order than meets the eye. If this should prove to be correct, a theory of artistic experience arrived at by the method of science ought to be able to verify some of the truths in these theories and to inform them with clearer understanding; and, by demonstrating the distortions which result from philosophical method, it might be able to reconcile some of the differences among them. If we could understand and classify some of the leading features of artistic experience objectively, perhaps we would have a basis for construing whatever better order this apparent chaos may contain. The features of the esthetic transaction which I shall attempt to explain in this way are the spirituality and the sense of beauty which esthetic experience affords; and the orderliness, organic unity, and vitality which we demand of art.

The Spirituality of the Artist's Creative Experience

No matter what differences exist among theories of esthetics, or how widely men differ in their judgement of art, or how variously the maker and the appreciator describe their experiences, there is one point of agreement among all: the "spiritual" quality of artistic experience. The evidence presented in my paper on "The Cultural Lag in Aesthetics"[8] demonstrated that on account of the cooperation of cultural and individual factors, the philosopher, the artist, the sensitive appreciator, as well as the man in the street, all hold that artistic experience is an exercise of the spirit, and that art is a "spiritual language". It would be remarkable, indeed, if these theories did not agree at least concerning the factor of spiritual pleasure.

When we examine the authoritative, i.e. the culturally approved, philosophical theories of esthetics for their explanations of what leads to a spiritual kind of satisfaction from art, we find that *this is always described as resulting from one's reaction to something outside one's self.* The outer stimulus that is said to evoke true creativeness as well as mere rendering is, ultimately, a supernatural one. Most frequently, this is stated to be the beauty of nature; but "beauty of nature" here

---

[8] Cf. footnote 1.

refers directly, or ultimately, to Beauty of Nature as a manifestation of the Beauty of God; it represents the divinely Perfect and Ideal. The beauty of the work is frankly stated to be its "soul", and to be "divine". Thus, the stimulus for the activity of the artist is claimed to arise from an external source which is said to reflect the Beauty of God; or else, it is ascribed to the promptings of another manifestation of the supernatural—the Muse. These theories allege that the artist is endowed by constitution with an extraordinary sensitivity to the Beauty and Perfection of God reflected in Nature; or, as it is stated sometimes, that the maker of art possesses special capacity for perceiving the ideal in the commonplace. The sensitivity of the artist is said to derive from "a spiritual need for order", one that is excited by his special sensibility to Beauty in Nature, that evokes an "esthetic impulse" which moves him in mysterious ways to make art, and which results in a spiritual or religious kind of satisfaction. His transcription of Divine Beauty into the work of art is then said to serve those less sensitive appreciators than the artist as the effective stimulus for evoking in them some apprehension of this Beauty transcribed in the work. Thus, the work of art yields the less sensitive percipient a measure of the same "spiritual" satisfaction as the artist enjoyed in reacting directly to the Beauty he is gifted to discover in Nature. If the reader will read this paragraph again he will observe how closely these theories have claimed the functions of the artist to resemble those of the minister of religion as a specially gifted mediator between God and man; and how closely they claim the experience of the contemplative appreciator to parallel the experience of those who seek spiritual satisfaction from a religious ritual officiated by a minister of God. It is evident that theories which explain artistic experience as the particular echo of the universality of the One are but lightly revised editions of an ancient esthetics that frankly declared the enthusiasm of the artist to be the result of divine possession.

Spiritual pleasure does not follow upon our perception of some evidence of God's handiwork. If it did, the artist endowed with "a spiritual need for order" and in the presence of natural beauty would not so often be at the mercy of inspiration and unable to do creative work. Spiritual pleasure occurs, rather, when a man, weighed down with an acutely increased unconscious sense of guilt, is unconsciously moved to achieve a reconciliation with conscience. The artistic or non-artistic activity which a man chooses for achieving reconciliation depends upon his kind of mental organization, the relative intensity of guilt feeling, and the nature of his transgression. Many kinds of reconciliation afford only a feeling of moral superiority. The reconciliations which yield pleasure of spiritual quality are those that require either religious experience or artistic experience for the liquidation of the acutely increased unconscious sense of guilt. The reconciliations which yield pleasure of a spiritual quality, and which require artistic experience in order to liquidate the guilt, are of several kinds. *It is from failure to differentiate these kinds that much of the confusion and obscurity in esthetics derives.*[9]

There are times when man is powerfully drawn towards art purely for the satisfaction afforded by its intrinsic values, and without knowing why. He feels compelled then to seek esthetic experience in making or appreciating, and to lose himself in close communion with a work. He cannot govern or predict the occurrence of these moments of increased esthetic sensitivity which are among the most valued in life. On such occasions he is seized by what we can call an urgent *hunger* for esthetic experience. I wish to describe what this condition reveals about the problems of spirituality, artistic beauty, and vitality, when the mental processes which are associated with esthetic experiences are observed according to the psychoanalytical method. Every patient whom I have so observed, sought esthetic experience when this activity was required by his kind of mental organization for the self-healing of a then disordered state of his mind. These patients included artists creative in the various arts as well as sensitive appreciators who are not artists. Therefore, I state that hunger for esthetic experience arises from an unconscious inner need, and not from our excitement with sensations perceived in a work of art or natural objects; and that when this hunger finds what it seeks, it is dissipated by an exercise of the spirit, a reconciliation with conscience and so affords a deep experience of beauty accompanied by the pleasure we call spiritual.

This "hunger" is one of the most arresting peculiarities of artistic experience, and one that is not explained by theories of esthetics. I refer to the marked variability of both the quality and the intensity of our appreciating activities in the presence of the same creative work of art at different times. It is even more remarkable that this extensive variability of appreciation for a given work holds also for the artist who created it. For a creative work is no fixed thing. It can be many things to many men, and many things to the same man at different times. With-

---

[9] Lee, Harry B.: On the Esthetic States of the Mind. *Psychiatry*, X, 1947, pp. 281-306.

out our willing it, the work of our preference moves us differently at various times, *depending upon our state of mind*. A similar variability characterizes the artist's experience in making; he cannot do creative work whenever he wills to; neither can he produce something made only with an everyday deadly competence when he is overtaken by a creative mood. In brief, the kinds and extents of esthetic activity at a given time depend upon the unconscious dynamic needs which motivate an esthetic hunger at that time. Elsewhere, I have classified and described, according to the unconscious mental processes observed in each, the various esthetic states of the mind which call forth particular esthetic activities which then liquidate them.

The ego is a clearing house for our unconscious instinctual tendencies and the demands of reality. The governor of this clearing house is conscience, our moral control against instinct. As Freud first demonstrated, this inner check is composed from the psychic representations formed early in life of one's parents and other moral authorities. When the ego wishes to gratify forbidden instinctual tendencies, whether actually or in fantasy, a state of tension arises between it and conscience. We call these states of tension a feeling of guilt and a dread of the loss of being loved by conscience. We suffer from them an inordinate amount of pain because conscience is largely an unconscious institution, and one whose demands are more harsh and exacting than were the prohibitions, threats, and punishments of parents in our early years when conscience was being formed. When guilt and alienation from conscience are painful enough, we find some relief by repressing it; but this relief is incomplete since the ego must continue to deal with the now unconscious tension by maintaining it in repression.

Some of the most fascinating discoveries of psychoanalysis concern the various techniques with which we liquidate guilt. When it is repressed, the sense of guilt takes the form of an unconscious striving for self-punishment. It can then be recognized only from its effects upon mood, thinking, behavior, and the function of bodily organs. As an unconscious need for punishment it may cause us to feel depressed, "blue", discouraged, without knowing just why; it can slow our sensory, thinking and motor functions; it weighs us down with mental fogginess, irritability, unaccountable feelings of unworthiness, and a sense of doom; and it finds expression in such alterations of bodily function as insomnia, or in headache, vomiting, and other psychosomatic symptoms. As a sense of messiness and of disorder, it may lead us in dreams and in waking life to employ unusual measures in order to achieve an overscrupulous, i.e. "crazy-clean", cleanliness of our bodies and belongings; or into flurries of putting into a perfect order the things and social affairs we had neglected. In short, when the sense of one's guilt is repressed into the unconscious it is dismissed only from one's sight, but it remains active in one's mind and strives incessantly for liquidation.

My observations of creative artists reveal their mental organizations to be characterized by the special importance of mothers in the formation of their conscience; such self-love that they react with excessive rage to any thwarting of self-esteem; strong jealous hatreds that judgment cannot cure; the unconscious need to treat guilt over destructive impulses as if these had been directed against the mother; and by the dynamically consequent ability to employ artistic experience as a supplemental unconscious means of liquidating the guilt and of suing conscience for the return of its love and approval. The artist becomes creative when, unwittingly, he needs to become creatively formative in a way that is the dynamic antithesis of his destructiveness. When depressed with the worms of conscience, he requires and seeks a contemplative kind of artistic experience on account of its remarkable efficacy for restoring his lapsed identification with ideal aims, and for so harmonizing his relations with conscience. At these times, he is beset not only with what could be described as "hunger" for esthetic satisfaction arising from an urgent need to discharge the worms of conscience; but also with the need to demonstrate grandly to the maternal representative in conscience that the relaxed function of pity has been restored and that the ego is, therefore, again worthy of its love. *Creativeness, we shall see, bears the same antithetical relation to destructiveness as pity does.*[10]

I have described elsewhere, in considerable detail, the psychology of the creative artist, both as a citizen and a maker.[11] The man within the artist is one who suffers a particular variety of neurotic depression when he has relaxed the function of pity sufficiently to permit an outburst of destructive rage. At such times, on account of the intensity of guilt aroused, and because the relative weakness of his ego does not permit him to deal with it effectively by other means, he becomes depressed since conscience turns against him the same rage as he had vented upon another. He withdraws a large share of interest from the environment

---

[10] Lee, Harry B.: Spirituality and Beauty in Artistic Experience. *Psychoanalytic Quarterly*, 1948.

[11] Cf. footnote 7.

which he now devotes to healing the dis-order among the institutions of his mind. The first steps in this self-healing consist in employing mental processes which are commonly used to liquidate guilt, such as satisfying unconscious demands for punishment. But the neurotic depression of the creative artist is unique in its extensive sense of loss due to the withdrawal of love and approval by the maternal representative in conscience. This results from the special importance in his conscience of an idealized representation of his mother, and from the consequent unconscious experiencing of guilt particularly towards her when destructive rage is expressed against anyone. Now, in the course of healing himself of a depression, when a point is reached where self-arranged suffering has liquidated much of his guilt, the depressed artist is able to muster in a special mental process which rapidly completes his cure; he begins to sue with the psychic acts of reparation and restitution for the return of love and approval from the maternal representative in conscience, whom he construes consciously, in projected form, as his Muse. His suit begins when these psychic acts, as "inspired" creative conception, demonstrate such reparative and restitutive intentions as testify conclusively that the function of pity has been restored; and it succeeds only when these intentions are signified more extensively by embodying them in a creative making. This testimony is contained in the esthetic meanings of what the artist creates; his work is a symbolic expression of intense pity and love, of reparation and restitution, of his devotion to ideal ends, of all that is opposed to destructiveness. This is the dynamic basis of the artist's contemplative mood, of his creative intention, and of his deliverance from mental depression.

In redeeming himself with conscience, the artist achieves not only a rare sense of unification among the institutions of his mind and with the alienated wide world; but, more than this, for the restoration of love and approval from conscience is felt as a lyrical kind of at-one-ness, and as an exhilarating rapture called spiritual pleasure. A marked elevation of self-esteem results from recapturing the flavor of those moments in early life when, guilty to his mother over destructive rage, the child regained her love, approval, and gratitude in the reconciliation that occurred when appropriate actions demonstrated his renewed allegiance to her teachings of pity. He experiences not only a moving sense of order, peace, and wholeness, but is flooded with his most passionate experience of spiritual pleasure and with his most intense experience of vitality and of becoming.

At the same time, the ego is reconciled also with its projections of conscience as God and Muse, feeling no longer alienated from them, but especially loved. The inspired concept which flowers ready-made from the unconscious of the artist is not attributed to these supernatural sources because culture provides that lore and that word, "inspiration", which conceive creativeness to result from a special relationship with a supernatural Being. The ego does not view its creative mental processes as revealed only to explain in a self-aggrandizing manner what it cannot account for from the data of consciousness: the mystifying compulsive nature of the creative process in which, as a seemingly passive vessel, the artist is able to make with ease works with formal and technical qualities such as he never achieves at other times, even with arduous labor. *It is the reconciliations with conscience, and with its projections as God or Muse, which permit the creating ego to view its work as revealed from an outside source, and which result in the pleasure of the quality we call spiritual.* If the artist has acquired extensive projections to God, he describes the quality of his pleasure as a religious one. Although there are atheists and agnostics among artists, none is without a secret belief in his Muse, and in the efficacy of his magical techniques for invoking and controlling Her. The Muse is, of course, none other than a projection to the supernatural of the idealized mother of the artist's childhood—one of whom Hesiod sang:

"Muses, who make man's mind widen with knowledge, and his tongue speak from heaven."

Thus, the states of inspiration and creativeness recapture for the ego some delights of the heaven that lay about it in infancy before it acquired a God. This, also, was a passive heaven tended by a powerful and good mother who "possessed" it, and fed its self-esteem, even as her images in conscience and in God or Muse do to an equal extent during inspired creativeness. Here, too, was one omniscient enough to divine its wishes and to reveal them to an ego that was then little differentiated from an outer world consisting largely of mother. This is what the inspired artist construes as a sense of the immediacy of some supernatural power. It moves him to declare that he is drawing inspiration from an external source: from God, Supernal Beauty, Mother Nature, the Universe, or just his Muse. It leads him to believe that he is tuning-in on transcendental truths, and that he is endowed with the capacity for expressing them in his art during these moments. The rare harmony now existing among the institutions of the maker's mind is felt as an unusual exaltation and at-one-ness called rapture, transport, "mysterious emotion", enthusiasm, ecstasy, elevating excitement of the soul, or "oceanic" feeling.

It is now plain why the artist tells us that the delight of his contemplative moments is spiritual or religious; and that he is not reciting what he has learned from cultural indoctrination. His is an interior experience of God if we are mindful that it is an unconscious one consisting in being loved intensely by an idealized image of the mother who was his first ideal of beauty, and was projected to the heavens as God and Muse. It is in this sense that "poetry redeems from decay the visitations of the divinity in man".

We may conclude that the spiritual character of the pleasure from creative artistic experience does not derive from a belief in values that transcend human life, but from this kind of healing restoration of inner harmony among the institutions of the mind. Experience of a contemplative kind is not evoked in the creative artist in the manner described by philosophical esthetics, as his reaction to an external stimulus that he regards as beautiful, such as the beauty of art or the beauty of nature; rather it occurs when, as the result of a pressing inner need again to become lovable to conscience, the depressed artist engages in esthetic activity on account of its superior capacity for demonstrating to conscience his renewed allegiance to ideal aims. It is because the contemplative experience of creating art is one which is unconsciously mustered by the state of mind just described that it is only an occasional unbidden experience; that the artist can only then express in his work the most intense love; that he can achieve only then, spontaneously and with relative ease, work of which he is incapable at other times, even with hard labor and after discouraging trial and error; that he cannot govern or plan its occurrence; and that neither he nor we are able to explain this experience merely from the data of consciousness, or from its subject-matter.

Contemplative creating and contemplative appreciating visit the artist only occasionally. Between these visitations he must be content, like sensitive non-artists, with other and less extensive kinds of esthetic experience. I have described and classified elsewhere the kinds of spiritual pleasure afforded by the various kinds of making and appreciating, and the unconscious dynamic contexts which call forth these activities. The spiritual pleasures which result from these non-contemplative esthetic activities are less extensive because they are called forth by, and resolve, less disharmonious states of mind.

The Experience of Beauty in Artistic Creation

We have seen that the depressed artist becomes an earnest suppliant in order to heal an alienation from conscience. His contemplativeness is an emotional activity, and not a sensory or intellectual one. It consists of such an orientation to a sample of the material world as will redeem him and attest to his loveworthiness. The unconscious object of esthetic emotional activity,—art, invention, theoretical activity— is to create something freighted with such convincing overcompensatory signs of integrity, perfection, aliveness, and love, as will convince conscience. When this esthetic synthesis of the institutions of the mind succeeds, the artist experiences spiritual pleasure and beauty. This view differs from those of philosophical esthetics where beauty has been confused with pleasure, religious feeling, knowledge, play, the sensible imitation of natural objects, truth, goodness, the contemplation of passion, "intransitive love", and morality. It differs, too, with the traditional view of esthetics that the experience of beauty is evoked by an outer stimulus that we judge to be beauty-full, such as the beauties of art and nature. It informs with scientific insight the wisdom of Plotinus: "The soul does not see beauty if it has not become beautiful itself."

In the fantasies which occur during inspiration, the ego experiments with, i.e. contemplates, treating the destroyed or damaged object in the way it hopes to induce conscience to treat the ego; as if the ego intends to restore the object not only perfect and undamaged, *but to a unique organic unity;* and as if the ego intends the object not only to live, *but to be animated with an unusual sense of aliveness.* The ego's elaboration of fantasy expressive of intentions to regenerate a recently hated object, and to pity and love it, earns some of the approval for which it sues. Partly redeemed, the artist becomes more alive; self-esteem returns; hebetude disappears, and is replaced with a new energy and pressure to activity.

When inspiration is successful, the ego centers its activities upon the pursuit of these salutary gains with increased expressions of the same intentions. This activity is creativeness. It restores, magically, a substitute for the destroyed object convincingly enough to influence conscience and win complete redemption. The artist wields this magic by taking a substitute for the destroyed object, some dead matter, and loving it passionately until he has transformed it with an overco pensating sense of unification, perfection, aliveness, and lovability. The experience of beauty begins during inspiration which attempts in fantasy to restore the object with these characteristics, and to ac eve progressively deeper identifications with it. Delight with its b(uty reaches greatest intensity when creativeness furthers the expressio of these ideal intentions by embodying them in symbol in the foi mal features of the work, and by loving treatment of the dead materials. The experience of beauty during inspiration and creation results from this magical regeneration of the object in a substitute, and the artist's loving union with it. This complete and positively toned absorption with the object is known as "contemplative" in the literature of esthetics.

The contemplative experience of artistic beauty is a supreme example of the integrative function of the ego. It achieves a synthesis of the institutions of the mind by liquidating with esthetic experience the artist's guilt over destructive rage. Inspiration is the contemplative activity that experiments in fantasy with intentions to renew allegiance to the ideal aims of conscience. Creativeness is the contemplative activity that completes the expression of these values by transfiguring dead matter with qualities which demonstrate to conscience the artist's wish for the wholeness, perfection, aliveness, and lovability of the object. His experience of beauty is the most extensive during creativeness as he extends this kind of identification with the object he is "bodying forth".

During inspiration and creativeness, the ego is first delighted with an experience of beauty from identification with the unique perfection of the restored object; and then from being found loveworthy by conscience and its projections as God or Muse. Thus, the experience of beauty is a fusion of narcissistic delights arising from separate psychic activities. One is identification. The other is as the love-object of conscience. Artistic beauty is not, as philosophical esthetics has claimed it to be, the expression, in matter, of reason which is divine.

Since we see the world as we are, it is small wonder that the artist, now keenly attuned with conscience and God, sees the ideal in the real; and that he sees hidden in the natural many intimations of the Beauty and the Perfection with which he had invested his projected representation of parent-images as supernatural beings. He perceives all objects as he has conceived the restored and idealized one—as they ought to be, not as they are; and, in the work he creates, he is able only to re-present the real with the ideal values which are then organic to his personality.

We may conclude that contemplative artistic activity is not evoked by an outer stimulus, but by an inner one: an unconscious sense of guilt over hatreds so strong that judgement cannot cure. The values of this experience for the individual are healing and ethical; they derive from its power to convert certain discords within his being into peace. He seeks it in order to liquidate an unconscious sense of guilt over destructiveness. He achieves it by celebrating in a substitute the magical restoration of a destroyed object to organic integrity, life, and lovability. This restitution is made through a series of form-giving projections and identifications. By restoring the fullest function of love and pity for objects, it transacts an esthetic synthesis of the mind that results in the fullest conspiration of instinct and conscience. This renewal of the inner check of pity assists the artist to recover, only temporarily, a better self-control; but it does not change him into a fundamentally righteous man.

Creativeness, like pity, is a dynamic and antithetical reaction against unconscious impulses to destroy. Pity is a constant inner check against the expression of these impulses. When rage overwhelms pity so that the impulse to destroy enters consciousness, the ego is disorganized from the effects of guilt. The creativeness of the artist is a most efficient technique for liquidating guilt and re-establishing the function of pity. He is able to use this technique because his emotional development in early childhood produced the special mental organization I have described. This mental organization is a fortunate one for the artist in the man; but it is an unfortunate one for the man in the artist since it afflicts him with his emotional immaturity, exquisitely narcissistic character, maladjustment to life, and recurrent neurotic depressions.

With this understanding of the dynamics underlying the need and the purpose of the artist's creativeness, psychoanalysis offers to esthetics, psychology, and art criticism, a more objective directive for their efforts and a basis for classifying psychologically the varieties of artistic experience. It may help to inform some of their conflicting theories with a more orderly relation by illuminating the distortions which arise from subjective factors. It helps us understand, too, since conscience is also our faculty of moral control, why the boundary between esthetics and ethics is confused, and why our experience of beauty is claimed to have moral qualities.

The Melancholy of Art and Artist

> "Ay, in the very temple of delight
> Veil'd Melancholy has her sovran
> Throne." (Keats)

The creative artist has been described as a melancholic person since ancient times. Aristotle stated that poets were persons of melancholic temperament with exactly the proper proportion of black bile. We accept as characteristic traits of the creative artist his sadness, forlornness, loneliness, and nostalgia, and the "sweet melancholy" of his work. Even so, his depression, its recurrent nature, its symptoms of suffering and inhibition, and its relation to his creative mood, are not often recognized for what they are. The artist, his friends, and those who are interested in the theory of art, regard these symptoms as manifestations natural to what they call an "esthetic retreat"; or as the due expression of a temperamental, because gifted, nature; or else they attribute his depressive hebetude and despondency to external circumstances, such as overwork with creative effort, or a presumed organic illness. Nor are his desolation, self-arranged suffering, and inability to work recognized by psychologists as the symptoms of mental depression. They usually dismiss them with classification as periods of "artistic brooding", "esthetic reverie", "contemplation", "musing", "incubation", or "germination".

The poet sometimes describes his depression, as Wordsworth:

"The Poet, gentle creature that he is
Hath, like the lover, his unruly times;
His fits when he is neither sick nor well,
Though no distress be near him but his own
Unmanageable thoughts." (*Prelude*, Book 1)

Not infrequently, he addresses poems to Dejection or to Melancholy, and associates her with Beauty, as, for example, Keat's "Melancholy Dwells with Beauty".

There are also numerous testimonies by creative persons which explain their creativeness as the way in which they heal themselves of a depression. A few examples will recall others to the reader. Burton: "Melancholy advanceth men's conceits more than any humor whatever." Burton stated that he wrote *The Anatomy of Melancholy* in order to cure himself of melancholy. Goethe tells us that his writing of *The Sorrows of Werther* rescued him from a depression with suicidal impulses; and that when he finished the work he "felt free and joyful, and entitled to a new life". "Poetry," Byron wrote, "is the lava of the imagination whose eruption prevents the earthquake. They say poets never or rarely go mad .... but (they) are generally so near it that I cannot help thinking rhyme is so far useful in anticipating and preventing the disorder;" also: "It comes over me in a kind of a rage now and then .... and then, if I don't write to empty my mind, I go mad." Shelley wrote:

> "Most wretched men
> Are cradled into poetry by wrong;
> They learn in suffering what they
> Teach in song." (*Julian and Maddalo*)

Beethoven overcame mental depression with composing. A composer recently described how mostly unconscious musical composition delivered him from "an overwhelming depression".[12] An interesting comment upon how the depressed artist's melancholic mood finds expression in the work he creates comes to us from Vasari.[13] He writes that while Leonardo was painting Mona Lisa's portrait he took the precaution to keep someone constantly near her to sing or to play on instruments, etc., so that her face might not exhibit the melancholy expression often *imparted by painters* to the likeness they take. Addison writes: "Thus, in Painting, it is pleasant to look on the Picture of any Face where the Resemblance is hit, but the Pleasure increases if it be the Picture of a Face that is Beautiful, and is still greater, if the Beauty be softened with an Air of Melancholy or Sorrow."[14] Burke: "The passion excited by beauty is in fact nearer to a species of melancholy, than to jollity and mirth."[15]

We may summarize the foregoing by saying that the artist has long been known to be subject to mental depression, and that he is depressed more frequently than is recognized; that he has often referred to creativeness as the way in which he heals himself of a depression; and that the overtone of melancholy characteristic of many works of art expresses the residue of depression present during inspired creativeness. Although this melancholy is accentuated in romantic artists and their art, it is present also in classical art. The melancholy even in Homer and in writings of the later Greeks is well known.

---

[12] Krummeich, Paul: Original Sketches, pp. 461-471, in Flaccus, Louis W.: *The Spirit and Substance of Art.* New York: F. S. Crofts and Co., 1937.
[13] Chambers, Frank P.: *The History of Taste.* New York: Columbia University Press, 1932, pp. 62, 210.
[14] Addison, Joseph: *The Spectator.* (1712) p. 418.
[15] Burke, Edmund: *A Philosophical Enquiry into the Origin of Our Ideas on the Sublime and Beautiful.* (1756) xxv.

The Vitality of the Artist During Creativeness

Creativeness transacts for the artist the psychic labors of restoring with an overcompensatory semblance of aliveness, in a substitute, the person he destroyed in fancy. All of his attention is so passionately absorbed in "bodying forth" an object transfused with his sense of its life that the ordinary distinctions between himself and the work disappear.

> "I fused my live soul and that inert stuff
> Before attempting smithcraft . . . . "
> (Browning: *The Ring and the Book*)

This contemplative identification continues despite exertions and fatigue until conscience judges the work to be an unquestionably animated and loved object. The increase in his own vitality then experienced by the artist derives from his identification with its sense of life. Another increase in his vitality flows from the inflation of his self-regard and feeling of power when conscience finds him again loveworthy. A third source of increase in vitality comes from being flooded with energy now released from the tasks of repression and self-punishment. This access of energy transfigures the recently depressed artist with an exhilarating feeling of muscular power, an acute sharpening of sensory functions, and a heightened sense of reality. To sum up, his increased vitality results from an absorbing identification with the overcompensatory sense of aliveness he imparts to the work, from the sense of omnipotence he experiences in being intensely loved by conscience, and from flooding of the muscles, sense organs, and mind with energy released from the tasks of repression.

The Orderliness of Art

The true intention of the creative artist is to make restitution in order to liquidate an unconscious sense of guilt over destructive impulses, and so restore the love and approval of conscience. He achieves this by magically regenerating a destroyed or damaged object in a symbolic substitute, investing it with overcompensatory signs of organic integrity, perfection, and aliveness. He transcribes within matter, as esthetic content, the active balance of a rare harmony that exists just then among the institutions of his mind; and it expresses the intense love for objects which is his dominant mood during inspiration and creativeness. These are translated into the formal properties of the work as conspicuously fine orderliness. It is order of an ideal kind, and freighted with unconscious magical significance. The philosopher, the esthetician, the artist, the psychologist, and the man in the street fail to explain the significance of this "beauty-full" orderliness because they do not understand the unconscious dynamic motivations which propel to the creation of exquisite order one who is noted for the chronic dis-order of his person, property, and social relations.

The evidence of myths suggests that ancient man employed this restitutive technique collectively, and from similar unconscious motives. For example, the myth concerning Osiris: when Horus, son of Osiris, felt compelled to seek revenge for his father's death, the collective conscience imposed upon him the duties of putting together the fragments of the body of Osiris, of making a mummy of his remains, and of performing the necessary ceremonies to reanimate the mummy, all in order to secure the continuation of his own existence; or the Tannhäuser theme whose original significance can be seen in the African tale of a murderer who was promised a pardon by the judge on condition that the withered branch with which he had murdered should produce new shoots.

As I have described elsewhere, the failures of science to understand the meanings of the order expressed by the artist are due largely to a faulty conception of the problem dictated by culture in its philosophical directive. Each philosopher tests his metaphysics on the proving ground of esthetics, and he explains the meaning of the orderliness in art, i.e. its beauty, in terms of the archetypal Order his metaphysical hypothesis has assumed. Estheticians have frequently enjoyed flashes of insight into the meanings of the ideal order that is art; but these have been distorted with unscientific conceptions of the mind as soul, and with shoehorning their *aperçus* into consonance with a philosophical directive which refers more to the quaint realm of essences than to our experiences of art. Thus, there arose among theories of esthetics endless conflicts which reflect chiefly those existing among the philosophies which fathered them. In brief, the meanings of orderliness in art were lost in a conceptual analysis of art, in discouraging inquiry by pronouncing beauty to be an unanalysable ultimate, and in psychologies of the conscious which viewed the mind as soul and ignored the dynamic role of the unconscious in mental life.

The following samples illustrate how philosophy has directed our thinking about artistic ordering as if it were (1) a conscious activity, (2) an intellectual activity, and (3) an activity which is but the particular reflection of an archetypal order: "We are framed by nature to relish order and connection."[16] Art is "the perception through our sensibilities, more or less guided by intellect, of universal order, and its expression in terms more directly appealing to some particular phase of our sensibilities."[17] "This craving for order appears to be one of our basic wants, quite possibly the most distinctly human of all."[18] "The eye no longer translates to the mind alone: it is consciously stimulated to convey a manifestation of order of a super-natural character."[19] "Art is the living and concrete proof that man is capable of restoring consciously, and thus on the plane of meaning, the union of sense, need, impulse and action characteristic of the live creature."[20]

The view of artistic experience as an unconscious mental process was first emphasized in philosophy, and by von Hartmann, who, in *The Philosophy of the Unconscious* (1884), localized esthetic judgement in the unconscious part of the mind:

> "The discovery of the beautiful and the creation of the beautiful by man proceed from unconscious processes, whose results, the *feelings* of the beautiful and the *discovery* of the beautiful (conception), are presented in consciousness."[21]

But von Hartmann's was a purely metaphysical conception of unconscious mental life. He claimed that the Absolute, or the foundation of all existence, was in the Unconscious. His concept yielded no fruitful results for esthetics.

Artistic order does not reflect the universal order created by God. The spirituality of art is not a participation in a universal Spirit. Instead, it expresses the restored inner harmony among the institutions of the mind of the creating artist. Both the child and the creative artist re-present what they feel, not what *you* see. Since the meanings of orderliness are chiefly emotional, and chiefly unconscious, they can be understood only by observing the mental processes of the artist while

---

[16] Home, *Elements of Criticism,* New York, Mills, 1933, p. 22.

[17] *Artists on Art.* Edited by Goldwater, Robert, and Treves, Marco. New York: Pantheon Books, 1945, p. 473.

[18] Calhoun, Robert Lowry: Theology and the Humanities, pp. 119-150, in *The Meaning of the Humanities,* Greene, Theodore Meyer, Editor. Princeton: Princeton University Press, 1938, pp. 123-124.

[19] Cheney, Sheldon: *Expressionism in Art.* New York: Liveright Publishing Co., 1934, pp. 124-125.

[20] Dewey, John: *Art as Experience.* New York: Minton, Balch & Co., 1934, p. 25.

[21] von Hartmann, Eduard: *Philosophy of the Unconscious.* London: Routledge and Kegan Paul, Ltd., 1931, vol. 1, p. 291.

the work is *in statu nascendi,* before and during its creation. They cannot be understood by an examination of the work itself, witness the failure of all speculative and experimental attempts to do so.

Orderliness has such obvious utilitarian advantages that it has always been an important requirement of civilization. The regulation, convention, and tradition which characterize the orderliness of social relations contribute to peace of mind from lending considerable stability to our affairs, and in saving much of our energy.

In ancient times the strict orderliness of ritual had a magical significance. The chief concerns of rites were the dead and fertility. The ritual drama, ritual dance, and ritual funerary games all served important magical functions. Men driven by inner need to safeguard life purchased mental peace with rites of supplication and propitiation which were intended to influence natural and supernatural forces in their favor. Primitive consciousness is exceedingly conservative and requires strict adherence to the rigid regulations dictated by custom for enacting a ritual. The order of all details of the ritual was considered absolutely important for its efficacy. Even special magical rites were required to propitiate the proper deities. Only what the forefathers had done to influence supernatural forces must be repeated; and to be successful it must be repeated in exactly the same way. The time-honored orderly sequence itself was endowed with such magical significance that any infringement of the customary order of enactment was prohibited at the peril of life, lest the dis-order of the smallest particular invite chaos and disaster. Although modern man has arrived at a weaker belief in magic, the tendency of his religions is to continue to enact ritual in its ancient forms, and with scrupulous observation of its ancient order, even though we are less consciously aware of the magical motive. For example, the Mass has undergone no important changes in thirteen hundred years.

Many of our games, folk dances, and sports are the more or less corrupted secular survivals of ancient religious ritual that was believed to possess magical efficacy as supplication and propitiation. Children reveal to us how our minds today still apprehend the magical quality of order, as when they demand that something must be read or enacted over and over with strict adherence to its order; neither deletions nor changes in sequence are tolerated.

Ritual and art are close kin. Our arts themselves arose from the drama of the ancient Greek religion. Primitive dances, poetry, drawing, music, and sculpture originated from magical rites which were employed for ensuring fertility and for appeasing the dead. The history of Western culture traces art and ritual back to an intimate relationship in the ancient Greek religion where they existed as an organic unity, and when the arts had not yet been differentiated from the ritual of which they were an organic expression. Both have magical intention, are called forth by inner spiritual needs, involve us in an experience of an ideal kind of order, and result in spiritual pleasure.

There is an impressive analogy between the mystical character of creative artistic experience and what is reported by the mystic about religious inspiration.[22] The mystic divides his experience into four stages: quiet, union, ecstasy, and spiritual espousal. The *quiet* refers to his habit of "retiring voluntarily" into solitude and obscurity in order to solicit inspiration and to await the inner call. This resembles the artist's self-isolation whenever he is overtaken by a neurotic depression. The descriptions of self-punishment followed by *union, ecstasy, and spiritual espousal* resemble the events and the sequence of events in the artist's self-healing of a depression. In both the religious mystic and the creative artist, inspiration follows a period of self-punishment in a person who is enough maladjusted to withdraw from his fellows periodically in a depressed state. In both, inspiration is sudden, passive, transient, ineffable, yields a spiritual quality of pleasure and the experience of beauty, results in an increased sense of vitality, and has noetic features that are employed to solve a problem with an ideal aim.[23] The inspired state of each is contemplative; the mystic aims at complete absorption of himself into God, and projects his inspiration as revealed; the artist arrives at complete absorption of himself in the work of art, whose ideal aim I have described as symbolizing an orientation to objects that is consonant with the dictates of conscience.

It is my thesis that the significance of order in religious ritual, and in art as a purely secular activity, serve the same unconscious defensive needs: to liquidate guilt over destructive impulses by celebrating the renewal of an identification with the ideal aims of conscience.

As Freud[24] has pointed out, art is the only field in which belief in

---

[22] For an interesting discussion of this subject, see: Merton, Thomas: *Figures for an Apocalypse.* Norfolk: New Directions, 1927.

[23] James, William: *The Varieties of Religious Experience.* New York: Random House, 1902, p. 371.

[24] Freud, Sigmund: *The Basic Writings of Sigmund Freud,* edited by Brill, A. A., New York: Random House, 1938, p. 877.

the magical omnipotence of thought has been retained in our civilization. The magical reference of the orderliness of ritual is retained in the ideal order of the secular arts descended from ritual. We still speak of "the magic of art", and it is one that is understood by all: by child and adult; by the art-sensitive in every level of society, and of all creeds; by people who do not understand each other's languages; by people of different historical periods; by the contemporary primitive and the civilized.

Works of art are marked by a fine order called a unity, one that results from the consenting together and the interdependence of its parts. Our interest in art derives from the ways in which the orderliness of the design organizes its forms with balance, rhythm, and repetition. What is really remarkable about this unity is that, in a creative work, it is *an organic kind of unity* like that of a living organism whose parts are in vital and structural relation to the whole. The organization of the work integrates all tributaries to form in those ways which express most effectively the current emotional attitudes of the artist. We have had no satisfactory explanation of why, since the time of Plato[25] and Aristotle,[26] we need to apply to the work of art the concept "organic" taken from biology. As we shall see, this is not a matter of indifference.

The design of a creative work contains two kinds of order, of which I shall offer psychodynamic descriptions. This should not be confused with the many classifications of artistic beauty[27] into two kinds, which ignore the fact that the same creative work contains one or both kinds of order for us on different occasions. Those do not differentiate, as I have, two classes of order contained *within the same work of art*.[28] They distinguish among different works of art (1) those notable for their sensuous order and interrelation, and (2) those notable for the quality of vitality. Since these classifications are based upon speculative and pseudo-scientific approaches to the problem, they fail to give us adequate explanations of the moving ways in which a work of art of

---

[25] Phaedrus 264c.
[26] Poetics 1450b. See also: Butcher, S. H.: *Aristotle's Theory of Poetry and Fine Art*. London: Macmillan and Co., 1923.
[27] Such classifications as into easy and triumphant beauty; surface and expressive beauty; subjective and objective beauty; natural and essential beauty; free beauty and adherent beauty.
[28] An exception is Brown J. Warburton: Psychoanalysis and Design in the Plastic Arts, *Int. J. Psa*, X, 1929, pp. 5-29.

either class affects us, and of why a given work affects us in both ways at different times.

Ross stated that order is a principle common to all of the arts; that a work of art is of value in proportion to the number of orderly connections its contains; and that Beauty "is a supreme instance of Order". He wrote: "Beauty might supervene on order and glorify it, but the artist could not encompass and assure the glorification. Beauty is not within his grasp."[29] Beauty he can only "hope for"; order he can "aim at" and achieve. I would add that art criticism, esthetics, and the psychology of art will remain as perplexed and helpless as the artist about this mystery so long as the ideal order that is artistic beauty is dismissed as the *"je ne sais quoi"* of art— a mystery beyond human ken.

One of the most arresting facts concerning esthetic experience is the marked variability in the quality and intensity of our enjoyment of the same creative work of art. Our day to day appreciatings of it reveal on different occasions the most extreme variations in the kind and extent of our satisfaction. We cannot govern or predict these variations; and we are not much informed about the reasons for all this by going to the vast literature about art. It is not very helpful, for example, to philosophize about this mystery with Schopenhauer: "You must treat a work of art like a great man: stand before it and wait patiently till it deigns to speak;" or to accept the reassurance of the psychologist that "the appreciation of beauty comes when the bid is accepted";[30] or to assume an "esthetic impulse" with the artist, art-critic, and esthetician, who described artistic vitality as "a mysterious quality" and stated that "man's esthetic impulse gives to works of art their spiritual significance";[31] or, to the art critic who assures us that "the ultimate object of the artist's emotion will remain forever uncertain";[32] or, with the philosophical esthetician, to dismiss artistic vitality as an unanalysable ultimate:

> "That elusive something which we entitle artistic 'vitality' or 'perfection' remains, like other ultimates, as inaccessible to conceptual analysis, as its appearance is unpredictable. All that reason can do in its presence is to exercise its peculiar prerogative of self-limitation, i.e., to confess its own impotence and to acclaim the power of disciplined and oriented artistic intuition to discover,

---

[29] Ross, Denman W.: *A Theory of Pure Design.* Boston: Houghton, Mifflin & Co., 1907, p. 189.
[30] Ogden, Robert Morris: *The Psychology of Art.* New York: Charles Scribner's Sons, 1938.
[31] Fry, Roger: *Last Lectures.* New York: Macmillan Co., 1939.
[32] Bell, Clive: *Art.* New York: Frederick A. Stokes Co., 1913, p. 37.

enjoy, and appraise artistic beauty in its innumerable specific manifestations."[33]

To return to my argument: the design of a creative work contains two kinds of ideal order. I classify these according to the ways which the observation of unconscious mental processes reveals that a percipient is affected by them on different occasions. One is the merely *harmonizing experience of orderliness* which, from a relatively superficial identification with the ideal order contained in the organic unity of the work, relieves a moderate amount of anxiety, restores us to inner security, and so makes for better peace of mind. The other is an *animating experience of orderliness* which, from a much deeper identification with the work, gives us a sense of aliveness in its esthetic features and floods us with a feeling of our own vitality. It is the emotional condition of the artist, or of the appreciator, that is the variable in every esthetic transaction. The kind of experience one has of art is determined chiefly by one's unconscious emotional attitude at the time, and only secondarily by intellectual or sensory factors, or by one's physical condition. As Whitman noted: "Architecture is what you do when you look upon it." As Picasso observed: "A picture lives a life like a living creature, undergoing the changes imposed on us by our life from day to day."

By an animating kind of orderliness I do not mean the clever semblance of life for which representation has been praised in the arts since ancient times, especially by those who adhere to the theory that art imitates nature. It is not the illusion of life to be found in subject-matter that imitates life, and is lauded as "lifelikeness", "truth to life", "living impression", and "living embodiment". The orderliness which I call animating is that contained by the emotional elements of the design. It is one that has been accepted as the distinguishing characteristic of art since Plato and Aristotle observed that a work ought to possess "an organic unity *like that of a living organism*".[34]

The capacity of the esthetic features of the creative work for animating us has been known for so long that it has become one of the commonplaces of criticism. It is, in fact, difficult to find critical comment, lore, or even theoretical writings about art which do not estimate the merit of a work according to its animating effect. For example: "It is alive with rhythmic vitality;" "he puts life into the work;" "the living jet of in-

---

[33] Greene, Theodore Meyer: *The Arts and the Art of Criticism*. Princeton: Princeton University Press, 1940, p. 422.
[34] Cf. footnote 25.

spiration;" "a living embodiment of . . . ;" "livingness;" "life-communicating;" "life-enhancing;" "the dynamic life of forms;" "living form;" "living rhythms;" "vivid values;" "the vivid consciousness of esthetic experience;" "vivid characterization;" "vivid tones;" to "perceive vividly;" "poems are made of quick works;" "the divinity that animates the poet's breast . . . ;" "the animation of the picture plane;" "the poem is animated with . . .;" "dead" spots in painting; a "cold" palette; Schopenhauer's statement that music must symbolize life, else it could not move us as it does; and the theory of empathy. In descriptions of art, and in the literature of esthetics, these references to vitality are sometimes repeated so frequently within the same sentence, and also in the sentences of the same paragraph, that they constitute a veritable incantation upon the animating benefits of art.[35,36]

The artist testifies frequently about the quality of vitality. The following are typical examples, and will help the reader to recall others:

"Spirit, substantial form, with matter joined,
Not in confusion mixed, hath in itself
Specific virtue of that union born,
Which is not felt except in work, nor proved
But through effect, as vegetable life
By the green leaf."
(Dante, *Divina Commedia*, Purgatory, XVIII, 47)

"I will say of it,
It tutors nature; artificial strife
Lives in these touches, livelier than life."
(Shakespeare)

" 'Tis to create, and in creating live
A being more intense, that we endow
With form for fancy, gaining as we give
The life we image, even as I do now."
(Byron, *Childe Harold*, iii, 6)

"But from these create he can
Forms more real than living man,
Nurslings of immortality."
(Shelley, *Prometheus Unbound*, Act 1, Sc. 1)

"What would live in song immortally
Must in life first perish."
(Schiller)

---

[35] Schoen, Max: *Art and Beauty*. New York: The Macmillan Co., 1932, pp. 129-130, p. 47.

[36] Centeno, Augusto: *The Intent of the Artist*. Princeton: Princeton University Press, 1941, pp. 9, 11, 14, 19.

"In placid hours well pleased we dream
Of many a brave embodied scheme.
But form to lend, pulsed life create,
What unlike things must meet and mate."
(Melville)

"The poet's page exalts her to the sky
With life more living in the lifeless tomb,
And death translates her soul to reign on high."
(Michaelangelo)

"Any object seen in nature or any object seen in the mind must be re-created to live with and on the surface it's to exist with and on to be—right—

"These drawings are made in the effort to put down the different Street and City movements as I feel them in such a way that what appears on the paper shall have a life of its own akin to the movements felt."
(Marin)

"Impressed by the vastness of nature, I was trying to express its expansion, rest, and unity. At the same time, I was fully aware that the visible expansion of nature is at the same time its limitation; vertical and horizontal lines are the expression of two opposing forces; these exist everywhere and dominate everything; their reciprocal action constitutes 'life' . . ." (Mondrian)

"A line is a living wonder." (Kandinsky. See also p. 91 in his *On the Spiritual in Art*.)

The following random extracts from the writings of estheticians and art critics also describe our need for art to be not merely an organic unity, but an organic unity *like a living organism*:

Abell: "Form is not essentially tangible or physical or plastic in its nature. It is not a kind of body opposed to a content or spirit. It is rather a life in forming a body, an organizing principle which brings elements into significant relationship with each other."[37]

Alexander: "And as has been said before, metre with its repetition is a potent means of compacting words into the expression of spontaneous life." Also: "On the other hand, concrete authentic life, life as of a real living being, is a description of poetry quite in keeping with its instinctive origin."[38]

---

[37] Abell, Walter: *Representation and Form*. New York: Charles Scribner's Sons, 1936, p. 165.

[38] Alexander, S.: *Beauty and Other Forms of Value*. London: Macmillan and Co., 1933, p. 122 and p. 123.

Barton: "Art itself is intelligent vitality, communicated to us from the vitality of others who are richly endowed with the gifts of living, feeling, and seeing."[39]

Bosanquet: "It is the sense of the special difference made in the vitality of our body-and-mind by living in a certain experience." Also: "But when you push home your insight into the order and connection of parts, not leaving out the way in which this affects the parts themselves; then you find that the form becomes (as a lawyer would say) very material; not merely outlines and shapes, but all the sets of gradations and variations and connections that make anything what it is—the life, soul, and movement of the object."[40]

Cassirer: "A great painter or musician is not characterized by his sensitiveness to colors or sounds but by his power to elicit from this static material a dynamic life of forms. Only in this sense, then, can the pleasure we find in art be objectified."[41]

Centeno: "Art italicizes the livingness of life." Also: "Art is a symbolic possession of life..."[42]

Cheney: "The painter's problem is to vivify the picture-field..."[43]

Coleridge: "When a human and intellectual life is transferred to them from the poet's own spirit, these lines become imaginative and rise into semblance of poetry."[44]

Collingwood: "The experience of beauty is an experience of utter union with the object; every barrier is broken down, and the beholder feels that his own soul is living in the object, and that the object is unfolding its life in his own heart..."[45]

Croce: "What we seek and enjoy in art, what makes our heart leap up and ravishes our admiration, is the life, the movement, the passion, the

---

[39] Barton, J. E.: *Purpose and Admiration*. New York: Frederick A. Stokes Company, 1933, p. 21.
[40] Bosanquet, Bernard: *Three Lectures on Aesthetic*. London: Macmillan and Co., 1931, p. 19 and pp. 15-16.
[41] Cassirer, Ernst: *An Essay on Man*. New Haven: Yale University Press, 1945, p. 160.
[42] Centeno, Augusto: *The Intent of the Artist*. Princeton: Princeton University Press, 1941, p. 19 and p. 9.
[43] Cf. footnote 19, p. 133; see also; *J. Aesthetics and Art Criticism*, Fall 1941, No. 1 and 2, p. 409, pp. 107-109, 328, p. 130.
[44] Quoted by Lucas, F. L.: *The Decline and Fall of the Romantic Ideal*. New York: The Macmillan Co., 1937, pp. 171-172.
[45] Collingwood, R. G.: *The Principles of Art*. Oxford: The Clarendon Press, 1938, p. 138.

fire, the feeling of the artist;"[46] Also: "A work of art has, certainly, value in itself; but this self is not something simple, abstract, an arithmetical unity; it is, rather, something complex, concrete, living, an organism, a whole composed of parts." And: "Life circulates in the whole organism: it is not withdrawn into the several parts."[47]

Dewey: "Art is the living and concrete proof that man is capable of restoring consciously, and thus on the plane of meaning, the union of sense, need, impulse and action characteristic of the live creature."[48]

Eastman: "Of all things poetry is most unlike deadness. It is unlike ennui, or sophistication. It is a property of the alert and beating hearts."[49]

Edman: "It is one of the chief functions of the artist to render experience arresting by rendering it alive."[50]

Flaccus: "There must be life and sparkle in a painting or a poem. The individual life breathed into artistic form differs from artist to artist . . ."[51]

Fry: ". . . if we find aesthetic satisfaction in a work of art it is probable that our satisfaction will be heightened if the images which arouse it suggest vital energy."[52]

Gentile: "For its artistic character is to be found in the feeling that animates it, in the soul that governs it and that makes us feel something inwardly alive, for which our hearts beat with that secret passion which is the very passion of life."[53]

Gill: "What is a work of art? A word made flesh."[54]

Greene: "A work of art which arouses interest is often said to be 'alive'; its 'vitality' is frequently made the measure of its artistic merit. To de-

---

[46] Croce, Benedetto: Quoted by Carritt, E. F. in *Philosophies of Beauty*. New York: Oxford University Press, 1931, p. 244.
[47] Cf. footnote 2, p. 79.
[48] Cf. footnote 20, p. 25.
[49] Eastman, Max: *Enjoyment of Poetry*. New York: Charles Scribner's Sons, 1918, p. 168.
[50] Edman, Irwin: *The World, the Arts and the Artist*. New York: W. W. Norton and Company, Inc., 1928, p. 37; see also: *Arts and the Man*, p. 17.
[51] Flaccus, Louis W.: *The Spirit and Substance of Art*. New York: F. S. Crofts and Co., 1937, p. 232.
[52] Cf. footnote 31, p. 48.
[53] Quoted by Carritt, E. F., Editor: *Philosophies of Beauty*. New York: Oxford University Press, 1931, p. 327.
[54] Quoted by Goldwater, Robert and Treves, Marco: in *Artists on Art*. New York: Pantheon Books, Inc., 1945, p. 457.

scribe a work of art as 'alive' is, of course, to resort to metaphor, but the application of the concept of vitality to art is appropriate and illuminating."[55]

Heyl: "Berenson, a very different critic, shares the laudable trait of making evident his principal standard for evaluating painting: a life-communicating quality which is expressed mainly by tactile values, movement, and space composition. How helpful in explaining divergent judgments such criteria may be is evident from Berenson's comment regarding the bandages about the heads of figures on the Sistine ceiling: 'To Ruskin, I am told, these were a source of great offence, but to me they are a source of delight, for they communicate an ideated sensation of pull and resistance which vitalize the forms they enclose, and make me feel more alive.' "[56]

Hulme: "The worth of a line or form consists in the value of the life which it contains for us."[57]

Kant: ". . . Beauty brings with it directly a feeling of vital stimulus, and so can be united with charm and play of imagination."[58]

Lange: "Even in the abstract arts, such as music or architecture, art consists of the 'illusion of feeling,' the sense that these artistic creations palpitate with human emotions and are instinct with a kind of life."[59]

Lipps: Presupposes that the work of art represents a living object.

Listowel: "But the real essence of the experience of beauty is not captured until the bare form has been transformed, until the skeleton has become alive, until by the superabundant force and exuberance of our own vitality, we have animated the inanimate, etc."[60]

Ortega y Gasset: "A picture or a poem where no 'lived' forms were remaining would be unintelligible..."[61]

Parker: "The content of music becomes not a mere form of life, but life

---

[55] Cf. footnote 33, p. 392.
[56] Heyl, Bernard C.: *New Bearings in Esthetics and Art Criticism.* New Haven: Yale University Press, 1943, pp. 128-129.
[57] Hulme, T. E.: *Speculations.* New York: Harcourt, Brace & Co., 1936, p. 85.
[58] Quoted by Carritt, E. F., Editor: *Philosophies of Beauty.* New York: Oxford University Press, 1931, p. 117.
[59] Quoted by Rader, Melvin M.: *A Modern Book of Esthetics.* New York: Henry Holt and Co., 1940, p. 4.
[60] Listowel, Earl of: *A Critical History of Modern Esthetics.* London: George Allen and Unwin, Ltd., 1933, p. 274.
[61] Quoted by Rader, Melvin M.: *A Modern Book of Esthetics.* New York: Henry Holt and Co., 1940, pp. 350-351.

itself" . . . "Works of art become alive and actual only as they are experienced."[62]

Read: "It was also a bronze . . . It was vital: I almost felt, as it fused into my consciousness, that it was alive."[63]

Richards: "But 'organisation' for me stood for that kind of interdependence of parts which we allude to when we speak of living things as 'organisms'; and the 'order' which I make out to be so important is not tidiness."[64]

Santayana: "The expressiveness of forms has a value as a sign of the life that actually inhabits those forms only when they resemble our own body; it is then probable that similar conditions of body involve, in them and in us, similar emotions; and we should not long continue to regard as the expression of pleasure an attitude that we know, by experience in our own person, to accompany pain."[65]

Schiller: defines beauty as "living form".[66]

Schoen: "The beautiful is thus a life-giving, and a life-saving influence."[67]

Spengler: "Arts are living units, and the living is incapable of being dissected."[68]

Spingarn: "What vital and essential spirit animates his work . . .?"[69]

Sully: "Just as there is a rudiment of ideal significance in colour, so form, even in its more abstract and elementary aspects, is not wholly expressionless, but may be endowed with something of life by the imagination."[70]

---

[62] Parker, DeWitt H.: *The Principles of Aesthetics.* New York: Silver, Burdett and Co., 1920, p. 168; and *Encyclopedia of the Arts.* New York: Philosophical Library, Inc., 1946, pp. 14-15.

[63] Read, Herbert: *A Coat of Many Colours.* London: George Routledge & Sons, Ltd., 1946, p. 2.

[64] Richards, I. A.: *Practical Criticism.* New York: Harcourt, Brace and Co., 1946, pp. 285-286.

[65] Santayana, George: *The Sense of Beauty.* New York: Charles Scribner's Sons, 1908, p. 203.

[66] Schiller, Friedrich: *Letters on the Aesthetical Education of Man.* Letter xxv, p. 109, New York: P. F. Collier & Son, 1922.

[67] Schoen, Max: *Art and Beauty.* New York: The Macmillan Co., 1932, p. 156; see also: *J. Aesthetics and Art Criticism,* No. 6, p. 19.

[68] Spengler, Oswald: *The Decline of the West.* New York: Alfred A. Knopf, Inc., 1939, p. 220.

[69] Spingarn, J. E.: *The New Criticism.* Criticism in America, New York: Harcourt Brace and Co., 1924, p. 24.

[70] *Encyclopaedia Britannica,* Article on Aesthetics, 11th ed., p. 284.

Woodberry: "The essence of the work, its living power for us, is not what the artist put in it..."[71]

It is noteworthy that, while the Chinese concept of artistic unity differs from ours, "the life rhythm of the birds and the ink bamboo is the characteristic above all others which artistically matters".[72]

The literatures of esthetics and criticism confuse the vitality of art with divine breath, perfection, divine energy, spirit, purity, soul, and "inner form or soul".[73] They call this quality a mysterious one, state that it is beyond conceptual analysis, and offer only vague speculations to explain it. Barnes writes: "The form is the living body, and the symbol is the bare skeleton."[74] Bosanquet states: "Form and substance are one, like soul and body."[75] Drew and Sweeney declare, in *Directions in Modern Poetry* (1940), that,

> "One of the impulses behind his (the poet's) writing of poetry is not only to interpret experience to others but to clarify and objectify it to himself, to incarnate his consciousness in a verbal pattern which shall give, as it were, another body to his own spirit. But his own spirit does not function in a vacuum, but in an environment. Whitman's "O Me! O Life!" is every poet's motto, and "life" means that he is alive at a particular epoch of the world's history..."[76]

Fry, speculating upon the quality of vitality, stated that the emotional elements of design are connected with the essential conditions of our physical existence—rhythm, mass, space, light and shade, and color;[77] but when he attempted to understand the nature of artistic vitality he concluded his speculations with the guess that "the graphic arts arouse emotions in us by playing upon what one may call the overtones of some of our primary physical needs." In *Last Lectures* (1939), he concluded

---

[71] Woodberry, George E.: *Two Phases of Criticism: Historical and Esthetic. Criticism in America*, New York: Harcourt Brace and Co., 1924, p. 70.
[72] Cf. footnote 56, pp. 136-137.
[73] The writer is preparing a study of the psychological history of the confusion of these ideas with that of vitality.
[74] Barnes, Albert C.: *The Art in Painting*, New York: Harcourt, Brace and Co., 1925, p. 39.
[75] Cf. footnote 40, pp. 16-17.
[76] Drew, Elizabeth and Sweeney, J. L.: *Directions in Modern Poetry*. New York: W. W. Norton & Company, Inc., 1940, p. 23.
[77] Fry, Roger: *Vision and Design*. New York: Coward-McCann, 1940, p. 37.

that it was impossible to define the quality of the "mysterious" vitality in artistic images, and that "sensibility is the spiritual need for order".[78] Dewey's speculations upon this point are interesting: "The native constitution of the artist is marked by a peculiar sensitiveness to some aspect of the multiform universe of nature and man, and by urge to the remaking of it through expression in a preferred medium."[79] But he does not tell us why the artist feels that it needs to be re-made. Dewey refers to the dynamic role of conflict in our need for order, but this does not explain the ideal order that is the art in art: "For only when an organism shares in the ordered relations of its environment does it secure the stability essential to living. And when the participation comes after a phase of disruption and conflict, it bears within itself the germs of a consummation akin to the esthetic."[80] Carpenter discusses the role of "instinct": "Yet something in the contemplation of pattern goes as deep as our instinct against bodily deformity and approval of fully and evenly developed things, whether they be flowers or children or our lovers' bodies."[81] Alexander explains the quality of vitality as follows: "The artistic disposition vibrates more easily to the life about him, and feels the life of things or animates them with the life he feels in himself."[82] Listowel speculates: "But the real essence of the experience of beauty is not captured until the bare form has been transformed, until the skeleton has become alive, until, by the superabundant force and exuberance of our own vitality, we have animated the inanimate."[83] Bell[84] states that the emotion comes to the artist from the apprehension of the formal significance of a material thing, i.e. of that thing considered as an end in itself.

Whether the esthetic transaction apprehends in a work of creative art only the harmonizing kind of order, or both the harmonizing and animating kinds, depends upon the esthetic sensitivity of the percipient at the time. The kind of communicative activity we have with art depends upon our unconscious intention as well as our conscious reason for seeking it. The esthetic and sensory features of a work are fixed factors. The

---

[78] Cf. footnote 31, p. 40.
[79] Cf. footnote 31, p. 265.
[80] Cf. footnote 20.
[81] Carpenter, Rhys: *Studies in the Arts and Architecture*. Philadelphia: University of Pennsylvania Press, 1941, p. 61.
[82] Cf. footnote 38, p. 124.
[83] Cf. footnote 60, p. 274.
[84] Cf. footnote 32, p. 69.

sensitivity of the percipient is a widely variable factor; and this is true even for the artist who created the work. As I have described elsewhere, the esthetic sensitivities of the percipient—i.e. his esthetic hungers and even his appetite for this or that mode of appreciating or of making at a given time—depend upon the extent of his unconscious sense of guilt just then, and upon failure of the ordinary means of defense to contain an acute increase of this tension. Through making or appreciating an external focus of ideal order, we dissipate the acutely increased dis-ease in our minds and replace it with an inner harmony. Whether we collect from the orderliness of the work of creative art only a sense of harmony, or of both harmony and vitality, depends upon the degree of the dis-order existing among the institutions of the mind, i.e. the degree of our alienation from conscience.

A sense of disorderliness, and the unconscious fears of disapproval and of being found out, are relatively superficial alienations from conscience; consequently a relatively superficial apprehension of the orderliness in the creative work is required for restoring harmony among the institutions of the mind. This yields a harmonizing sense of orderliness in oneself from art. It is an identification that does not extend much beyond the sensuous order gleaned from the organic unity of the work, but is sufficient to resolve the disharmony between conscience and the ego.

When the unconscious tensions from guilt over an impulse to destroy are only moderately increased, they are able to find conscious expression as feelings of disorder and messiness. The repressed sense of guilt is misconstrued in this way because consciousness finds it less painful to tolerate, and simpler to deal with. These feelings are now entirely disassociated from their cause, and the guilty person treats his irrational sense of messiness and disorder as if it had a full basis in reality; he engages in compulsive behavior which is logically sequential to his conscious false premise that he is actually dirty and disorderly, instead of being so only figuratively. He then feels compelled to transcend his discomfort with a conspicuous interest in promoting external cleanliness and orderliness. In *On the Esthetic States of the Mind*,[85] I have described how, unconsciously, we often require and seek an esthetically superficial appreciating experience of art when we are visited by a guilt-driven compulsion towards orderliness. At these times, we are able to

---

[85] Cf. footnote 9.

reduce our sense of inner disorder by identifying ourselves with the orderly properties in the organic unity of the work. This identification is a relatively superficial one as compared with the deeper contemplative one. The orderliness in the work of art is here unconsciously sought for its stabilizing effect. It offers peace of mind, and even a mild spiritual pleasure, but little experience of the work's vitality. As compared with the more extensive contemplative and re-creating appreciation it is esthetically superficial because the appreciator need not plumb the work further than the orderly connections of its organic unity for the peace this lends against his dis-ease.

The harmonizing experience or artistic orderliness is sought not only to relieve one's guilt when this finds expression as a conscious, but irrational, sense of disorderliness and messiness. The guilt manifests itself also in unconscious fears of being found out and of disapproval. The unconscious needs here are to deny to conscience that one has felt a destructive hatred, and to affirm allegiance to its dictates. These are met by artistic activity since it enables us to identify ourselves with the ideal order embodied in the organic unity of a work of art, and because of the high value which culture places upon artistic activity.

When we are only moderately disturbed by a repressed sense of guilt—which can manifest itself as a sense of disorderliness, or be repressed as fears of being found out or of disapproval—we are often able to find peace of mind from the harmonizing effect upon us of a work of art. We require at these times to capture from its unity an identification with the ideal aims of conscience which its order expresses. This identification resolves our disharmony with conscience because the ideal order in art is a repository for, and is expressive of, the command of conscience to pity and love objects. On these occasions, our needs are not to identify ourselves with mere order and stability, such as we find in a kaleidoscope, the alphabet, a crystal, or a flag; but what we hunger for then is to identify ourselves with the idealistic significance of the order in art because this activity, from expressing allegiance to the aims of conscience, possesses the magic power of harmonizing our inner disorder. Neither are these needs satisfied by the sensuous charm we find among the orderly patterns of living organic unities such as the rose, the human body, or the wing of a butterfly; since these do not of themselves express order with ideal significance, they lack the magical power possessed by an artistic unity for avowing an identification component with the dictates of conscience.

When we are more heavily laden with guilt over our destructiveness, and become mildly depressed, our unconscious needs resemble those which compelled the artist to create. At these times, we orient ourselves to the work of creative art in order to seek from it what I have called the animating kind of orderliness, and which is a more extensive identification with the ideal meanings of order in art than the one just described. It is a form-making experience after the manner of the artist in creating the work. When we are unconsciously propelled to redeem ourselves with conscience through this formative activity, we require to identify ourselves much more extensively with the deeper meanings its ideally significant order possesses. We require to apprehend then the symbolic meanings a creative kind of orderliness possesses for avowing the intention to restore an object with unmistakable signs of life and perfection, and the intention to love it. This kind of appreciating is contemplative, and its activity is formative. It re-creates of the work the esthetic content which the artist has infused with his intention to endow an object with overcompensatory signs not only of restored organic unity and perfection, but also of aliveness and lovability. It does not merely say to conscience, as does the harmonizing experience: "My love for the ideal order in the organic unity of this work demonstrates love and pity towards humans, therefore, you need not suspect me of having entertained recently an impulse to destroy someone." Instead, the animating experience deals with the deeper ideal meanings of the work's organic unity, i.e. *an organic unity that is like a living organism,* and not merely a harmonious organic unity. This activity indicates to conscience: "See how worthy I am of redemption now, after suffering for my guilt, and after re-creating the object I have destroyed. See how I have given the object unquestionable life and perfection, and how intensely I love it again". This contemplative appreciating re-creates the work by projecting upon it one's own current compulsion to formativeness. It achieves in this substitute for the actual object symbolic restitution of the same kind as moved the artist to create the work. It proceeds, as did the maker, largely with haptic experiences of the emotional elements of the design; and it transacts among these, by projection and identification, the unconscious need to give form in order to restore a destroyed or damaged object. Thus, the more extensive and animating experience of the orderliness in a creative work yields a deeper spiritual pleasure and sense of vitality than our merely harmonizing experience of the same work because the alienation from conscience is greater, the psychic task more extensive, and the reconciliation more passionate. It is animating because the form-giving extent of order that this identification is able to seize re-creates for us the artist's sense of life in the work. The more extensive alienation from conscience requires for its cure that we apprehend from the same creative work a more extensive experience of its esthetic features. We are then unconsciously compelled not merely to identify ourselves with the harmony of the sensuous order in the organic unity of the work, but also to seize those emotional elements of the design which re-create it into *an organic unity like a living organism*. When the appreciator is overtaken at times with an urgent hunger for esthetic experience motivated by unconscious dynamic needs that are similar to the artist's in his creative moments, his appreciating is of the kind called contemplative. He feels compelled to discover among the formal properties of the work an objectification of his needs just then to give form as an avowal of his restitution of the object, and of love restored to it. Thus, emotional necessity dictates the psychic tasks of re-creating an object and of treating it with pity. As the sculptor projects into a stone the forms that are in his mind when he feels compelled to give form, so contemplative appreciating is not merely passive and receptive perception but consists in our passionate *interaction* with an object in whose esthetic content we can express re-creative and loving intentions. We discover among its qualities those which satisfy our guilt-driven need to symbolize in a substitute for an object our regard for its life, perfection, and lovability. The appreciator sensitized with this need orients himself to an esthetic content rich in the symbolization of these qualities, and then employs it as a focus within which, by projections and identifications, he can articulate his need to give form and life. Because the work of creative art is for him an ideal order of congruous forms and relations that already expresses these ideal aims of conscience, his absorbing identification with its order results in the delights he perceives as beauty and spiritual pleasure, and a sense of vitality both in himself and in the work. He is able to re-create the signs of life contained in the emotional elements of the design because his unconscious needs just then are dynamically similar to those of the artist at the time he required to create an ideal order that would signify his intentions to restore life, pity, and love. Since the rconciliation with conscience is more impassioned in this kind of appreciating, it affords much greater spiritual satisfaction and sense of vitality than does the harmonizing sense of orderliness where the pleasure consists largely in a feeling of moral superiority.

Re-creative appreciating is an activity which rapidly enlarges our sympathy to an increasing sense of union with the work. It expresses for us what Tolstoy described "as if it were something one had oneself been longing to express". A day or a year later, unless the worms of conscience again compel him to make restitution, the appreciator will not be able to recapture this deeply moving experience of the same work at will. His pleasure will now derive largely from non-esthetic features of the work, and from remembered echoes of the contemplative experience. One of the most impressive facts I have learned from creative artists is that they, too, are unable to enjoy this animating experience of a creative work at will, even of their own work; and that, like the non-artist, they are able to enjoy it deeply only when they are overtaken with a need to resolve mental emergencies of the unconscious and dynamic nature I have described. So are we judged by the creative work of art.

It is no matter of indifference that the artist requires to construct "an organic unity *like that of a living organism*", one vibrant with the illusion of life; and that we are able to apprehend a sense of its life from its esthetic content on those occasions when similar unconscious needs compel us to experience the deepest reaches of its order. The harmonious dynamic balance between the institutions of his mind, intense pity for the object, and overcompensatory need to endow it with life and lovability, are all translated into the design of *an organic unity like a living organism*. The elements of the design created in this mood are freighted with meanings which are the dynamic antitheses of hatred and destruction; it is for this reason that the creative degree of orderliness in art has an ideal significance, and is so valued by all cultures. We call it a vital design. Its organization and sense of life register emotional attitudes which the artist's conscience judges sufficient for his redemption. We apprehend the vitality of its lines since lines are sensitive signatures which register the redeeming emotional attitudes of the artist at the moment, his own feeling of vitality, and his unconscious freedom; and because these lines were not planned and labored, but were unconsciously propelled to express his wishes for the wholeness, perfection, aliveness, and lovability of the object. We apprehend the semblance of life in the mobile order, the pulsating rhythm, and the illusion of movement in its rhythms of repeated lines and forms and relations to space. There is a sense of life in the tactile values of created design; in the dynamic balance of created forms, and in color when it is employed caressingly to contribute to the design. Even the abstractions of the object which the artist selects unconsciously when in creative mood lend power and life from omitting the unessential, and from representing "the inward significance of things" by expressing only their "vital" characteristics. The accurate rendering of an object does not move us in the same way or to the same extent as the abstraction of one when it is esthetically coherent with the design. This is particularly true of the representation of the human body. As others have noted,[86] the animation of the design is more intense when its emotional elements include the appearance of the human body. I do not refer to lifelikeness of the subject-matter but to the animation its formal properties lend to the design. Exact likenesses of living things may be devoid of life. A dead animal may be represented with as much artistic life as a living one.[87] A preliminary study made during creative mood expresses a sense of life that is frequently lost in the work done from it or days later. It is for this reason that the truly creative artists are reluctant to revise, re-touch, or complete their work because "it will lose a certain freshness and power". Likewise, a copy of his creative work by the artist himself is "not right".

THE EMOTIONAL POWERS IN ART

Until as recently as the latter part of the nineteenth century, the traditional esthetic received from philosophy directed us to believe that the artist's function is to reveal in the likeness of natural objects their pale reflection of a universal Beauty. His function was conceived to be the copying of nature according to principles laid down by the church, taught by the university, and promulgated by the academy. During a period in which the prestige of science was great, and when philosophy was generally scorned, Veron, a scholarly journalist, and Tolstoy, the writer, were bold enough to revolt against this view. They advanced theories of art as art, and not of Beauty as a Divine Essence. They insisted that the artist expresses human feelings and earthly values in his work, and not the otherworldly Beauty in the sacred triad.[88]

Veron's *Aesthetics* (1878) declared that "the only beauty in a work of art is placed there by the artist"; and that art is a universal language of the emotions.[89] Tolstoy's *What is Art* (1896) criticized the metaphys-

---

[86] Cf. footnote 77, p. 38.
[87] Siren, Osvald: *Essentials in Art*. New York: John Lane Company, 1920, pp. 27-28.
[88] I have described the otherworldliness of theories of esthetics even today in, The Cultural Lag in Aesthetics, *J. of Aesthetics and Art Criticism*, 1947, 6:120-138.
[89] Veron, Eugene: *Aesthetics*. London and Philadelphia: Chapman and Hall and J. B. Lippincott & Co., 1879.

ical concept of Beauty as a Divine Essence, and agreed with Veron.[90] He added that the activity of the artist is not merely to express human emotions, but also to infect others with his emotion; that the stronger the infection, the better the art; and that the artist expresses values rooted in human feelings, and not in the heavens, or in academic canons of beauty. The acceptance of Tolstoy's theory was delayed because he introduced into it a moral bias in asserting that art should promote the Christian virtues and the brotherhood of man.

Freud made impressive contributions to our understanding of the themes of art so that today it is almost trite to repeat that subject-matter expresses the unconscious emotional attitudes of the artist. He gave us a scientific concept of the unconscious that associates our instinctive life and emotions with the imagination. He demonstrated the unconscious to be the fount of the creative imagination. He discovered that the emotions expressed in the subject-matter of art were the same as those expressed in dreams and daydreams, and were subject to the same unconscious mental processes. Freud called attention also to the ubiquity of the Oedipus theme in works of art. He gave us valuable insights into the psychology of the artist as a citizen, and concerning the themes of art, but his general theory of sublimation did not explain satisfactorily the special problems of artistic sublimation.

Although the new concepts which Vernon, Tolstoy, and Freud gave us could constitute the secure cornerstone for a science of esthetics, the central problems of artistic experience remained as unsolved as when art was considered by everyone to be a special way of knowing God.

Fry, the esthetician, was much influenced by Tolstoy's theory that art expresses human emotion, and commented: "I think that one may date from the appearance of *What Is Art?* the beginning of fruitful speculation in aesthetic."[91] Veron had stated that the emotions expressed by art were the everyday ones of joy, happiness, pleasure, grief, sadness, and fear. Tolstoy had stated that the artist expressed remembered emotions, the everyday ones of patriotism, self-devotion and submission to fate or to God, and the raptures of lovers. But Fry, the artist, knew that while the themes of art express these emotions, we value art much more for its power to move us with a unique feeling that is different from the everyday emotions. He called this profound affective quality "aesthetic emotion." While Fry criticized the error of confusing every-

---

[90] Tolstoy, Leo: *What Is Art?* London: Oxford University Press, 1930.
[91] Cf. footnote 77, p. 236.

day emotions with esthetic emotion, in his speculative attempts to explain esthetic emotion he confused it with sensibility—"the need for spiritual order"—and with vitality. As we have seen, "sensibility" is an occasional esthetic state of mind which is required to heal our inner disorder when we are sensitized with the need to give form; the condition of spiritual order we achieve through giving form results in our esthetic emotion, which is a mixture of spiritual pleasure and our inner experience of beauty; and the vitality in art results from the form-giving achievement of spiritual order among the institutions of our mind. One must re-create forms in order to be quickened with their vitality.

Although Fry criticized the moral bias of Tolstoy's theory, he stated that esthetic emotion resulted from the reaction of the sensitive to what he called *pure form*. Fry was correct, however, about the significance of the emotional elements of the design for the art sensitive, and about the unconsciousness of our reaction to them. Bell differentiated between "beautiful form" and "significant form". He stated that esthetic emotion is the emotion that is excited by significant form; that "significant form conveys to us an emotion felt by its creator"; and that "beauty conveys nothing".[92]

The artist's aim when he is truly creative is to make an object whose orderly qualities are organized into a design that expresses towards the object the emotional attitudes I have described: a sense of its life, its perfection, and its lovability. Although he regards his work as "a creature of flesh and blood", his rapt interest in it is dissipated as soon as the psychic tasks of restitution have been completed. The emotion he expressed in creating the mobile order of its esthetic content is not lost on the sensitive appreciator. As I have described elsewhere, it is when the appreciator's inner life is dis-ordered that he feels compelled to seek an absorbing experience of a work; it is then that art invites him to a contemplative participation in its power for unifying his personality. When inner needs require esthetic activity for their liquidation, he is able to tune-in, with a recently heightened sensitivity, the deeper beauties of a work's orderly relations and coherence. His activity then consists in an imaginative absorption with the ideal significance of its esthetic content.

The esthetic content of a work of art results from an unconscious need to re-present an object distorted with a passionate idealization of

---

[92] Cf. footnote 32, pp. 49-50.

its sensible qualities. As Leonardo put it: "A good painter has two chief objects to paint, man, and the intention of his soul; the former is easy, the latter hard, because he has to represent it by the attitudes and movements of the limbs." Thus, the artist gives us the living forms which are just then his imagined and idealized conception of the real. These are distorted with convincing overcompensatory signs of organic integrity, perfection, aliveness, and lovability, all dynamically antithetical to those of an object hated and destroyed. The formal properties of the work constitute a dynamic harmony infused with the esthetic emotion which possessed the artist during moments when he was in a state of creative excitement. These hold in equilibrium emotionally charged forms and relations that contain the power of formativeness for an appreciator when he is sensitized with restitutive needs similar to those which prompted the artist to create form. The appreciator is sensitized, and seeks art contemplatively, only when he requires to draw from its formative and animative capacities a renewal of his lapsed identification with the dictates of conscience. To sum up: the contemplative kind of appreciating re-creates the esthetic content of a work, and so affords a measure of the esthetic emotion the artist experienced and embodied in the work.

The esthetic content of the creative work—both its forms and its subject-matter—is potentially formative for those who come sensitized with the need to transact the contemplative mode of esthetic activity with it. *A creative work embodies two kinds of emotion.* One is the esthetic emotion of the artist, that lies latent in the emotional elements of the design, that registers the rare moments of spiritual harmony he enjoyed during its creation, and that can be recaptured intuitively and in extent, whether by the artist or by others, only occasionally. Also the subject-matter of a creative work contributes to the esthetic content of the design. The other kind of emotions expressed in the work, the non-esthetic emotions, are the everyday unconscious ones which are manifest in the thematic properties of the work, and which are legible at any time. One of the major confusions in esthetics arises from our failure to distinguish between these two classes of emotion, and from attempts to explain esthetic emotion by the emotion described in the literary content of subject-matter.

In our day to day experience, we take notice of the creative work mostly as a physical object with certain sensory, orderly, and literary qualities, and as a constant and fixed thing. We may recall the delight of our occasional passionately absorbing experiences with it—contemplative experiences that we are unable to recapture at will. Our everyday pleasure from the work flows largely from unconscious resonance with some personally significant emotive fragments of its theme; and this concerns sensory, cognitive, and associational values, rather than an intuitive apprehension of the forms. Preference for one of the arts, and taste for works of a particular style, depend upon the special value they possess as a focus upon which we can project our own relevant fantasies; for our taste in subject-matter is a judgement which is determined by personal unconscious accents upon this or that infantile interest, and upon one or another variation upon the oedipus complex. Because the subject-matter we prefer has an expressive appeal to our dominant unconscious interests, it enables us to reveal personal and everyday unconscious drives to ourselves by projecting them upon a relevant and culturally valued focus in which we then discover them. But this activity has little to do with the esthetic emotion that animates us with a sense of life in the work.

The thematic properties of a creative work are employed by the artist for their contribution to the restitutive meaning of the design, i.e. its esthetic contribution, and not primarily to ventilate his everyday unconscious instinctual tendencies. The need to make restitution governs the art of the work, and it exploits whatever potentialities a personally significant theme has for contributing to the total design. Thus, the art in art consists in expressing an everyday unconscious instinctual tendency with such love and pity, and as an integral part of such an exquisitely organized and animated unity, that it commands lasting interest for the same theme which leaves us cold in the non-creative work.

The subject-matter of creative art treats of no theme that cannot be found in the prose of non-creative work, dreams, and children's fantasy; but we identify ourselves deeply with it, and return to it again and again, when we intuit the art of its contribution to the total design. When subject-matter is conceived formatively it is largely the product of unconscious elaboration, and is expressed with unconscious freedom; its forms, and not its themes, are tributaries to the esthetic content. It is able to re-present in living images both live and dead things. Whereas, in the non-creative work, the theme is the central point of interest; it is not conceived with intense love and pity; and it is largely the result of conscious elaboration. Here, theme, sentimentality, novelty, and technical virtuosity are overworked to compensate for an internal lack of unity and life, and to seduce our interest for something esthetically anemic. As regards the relatively subordinate value of the theme in art, many have pointed out that it gives most pleasure when it is only generally, and not perfectly, understood; and that "perfect understanding will sometimes extinguish pleasure" (Coleridge).

Conclusions

We may conclude that the good of art derives from its power to convert certain of our inner discords into peace; and that our esthetic activity with a creative work is dominantly an unconscious emotional experience, and not a rational, intellectual, or "knowing" process. Its value is human and mentally hygienic, not cosmic and heavenly hygienic.

We do not value this activity because we recognize in art an independent reality of eternal and ultimate values identified with Deity. Nor do we seek it primarily for the pleasure it promises; the pleasure is a secondary gain from the state of grace that we are compelled to achieve with our conscience in apprehending the magical meanings of the order and the vitality in art. The occasional unconscious need for either the harmonizing or the animating esthetic experience is the largest factor governing the variability in our evaluations of the same work at different times.

Esthetic activity does not interest us from a belief in values that transcend human life, or because Beauty has moral qualities. As an unconscious means to good states of mind, and just because its motivations are ethical and healing, it requires no moral justification. Esthetic synthesis of the mind restores to fullest functioning our love and pity for objects, and so achieves the most salutary conspiration of instinct and conscience. Thus, conscience is not only an important faculty in our moral control, but also in our esthetic activity.

Part Three

HISTORY

FREUD'S *MOSES* AND BISMARCK*

By Henry Lowenfeld, M.D. (New York)

The task which I have set myself in the following essay is a twofold one. By means of an historical example I should like to offer a contribution to the question of whether and in what way psychoanalysis can add to the better understanding of historical processes. The example itself, the figure of Bismarck, casts its shadow into the present; hence a closer understanding of Bismarck's effects on and repercussions in the German people may illuminate certain experiences of the immediate past.

The difficulties and pitfalls into which one gets by subjecting historical phenomena to psychological investigation are well known. They should be recognized, yet they ought not to deter the investigator. The chief danger lies always in a one-sided approach; it is a danger that is present in most conceptions of history, which generally neglect the majority of factors in favor of a single determining force. Avoiding always the one-sidedly psychological approach, one ought to attempt a psychoanalytic investigation of the psychological factors within historical developments. Psychological concepts, it may be recalled, are implicit in all theories of history, even where they are not specifically treated. Psychological analysis is not only possible but necessary in dealing with such questions as national character, the content and function of a tradition, the meaning of the Leader, and kindred problems involving psychological processes. No attempt will be made here to replace the materialistic conception of history by a psychological one, as that would be like jumping out of the frying pan into the fire. Economic and political developments confront peoples or classes with problems which, while they must be solved, nevertheless admit of different alternatives and different attempts at a solution.

---

* This paper was written in 1942 and therefore does not take into account conditions in post-war Germany.

Freud has given us a magnificent contribution to the analysis of history, one that may not yet have borne full fruit. In the following pages I shall use Freud's *Moses and Monotheism* (1) as a point of departure to the extent to which that work bears on my subject.

The difficulties of the *Moses* work lie in the paucity of historical information. Freud has compensated for the lack of historical data by applying psychoanalytic interpretation to the little evidence that is authentic. From the results of this interpretation he then draws his conclusions for subsequent history. Such conclusions, therefore, can be regarded as neither proved nor provable; their decisive value lies in the suggestions they contain. The same method of historical interpretation, which in the case of such early, legendary events cannot be verified, ought to be applied to the examination of recent or present periods of history, thereby allowing at the same time a test of the method itself. It would soon become evident, however, that the difference between the legendary event on the one hand and the historically recent event on the other is not nearly so significant as one might expect. The absence of reliable sources for the early material is compensated for in the historically available matter by the quarrels of historians, the varying interpretations of documents, and one's personal bias. Nevertheless, it is possible to inquire whether the application of analytical concepts to known yet strange, hitherto inexplicable developments in the history of nations will not perhaps yield better understanding and more plausible solutions.

The development of Germany has raised just such questions, and most previous interpretations consist either in the denial of obvious facts that do not seem to fit into the picture, or in oversimplifying generalizations that do equal injustice to the facts.

At this point I should like to recall Freud's conclusions in his *Moses*. Freud assumes that Moses was a noble Egyptian who chose a people, the Jews, and appointed himself their leader. He derives this conclusion from his analysis of the exposure myth. Moses became not only the political leader of the Jews but their lawgiver and educator. The monotheism of the Jewish religion, which shows significant traits of the Egyptian cult of Aton (of only short duration in Egypt itself), is linked to the figure of Moses. Moses is described as extremely ambitious, irascible, hot-tempered and autocratic. This founder of the Jewish religion met a violent end in a rebellion of his obstinate people. The legendary figure of Moses is a fusion of two historical personages, namely that of the Egyptian Moses, that fierce leader and lawgiver, and the figure of a Midianite priest, a mild man, who served the local volcano god Jahve and lived two generations after the first Moses. Certain traits in the Jewish conception of God, such as his sternness and mercilessness, seem to be derived from a recollection of the first Moses. In the uprising in which Moses perished the religion was likewise abandoned. This tradition is the basis for all later Messianic expectations (Sellin).

The later development tends toward a harmonization of the Jahve cult with the original religion of Moses and toward the creation of a common mythology. In the adoption of a common religion the Jewish tribes were thus united. "The tradition itself remained and its influence reached . . . the aim that was denied to Moses himself." The emergence of the prophets was the decisive element in this process. Thus the most powerful effects of the Moses episode became noticeable only at a later date. Yet the figure of Moses remains the determining force in a development which, without him, would have taken an altogether different course. The remarkable thing in this process is the latency period, during which the ancient experiences, preserved by oral tradition, became ever more powerful. Only after this latency period did the Moses religion unfold its true influence. Here lies the analogy to the development of the neurosis: the return of the repressed gives religious phenomena their compulsive character. The traumatic experience in Jewish history, the killing of Moses, derives its great significance from the fact that it is the re-enactment of the assassination of the primeval father and recalls forgotten memory traces of that archaic heritage. Freud emphasizes that a tradition based solely on word-of-mouth information would not be capable of producing such powerful effects. Rather, it must first have suffered the fate of repression, the state of being unconscious, in order to force the masses under its spell.

From the above reflections Freud draws some decisive conclusions as to the Jewish national character which, he believes, is shaped by the Jews' relationship to the only God and, conversely, by that of God to them. As Freud puts it: "It was one man, the man Moses, who created the Jews."

We have here, then, the one man Moses uniting the Jewish tribes and giving them his law. The parallel in German history is the one man Bismarck who united the numerous German peoples and states and thereby exercised a profound influence on the further development of the German character. With the waning significance of the religious experience, the functions that were once vested in religious mass movements have, in the modern world, been taken over by nationalism. It is not surprising, therefore, that the modern parallel to Moses should be a national leader.

I am following Freud in not attempting to define the concept of "national character", but rather in employing it as it is commonly used. However difficult an exact definition of this concept may seem, one cannot deny that there exist national characteristics which, in certain peoples and at given periods in their history, predominate and prevail. It is more difficult to speak of a typical German than, for instance, of a typical Englishman; if one is to regard the Nazi as typical, one cannot easily account for such phenomena as German music and poetry. We may more nearly approach an explanation if we remember that Germany, during the last centuries, was subjected to tremendous historical experiences and changes; France and England, during that period, while they suffered phases of greater and lesser power, experienced nothing as overwhelming and decisive as did Germany. The peculiar structure of the Holy Roman Empire, with its hundreds of sovereign lords autocratically meting out punishments and favors, collapsed during the reign of Napoleon. The German Reich, the work of Bismarck, was created roughly eighty years ago. Many contradictions in the evaluation of the Germans are caused by the neglect of such important factors as the founding of the Reich, the union of German peoples and states under Bismarck's leadership. In Germany itself many have pondered this problem. But the tendency is still to overlook the real change in the dominant character of the German people that took place under the influence of Bismarck's powerful leader personality. Out of the multitude of contradictory traits among the German tribes, a single element prevailed, either suppressing or destroying others. It was a development which, though favored by numerous other factors, was basically determined by the figure of Bismarck.

The change in the dominant German character has been treated time and again by German historians, enthusiastically by some, critically and with concern by others. The Swedish sociologist Steffen writes: "Bismarck's spirit left its mortal shell only to permeate the German soul. The latter absorbed his brutality and indifference to justice, as well as his magnificent conception of the state (*Staatsbewusstsein*)." (2)

A critically inclined democratic author, Robert Riemann, says: "Metternich cast free men in chains; Bismarck inoculated them with the slave mentality which loses even the will to rebel and pays homage to the victor out of conviction." (3)

The result of this development was a complete change in the orientation of the formerly liberal bourgeoisie, of professors, students and merchants, as compared to the attitude maintained by those same groups before 1866. It is true that, as in all industrial countries, economic factors helped to change the position of the middle class and to influence its thinking; yet in Germany it was the towering figure of Bismarck that gave this development its special character.

In a nation newly emerged under a leader, the conditions of "group formation" exist to a striking degree, in that the leader becomes part of the superego of the individual: the group, as Freud phrased it, "replaces its ego ideal by the object". (4) The German as a member of the national "group" is indeed vastly different from the German as an individual, as puzzled observers have pointed out many times.

Various factors were decisive in the overwhelming influence of Bismarck: his role of founder and father of the Reich, certain traits of his character and, above all, the hostility of the people toward him, which was later to be effaced by the legend.

Bismarck pursued his opponents, who included everybody at one time or another, with an indomitable hatred (5, 6, 7, 8, 9).

Thus one of Bismarck's most enthusiastic followers, the son of an intimate friend, Siegfried von Kardorff, writes about him: " . . . One thing, however, must be frankly admitted; there was one blemish on his character: Prince Bismarck possessed a demonic hatred . . . we feel the after-effect of this hatred, with which he pursued his opponents, even to this day (1929) in the maliciousness of our public life." (5)

Bismarck himself once said that Goethe was wrong to maintain that only love beautified our lives, for hatred, he thought, served the same purpose: "Indispensable to me are: for love, my wife; for hatred, Windthorst." (Windthorst was the leader of the Catholic Center Party and one of Bismarck's opponents.)

The above-mentioned Kardoff begins his book with the statement that Bismarck was an extremely irritable person. From 1866 on, he is to be considered a sick man. Bismarck says of himself: "My nerves are always troubling me; I am continually upset, like a grenade that is in constant danger of exploding." He ate and drank to excess and was plagued by insomnia. His irritability, his misanthropy, his contempt for human beings, were particularly evident in his attitude toward the representatives of the people. In the tremendous Bismarck literature, written for the most part by admirers, there are innumerable remarks of this kind: "There are two things from which he cannot abstain: lying and vengefulness." He himself remarks that he could never forget an insult.

Briefly summarized, the development of the popular attitude to Bismarck may be described as follows:

In the years after 1848, undivided hatred; after 1866, ambivalent admiration, which with the years turns more and more into hatred of the dictator; finally, after his fall and then his death, a strong reaction, guilt feelings, and "deification" of the now legendary figure. The climax of the actual "experience", the traumatic part of this period in history, was the fall of Bismarck. As a background for this experience. I should like to interpolate a short résumé of the historical events:

The large majority of Germans, particularly the leading circles (Bismarck referred to them as "the thinking stratum" of the nation), were, since the Napoleonic wars, both liberals and nationalists. This development reached its climax with the Frankfort Parliament, in which, indeed, the flower of the nation was represented. The plan which was there accepted, after long negotiation, provided for the unification of Germany under the leadership of Prussia, in close association with Austria. The original idea of incorporating Austria into Germany had been abandoned, partly in view of the non-German regions of Austria, and partly because of the opposition of the neighboring countries, particularly of Russia, the leading nation in continental Europe since the Napoleonic wars. In 1849, in Berlin, the delegates of the Frankfort Parliament offered the German Imperial crown to King Friedrich Wilhelm IV, who refused it. He did so partly from fear of a democratic solution of the problem of unification, and partly from doubt of the reaction of his more powerful neighbors. Bismarck was at that time one of the strongest, most notorious and worst hated representatives of reaction and the dynastic principle. In arguing against the acceptance of the crown, he said, among other things: "I am seeking Prussia's honor in having her avoid, above all, any disgraceful contact with democracy." The tragedy of the subsequent development was that, while the democratic forces did not gain their ends but succumbed to the dynastic powers, Bismarck did achieve the goal of unification with the aid of the Prussian dynasty and through his influence over the King; he imposed it from above and carried it out with "blood and iron". But because, in his fight for the Prussian dynasty, Bismarck had had to destroy many other dynastic-legitimist perogatives, he had no choice but to seek the support of the liberal and nationalist popular forces. Although he was thus dependent upon the liberal elements in decisive matters, particularly in questions of foreign policy, he relentlessly fought these groups whenever he did not need them for the realization of his aims. He frequently told them that they had the words, he the power. Liberal officials were constantly harassed by chicanery, enforced transfers, and the like. His treatment of the parliamentarians "was enough to make the most moderate man's blood boil," as his celebrated biographer, Max Lenz, puts it (7). The liberal elements were, politically as well as psychologically, in a very difficult position. They were incapable of overthrowing him and completing the unification of Germany under liberal leadership. "Whoever did not wish to spend his effort in fruitless negation had to follow the trail-blazer" (7).

Professor Hans Delbrück (8) describes the situation in 1866 as follows: "Every aspect of political life and thought depended ultimately upon the person of Bismarck alone, with popular hatred of him rising to such a pitch that, in the midst of the crisis of May 7, 1866, an attempt was made on his life and inexplicably failed; the people regretted only, however, the fact that the great villain had escaped."

And, after the War of 1866: "Elements which had until now been deadly enemies, antagonists as bitter as good and evil, Heaven and Hell, were now to be fused into an organic whole." To the great majority, this unification was possible only through complete inner submission to the hated victor.

The famous jurist, Professor R. v. Ihering, wrote of Bismarck, in 1866: "Probably never has a war been provoked with such shamelessness and such frivolity . . . One's innermost feelings are revolted by such an outrage against all principles of law and ethics . . . the simple understanding of an honest man cannot reach or even comprehend such depths of perfidy. What a frightful future lies before us!"

Two months later, the same man writes: " I bow to the genius of a Bismarck. I have forgiven him everything he has done until now. For such a man of action, I should give one hundred men of impotent honesty" (3, 10).

The years from the founding of the Reich to the fall of Bismarck were more or less a dictatorship. Bismarck needed the support of the parliamentary parties for the passing of his budgets. He employed in domestic affairs the same principles that had proved so successful in foreign policy, conducting a series of enervating wars, always changing allies and aiming at the destruction of his opponents. I need mention only the extraordinary edict against the Socialists, which remained in force for twelve years, and the so-called *Kulturkampf* against the Catholics. Kardorff, the ardent admirer of Bismarck, writes: "The consequences of the *Kulturkampf* were catastrophic . . . This struggle inflicted the severest imaginable wounds on the Catholic population. Even today (1929), these wounds have in many cases not healed. Of 4,000 parishes, about 1,200 were totally or partially orphaned. In more than 400 parishes, no services were held, no masses read, no sacraments given. Thousands upon thousands of Catholics died in those years without receiving the last rites . . . Most bishops' sees were left vacant: the Archbishop of Posen-Gnesen, the Archbishop of Cologne, and the Bishops of Muenster, Paderborn, and Trier were arrested and imprisoned, to the profound indignation of the Catholic population; the Prince-Bishop of Breslau and the Bishop of Limburg were removed from office . . . Numerous priests were banished, some from their home districts, others from the country . ." (5).

With an even more personal hatred he pursued the liberals, and even those parties with which he was closest in thought and feeling, the various shades of conservatives. He haunted them with lawsuits, asked for a boycott of their leading newspaper, and in the end had hardly a friend left among them.

It is impossible in this space to go further into these struggles, which covered two decades. Two facets of this conflict should be emphasized; on the one hand, the hatred and violence with which Bismarck carried on the fight; on the other hand, the extreme difficulty that his opponents, the great mass of the people, found in expressing themselves, partly because of the moral authority emanating from the founder of the Reich, partly from fear of his actual power that he so relentlessly exploited, and partly also through the magic of his powerful personality.

The liberal bourgeoisie was, nevertheless, able for years to form the most powerful parties in parliament. Among them were the most eminent minds of the nation, such as Virchow, Mommsen, and Lasker. But these parties were internally divided, and they had for years demonstrated their impotence in the war against the dictator. The possibility of success of a liberal democratic solution of the German question could obviously not be tested.

In 1890, Bismarck was dismissed by the young Kaiser Wilhelm II under embarrassing circumstances. Bismarck did not want to go. The day of his departure marked the beginning of the Bismarck legend, a term used by both his admirers and critics. The first reaction was one of general relief, as these quotations from contemporary newspapers show (11):

"The fall of Bismarck will be felt as a deliverance" (*Frankfurter Zeitung*). "It is a joy to be alive; never since 1880 has such happiness prevailed among large sections of the people." The consensus was that the general discouragement was giving way to a new hopefulness, since Bismarck's omnipotence no longer obstructed and condemned to failure all liberal efforts. Eugen Richter notes the general joy over Bismarck's retirement: "Thank God that he is gone." The *Sozialdemokrat* writes: "It fills us with the deepest satisfaction that this man should have fallen in such an undignified way." The *Vossische Zeitung* compares the fall of Bismarck to the death of Frederick the Great: "The nation sighed with relief as though liberated from a heavy burden."

Wilhelm Mommsen, in his well known book on the fall of Bismarck, gives the following summary: "All shades of opinion, from bitter derision to petty reserve and tactical exploitation by the various political parties, were represented. As everyone had at some time been the target of Bismarck's hatred and scorn, objective motives dropped into the background. And as many of the party leaders had fought him not alone for motives of principle, but for personal reasons, they now lacked the inner strength and the courage to acknowledge openly their own actions and convictions" (11).

Bismarck himself considered his dismissal his death sentence (12). The official award of a title and similar honors he referred to as a "first-class funeral". "In life I am given the honors of death; I am buried like Marlborough." To a friend he complained: "My trumpet has been silenced. It has been shot through." His peers avoided him and his son. No one called on him. The Reichstag refused to congratulate him on his eightieth birthday. Now, however, a curious reaction set in among the people, who suddenly began to glorify him. Bismarck himself describes it in the following words: "Formerly, my whole life was devoted to strengthening the people's feeling for the monarchy. I was feted at court and in the official world and overwhelmed with gratitude. The people would have liked to stone me. Yet today the people acclaim me, whereas the other circles anxiously avoid me. I believe that is what is called the irony of fate." On a trip through Germany, in the course of which he delivered several speeches, he was warmly cheered by the populace; curiously enough, this was especially true in those regions against which he had formerly made war and where hatred and fear of him had therefore been strongest.

From this time on, there developed a complete transfer of allegiance to Bismarck and his legend on the part of the educated group, the professors and students, as well as of the petite bourgeoisie; it signified the collapse of liberalism, whose representatives in the Reichstag, which they had formerly ruled, shrank to an insignificant number. The people were gradually imbued with the ideology and characteristics of Bismarck, especially with those of his traits that would strike a more remote observer. Despite the existence of excellent biographical information, the figure of Bismarck underwent a process of simplification in the course of the development of the Iron Chancellor legend. Side by side with historical research, and independent of it, there continues even today the formation of new myths, capable of exerting a decisive influence on the fate of a people.

The great mass of the people and the bourgeoisie, whose former attitude toward Bismarck had been ambivalent or frankly hostile, now completely embraced him and blamed the Kaiser for the dismissal which most of them had once longed for. The guilt-feeling engendered by years of hatred of the founder of the Reich led them to project this guilt onto the Kaiser and onto Bismarck's successor in the Chancellery, and caused them to identify themselves with "the Old Man of the Saxon Forest". His ideology was accepted in "deferred obedience" and all inner resistance was discarded. All the aims of the liberals, which already suffered under the curse of impotence and defeat, now acquired the added stigma of guilt toward the great man.

I again quote Professor Delbrück: ". . . The idea now taking shape that he, the creator of our greatness, the father of the Fatherland, had been felled by insidious intriguers, rewarded with black ingratitude and condemned to end his days in disfavor and inactivity, only made the hearts, even in the ranks of his opponents, beat with greater veneration for him and turned Friedrichsruh into a national shrine" (8). The historian has described this phenomenon very clearly; we can add that it was precisely this guilt-feeling toward the hated father that contributed to such national mourning and veneration and helped to build Bismarck's enduring influence. Now all parties began to wipe out the traces of their opposition to Bismarck and to blame his fall on the impetuous temperament of the youthful Kaiser. Even the Social Democrats, while continuing the fight, remembered the old conflict with Bismarck only as part of the class struggle; the person of Bismarck, as the hated and feared antagonist, disappeared in the course of the routine application of the materialist doctrine, which thus fulfilled the function of exculpation by escaping into theory.

In the decades after Bismarck's death, the effects of the experience increased with its growing remoteness in time. The so-called nationalist circles, which had once betrayed him, now appealed openly to him and wished to be regarded as the perpetuators of his work and his glory, and as his successors. But even the forces of the Left were permeated with his intellectual heritage and in this respect differed widely from their comrades in other nations. In the war of 1914-1918, the proponents of the most diverse demands based themselves on Bismarck in an attempt to gild their requests with historical and emotional dignity. The idea of the "Chosen People" (the *Herrenvolk*) came to the fore.

Where does the parallel with Moses lie? To be sure, Bismarck was not killed but merely, as we said above, "felled by insidious intriguers". But just as he himself considered his dismissal his death sentence, so the masses regarded his fall as the fulfillment of their death wishes. They were no longer willing to tolerate him, but they were prepared to mourn him. Nor could they do otherwise. The actual traumatic experience, their own participation and guilt, is repressed more and more deeply, and the figure of Bismarck, more and more depersonalized, becomes the essence of the national ideology.[1]

At the end of the war, in 1918, when Wilhelm II lost his throne, many regarded his downfall as his just punishment for the fall of Bismarck. For the great mass of the people it was the renewal of the traumatic experience, the repetition of the patricide. For with the Kaiser went the generals, the whole hierarchy of the military leaders, who in the meantime had become the strongest followers and successors of Bismarck.

In the rise and the propaganda of the National Socialists, the figure of Bismarck played an important role; the Third Reich was to be the

---

[1] We cannot dwell more extensively on the historical details which form the dramatic background for these years. It may be worth recalling, however, that the son of the old *Kaiser Wilhelm*, with his friends, had been anxiously waiting for the death of his father, and that in turn, when he himself fell ill, his son began to wait openly and unashamedly for his death. The death of *Kaiser Friedrich* itself became the object of heated debates, in which each party declared the other guilty of the Emperor's death. All these national events, which provoked such violent repercussions in public opinion, formed the background of the chain of events culminating in the **fall of Bismarck.**

true fulfillment of the Bismarckian State. On the placards of the Nazi rallies, Hitler ordered himself painted with a shadowy and giant Bismarck in the background or, occasionally, with Frederick the Great.

As I have said above, it was undoubtedly not only the Bismarck experience—which lasted fifty years!—but powerful economic factors which contributed to the collapse of German liberalism and brought about a change in the dominant part of the national character. But these factors, especially the rise of the working class, were similar in other countries and yet did not lead to the suicide of liberalism; on the contrary, liberal forces frequently succeeded in imbuing the workers with liberal thought.

The rise of industrialism presented the Germans, as it did other nations, with new tasks, demanding new ideological solutions along with the change in material conditions and working methods, and a new function of the individual in the process of work. But the Bismarck experience limited the range of possibilities; with its overwhelming influence, it excluded all liberal-humanist solutions, burdening the Germans with guilt and forcing upon the consciousness of the nation only violent solutions. The assimilation of this experience continues even now.

I should like to discuss briefly the role of the leader in the shaping of a national tradition and of the dominant characteristics of a people, particularly of those that prevail in the sphere of politics. Tradition limits ever more the possibilities of a leader. Extraordinary circumstances may break this chain. In Germany of the nineteenth and twentieth centuries we may clearly observe the operation of this limitation by tradition. The leader with the greatest chance of success is the one who, in difficult situations, knows how to appear as the successor or regenerator of ancient leader personalities, and to impress himself on the unconscious of the people as a link in a chain of legendary figures. But all these heroes—the old Barbarossa, the *Alte Fritz* (Frederick the Great), the Old Man of the Saxon Forest, the old Hindenburg—are men armed with power, once feared and hated but now seen in the conciliating light of age. Bismarck himself considered himself a perpetuator of tradition, or rather of certain features of that tradition. "The Old Man of the Saxon Forest", as he was called, derived from the Kyffhäuser legend, according to which the old *Kaiser Barbarossa* is waiting inside the mountain to rise from the dead and lead his people to glory. (It is the messianic idea of Judaism.) The *Propyläen Universal History* says of him: "As the Barbarossa of the Kyffhäuser, his figure was capable, despite changed ideals, of driving and inspiring guidance, even in the nineteenth century of the German unification movement". The figure of old Bismarck acquired the same legendary power. The nineteenth century was in general a period of revival of ancient experiences: thus, for example, the old *Nibelungenlied* once more became the property of the nation. Bismarck, in his Nibelungen-like loyalty (*Nibelungentreue*), as it was called, to the old Kaiser was thus reliving an ancient ideal. This amalgamation of traditional heroes (13) points to the importance of the leader in historical development as well as to the limits of his possibilities. He has to have been feared and hated at one time, to have, as it were, risen from the dead, and to represent the rebirth of a legendary ancestor, in order to play so fundamental a part in the life of a people, and to exert a permanent influence on the nation in forming its tradition and character. Bismarck was such a phenomenon; it was his peculiar fate, after his fall and resurrection, to witness his own mythification.

The Siegfried-fate that is attached to Bismarck's name, death at the hand of a friend, again appears in the famous "stab in the back", by which Ludendorff, Hitler and others justified the defeat of 1918. With this slogan, the propaganda of the nationalists succeeded from the outset in instilling in the Republic and its followers a profound feeling of guilt, which paralyzed its power or resistance. At the same time, the latent conflict with the founder of the Reich was revived—experiences which, as Freud suspected, derive their decisive and lasting significance from the fact that they evoke recollections of the archaic heritage, the killing of the primeval father.

Summary

The analytic investigation of significant experiences which a people undergoes can contribute to an understanding of character development and character traits typical for a people in a national "group". The phenomenon of a leader can be such a decisive experience. Thus, the role of the great man in history is a special field for analytic investigation.

In the case of Germany the analytic interpretation of the Bismarck experience makes comprehensible certain contradictions that have struck all observers of the development of the German character. In the nineteenth century, the founding of the Reich by the one man, Bismarck, fulfilling the desire of all groups, exerted a decisive influence on the development of the German character, rendering preponderant certain traditional elements. Germany since Bismarck is a different country from the pre-Bismarckian Germany, just as the character of the Jews changed with Moses.[2]

Contradictory elements in the German character may be explained as an alloy of various traditional elements in the superego. Certain elements are superimposed on others as the result of a traumatic experience. This explains the striking discrepancy between the behavior of the Germans as individuals and as a national "group".

REFERENCES

1. Freud, *Moses and Monotheism.* New York, 1939.
2. Steffen, *Der Imperialismus.* Jena, 1915.
3. Robert Riemann, *Schwarz-Rot-Gold.* Leipzig, 1923.
4. Freud, *Group Psychology and the Analysis of the Ego.* London, 1922.
5. Siegfried von Kardorff, *Bismarck.* Second edition. Berlin, 1930.
6. Emil Ludwig, *Bismarck.* Berlin, 1926.
7. Max Lenz, *Geschichte Bismarcks.* Fourth edition. Leipzig, 1913.
8. Hans Delbrück, *Bismarcks Erbe.* Berlin, 1915.
9. Hermann Kantorowicz, *Bismarcks Schatten.* Bielefeld, 1921.
10. Fr. W. Foerster, *Europa und die Deutsche Frage.* Luzern, 1937.
11. Wilhelm Mommsen, *Bismarcks Sturz und die Parteien.* Berlin, 1924.
12. Paul Liman, *Fürst Bismarck nach seiner Entlassung.* Leipzig, 1901.
13. Ernst Kris, Zur Psychologie der älteren Biographik. *Imago,* XXI, 1935.

---

[2] H. Sachs has analyzed a dream which Bismarck describes in his *Gedanken und Erinnerungen,* and in which he actually identifies himself with Moses. Sachs writes: "With the leader Moses, who was rewarded with rebellion, hatred and ingratitude by the people whom he came to free, Bismarck, during his period of conflict, could readily compare himself." (See Freud, *The Interpretation of Dreams,* London 1932.)

Part Four

SOCIOLOGY

HITLER'S TWO GERMANIES

A SIDELIGHT ON NATIONALISM

By Gertrud M. Kurth, Ph.D., M.S.Sc. (New York)

The application of psychoanalysis to problems of group life appears to have been determined not only by a natural development of the science itself, but also by the impact of historical events which served as stimuli to the unconscious of the probing investigators. Thus in Freud's *Totem and Taboo* (18)—the first milestone in the field—psychoanalysis, while still concerned primarily with the study of the abnormal individual, tried to elucidate certain phenomena of primitive groups which, if not abnormal in the strict sense of the word, were at least very strange. But this attention to the apparently remote problems of primitives was distracted to problems nearer at hand by the aftermath of the first World War, the rapid disintegration of a form of society previously taken for granted, the overthrow of monarchies and the Russian Revolution with its reverberations throughout Central Europe. Freud's *Group Psychology and the Analysis of the Ego* (16) directed psychoanalysis to the study of mass-movements of our own culture and was followed by a crop of studies on revolution, the personality of revolutionaries, youth movements and the like [cf. (3), (4), (32), (46), (47)].

So far this development of research shows a logical correlation with historical events. It is its next focus of interest which is somewhat puzzling.

The tremendous upsurge of nationalism throughout Europe, culminating in Hitler's rise to power, evoked a one-sided reaction. With Freud's *Moses and Monotheism* as a beacon (17) psychoanalysts probed and probed successfully, the nature and various aspects of the persecution of minorities as a grave symptom of mass regression [(cf. (7), (31), (33), (42)]. Yet they devoted almost no interest to the equally urgent manifestations of nationalism. Doubtless certain forms of nationalism are age-old. But the type of nationalism which has been the sorest affliction of Western civilization in the hundred and fifty years since the French Revolution, has been accepted relatively unquestioningly by otherwise enlightened spirits. And yet this is a nationalism *sui generis*—a type all-pervading, narcissistic and paranoid in its manifestations.

Only Federn (12)—a pioneer here as always—was stimulated to a study interpreting the normal identification with one's nation, the pride in one's nationality, as a part or extension of the individual's healthy narcissism. On this basis he pointed out that excessive nationalism parallels a distortion of narcissism, a disturbance which readily accepts reinforcements from aggressive tendencies.

In Fessler's study (13)[1], there are certain conclusions which are pertinent to this topic. He considers that the equating of a mere passive and automatic membership in a nation with achievement results in a lowering of the ego-ideal and/or of superego demands. That nationalism can reduce anxiety (that "scourge of mankind") (13) goes far to explain the power of its attraction. But as all group-phenomena share this essential element, this factor alone cannot explain the specific features of nationalism and related ideologies.

Considering the magnitude of the threat, it is indeed appalling to realize how little has been done to investigate the nature of what is "clearly an extremely complex sentiment. If it were a new lethal chemical in the hands of an enemy," Stuart and Marian Chase say in a recent study (8), "we would spare no expense to learn its nature. Teams of experts would be probing the unknown with microscopes, spectographs, and other stupendous apparatus. But no such attention has ever been given to a sentiment stronger, more dangerous, and more mysterious than any military weapon—although modern demagogues have learned (and put to use) a few of the techniques by which it may be manipulated."

Since the study of the abnormal has yielded insight into the working of the normal mind, some answer to these problems might be found from a closer scrutiny of the "lunatic fringe" of the nationalist movement, of those demagogues who, as the Chases point out, possess the skill of manipulating the mysterious forces inherent in nationalism.

---

[1] In general, the author's concept of nationalism is not clear cut since it includes criteria of totalitarianism. Therefore the applicability of his findings to this study is limited.

My own attention was first drawn to this aspect of the problem here to be discussed by an author of obviously nationalistic leanings and with no remotest connection with psychoanalysis. Theodore Heuss'* book on Hitler (22) was published in Germany in 1932, shortly before the Nazis' assumption of power. By and large it is a kind of psychological evaluation of Hitler's personality and as such is remarkable both for its comparative objectivity and the astuteness of its observations. Discussing Hitler's conception of and relation to the people, the author says:

"He has two concepts of the people at his disposal. The one is romantic, a list of virtues: faithful, courageous, simple, pious, industrious . . . the German people is the Chosen One. This series of images is entirely genuine and authentic, he believes in it. His self-identification with this concept of the people, as performed in his ecstasy of spiritual devotion, is equally genuine and naive. Naturally, through repetition, this ecstasy has increasingly become a technique. But it would have run out long ago, were it not kept alive by an *original force*.[2] On the other hand, however, he operates with a modification of this ideal type. . . . When he conceives himself in the role of a martyr . . . he speaks contemptuously and cynically of the masses, conceives them as feminine, clay in the skillful hands of the propagandist . . . " But: "He who pretends to despise the masses cannot be without them. He needs them to find himself, he derives his enhanced sense of life from the instincts, friendly or hostile, that he physically feels emanating from the masses and affecting him. . . . In mellow moments he speaks of the efforts and sacrifices of his life devoted to agitation. . . . "

The triad, *admiration-contempt-sacrifice*, constitutes a syndrome familiar to psychoanalysts and indicates that the "original force" which kept Hitler's ecstasy alive was a specific conflict of unconscious ambivalence they so frequently encounter. A random sampling of the formulations of these concepts will serve to clarify the nature of the conflict, particularly if we keep in mind their underlying "personification."[3]

---

*As this paper goes to press, Heuss has just become president of the West German Republic!

[2] Italics mine.

[3] The samples were chosen to represent a large number of equally revealing phrases. *Mein Kampf* (25) as well as the various collections of Hitler's Speeches, cf. (6), (9), (23), (24), (26), (37) yielded quantitatively satisfactory evidence.

Here are examples from the "catalogue of virtues":

"There is hardly a people on this earth that has capacities of wider range than has the German people ... "

" ... I never doubted the qualities of the German people ... "

" ... the goodness of our people ... its efficiency ... its loyalty ... its decency ... its industry ... its sense of order ... "

"He who seeks loyalty and faith, confidence, fanaticism, and resolute devotion, must seek them where such virtues still are to be found. And they are to be found only in the great mass of the people ... "

"Where, then, can any strength still be found in the German people? It is to be found as always, in the great masses ... "

In the opposite mood, this is what Hitler had to say about the very same people, the very same masses:

" ... the broad, groping, erring masses ... "

" ... the rule of the people is ... in reality the rule of stupidity, of mediocrity, of half-heartedness, of cowardice, of weakness and inadequacy ... "

"The great masses ... only want bread and circuses; they have no understanding for ideals of any sort whatever ... "

" ... the German people lies broken down, exposed to being trampled under the feet of the rest of the world ... "

"The German people lay prostrate, completely wrecked and shattered ... "

" ... the people of dishonor and shame, of self-castigation, of discouragement and hopelessness ... "

"(one sees) an example ... of fatal decay in the Reich of today ... "

Hitler's contempt culminates in his well-known theoretical concept of the masses, as laid down in *Mein Kampf* (25): "The psyche of the great masses is not receptive to half measures or weakness ... Like a woman, whose psychic feeling is influenced less by psychic reasoning than by an undefinable sentimental longing for complementary strength, who will submit to the strong man rather than dominate the weakling, thus the masses love the ruler rather than the suppliant, and inwardly they are far more satisfied by a doctrine which tolerates no rival than by the grant of liberal freedom, they often feel at a loss what to do with it, and even easily feel themselves deserted. They neither realize the impudence with which they are spiritually terrorized, nor the outrageous curtailment of their human liberties, for in no way does the delusion of this doctrine dawn on them. Thus they see only the inconsiderate force, the brutality and the aim of its manifestation to which they finally always submit..."[4]

However, it is in speaking of his own attitude to this double-faced object, that Hitler reveals most clearly its origin and meaning.

"We have only one interest and that is our people. We love our people fanatically . . . We can go along as faithfully as dogs with those who are serious about our love for our people, but we can persecute with fanatic hatred those who think they can take advantage of this love . . . "

"All peoples on earth are a matter of indifference to us, but in relation to one people we are full of passionate love, namely, in relation to our own people . . . "

"I beseech the entire German people, if I should ever fail . . . then let the people execute me. I will offer no opposition. Never will I do anything that will violate my honor or the honor of the nation. I should not like to have a hand in disgracing the German people . . . "

"I am a child of the people and I will remain so forever and if necessary I would let myself be cut into pieces for this people . . . "

"The people as such is . . . the eternal source and the eternal well which gives new life constantly . . . "

"I receive my strength from the people . . . the power of the people is my power and its strength is my strength . . . "

"He who loves his people can prove it only through the sacrifices he is ready to bring for this people . . . "

"I have taken over my office to save the German people."

"He who wants to save a people cannot but think heroically."

It seems, then, that Hitler's concept of the people (the nation, Germany, the masses, terms which he uses interchangeably) is that of a woman, on the one hand a woman of outstanding character, on the other a "loose" and despicable creature. Nevertheless he professes to

---

[4] Cf. also the passages on syphilis in *Mein Kampf* (25), pp. 340-349. Even though this may only be a rehash of Le Bon's ideas, Hitler's selection of them remains significant.

love this image "passionately," "fanatically" and to be ever ready to "sacrifice" himself to "rescue" her.[5]

Freud described this syndrome in the first of his three "Contributions to the Psychology of Love" (15) under the title: "A Special Type of Choice of Object Made by Men," and analyzed it more fully in the second, entitled: "The Most Prevalent Form of Degradation in Erotic Life." Both papers discuss a certain form of psychic impotence in men, which Freud succeeded in "reducing to the non-coincidence of the tender and sensual tendencies in love and in explaining this inhibition in development itself from the strong childhood fixations and later frustration in reality by interference of the incest barrier."

More precisely, Freud found in almost all of his patients who suffered from disturbences of potency that they had two love objects. The one they admired but were unable to enjoy sexually, the other, of a lower type, was in a way "despised" but therefore could be enjoyed sexually without inhibitions. Freud furthermore found that this type of man will choose as his sexual object a woman who is, either in reality or in his fantasy, promiscuous, and whom he then feels compelled to "rescue" or "rehabilitate." The origin of this conflict Freud traced back to the time when the boy becomes aware of the fact that his mother who hitherto had been the image of purity for him actually has sexual intercourse with his father. Since the child usually equates sexual intercourse with an aggressive assault of the male upon the female partner, the little boy wishes to rescue and protect his mother from this danger. The conflict is revived with particular intensity in puberty, when it is strengthened by the re-awakened oedipal jealousy so that the boy at this time is inclined to minimize the difference between his mother and a harlot. Both, he feels, do practically the same thing and this is the period when the element of contempt enters his psychosexual attitude.

In the light of this analysis and from what is known of Hitler's psychosexual structure, one is justified in asserting that he suffered

---

[5] Obviously, such an interpretation is, to a certain extent, based on style, on the choice of words and metaphors, their flavor, connotations and possibly their double meaning, all of which is partly obscured in translation. The reader is therefore referred to Heuss' impartial evidence and to the corroborating material in the following pages.

from this ambivalence conflict and projected it into his nationalistic ideology.[6]

Were this trait restricted to Hitler's enunciations, it would certainly not permit broader conclusions about the nature and function of nationalism. This, however, is not the case. On the contrary, the triad runs, as a sort of *leitmotif* through all of Nazi propaganda. One of the most transparent and characteristic examples is the first Hitler biography, Georg Schott's notorious *Volksbuch vom Hitler* (41) which received its subject's official and enthusiastic sanction. It is conceivable that Hitler may have influenced formulations to a certain extent. Yet the author's style of adulatory hero-worship, spiced with romanticism and blood-and-soil ideology, is so much his own that these doubts can easily be dismissed. Some of the characteristic passages are well worth quoting:

"As to Hitler's role in respect to Germany, the fatherland, the tragic case is quite clear. The entire case history is in his hands. He is the physician, standing at the patient's bedside and feeling her pulse. Everything is not yet lost. But the danger is greater than anyone realizes. The doctor, however, knows everything, from her face, from her eyes, he reads everything, all the time, not only her physical, but even more her spiritual suffering. A child, a king's child, in fever delirium; victim of a debauchee, rended, torn, *raped*.[7] And as soon as the doctor were to turn his back, she would again be in danger of being raped and by the same villain. That is Adolf Hitler's concept. *That is reality!*"[7]

"The soul of the people is reflected in him . . . its beauty, strength, and chastity . . ."

" . . . the deadly threat to the German people . . . recognized by Hitler . . ."

---

[6]For his positive relation to his mother, cf. *Mein Kampf* (25), Chapter I, also Bloch (5), and Erikson (11); for his negative, contemptuous attitude, cf. *Mein Kampf* (25), Chapter II, also Kurth (31). In his later private life, exalted mother figures, like Frau von Bechstein, or Cosima Wagner (cf. 21 and 36) always played a role, whereas his sexual perversions revealed his aggressive and degrading tendencies. It is also significant that at the beginning of his nationalism, he made a split between the racially "promiscuous" Austria and the "great" Germany and furthermore that this occurred, true to clinical type, in his adolescence.

[7] Italics mine.

"Hitler . . . destined to be the 'savior' of the German people . . . the German people believes in redemption through him . . ."

(His is the task) . . . " to lift a people up from bottomless filth and slime . . ."

"We were confronted with a plunge into the abyss . . . Hitler has led us back to the path from which we had deviated . . ."

It is hardly necessary to list further verbatim samples of this concept and its uniform imagery. The voluminous Nazi propaganda of which the *Voelkischer Beobachter*,[8] the official party organ, is only one sample will yield ample proof of the persistence of this triadic image: Germany, the greatest, the worthiest of all nations; the people lost, fallen, submerged in "shame and dishonor;" Hitler's role as the protector, the rescuer, the "savior," the rehabilitator, destined to "restore" her "honor."[9]

In order to answer the question whether this triadic imagery is a German characteristic or is the characteristic of a specific ideology, I have drawn upon material stemming from another representative of the "lunatic fringe" who is a member of an essentially democratic society. I labored through the speeches of Gerald L. K. Smith who has been called the "American Hitler" and whom the late Huey Long personally conceded to be the "better rabble rouser."[10] The speeches

---

[8]Cf. this writer's study of *The Image of the Fuehrer*, (30) culled from the annual Hitler-birthday issues of the *Voelkischer Beobachter*, particularly the reference to the erotization, if not sexualization of the Fuehrer-people relationship, p. 90, footnote 10a.

[9]It may be mentioned here that in Hitler himself this dichotomy apparently maintained its role and its intensity up to the very end. As early as 1942, when defeat began to loom, the Fuehrer was ready to blame the people for "failing" *him*. After the attempt on his life, on July 20, 1944, Trevor Roper reports that he exclaimed: "I'm beginning to doubt that the German people is worthy of my great ideals!" Immediately before the surrender, in the bunker underneath the Reichs Chancellery, when he decided upon his suicide, he is alleged to have said: "If the war is to be lost, the nation will also perish . . .The nation has proved itself weak . . ." And like the lover who in the rage of despair and disappointment in the woman he was unable to "rescue" destroys her together with himself, "he was deliberately attempting to let the people perish with himself . . ." [For the last quotes, cf. (45), pp. 32, 82, and 78, resp.] Whether this destruction could have been the ultimate unconscious aim—inherent or dominant in the ambivalence—is a guess. Cf. Bateson (2) ". . . through preliminary victories to defeat . . ," (p. 10)

[10]Smith started as Long's lieutenant.

from which I quote were delivered shortly before and after the outbreak of World War II (43).

Smith's opinion of the "people" is also not very high, at least at times:

"Not until the storm breaks, do the sleeping masses awaken, yawn, stir themselves and look about at the wreckage and carnage, after it is too late to help matters. . .

"International conspirators always find it to their advantage to lull the people to sleep . . . A man in a stupor is harmless. . ."[11]

"The despoilers have a way of keeping the popular mind befuddled and drugged under the influence of opiates. Propaganda is a powerful weapon in the hands of wicked men. Yet, the thinking of a whole nation may become warped in a comparatively short time . . ."

"By degrees, these ideas sink into the mass-mind and a community is moulded accordingly. Then the people take the things they have been taught for granted, little suspecting that, parrot-like, they are merely chattering about false notions, which have been insinuated into their mental processes. . ."

On the eve of an election, Smith said: "I shudder tonight to think what is going to happen if America fails to awaken. Oh America, tonight is your awful hour. This is your night to fight. This is your day to pray. This is your hour to protest against any conspiracy. . ."

At other occasions, he is as fervent as Hitler ever was in protesting his love of his country. Immediately upon the outbreak of war, he said:

"We mumble not nor do we complain when it comes to standing for our beloved America. For God, Home and Country, we gladly give all. No sacrifice is too great. We love our soil, institutions and liberty. We love and cherish the great American heritage more dearly than life itself . . ."

"All Americans love America enough to pay any price necessary to attain victory . . ."

---

[11]Cf. the Nazi battle-cry: *"Deutschland erwache!"*

"Americans love their native land. They are willing to make any sacrifice necessary to protect the Stars and Stripes."

"We Americans do not want to possess the world. We do not want to police the world. We do not want to rule the world. We resist this temptation as did Christ.[12] We want to preserve America and her traditional way of life, and we refuse to share our American independence with friend or foe."

At times, Smith's lyric imagery becomes quite transparent:

"Love of one's country is like love of one's mother—as long as one has a sweet mother, with her eternal forgiveness, her loving caresses, her patient indulgence, one is inclined to take these gifts for granted." He goes on to depict dramatically the self-accusations in the wake of this mother's sudden death: "Oh God, why did I take my mother for granted? Why did I let her slip away from me without manifesting a greater appreciation for her *godlike*[13] love and affection?" Finally he concludes: "Democracy is dying in America . . . . Ruthless and hard-headed individuals are taking advantage of the lethargic indifference of cowardly and selfish and neglectful Americans. All mothers must die sometimes, but Americanism need never die. The America we know, this beautiful design of life which was handed us by our founding fathers . . . need never die. . ."

Right after Pearl Harbor, he said: ". . . my followers . . . know I love America, they know I put America above any personal, partisan, political consideration. This is a war that makes a simple appeal to the father to defend his home, to a husband to defend his wife . . . to a brother to defend his sister. It is as justifiable as for a brother to step into the breach of assault to save his high-school sister from an unprovoked (sic) attack by a sensual beast."[14]

I intentionally disregard the interesting points of departure from German nationalistic propaganda to emphasize the parallels. Like Hitler, Smith divides the American people, or America, into an exalted and a degraded image, the fervor of his love matches Hitler's, so does his ardor to "rescue" this beloved creature whom he consciously identifies as "mother", and like Hitler he casts either the non-

---

[12] Just for curiosity's sake be it noted here that Hitler, also, occasionally identified himself with Christ.

[13] Italics mine. Cf. Federn (12).

[14] Cf. Schott's "king's child"!

Americans or the "bad" Americans into the role of seducers and rapers.[15]

Since, however, I have no objective data on the "American Hitler's" personality structure, I should like to supplement this material by the findings which R. Nevitt Sanford has published in a paper, entitled: "Identification with the Enemy: A Case Study of an American Quisling" (39). Sanford chose this case for study because "the subject revealed a pattern of social and political attitudes and a syndrome of personality characteristics that were very similar to those of men scoring at the high extreme on the University of California Public Opinion Study Scales for measuring anti-Semitism, general ethno-centrism, and related anti-democratic trends . . . it seems probable that the factors which have determining significance in his case will be among those which will differentiate statistically between prejudiced and non-prejudiced individuals."

Of his case, Sanford stresses in particular: "Women were seen as of two kinds: the virtuous woman who belongs on a pedestal and the low woman who can sometimes be helped and sometimes be treated as if she were beyond help." And: "At the deepest level, *our subject was identified with his mother and America.*"[16] Finally: "The pathology of our case lies in its extremeness, rather than in its quality. The variables that operated as crucial determinants in this case are distributed widely in the population at large, and they can be expected to have similar, if less dramatic effects wherever they occur."

This material, we feel, provides ample foundation for the following conclusions and hypotheses in regard to the psychology of nationalism.

(1) First—in regard to the mechanism of projecting an ambivalence conflict, let us quote Kris (28) who says: "Agitators are persons whose early experiences have created a predisposition for intense ambivalence. . . In order to escape that ambivalence they tend to polarize positive and negative attitudes . . . the mechanism of pro-

---

[15]To the best of my knowledge, it has frequently been advanced and possibly even been established that Smith drew on Hitler's speeches liberally, to the extent of quoting him verbally. But it should again be emphasized that the voluntary choice of similes is as indicative of the underlying unconscious factors as spontaneous production would be.

[16]Italics mine. Cf. Heuss (22) on Hitler's identification with the concept of "virtues".

jection provides for them the solution of personal conflict. . ." It seems clear that the basic ambivalence conflict which nationalistic agitators project is that between sensual and tender strivings and our conclusion is shared by Flugel who linked nationalistic enthusiasm to the rescue fantasy, using Byron as example (14).

(2) In regard to the social effects of this mechanism of projection we would again cite Kris (28) : ". . . the mechanism of projection alone does not constitute the agitator. He is also a man . . . who has the uncanny ability to convince others of his views. . ." In other words this "uncanny ability" of the agitator to persuade others serves to attract to their groups those individuals who are under the sway of the same intense ambivalence conflict and who also find in the agitator's ideology their own solution by projection. This would then be one factor in what Hartmann has called "social compliance" (20).

(3) So far, the attractiveness of nationalism has been ascribed to its function as an outlet for aggression (13) and as a means of ego aggrandizement based on identification with the mother (12). But this identification has been tacitly accepted as based on the projection of the love or positive feelings toward the mother. Our material, however, demonstrates that nationalism also contains a projection of the negative feelings toward the mother, a factor of considerable significance in its social results.[17] It goes without saying that all these unconscious motives must be simultaneously effective, correlated and mutually interdependent.

Manipulators (i.e., propagandists or demagogues) show particular skill in blending these ingredients so as to channelize emotions in a

---

[17]Not only nationalism but every other kind of social prejudice seems to constitute a projection of an unconscious ambivalence conflict (49). However, we know very little about the subtle interplay of dynamics and psychic economy which differentiate various manifestations of social prejudice. From Brunswick-Frenkel's and Sanford's classical report (42) on the Anti-Semitic Personality, for instance, one might conclude that in anti-Semitism the projection of only the negative, ego-rejected part of an ambivalent attitude provides a solution whereas nationalists appear to project both the positive and negative components. In the case of anti-Semitism it seems as if the afflicted individual could himself play the role of the angel as long as the role of the devil can be delegated to another actor; whereas in nationalism the entire drama is projected onto a vast stage on which the actor takes the role of defender of his projected object. These relations between the individual structure of the conflict and access because both factors are in a state of constant flux. Cf. (34).

desired direction. That is why for such types, as Sanford puts it, "different groups of people could at different times have one or the other role" (39). Nazi nationalism offers an excellent illustration: according to expediency, the roles of the two Germanies were assigned —more or less consciously—to either of two groups of contemporaries, those who accepted defeat (in World War I), and those who refused to accept it; after 1933, the differentiation referred to Nazis and dissenters. At the peak of power, the assumption was upheld that National Socialism and Germany were identical. The split was conceived historically, Germany past and present, with the "Germany of shame and dishonor" being a thing of the past. Yet, as breakdown approached, "Germany and National Socialism become subtly differentiated in propaganda practice. National Socialism stands at the center of achievement in times of victory but tends to separate itself from the *suffering body*[18] during times of defeat. The interrelation of the two ideas is obscured by the shadow of mysticism: the words may not change very much, but the impression is different. The leader of National Socialist Germany tends to become the martyr *for* Germany at large" (29). Apparently what struck the propaganda analysts as mysticism, was nothing but the re-emergence of the "two Germanies" in still another disguise.

A qualification of our conceptualization seems called for at this point. Webster's Dictionary defines a nationalist as "one who advocates the national independence and unity of his country," whereas the characteristics of a patriot[19] are defined as "love of one's country; the passion which influences one to serve one's country, either in defending it from invasion, or protecting its rights and maintaining its laws and institutions in vigor and purity." But today the definition of the patriot is tacitly assumed to apply to the nationalist. The historical development of the Western concept of nationalism is reflected in the scope of the two definitions. In its beginning—in the French Revolution—nationalism meant the right to sovereignty and self-government of a people in the same ethnic group, while today the concept has changed to an impassioned, somewhat hysterical and highly emotional worship of an unambiguously maternal symbol of

---

[18]Italics mine.
[19]I am indebted to Dr. Ludwig Jekels for pointing out to me the implied meaning of the word "fatherland": It is, indeed, the mother who is "father's land"!

a country. Moreover this country need not necessarily be that of one's birth as evidenced by Hitler and numerous other "Quislings". In fact, the very phenomena of treason and Quislingism are probably merely sub-types of the basic solution of the same underlying ambivalence conflict.[20]

In its function of polarizing the exaltation-degradation conflict nationalism is not unique. The same bait is employed by manipulators today to secure allegiance whenever a movement or a Party is invested with maternal symbolism. Bateson has given us a particularly illustrative example of this in his analysis of the Nazi motion picture, *Hitlerjunge Quex* (2), in which Nazism is identified with "pure", idealistic love and Communism with the crude, sensual type. Moreover, the motif, in this picture, appears on two levels: the one where the two girls represent the two political movements, and the other in the protagonist's family life. In his family life the mother is worshipped (indicating the origin of the fantasy) yet has to be "rescued". In the political scenes, it is the self-sacrificing hero's inspiring example which "reforms" the Communist girl. According to Bateson, the same motif is repeated in other Nazi films.[21] One may also suspect that the ease with which Party allegiance was switched to national allegiance in Russia during the last war was effected by means of the same transfer of symbols from Party to Nation.[22]

Let us now consider the possible objections to our thesis that this particular ambivalence conflict plays so determining a role in the psychology of nationalism. It may be suggested that the qualitative and quantitative importance of the conflict between tender and sensual

---

[20] Though it seems self-evident, it may be advisable to emphasize that both, definition and conclusions refer to Western civilization only. Other cultures may present differently structured types of nationalism to which this study then obviously does not apply. Geza Roheim's writings contain a wealth of material about nationalism among primitives; for the problem of the origin of nationalism, the reader is referred particularly to his *War, Crime and the Covenant*, Journal of Clinical Psychopathology Monographs No. 1, Monticello, N. Y., 1945.

[21] *The Street, Faehrmann Maria.*

[22] We are here reminded of the easy and superficial generalization which claims that modern political movements, particularly those of the totalitarian type, are substitutes for religion. A study such as the present indicates one reason why this is not so: religion operates on a high level of sublimation and therefore offers steady support to the individual harassed by his drives and the external world; while political ideologies offer no more than piecemeal and constantly shifting pseudo-solutions. For a more profound discussion of this problem, cf. (34).

strivings in love has been exaggerated for purposes of the thesis. In refutation I would quote Freud whose clinical experience led him to say of the role which this conflict played in individual lives as well as in culture as a whole (15): "I shall put forward the proposition that . . . psychical impotence is far more wide-spread than is generally supposed, and . . . that some degree of this condition does in fact characterize the erotic life of civilized people. . ." And: ". . . we shall not be able to deny that the behavior in love of the men of present-day civilization bears in general the character of the psychically impotent type.[23] In only very few people of culture are the two strains of tenderness and sensuality duly fused into one; the man almost always feels his sexual activity hampered by his respect for the woman and only develops full sexual potency when he finds himself in the presence of a lower type of sexual object."

It is noteworthy that this was written in 1912. Thus we cannot avoid raising the question, whether anything has happened in the last forty years further to increase the impact of this conflicted situation.

I believe such a factor can indeed be adduced. What has been called the "emancipation" of women has made momentuous strides during this period. But there are no such rapid changes in the archaic imagery of the unconscious which would enable such imagery to keep pace with the overwhelmingly accelerated change of reality.[24] Glaring inconsistencies and incongruities in the prevailing picture of reality reveal, like symptoms, the great (unconscious) tension caused by this type of "cultural lag". To condense these reality changes, we may offer the following brief formulation: In this "man's world" of ours women smoke, drink, propose, support their families, fly airplanes, split atoms, and rebuild war-devastated cities but are still scorned for bearing children out of wedlock. Yet the image of woman as helpless, motherly and self-sacrificing is tenaciously maintained and inculcated by our education from the nursery on. It dominates our sex mores, popular fiction, the movies, and so on.

Let us, however, contrast this image with psychic reality. Within two generations, women have attained in this "man's world" all the attributes of masculinity previously denied them. If we accept the

---

[23]It may be both permissible and advisable to qualify this statement by inserting the word "Western" before "civilization".

[24]For a discussion of the significance for individual development of a rapidly changing environment see (34), also (10).

psychoanalytic formulation that the valuation of the sexes is unconsciously based on the possession or non-possession of a penis and its corollary, that women must have envied men their prerogatives, then we would expect them to show an exaggerated reaction to suddenly attaining so much of what they had craved. The natural reaction would be that of a "nouveau riche"—a vehement rejection of the former status, and an inflated attitude toward the present one. This aggressiveness of women has forced men into a correspondingly defensive and passive role.[25] That such a situation reinforces homosexual strivings in both sexes is also an important factor in the vicious circle. But further discussion of this element is beyond the scope of this paper.

Our culture tends to confuse the growing child about the role and function of the sexes, and this confusion and the resulting tension are considerably increased by the sharp contradiction between the reality of the roles and their archaic imagery in the unconscious. Juvenile and divorce courts, the psychiatrists' consulting rooms and the mental hospitals are indications of the unhappiness and misery which result from conflicts such as the one under discussion. And it would seem that as tension in individual lives increases, it finds an outlet in mass movements, in various social institutions and political ideologies of various types.[26]

---

[25] For support of this analysis, may I here refer to several authors (whose views I have condensed) who offer a more detailed foundation for these conclusions, such as Lundberg and Farnham (35), Philip Wylie (48), Geoffrey Gorer (19); the work by Lundberg and Farnham offers a wealth of bibliographical material as docs also (27). As convincing evidence I also quote James Thurber's witty and amusing report on the soap opera (44): "Good women dominate most soap operas . . . Their invariably strong character, high fortitude, and unfailing capability must have been originally intended to present them as women of a warm, dedicated selflessness, but they emerge, instead, as ladies of frigid aggressiveness." And: "When their men are stricken, the good women become nobler than ever. A disabled hero is likely to lament his fate and indulge in self-pity now and then, but his wife or sweetheart never complains. She is capable of twice as much work, sacrifice, fortitude, endurance, ingenuity, and love as ever before . . . The man in the wheelchair has come to be the standard Soapland symbol of the American male's subordination to the female and his dependence on her greater strength of heart and soul" (44). Cf. also Wylie (48), particularly Chapter XI.

[26] It may be objected that mass movements such as nationalism count many women among their followers and that therefore our conclusions cannot apply to them. It would lead too far to disprove this objection in all its aspects (Cf. 14). Suffice it to point out that, to date, such movements are led, practically exclusively, by men and that therefore women's reasons, conscious and unconscious, for adherence are probably of a somewhat different nature.

Nor would it be the first time in history that men have attempted to solve personal conflicts by projection into the public domain and by creation of irrational and therefore all the more irrepressible mass movements, particularly when external circumstances favored or facilitated such reactions.

A study which correlated the prevailing intra-family situations with the outbreaks termed mass-hysteria, would probably reveal the prevalence of specific unconscious conflicts whose discharge by projection made participation in such movements so irresistible. Some of the persecutions of minorities have been studied from this viewpoint [cf. (14), (42)]. It seems relevant to speculate whether the age of witch trials did not have factors in common with the problem here discussed, namely the ambivalence conflict between the good mother and the witch-mother, whose image was then exterminated with such vicious ferocity.

Here I would refer to Stephen Schonberger's study of the nightmare syndrome (40) in which the author links "ideas and images . . . of witches and their activities . . ." to "well-definable instinctual impulses and traumata, likely to occur in every age and every person . . . The image of the witch has, indeed, caused many a grave epidemic to mankind; from time to time, men set about to persecute, slay and exterminate the witches . . . Very often these epidemics coincided with social crises . . . We know that social crises are the superstructure of economic crises, that is of crises in production and consequently in consumption. Except for a very small part of the population, people perceive the economic crises obviously as crises of consumption . . . As a result, mankind is prone to experience these social and economic crises as oral traumata, reactivating the reactions and states once developed in response to oral traumata . . . In times of social and economic crises, on account of the prevailing oral-traumatic character of these crises, men are again inclined to believe that it is some oral-sadistic image, as for instance witches, that has brought the hardship upon them, just as the 'starving' infant thinks the cause of his miserable state is the mother who has changed into a witch." I quote this hypothesis, which I am not inclined to accept as a whole, only because of its relevance to the problem of how individual psychic reactions are related to mass movements.

Since highly speculative hypotheses such as the present one are very conducive to misinterpretation let me here intercept one such possible misunderstanding. In linking ideologies of the type of nationalism, which are manipulated by means of maternal symbols, to the emancipation of women, I do *not* have a cause-and-effect relation in mind. Historically speaking the two phenomena are of common origin. The French Revolution gave rise to modern nationalism by evolving the principle of "national" sovereignty, simultaneously, it was of powerful impact on man's concept of woman and of woman's concept of her own role.[27]

Again, the ensuing rapid development of science and technology was of dual influence: on the one hand it "liberated" woman, from the major part of her daily chores as well as sexually, by taking the "danger" out of sex life and, more important, of childbirth.[28] On the other hand, this same rapid expansion of technology created economic pressures and crises which, in turn, not only re-enforced individual conflicts but also, in the long run, swelled the rising tide of nationalism. Thus, certain processes of public and private life that originated independently have, in the course of time, become so intricately intertwined that they appear almost inseparable. They cannot and should not be considered separately.

Moreover, to take into account the impact of unconscious engrams on social behavior[29] means at the same time to face realistically the main, if not the only, line of attack. In the following I quote Bateson and Erikson who have both, independently, pointed out the devastating influence of over-aged and unadjusted family patterns in Germany. "The old German family pattern," says Bateson, "with all its ambivalences may have provided a stable base for German society in the nineteenth century but it would not provide such a base today . . . the roles of the father and the mother must be modified in some way or other . . ." (2) And Erikson concludes that "it will be one of the functions of psychology to recognize in human motivation those archaic and infantile residues which are subject to misuse by demagogic adventurers" (11). [Cf. also (38)].

---

[27]Mary Wollstonecraft's *Vindication of the Rights of Women* was published in 1792.
[28]Ernst Kris, in a private communication, drew my attention to the crucial importance of Semmelweis' introduction of asepsis for the emancipation of women.
[29]Cf. de Saussure's paper on "Psychoanalysis and History," *this volume,* p. 7. Also Alexander (1), cited by de Saussure.

In conclusion, I should like to return to the most formidable objection to be expected, namely, that I may have grossly overrated the significance of one such "archaic and infantile residue" responsible for the attractiveness of, say, nationalism. Again I can do no better than to quote Freud (15) who assigned such crucial importance to the unresolved conflict between tender and sensual love that it induced him to the statement: "So perhaps we must make up our minds to the idea that altogether it is not possible for the claims of the sexual instinct to be reconciled with the demands of culture, that in consequence of his cultural development renunciation and suffering as well as the danger of his extinction at some far future time, are not to be eluded by the race of man. . ."

Confronted with a world toying with the threat of total extinction in the near future, one may speculate whether Freud's gloomy prognosis might not come true through the aid of just some such disastrous projection.

BIBLIOGRAPHY

1. Alexander, F. Mental Hygiene in the Atomic Age, *Mental Hygiene,* 1946.
2. Bateson, G. *An Analysis of the Nazi Film, Hitlerjunge Quex,* New York, 1945. Not for publication.
3. Behrendt, R. Das Problem Fuehrer und Masse und die Psychoanalyse, *Psa. Bewegung,* I.
4. ―――. *Politischer Aktivismus,* Leipzig, 1932.
5. Bloch, E. My Patient Hitler, *Collier's,* 1941.
6. Boepple, E., Ed. *Adolf Hitlers Reden,* Munich, n. d.
7. Brown, J. F. The Origins of the Antisemitic Attitude, in Graeser, I. and Britt, S. H., Eds. *Jews in a Gentile World,* New York, 1942.
8. Chase, S. and M. When the Flag Goes By, *1947,* December 1947.
9. de Sales, R. de Roussy, Ed. *My New Order,* New York, 1941.
10. Erikson, E. H. Ego Development and Historical Change, *The Psychoanalytic Study of the Child,* II.
11. ―――. Hitler's Imagery and German Youth, *Psychiatry,* 1942.
12. Federn, P. Vom Nationalgefuehl, *Almanach der Psychoanalyse,* 1931.
13. Fessler, L. Psychology of Nationalism, *Psa. Review,* 1941.
14. Flugel, J. C. *The Psycho-Analytic Study of the Family,* London, 1948.
15. Freud, S. Contributions to the Psychology of Love, *Collected Papers,* III.
16. ―――. *Group Psychology and the Analysis of the Ego,* London, 1948.
17. Freud, S. *Moses and Monotheism,* New York, 1939.
18. ―――. Totem and Taboo, in *The Basic Writings of Sigmund Freud,* New York, 1938.
19. Gorer, G. *The American People,* New York, 1948.

20. Hartmann, H. Psychoanalysis and Sociology, in: *Psychoanalysis Today*, S. Lorand, Ed., New York, 1944.
21. Heiden, K. *Der Fuehrer*, New York, 1944.
22. Heuss, Th. *Hitlers Weg*, Munich, 1932.
23. Hitler, A. *Adolf Hitler spricht*. Ein Lexikon des National-Sozialismus, Leipzig, 1934.
24. ———. *Ja aber—was sagt Hitler selbst*, Munich, 1931.
25. ———. *Mein Kampf*, New York, 1941.
26. ———*The Speeches of Adolf Hitler, April 1922—August 1939*, New York, 1942.
27. Klein, V. *The Feminine Character. History of an Ideology*. New York, 1949.
28. Kris, E. Notes on the Psychology of Prejudice, *The English Journal*, 1946.
29. ——— and Speyer, H. *German Radio Propaganda*, New York, 1944.
30. Kurth, G. M. *The Image of the Fuehrer*, Unpublished thesis at the Graduate Faculty of Social and Political Science, New School for Social Research, 1947.
31. ———. The Jew and Adolf Hitler, *Psa. Quarterly*, 1947.
32. Lasswell, H. D. *Psychopathology and Politics*, Chicago, 1930.
33. Loewenstein, R. M. The Historical and Cultural Roots of Anti-Semitism, *Psychoanalysis and the Social Sciences*, I.
34. Lowenfeld, H. Some Aspects of a Compulsion Neurosis in a Changing Civilization, *Psa. Quarterly*, 1944.
35. Lundberg, F., and Farnham, M. F. *Modern Woman, The Lost Sex*, New York, 1947.
36. Olden, R. *Hitler*, New York, 1936.
37. Prange, G. W., Ed. *Hitler's Words*, Washington, 1944.
38. Rees, J. R., Ed. *The Case of Rudolf Hess*, New York, 1948.
39. Sanford, R. N. Identification with the Enemy: A Case Study of an American Quisling, *Journal of Personality*, 1946.
40. Schonberger, S. A Clinical Contribution to the Analysis of the Nightmare Syndrome, *Psa. Review*, 1946.
41. Schott, G. *Das Volksbuch vom Hitler*, Munich, 1939.
42. Simmel, E., Ed. *Anti-Semitism. A Social Disease*, New York, 1946.
43. Smith, G. L. K. *Various Speeches*, from the Collection of the New York Public Library, 1940-41.
44. Thurber, J. Soapland, *The New Yorker*, May 1948.
45. Trevor Roper, H. R. *The Last Days of Hitler*, New York, 1947.
46. Williams, F. E. *Russia, Youth and the Present Day World*, New York, 1934.
47. Wittels, F. Politischer Radikalismus, *Psa. Bewegung*, III.
48. Wylie, Ph. *Generation of Vipers*, New York, 1942.
49. Zilboorg, G. Psychopathology of Social Prejudice, *Psa. Quarterly*, 1947.

VARIETIES OF GROUP FORMATION

By Roger Money-Kyrle, M.A., Ph.D. (London)

INTRODUCTORY NOTE

This paper was originally given as an open lecture at the British Institute of Psycho-Analysis in the Spring of 1939. (It was one of a series of six, delivered by different analysts which, but for the war, would have been published in book form.) The examples I chose to illustrate my particular thesis were the events and attitudes most familiar to an English audience at that critical period. The fact that they can now be considered in retrospect may in some ways be an advantage and, for this reason, I have not brought them up to date—except occasionally by adding an explanatory note in brackets.

As to the thesis itself, this is an elaboration Freud's theory as expounded in his *Group Psychology and the Analysis of the Ego* (1921). He then described a primary group as "a number of individuals who have substituted one and the same object for their ego-ideal (later called the superego) and have consequently identified themselves with one another in their ego". This formula, which I accept as fundamental, has been my starting point. But while Freud was concerned mainly with the paternal imago, we know that both parent figures must play some role. Moreover, they must do so in each of the two aspects—ideally good and ideally bad—into which they are split in the child's early unconscious fantasy. (This splitting of an object as a defense against the anxieties aroused by ambivalence towards it has been especially stressed by Melanie Klein.) Some elaboration of Freud's formula to include the roles of both parent figures, in their bad as well as good aspects, in the formation of groups does therefore seem to be required. To supply it is the primary aim of this paper. Of course, many other factors, both psychological and social, would have to be included before our theoretical picture or model of a group could be regarded as anything like complete. I have concentrated only on filling what seemed to me a particular gap.

The Family as the Prototype of All Group Formations

Man creates the society he lives in. Can he, like God, look upon his work and find it good? Sometimes he is complacent when it functions very badly. Sometimes he dislikes it even when it functions fairly well. But he seldom blames himself for its defects. He blames his ancestors, or those who seem to have imposed it on him, and overlooks his own share in the work.

The truth is, that in building his society he is influenced by unconscious as well as conscious motives, which are often incompatible with each other. For this reason he does not know exactly what he wants or why he fails to get it. If this is really so, some understanding of these unconscious motives is a first condition of the success of the societies he builds.

To uncover these unconscious motives we must go back to his early childhood. Here, in his relation to his parents, we shall find the model of all the varieties of social structure he will build in later life.

To be more exact, the basic model of all group formations is not quite the family as it really is, but the family as it appears in the child's imagination. Perhaps most of the troubles of society result from the fact that the two are by no means the same. The real family contains two parents; the imaginary one contains at least four—two good ones and two bad ones—who are the prototypes not only of divinities and devils but of our more abstract ideas of good and evil. This, of course, is not remembered, and some of it is never conscious, but it can be discovered by Freud's method of analysis, which Melanie Klein and others have applied to the direct study of very young children. We know, too, why it is that the child forms these contradictory pictures. When he loves his parents, he forms a good picture of them. But when they arouse his hate, he fears them and forms a picture of vindictive bad parents, who are different people altogether.

Moreover, in his efforts to disown his dangerous aggressiveness against one parent, he tends to attribute it to, or project it upon, the other. Then to reassure himself against these imaginary dangers he exaggerates his picture of the good parents into perfect and omnipotent beings. But paradoxically enough, they not only give but also need protection; for they are threatened by the child's aggressiveness which he projects upon the bad parent figures. Lastly, they are not only persons to be obeyed and followed; but also persons to be admired and imitated. To the boy, it is more especially the mother who has to be protected and the father who is both followed and admired.

These figures of the good and bad parents are incorporated in the child's unconscious fantasy and so give rise to that sense of inner goodness and inner badness, almost of spiritual possession, of which some people are quite conscious. But throughout his life he will also seek to rediscover the pattern of his imaginary family in the outer world. In particular, he will seek to impose it upon all the varieties of group formation he will enter, and so help to mould.

Types of Group Value

We may start our search for the elements of the family pattern in the group by looking for representatives of the good mother figure. In the person of a Queen Elizabeth or a Queen Victoria she may appear as the actual ruler of the group. Such queens have inspired a degree of self-sacrificing devotion that can hardly be explained in terms of the excellence of their real characters alone. A large part, at least, of this devotion must have sprung from their symbolic characters—although it is also true that each succeeded in identifying herself with the role she was cast to play.

But in masculine groups, at least, the good mother figure usually appears in a less concrete form. To most modern nations, for example, the concept of the Motherland has an enormous emotional appeal, especially when it is in danger. Frenchmen (in 1914) forgot their normal party quarrels and united as one man when France was threatened. And a French soldier, even when routed, returned immediately to the attack,if someone reminded him of his country. A scene from the last war (1914-18) was once described to me by an eyewitness. A French battalion had been attacked in the early morning before they were properly awake. At first they bolted crying, *"Tout est perdu"*, and it seemed that the Germans were certain to break through both the front and support line of trenches. But soon the routed battalion came charging back shouting, *"Vive la France"*, and attacked with such desperate vigor that they not only captured their own lost trenches, but the German front line as well. It was simply the recollection of their country as a symbol of the good Mother in danger, that produced this astonishing return of valor. [With such clear recollections of French patriotism in our minds, most of us were unprepared for the collapse in 1940. We did not realize that in a decisive minority of Frenchmen two fundamental changes had taken place: The good mother figure symbolized by their country was already so threatened that its defense seemed hopeless; and the bad father figure was being symbolized more by communism within, than by the national enemy outside their country.]

But the figure who is threatened may be a father as well as a mother, and is perhaps always, to some extent, what analysts call a "combined parent". To the Germans, Germany is the Fatherland more than the motherland—a fact that may explain some of the psychological differences between them and the French. Perhaps because the son's attitude is always more ambivalent towards the father, the Germans are overapt to think of their Fatherland as threatened even when it is not. If the internal figure of the father is not quite trusted there is a constant unconscious effort to keep him in check and hem him in. In dreams, for instance, he may appear as a dangerous lunatic who has been kept for years in a strait jacket, but who at any moment may be expected to break out. A people who identify their country with such a figure are certain to be over-suspicious of plots to encircle it and to prevent its natural expansion. Their sense of claustrophobia will breed a compulsive desire to break out, which will naturally alarm their neighbors, who are then likely to form just those encircling alliances they fear. Whether and under what circumstances the neighbors of such a state would be wise to try appeasement rather than encirclement is an old problem, to which we shall return.

Another form in which the idea of a persecuted good figure who should be protected appears is in the concept of a small nation threatened by a big one, or of an oppressed minority fighting to be free. We all know the enormous influence of this concept on the history of the world. We remember the national enthusiasm and sympathy at the time of Byron for the Greeks, or of Garibaldi for the Italians. We remember how Gladstone, in his Midlothian campaign, fired the country and altered its whole political complexion by his accounts of the Bulgarian atrocities. We remember the determined fury aroused in us by what is described as the rape of Belgium (1914). And, at least until recently, we liked to think that our pride in our country rested not in the size of its dominions, but in its constant preparedness to fight in the old battle of Freedom against Tyranny. On the other hand, we find it more difficult to realize that to Americans the Irish, and to Germans, the Boers (1899) have played this same role of a damsel in distress. We may think, too, that the concept of persecuted Germans in Czecho-Slovakia, or of persecuted Italians in Tunisia is pure moonshine. But whether or not such concepts have been artificially created for a sinister purpose, they belong to the same psychological category as those that have often led our own country into war. Since tales of atrocities against defenseless peoples correspond with a pattern in unconscious fantasy, we are over-ready to believe them. But it by no means follows that they are always false, or that our indignation is irrational when they are true.

The same concept of a good figure persecuted recurs in still more abstract form. Some groups are bound together, not by common blood and common land, but, by a common ideal, which may be religious or secular. I believe that such concepts as the Mother Church, or the Gospel which gives spiritual nourishment to mankind, are the psychological equivalents of the mother goddesses of earlier religions, and therefore of the good mother of unconscious fantasy. Even goddesses needed, as well as gave, sympathy and protection. Iris, Astarte and Aphrodite, no less than Mary, were represented as mourning for their loss; though by a curious twist of unconscious fantasy it was not the goddess but her divine son or lover who had been directly injured. Similarly, those religious ideals—which I suggest are more abstract symbols of the same figure—have usually been threatened, or persecuted, ideals—at least during their periods of most vivid life. Many of their adherents have gladly suffered death and torture in their defense; and seem sometimes to have provoked persecution in order to reproduce in the external world the central pattern of their unconscious fantasy.

Something rather similar to a gospel, but still further sublimated into a system of principles, is also the aim of political parties as we know them now. It may seem far fetched to claim that an abstract political ideal for which men sometimes give their lives is a symbol of the unconscious picture of the good mother. But it is no accident that Liberty, for example, is represented by a statue of a woman. Nor indeed is it strange that this should be so; for whatever is valuable on rational grounds tends to become associated with the earliest values, which we preserve in our unconscious, and from which it derives a great part of its emotional force.

Human history is largely an account of the conflict of groups each striving to defend their own values or ideals. Whether concrete or abstract, these symbolize good parent figures to be protected, and from this source derive their power. But can we tell whether this power is likely to be used for the benefit or for the destruction of mankind?

It is no part of psychology, or indeed of any science, to choose between ideals. Each, so far as it is neither based on falsehood nor contains an inner contradiction, is the equal of its fellow. But the attitude to ideals can be either pathological or sane. The dividing line is extremely difficult to draw. But the individual or the group who imagines attacks upon his ideals when they do not exist, or who provokes such attacks in order to realize his unconscious fantasy, is clearly on the wrong side of this line; for his inner life is full of unreal conflicts which he is compelled to reproduce in the external world.

But if the fanatic is unbalanced, it does not follow that the group or individual who abandons ideals too easily is necessarily more sane. If the good values we stand for are so threatened that we feel it hopeless to defend them, there is sometimes a tendency to devalue them, or even to feel that they are bad. I will try to make this clear by an example which is fresh in my mind. In the September (1938) crisis, it seemed likely that Czecho-Slovakia would become another Belgium in our minds. People who had hardly heard of it before were deeply stirred by the old ideal of a small nation in distress and prepared to take up arms in its defense. But as soon as they heard it was to be abandoned, many of these same people suddenly lost all interest in the Czechs. In some the change of feeling went further and they found themselves actively disliking the very nation they had been so anxious to defend. This seems hardly credible; but I saw the change occurring in several of my friends.

The tendency to abandon ideals too easily may result from the same internal disharmony as the tendency to propagate them with too much fanaticism. If in the internal picture the good parents are too much threatened by the bad ones, these symbols must either be defended with an indiscriminating zeal or abandoned altogether.

Which of these two alternatives is chosen by a given group is partly determined by the type of leadership it gets. If the leadership is fanatical, there is likely to be a fanatical response. If it is defeatist, there is usually a defeatist response. If it is resolute, and neither fanatical nor defeatist, there may be a balanced response. But, in the long run, the stability or lack of stability of the group depends upon the inner harmony or lack of harmony of the members that compose it. They tend to get the leaders they deserve.

Types of Group Enemies

The concept of a good parent figure persecuted implies, as we know, the concept of an enemy; and we know, too, that this enemy is the bad parent figure on to whom the child has projected his aggressiveness. Because this enemy is part of the unconscious pattern, there is always a tendency to rediscover him whether he is there or not; and for this reason he is a constant factor in almost all group formation.

In tribes or nations he is often real enough and takes the form of some other tribe or nation. If two groups live in an area that only provides sufficient food for one, it is perhaps inevitable that they should fight—unless they mutually agree to restrict their populations. Such examples once led us to believe that all wars were ultimately economic, that they were special products of the struggle for existence. This theory, of course, contains a partial truth. But it also serves to cloak the irrational motives, which are at least equally important.

To the extent to which as children we have unconsciously incorporated an imaginary enemy, we shall tend to find him in the external world. In extreme cases we may suffer from obvious delusions of persecutions and be classed as paranoiacs. If we are more normal, and so long as we are behaving as individuals, the slight degree of oversuspiciousness that may remain will be counteracted by the different attitude of our friends. If you do not share my irrational distrust of a mutual acquaintance I am likely to revise my view. But when we are acting not as individuals but as a group there is no such check. When two groups begin to distrust each other, the suspicion of the individual will be confirmed first by the similar suspicions of the members of his own group, and then by the defensive reaction of the other. To each the other becomes the personification of evil, and tension increases which may eventually explode in war.

For a nation to permit its suspicions of another nation to grow unchecked may therefore produce an actual danger which would not have otherwise arisen. But there is another tendency, which is also dangerous. This is to repress or deny suspicions that are well founded. There are in fact two ways of dealing with unconscious anxiety produced by unconscious aggression. One is to project the aggression and become excessively distrustful. The other is to deny it and become too trusting. It is not easy for individuals, and still less for nations, to keep the balance between these two extremes.

To take a concrete example, there is no doubt that Germany's sense of claustrophobia, and determination to break out before the war (1914-18) was fostered by the encircling alliances made against her. But can we be certain that by repressing our suspicions we should not have fallen into the opposite danger of denying and failing to protect ourselves against an actual threat? Or to come bluntly to our present problem, can we be certain that appeasement rather than collective security is likely to keep peace? Hitler's own answer is that it was tried six years too late.[1]

Psychology can only give an answer in more general terms. If owing to the conditions of their infancy or to some other cause a particular people have a very large fund of aggression which they must project, as the only alternative to internal disruption, they are likely to be militant whatever the attitude of their neighbors may be. If, on the other hand, the fund of aggression is small, much provocation will be necessary. To determine whether and at what time a nation is in one rather than the other of these categories is a problem of practical statesmanship, which practical statesmanship has often failed to solve.

So far we have discussed only one type of group enemy—namely a rival group. But this element in the unconscious pattern may take many other forms. Sometimes the enemy may be felt to be inside

---

[1] When British statesmen said that all problems were capable of solution by discussion, his answer was that there were "fifteen years for that before he came to power." Report of Hitler's speech in the *London Times*, April 3, 1939.

the group itself. From time to time during the Middle Ages the terror of witchcraft seized hold of nations. The group became as it were hypochondriacal, and like the individual hypochondriac, sought to cut out the supposed evil within itself. The vague and roving terror of internal enemies would be periodically focussed on some poor wretch, and momentarily relieved by his or her destruction, only to return once more to seek fresh victims. The witch, of course, was a symbol of the unconscious image of the "bad mother". But since she was endowed with phallic attitudes, a broomstick, a beak-like nose and chin, and was moreover possessed by the devil, she was also what psychoanalysts call a "combined parent" figure.

This same tendency to group hypochondria seems also to have been responsible for the burning of heretics as well as witches. The Church, and State united to it, could tolerate no foreign body within itself, and turned ferociously upon any that it found.

Coming to more modern examples, the same mechanism may, I think, be seen in those persecutions of minorities, both political and racial, of which we have heard so much. That the Nazi attitude towards Jews and Social Democrats is, at least partly, a symptom of group hypochondria seems to be confirmed by no less an authority than Hitler, who described them, in a speech I heard, as a cancer in the body of the State that must be ruthlessly cut out. But lest I should be accused of seeing faults only in our neighbors, I would suggest that in our own country there are many people for whom the wicked Bolshevik or the wicked Capitalist are overcast to play this role. Moreover, I do not wish to suggest that all dislike of minorities within a group is irrational, but only that the irrational component is often larger than it seems.

Among primitive peoples throughout the world, perhaps the commonest anxiety is that of physical possession by evil spirits or forces. All illness, when not caused by the loss of some good internal object, such as the soul, is caused by possession by a bad one. Thus primitive medicine consists mainly of magical rites to restore the good or drive out the bad. We now know, thanks mainly to the work of Melanie Klein, that such superstitions are not confined to savages, but form part of the unconscious fantasy of every child. We know, too, that those in whom the sense of inner evil is near consciousness, often find the presence of a real external enemy a positive relief—for this relieves the much greater terror of the imaginary internal one who cannot be destroyed except by suicide. For much the same reason, a real external enemy is often a condition of the solidarity—sometimes even of the continued existence of a group. If therefore some nation is ever driven by this motive into the conquest of the world, the result might be, not external peace, but speedy disintegration and collapse—that is, unless it could find an abstract enemy to take the place of the external concrete ones it had destroyed.

Some groups do have abstract or at least spiritual enemies. The Church, for instance, used to be vividly aware of the enmity of Satan; and although he has now been largely ousted by more abstract concepts such as sin, impurity and vice, these have much the same meaning to the unconscious. To primitive man guilt (at least that part of guilt which may be identified with persecutory anxiety)[2] is quite consciously treated as something invisible but concrete, which can be washed off, driven out by an emetic, or removed by some other purification. It was therefore quite clearly identified with the internal "bad objects" of the child's unconscious fantasy.

Since (persecutory) guilt is an internal "bad object" to the unconscious, we may expect to find the same principles of denial and projection at work as we have found elsewhere. Perhaps these principles may account for the excess of zeal with which such bodies as watch committees endeavor to discover vice outside themselves.

In this connection, it is interesting to speculate whether human freedom has gained or lost by the decline in the belief in Satan. To a degree varying with the intensity of their inner conflicts men have always sought relief by projecting the devils they feel within themselves into the external world. So long as they believed in the reality of Satan, there was less need to seek for more abstract evils in their neighbors, where minor foibles were not so much attacked. Perhaps more people were comparatively free; but those who were suspected of intercourse with Satan, were burnt as heretics or witches—instead of being merely prevented from drinking, or betting or undressing on the beach.

Flugel once suggested that the future safety of the human race

---

[2]The sense of guilt seems to be a compound of two elements: a persecutory element aroused by the sense of having offended a feared object, and a depressive element aroused by the sense of having injured a good one. While the response to the first is propitiation that to the second is reparation.

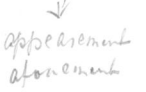

depends upon its ability to find the right object to attack. Some groups do in fact find their enemies in things that almost everyone regards as bad. To councils for the preservation of rural areas, the enemy is ugliness in many forms, which they sometimes attack with a commendable fanaticism. A similar, though perhaps even more abstract role, is played for the medical profession by "illness", and for educationalists by "ignorance", which both seek to banish from the world.

Like other psychological forces, the tendency to attack an inner evil projected into the outer world can be applied to ends that are generally acknowledged as either useful, useless or pernicious. To a great extent, no doubt, later education determines the choice. But the less exaggerated the unconscious picture of the inner evil, the more likely shall we be to find its symbols only in those things which on rational grounds seem to deserve attack. The real test is not whether one can think rationally as an individual, but whether one can also do so as a member of a group.

But is an enemy—abstract if not concrete—a necessary part of every group formation? A society without enemies, and in perpetual peace, has been the dream of the Utopists—a dream which is at least approximately realized by the Society of Friends. Not only are they pacifists who do not fight; but they do not even proselytize or attack other peoples' religious views. The whole emphasis seems to be on the control of their own conduct. As Rickman has pointed out, they do not, like other groups, project their inner sense of evil, but attack it only where it is—within themselves.

Types of Group Leaders

So far I have said nothing about the leader whose presence often distinguishes the group from a mere crowd. The leader, of course, is the good parent figure—but in another role, for we have already found this figure beneath the values that the group defends. In masculine groups, at least, these values usually symbolize the mother, while the leader is a father symbol, whose main function is to lead the group in their defense.

Since the sons' attitude to their father is always ambivalent, that is, a blend of love and hate, many groups have tried to dispense with leaders altogether. Nowhere has this attempt been more successful than in Central Australia, where the tribes are ruled not by chiefs but by committees of old men. Fathers indeed are brought so low that they are even denied their share in procreation; children being conceived, not by natural means, but by the entry of an ancestral totem. But although the father figure is in this way banished from the earth, it is not difficult to recognize him in the spiritual form of these very totems who play an enormous part in the beliefs and rituals of these people.[3]

Although in very small communities the father figure may be dispensed with, or rather banished into the spiritual realm, in larger communities this has always been impracticable. In a common type of primitive autocracy the father is still projected into the spiritual realm to become the tribal god; but the god exercises his authority through some man who is more or less identified with him. Extreme forms of such theocracies developed in Babylonia and Egypt, in China and Japan and in the old civilizations of Mexico and Peru. The king was not only the priest of the god, but often also the actual god in human form. This theory was revived by the Roman Emperors to strengthen their prestige, and lingered on in a weaker form in the doctrine of the divine right of kings. But with the secularization of monarchy, the old ambivalence became conscious once more, and some nations returned, not indeed to the leaderless democracy of Central Australia, but to a system of leadership by election rather than inheritance.

Intermediate between the inherited leader and the elected leader is what may be called the appointed leader, that is, a leader who is elected by a ruling oligarchy. The so-called Greek democracies, containing as they did large numbers of voteless helots, had leaders of this type. Among other examples is the Pope who is elected not by the whole Roman church but by the College of Cardinals; and a manager of a company who is elected by the board.

A fourth type is the elected or at least popular leader who becomes an autocrat. To distinguish him from the other three we may call him self-imposed.

From the point of view of the stability and efficiency of the group, each of these four types of leaders have their peculiar merits and defects. The hereditary leader may be badly adapted to this job— that is, he may fail to resemble the kind of ideal father his particular

---

[3]Cf. Roheim: *The Riddle of the Sphinx*, London, 1934.

VARIETIES OF GROUP FORMATION

group desires. But if he does satisfy this condition, his own security and the stability of the group is likely to be greater than in any other kind. For both in his own unconscious belief and in that of his followers, he already incorporates the spirit of his father and remoter ancestors, that is, of the previous leaders or father symbols of the group. Unlike other types of leader he inherits, as it were, a fund of prestige, which he can either squander or increase, but which certainly gives him a very great advantage. To the unconscious, at least, he still has something of the past divinity of kings.

An appointed leader is probably more likely to be competent than a hereditary one, but he does not start with the same psychological advantages and must be a better leader in order to achieve an equal prestige for himself and therefore of stability for his group. Sometimes, especially in religious groups, this disadvantage is overcome by a ceremony of investiture, which symbolically transfers to him the prestige, spirit, or *mana* of his predecessors.

An elected leader, for example, the President of a Republic, a Prime Minister or even an ordinary Member of Parliament, is usually more likely to start his career with the requisite prestige than an appointed one; but it is usually more difficult for him to keep it. If he did not start with the requisite prestige, that is, if he did not possess the qualities of a "good father" symbol, he would never have been elected. But unlike hereditary or appointed leaders, he is never free from rivals, to one of whom his group is apt to turn at the first sign of failure. Then, having ceased to symbolize the good father, he often comes to symbolize the bad one, and finds that the reverence he so lately enjoyed is turned to hate. These groups are often less loyal to leaders they chose themselves than they are to leaders thrust upon them. But the inconvenience of more frequent revolutions is offset by the fact that they are also bloodless. Our own constitution, as the late David Eder and also Jones have pointed out, has some of the advantages of both the hereditary and elective systems. For the fact that the Prime Minister has to take the blame for all misfortunes enables the King to remain a focus for the country's loyalty. This is probably one reason why a change of government is less of an upheaval here than in other democratic countries.

The difference between the elected leader and what I called the self-imposed one is of degree rather than of kind. At one end of the scale is the man who is elected by a group to preserve its existing values and ideals; at the other, the man who preaches an ideal and rallies a group in its support. He creates the group which follows him. To this type belong the founders of religions: Buddha, Christ, Mohammed; the founders of new political ideals and systems: Lenin, Mussolini, Hitler; and also religious or political revivalists.

Such leaders, so far as their ideals are aggressively promoted, may become the victims of their own creation. Napoleon III started as the popular hero destined to revive the lost spirit of French Nationalism. The enthusiasm he had himself inspired pushed him, it is said against his better judgment, into the disastrous war that ended his career. We have yet to see whether Hitler or Mussolini can check their expansive policies before these lead to war—that is, assuming that either wants to do so.

How far then is a leader the cause or the effect of the psychology of his group? If the inner conflict in the members of the group is severe, they are likely to be melancholic, or to quarrel among themselves, unless they have an external enemy to identify with the bad figure of their unconscious fantasy. They are likely to turn against a pacific leader, and to replace him by one who gives them that exaltation which is for them the only alternative to melancholia. If, on the other hand, they are at peace within themselves, they will still be capable, and perhaps with less anxiety, of defending their values and ideals; but they will not be compelled to create enemies who would not have otherwise existed. They will not be easily influenced without due cause, and are likely to choose a leader who is resolute rather than aggressive. In intermediate cases, however, when the members of the group have an average amount of inner conflict, the leader may have a very great effect. If he seems weak in the defense of their ideals, they will soon be plunged in defeatist gloom. If he is aggressive they may become fanatical. And if he is resolute he may keep them balanced between these two extremes.

Types of Group Standards

So far we have found three types of symbols of the various figures in the child's unconscious picture of his family. The "good parents", and more particularly the mother in her role as a figure to be defended, reappear as the values of the group. The "bad parents" in their role of persecutors reappear as the enemies against whom the values have to be defended. The "good parents", more particularly the father, in his role of defender, reappears as the leader or leaders of the group. But the "good parents" and to the boy more particularly the father, have one other role. As we said before, he is not only someone to follow but also someone to admire and imitate. He remains throughout life an unconscious model for his sons' behavior—a model which is only within limits modified by the later incorporation of other father figures. To the extent to which education, and the treatment of young children by their parents in a given group is homogeneous the models of behavior that different members erect within themselves will be similar, and the group will have what Roheim calls a well marked group ideal. This group ideal is the standard of conduct the group tries to live up to and must not be confused with the ideals the group defends. The group ideal of the Spartan, for example, was fortitude and courage; the ideals he defended comprised everything he meant by Sparta.

Small primitive tribes, who have had little contact with other types of culture, each develop characters, or rather standards of behavior, peculiar to themselves. So also, though to a lesser degree, do larger nations. The group ideals of different sections of the English population differ widely from each other; but there is a common element. hard to define perhaps, which is distinct from the group ideals of Frenchmen or Italians. Artificial groups, too, such as the medical or legal profession, the army or the church, have their typical group ideals of conduct, which are often very rigid.

Each group naturally feels that their own standards are superior, and often disapproves of those of other groups. It is not the business of psychology to make moral judgments which are necessarily subjective; but it can make medical judgments and say that one group ideal is pathological and another sane. Among some of the North American Indians described by Margaret Mead in *Sex and Temperament*, the ideal man was he who destroyed the largest quantity of his own possessions. He amassed wealth in order to prove that he could destroy more than his neighbors; and in his anxiety to defeat a rival, he destroyed not only his boats, his blankets and his oil, but sometimes even his wife and family as well. Without analyzing these people it would be difficult to say in detail how they developed this singularly masochistic ideal. But we know that one of the ways of dealing with inner conflict and anxiety is to develop a neurotic character, of which there are many forms. Something both in their treatment of their children and in their innate disposition must favor a form of inner conflict most easily relieved by the development of a masochistic character; and the very prevalence of this character, by making it a source of pride rather than of shame, must make it still easier to acquire. The tribe by its treatment of its children causes a mental illness, and then provides a rudimentary cure.

There is no guarantee that a man's actual character will correspond with the group ideal of his tribe or nation. If it does not, he will be maladjusted and probably unhappy. But he can sometimes join a congenial sub-group. If he has a strong need for reparative work he can become a doctor. If he has a sense of inner poverty, which can only be relieved by constant acquisition, he can become a predatory type of business man. If he can only deal with his unconscious anxieties by extreme asceticism he can become a monk. And if he is not happy in a community at peace he can join the Foreign Legion. Some societies tolerate a rich variety of sub-groups of this kind. Others, those who cannot endure divergent minorities within them, seek to mould their citizens in the image of one chosen type.

Since the group ideal and the group leader are both ultimately based on the unconscious image of the good father, we should expect a close connection between the two. To a limited extent the group ideal is modified to conform with the actual character of the leader. He sets the fashion in small matters if not in great ones. In the pre-war (1914-18) period, for example, there was an astonishing profusion of Kaiser Wilhelm moustaches in Germany and of Franz Joseph whiskers in Austria. Sometimes, indeed, he seems to transform the whole character of his group. But he cannot do more than bring out what is already latent in its members; and usually they refuse to follow him if he differs too much from their existing group ideal. Henry VI, for example, had he been an abbot would by his piety have won the devotion of his monks, but as a king he failed to live up to the bellicose standards of the time and was deposed to make way for the more aggressive Edward IV.

The group, therefore, must accept the main responsibility for its own character. If some of its members find this character too aggressive, or too acquisitive, or too ascetic, or marred by some other defect, they are unlikely to change much even by a successful revolution against its leaders, unless they can vary the conditions that form character in the early life of the child.

Summary

To sum up the main points in the argument: The child forms an imaginary picture of his family, which is more or less distorted and which he preserves in unconscious fantasy throughout his life. This picture contains good parent figures to protect, to follow and to imitate, and bad parent figures against whom they have to be protected. Moreover, he tends to reproduce this pattern in the external world.

When a number of individuals find common symbols for the elements in this unconscious pattern they form a group. They have common values to defend, a common enemy, a common leader and a common standard of behavior.

These four features recur in a great variety of group formations. The values a group defends may be its concrete possessions, its motherland or some abstract religious or political ideal. The enemy it defends them against may be another group, a suspected minority within the group, or some abstract but more or less personified principle of evil. Few, if any, groups have no real or imaginary enemies at all. The leader they follow may be of many types. Some groups have tried to do without him; but in a new form he nearly always returns. He may be an ancestral god, a priest or king who incarnates the god, or a hereditary monarch. He may be elected, appointed or self-imposed. And lastly the group ideal standard of behavior, depending as it does on education, may take any of an infinite variety of different forms.

A group like an individual may be either pathological or sane. If the individuals who compose it have severe internal conflicts they are apt to create enemies for themselves by suspecting enmity where none at first existed or to become depressed if they fail to get the fanatical leadership they need. Or they may relieve their inner tension by a character formation corresponding to a neurotic group-ideal. But if, as a result of a favorable environment in early life, or of later treatment, the individuals who compose a group are at peace within themselves, the group itself, whatever its form, will certainly be sane.